FLEMING'S FUNDAMENTALS OF LAW

MULTISTATE EXAMINATION WORKBOOK

Volume I

By

Jeff A. Fleming
Attorney at Law

Edited by

Susan P. Sneidmiller
Attorney at Law

Melody Lynne Jolly
Attorney at Law

LEARN TO WRITE . . . THE RIGHT WAY®

Published by:

FLEMING'S FUNDAMENTALS OF LAW
23166 Los Alisos Bl #238, Mission Viejo, CA 92691
(949) 770-7030 • (800) LAW EXAM
FAX (949) 454-8556
WEB www.lawprepare.com • EMAIL flemings1@aol.com

Distributed by:

LEGAL BOOKS DISTRIBUTING
4247 Whiteside Street
Los Angeles, CA 90063
(800) 200-7112

SUPERVISING WRITER AND EDITOR

Jeff A. Fleming
Attorney at Law

MANAGING WRITER AND EDITORS

Susan P. Sneidmiller
Attorney at Law

Melody Lynne Jolly
Attorney at Law

LAYOUT:

Donald F. Bayley II
IMAGEN Company Irvine, CA.

CONTRIBUTING WRITERS:

Professor Sam Frizell
University Of California, Hastings College Of The Law, J.D.

Jared Gross
University Of Santa Clara School Of Law, J.D.

Melody Lynne Jolly
Western State University College Of Law, J.D.

Dawn Marie Jolly
Western State University College Of Law, J.D.

Cameron Jolly
Western State University College Of Law, J.D.

Professor Philip Merkel
University Of Illinois, J.D.

Professor Jeremy Miller
Tulane School Of Law, J.D.

CONTENTS – Volume I

INTRODUCTION

THE RULES OF THE ROAD – AN INTRODUCTION TO THE MULTISTATE METHOD

As we traveled down the road of higher education, each milestone had a cryptic name – the PSAT, the SAT, and the LSAT, among others. Although each successive exam seemed to intimidate more than the last, with some determination, we arrive at the ultimate milestone – the Multistate Bar Examination, or MBE.

Created in 1972 by the National Conference of Bar Examiners (or NCBE), in cooperation with the Educational Testing Service, the MBE is a full-day, 200-question, mind numbing, multiple choice exam. One hundred questions are administered, randomly as to subject area, in two three-hour testing sessions. The exam seeks to cover a breadth of subjects that would be impossible to cover in a few selected essays.

The MBE has become the standard for most multiple choice exams that seek to test on legal reasoning skills, as well as familiarity with generally accepted legal principles. Presently, it covers the seven core areas of Torts, Criminal Law and Procedure, Contracts, Real Property, Constitutional Law, and Evidence. As constituted, the MBE is a major portion of the bar exam in virtually every jurisdiction, with Indiana, Louisiana and Washington being the exceptions.

The MBE has also been the model for countless objective law school exams, as well as the California First Year Law Student Exam administered by the State Bar (also referred to as the Baby Bar). However, the MBE is perhaps the most subjective objective test ever created. It attempts to test those analytical skills that we have honed and perfected, or have attempted to perfect, in the law school classroom through case study.

This introduction will review preparation methods and offer test-taking techniques that will also be of value to the law student facing objective testing in virtually any area of the law and California students preparing for the Bar and/or Baby Bar Exam. The methodology discussed herein can be applied to any multiple choice testing format that uses the MBE as a model.

RULE #1 – FAMILIARIZE YOURSELF WITH THE MBE TERRAIN

Material released by the NCBE indicates, in an almost lawyer-like disclaimer fashion, that the MBE is:

1. Not a multiple-guess test, or a test of test-taking skills, but of legal skills and knowledge, with a high correlation to performance on the essays;
2. Not a needlessly difficult, arcane or tricky test, but is designed to be a fair and unbiased index of whether the applicant has the ability to practice law, regardless or race or ethnicity;
3. Not a test in which time is a statistically significant factor, as the time allotted is sufficient for 99 percent of the test takers;
4. Not inferior to essay and performance exams as a measure of minimum competency to practice law, because the MBE can cover a greater breadth of subjects, can be scored objectively and scaled to account for variations in difficulty from test to test; and
5. Not getting easier from year to year.

Perhaps this last representation can go without dispute, but even the less gifted advocates among us may, after a trip down the MBE road, be able to raise an issue or two.

The landscape on the MBE road looks something like this:

A. **TORTS** (34 questions)

50% - Negligence, Proximate Cause, Damages (Apportionment), Defenses, Vicarious Liablility

50% - Divided among remaining Tort areas

Questions here are based on the common law, the majority rule, and, increasingly, on the Restatement 2d, Torts. The importance of Torts, and specifically of negligence, cannot be overstated. The remaining emphasis is primarily on the intentional torts and strict liability, with nuisance, defamation, privacy and misrepresentation also being represented. You can count on at least one question from each of these seven topics.

The specifications (i.e., subject matter outline) for the Torts MBE questions feature five main headings. Nuisance, defamation, privacy and misrepresentation fall under a single heading of Other Torts. Products liability is segregated from strict liability, and the Other Torts heading also includes intentional interference with business relations. The significance of the headings is that the examiners will always post at least one entry from each category. Of the 34 Torts questions, 50% will test on negligence.

B. **CRIMINAL LAW AND PROCEDURE** (33 questions)

15% - Pre-Commission Crimes
15% - Homicide
15% - Real/Personal Property/Theft Crimes
15% - Mena Rea, Defenses - Justification/Excuse
40% - Criminal Procedure - Fourth, Fifth and Sixth Amendment

The common law, the modern law, the majority rule, the Model Penal Code, and, sometimes, a statute contained within the problem form the basis for the Criminal Law questions. The decisions of the U.S. Supreme Court are the basis for the Criminal Procedure questions. In the other crimes area, theft crimes predominate. In Criminal Procedure, search and seizure issues are emphasized.

The MBE includes 33 questions in Criminal Law and Procedure, 40% testing on Criminal Procedure, the remaining questions divided equally among the four remaining areas of Criminal Law.

C. **CONTRACTS** (34 questions)

60% - Mutual Assent, Defenses, Warranties, Conditions, Breach, Remedies (U.C.C.)
20% - Consideration, Statute of Frauds, Third Party Rights
20% - Parol Evidence, Impossibility of Performance, Frustration of Purpose, Discharge of Contractual Duties

The source of law in this area is the common law, the majority rule, the Restatement 2d, Contracts, and the Uniform Commercial Code (U.C.C.) Articles 1 and 2. The bad news is that the questions in this area feature some of the longest, most complex fact patterns on the MBE; the good news is that the concepts tested generally tend toward the basic.

The MBE includes 34 questions in Contracts, roughly 60% covering formation, conditions and remedies, and with about eight or nine questions based on U.C.C. Articles 1 and 2.

D. **REAL PROPERTY** (33 questions)

75% - Interests in Land, Co-Tenancies, Landlord & Tenant, Ownership in Trusts, Easements, Profits, Licenses, Covenants, Servitudes, Water and Land Rights, Zoning, Fixtures (Article 9, U.C.C.), Adverse Possession, Deed, Conveyancing by Will, Recording Act

25% - Land Sales Contract/Risk of Loss/Marketable Title/Mortgages

The common law, the modern law, the majority rule, and the U.C.C. (Article 9 – Fixtures) are tested in Real Property. The problems are, along with Contracts, the longest and most complex on the MBE; unfortunately, most students would agree that the concepts tested are anything but basic. Traditionally, the lowest percentages come out of Real Property. On recent MBE's, there has been a significant rise in testing on mortgages.

The 33 Real Property questions will draw on the areas of ownership, rights in land and title for 75% of the questions, land sale contracts and mortgages for the remainder. Newly tested subjects include zoning, conveyance by will and ownership interests in trusts.

E. **CONSTITUTIONAL LAW** (33 questions)

50% - State Action, Due Process, Equal Protection, Privileges and Immunities, Bill of Attainder, Ex-Post Facto, Contract Clause, First Amendment (Speech, Association, Press, and Religion)

17% - Federal/State Conflict

16% - Separation of Powers

16% - Procedure

The principles tested in Constitutional Law are derived from the U.S. Constitution, the decisions of the U.S. Supreme Court, and, apparently, from obscure footnotes in Nowak's hornbook on Constitutional Law. The good news is that the questions in this area tend to be the most straight forward on the MBE, accounting for the highest percentage scores.

The MBE includes 33 questions in Constitutional Law, approximately 50% of which will test on "individual rights": due process, equal protection and first amendment freedoms.

F. **EVIDENCE** (33 questions)

- 33% - Hearsay
- 33% - Relevancy, Real and Demonstrative & Scientific Evidence, Authentication, Expert Testimony, Privileges, Best Evidence Rule
- 33% - Impeachment, Rehabilitation, Opinion, Burdens and Presumptions, Judicial Notice, Direct Examination, Cross-Examination

The questions are based on the Federal Rules of Evidence. Throw out those old outlines based on the common law, with one possible exception – From time to time, you may see a federal court sitting in diversity jurisdiction. In those situations, apply state rules of procedure that may be outcome determinative, including state rules of Evidence, as spelled out in the problem.

Note that if the questions testing on character evidence (from relevance and impeachment) are combined with the hearsay questions, the total is generally 60% or more of the testing in Evidence. The questions tend to be the shortest, yet most devious, on the MBE.

The MBE includes 33 questions in Evidence, one-third based on presentation of evidence, one-third based on hearsay, and one-third based on relevancy, privileges and writings.

The subjects of Crimes, Evidence and Torts tend to emphasize, and will likely continue to emphasize, the elements of the rule invoked by the facts; in Constitutional Law, Contracts, and Real Property factual analysis and reading comprehension is emphasized.

Unlike the essays, cross-over testing is the exception rather that the rule. This is due, at least in part, to the fact that the questions are drafted by individual committees, each responsible for one of the MBE areas.

Although Civil Procedure is not considered a testable subject, a recent trend has been to get to Torts by means of a motion for a directed verdict (known as a motion for judgment as a matter of law), a motion to dismiss, or a motion for summary judgment. For example, a question may require you to know that the doctrine of res ipsa loquitur will raise an inference of negligence sufficient to turn the matter over to the jury, and overcome a directed verdict motion.

Prior MBE questions have tested the Erie doctrine in Constitutional Law, have used a will or trust to get to an issue in Real Property, have used a federal court sitting in diversity jurisdiction to get to an Evidence issue, or have used a contract to get into a Real Property issue. Expect to see as many as three or four questions that could cross-over between Evidence and Criminal Procedure. Remedies, including damages and equitable relief, will arise in the context of in Contracts, Real Property (e.g., specific performance), Torts, and, possibly, Constitutional Law (e.g., injunctive relief).

It is highly unlikely that anything resembling a cross-over pattern will be seen on the Baby Bar, as the examiner is unable to assume that you have any knowledge beyond the Contracts, Crimes or Torts material covered in your first year of law school.

RULE #2 – PREPARE FOR THE LONG HAUL (or, You Have to Get out of the Driveway before You Can Ride the MBE Fast Lane)

The foregoing subject breakdowns are to be used as study guides, along with comprehensive outlines, such as the Gilbert series recommended by Fleming's Fundamentals of Law in the MBE areas. It is recommended that one outline be reviewed every one and one-half weeks for long term and review two outlines per week for short term. Greater emphasis should be placed on any weak or highly testable areas, combined with practice problems as discussed below.

The essentials of preparation for the MBE can be addressed in three words – **practice, practice, practice.**

In gearing up for the practice runs, the student must sort through a potentially overwhelming assortment of materials. At the outset, a schedule should be prepared that considers the outlines to be covered, as well as the practice problems to be done. A series of goals, both long term (overall) and short term (daily), will be helpful, but only if these goals are realistic and within reach.

A successful performance on the MBE requires more than the ability to regurgitate rules of law and a rote memorization of the outlines. An examinee must be able to master the rules, the exceptions, the exceptions to the exceptions, the footnotes in the hornbooks, the Restatement comments and illustrations, the ability to function in a stress-filled environment, the ability to think on one's feet, and the ability to apply all of this in 1.8 minutes per question.

Unquestionably, success on the MBE is grounded on a solid foundation of the black letter law. By itself, however, this is not enough. Each rule, as it is studied, must be put into a factual context so that the application of the rule is understood and the associative process is enhanced.

Generally, the commercial outlines, such as the Gilbert series, or the bar review outlines, will be a sufficient source of the law needed. Despite all of our experience with last-minute cramming, merely reading the outlines will not be enough to vanquish the MBE. The study of the law must be incorporated into an approach that contemplates problem-solving as the goal, rather than rote memorization.

The recommended **first step** is to break down each subject area into its component parts and to master each of these areas before moving on to the next. For example, one cannot learn Crimes without first mastering the general requirements of **actus reus** (the criminal act) and **mens rea** (the mental state) **before** moving on to homicide and theft crimes.

While studying the outline materials, take the time to discern the necessary elements of each rule reviewed. List these elements in your mind, on a piece of paper or on a flash card and then **contextualize**. This means putting the outline aside for a moment to consider or imagine a set of facts that will call up the rule, element or exception to be applied. For example, while reviewing contract offers, consider a number of situations in which an offer may or may not exist, such as Do you want to go to the movies? (merely an inquiry); If you pay for the movies, I'll pay for the food (possibly an offer, despite its indefiniteness, if another would be justified in believing that a power of acceptance has been created); or I'll pay you $5.00 an hour to come over at 7:00 P.M. this Saturday and watch my kids while I go to the movies (clearly an offer). If at first this seems difficult, there are a number of flash card sets, such as those published by Law-in-a-Flash or PMBR that list examples or hypotheticals that may prove helpful in helping initiate the process.

The **next step** is to turn to a source of practice questions, such as the Finz Multistate Method book utilized by Fleming's Fundamentals of Law, starting with the table of contents. You will see, for example, in the Criminal Law section, that following the heading **General Principles** is a listing of 13 questions that test in that specific area. Working questions in the subtopic immediately following its review will not only help you place the rules in context, i.e., to apply the rules, it will also help you to determine whether or not there is sufficient comprehension of the rules so as to allow you to move on to the next area of testing. Again, it is vital to achieve some sense of mastery in each area before moving to the next.

When taking the practice test questions, always time yourself, allowing no more than 1.8 minutes per question. If you are aware of the time pressure from the very beginning, then you will start to develop a rhythm or an almost instinctive awareness of the passage of time as you work the problems.

RULE #3 – KEEP YOUR EYES ON THE ROAD (or, the Zen of testing)

One of the attributes of the successful examinee is the ability to **focus**, to the exclusion of all else, while in testing mode. This can be thought of as finding a quiet place, both externally and internally, in which to perform. The distractions may be external, such as the continued groans of a neighboring test taker; or the distractions may be internal, such as wondering what impulse possessed you to sit for the exam.

The key is to block out everything but the test question, and to be able to do that for an extended period of time. By doing test questions in blocks of no less than 17 at a time, one half hour per set, you can consciously put yourself in the exam for that period of time to the exclusion of all else. Consider continuing to practice the half hour sets until you have mastered the ability to go for thirty minutes without thinking about anything but the test questions. Once you have mastered this ability, then expand to one hour of testing, or 33 questions, and so on, until you can sit for three hours without a significant break in concentration.

This does mean, however, that no matter how great the temptation, you cannot look at the answer key until you have completed the set. When you do review the answers, look at the explanations for both the correct and incorrect responses to ensure a well-reasoned basis for your selections and to reinforce your grasp of the rule being tested.

Some students will find it helpful to write out the rule on a flash card for those problems they got wrong. This, again, helps to reinforce your grasp of the rule, will help you keep track of areas of difficulty, and will create a valuable study tool.

It is also important to sit for at least one simulated exam so as to test your ability to focus over the long haul. Use the simulation as an opportunity to diagnose areas of weakness, not only substantively, but technically or procedurally as well, i.e., Does the brain completely fade somewhere around question 75? Does it take 10 to 15 questions to establish a rhythm? Does the brain think of nothing but lunch as the clock nears the noon hour?

As the exam draws nearer, the emphasis should shift from outline review to problem solving, with the outlines being used primarily as a refresher or supplement to the problems. Again, the exam is testing on problem solving skills, not the ability to regurgitate the black letter law. The final month should be devoted to doing practice MBE's.

RULE #4 – MAXIMIZE YOUR FUEL EFFICIENCY

As mentioned above, study time should be allotted to reflect the relative importance of each subject area. Of the 200 questions on the current MBE, there are 34 each in the areas of Contracts and Torts, and 33 each in the areas of Constitutional Law, Criminal Law and Procedure, Evidence and Real Property.

Factor in the testing on the essays, where typically three out of the six one-hour questions test on the same rules as the MBE, and that you cannot study law for the performance essays, and the result is that at least 75% of the black letter law needed to pass the California Bar Exam comes out of the MBE areas. This same basic principle, that studying for the MBE will help on the essays, also applies to the Baby Bar essay questions, but is limited to the topics of Contracts, Crimes and Torts.

Emphasis in study time for the California Bar Exam should be placed on the MBE areas. Generally, each MBE area should be studied three times as much as any individual essay-only subject, such as Wills or Community Property.

As we saw in the subject breakdowns, above, within each MBE subject can be found certain key areas, for example:

CONSTITUTIONAL LAW:.... Individual Rights And The First Amendment .... 16 Questions

CONTRACTS: .... Formation (Including U.C.C.), Defenses ... 15 Questions

EVIDENCE: .... Hearsay And Character Evidence .... 15 Questions

TORTS: .... Negligence .... 17 Questions

PROPERTY: .... Establishing And Conveying Title .... 20 Questions

(Note: While Criminal Law has a somewhat emphasized area, the general requirements and defenses will likely be tested directly or indirectly on the bulk of questions, and should therefore be considered key, both in study and in the review of the elements of each criminal offense.)

Obviously, the key areas require a greater expenditure of time. Again, the subject breakdowns will be an important tool in emphasizing specific areas, and getting the most efficient use of your study time.

RULE #5 – KNOW WHERE YOU ARE HEADED (Before You Leave the House)

In order to maximize your reading comprehension and initiate your analysis of an MBE test question, it will help to know the area of testing, and, if possible, to determine the rule of application, before you start to read the facts. The area being tested will not be specifically identified for you.

The typical MBE question is composed of three parts – the **root/stimulus** (fact pattern); the **stem** (call of the question); and the **options** (answer choices), as in the following example:

Question 1 is based on the following facts:

Archie, a candidate for Student Body President at the exclusive Riverdale Academy, was scheduled to debate the other presidential candidates before the assembled student body in the school's auditorium. After the students had taken their seats, Ms. Grundy, the faculty advisor, called Archie to the podium. Just as Archie was crossing the stage to get to the podium, his opponent Reggie stuck out his foot, causing Archie to fall off of the stage. As a result, Archie was deeply humiliated, but suffered no physical harm.

1. If Archie asserts a claim against Reggie due to the humiliation that he suffered, will Archie prevail?

   A. Yes, if Reggie knew that Archie had to walk across the stage in front of Reggie at the precise moment Reggie stuck out his foot.

   B. Yes, if Reggie carelessly failed to notice that Archie had to walk across the stage in front of Reggie.

   C. No, because Archie suffered no physical harm.

   D. No, only if in sticking out his leg Reggie did not intend to cause physical harm to Archie.

The answer to this example can be found in the Rule #7 Section that follows.

Prior to reading the facts, read the stem. In the above example, the asserts a claim language identified the area of testing – Torts. Now the root can be read with a eye toward the appropriate cause of action. This is essentially the same as issue spotting an essay. The facts are designed to trigger the application of a rule. The examinee's job is to recognize those trigger facts and apply the appropriate rule.

Getting a sense of the ultimate destination helps to initiate the reasoning process that goes into analyzing the facts. Again, this is the same process that goes into issue spotting an essay, i.e., Do the facts support a particular outcome or result? Have all elements been satisfied? Are there additional facts that must be evaluated? Are there missing facts that must be considered before the outcome can be determined? Is there an exception that will apply?

In the above Archie-Reggie example, once the area of law was established, we can now consider the various rules which might apply, e.g., negligence, intentional tort or strict liability. Which facts become significant? The facts state that as Archie was crossing the stage, his opponent Reggie stuck out his foot. There is no mention of whether or not it was intentional or accidental. It does not appear that any of the categories of strict liability (products liability, wild animals, abnormally dangerous activities) can be supported by the facts, so this area can be eliminated. Negligence is possible, but given the lack of physical harm, we will need to continue the search for a more appropriate rule. The claim asserted will likely arise out of the intentional torts, perhaps battery or intentional infliction of emotional distress. The facts must be scrutinized to see if they will support the claim, or if something more will be needed.

On occasion, the stem may go further in establishing the rule of application, e.g., if Defendant is charged with murder..., or if Plaintiff asserts a claim in strict liability due to the injuries caused by the defective product.... This may allow you to get further along in the distillation process, but it does not mean that your analytical skills will not be called into play.

In those problems where the root is followed by more than one stem, i.e., multiple questions follow a single fact pattern, try to read each stem so as to get a general sense of the issues or areas being tested. Later, when working through the responses, you can deal with each stem independently.

If the stem does not provide you with sufficient information to determine the area of testing, glance at the options. This means allowing your eyes to drop down an imaginary centerline through the potential responses, so that you recognize key words. This should be enough to enable you to determine, at a minimum, the area of testing. In the above example, you may have noted the words know and carelessly in the first two options, suggesting that the key, or correct answer, will be coming out of intentional torts or negligence, and may possibly require a distinction to be made as to those two areas.

Consider the following example:

2. In a common-law jurisdiction, Defendant should be found guilty of:

   A. Burglary only

   B. Arson only

   C. Burglary and arson

   D. Neither burglary nor arson

As you have likely observed, the stem did identify the rule of application, the common-law rules. It did not identify the rule of law; however, a quick glance at the options clarified the area (Criminal Law) and the crimes of burglary and arson. Once you have identified the rule or rules of application, your job may merely be the accounting of all essential elements.

In some examples, the stem essentially replaces or supplements the existing facts by asking you to assume additional facts. In this situation, reading the entire stem first may not be as desirable. It may be helpful to first read the last sentence or phrase of the longer stem, so as to learn the objective of the problem, and then read the additional facts contained in the stem. Consider the following example:

Assume for the purposes of this question only that instead of doing the job herself, Builder delegated the remodeling work to Framington, who was an experienced cabinetmaker. Although Framington had never worked on a job of this exact type, size and complexity, she eagerly accepted the delegation because she owed a sizable gambling debt to Builder. Builder did not inform Owner of the delegation. Builder then assigned the contract proceeds to Karman to pay off her car loan.

3. Will Owner be required to accept Builder's delegation of duties to Framington?

In this example, glancing at the last sentence identifies this stem as testing on a delegation of contract duties. By having this knowledge, the important facts are easily distinguished from those immaterial to the inquiry (e.g., that Framington was inexperienced with the type of job versus Framington's experience as a cabinetmaker or the assignment to Karman). Note also that where the stem instructs you to Assume for the purposes of this question only **do not** carry those additional facts on to other questions and **do not** allow the new facts to influence your reading of the basic fact pattern.

RULE #6 – USE ROAD MAPS

Reading the stem, or glancing at the answers, to establish the objective or direction the problem is taking will help boost your reading comprehension. This can be compared to using a road map to establish which direction to take in order to reach your ultimate destination, i.e., the objective of the problem.

Reading comprehension is enhanced if you have a sense of direction, that is, an idea of which facts are likely to be important and which facts are set forth as mere distracters. Whole paragraphs may be skimmed if you know in advance that such paragraphs will not have a bearing on the result. Parties are more easily identified, issues are more easily narrowed.

Once the objective has been established, it becomes easier to recognize the details that may be important in resolving the issues presented. For example, the fact that the plaintiff was an anticipated or known trespasser, and thus a duty was owed, may be determinative in Torts; or that the seller was an unemployed ballerina, and thus not a merchant, may help resolve the issue as to whether or not a written option contract not supported by consideration is enforceable; or that the seller was planning to sell, rather than presently intending to sell, may indicate that there is no offer on which to base a contract.

As indicated above, a fact critical to the outcome may be buried within the details of the fact pattern which, in essence, is identical to the essays. These details may be seen in adjectives, verbs, adverbs, times, dates, places, quotations, personal characteristics, names, or intentions. The question to ask is: What is the **legal significance** of each fact or detail as it relates to our inquiry or call of the question?

In some problems, but not all, a simple, quickly executed diagram may be helpful to set out, for example, the chronology or the relationships that are central to the question. This can be done right in the test booklet, or on the scratch paper provided by the proctors. Consider the following example:

Question 4 is based on the following facts:

Buss is the owner in fee simple absolute of Lakeracre, a 13,000 acre ranch in Kern County, in the state of Golden. On May 2, despondent over the playoff loss of her beloved Magicians basketball team to their archrivals, the Missiles, Buss conveyed Lakeracre to Johnson for the price of $150,000.00 by means of a quitclaim deed. Johnson did not immediately record this conveyance. On June 16, Buss conveyed Lakeracre by warranty deed to Nelson in consideration of a $250,000.00 debt owed by Buss to Nelson, which Nelson forgave. Nelson recorded this conveyance immediately. On July 1, Johnson recorded his quitclaim deed.

On July 10, Johnson conveyed Lakeracre to his friend Threatt as a gift.

Threatt recorded the conveyance immediately. On July 15, Nelson conveyed Lakeracre to Peeler by quitclaim deed for the price of $300,000.00. Peeler recorded immediately.

4. Assume for the purposes of this question only that Golden has a recording statute that reads as follows:

   > *No conveyance is good as against a subsequent purchaser for valuable consideration and without notice, unless such conveyance be recorded prior to subsequent purchase.*

   If all necessary parties are joined in a quiet title action, title will be found in which of the following of the following parties?

This problem can be diagrammed to strip the facts down to the essentials. The key is to identify the bona fide purchasers, and when each recorded relative to the other, so as to establish the absence or presence of notice in this race notice jurisdiction. A diagram may look something like the following:

B to J/BFP B to N, N rec J rec J to T/gift, T rec. N to P/BFP, P rec
–|––––––––––|––––––––––|––––––––––|––––––––––|–

Of course, the diagram can be distilled further by using arrows instead of to, or abbreviating recorded to the letter R, so long as there is no confusion as to meaning or a party.

The areas that are most likely to call on diagramming skills would be Contracts and Real Property. It is recommended that you practice diagramming, if that technique is to be employed, wherever appropriate in the practice questions. The objective to distill the information into a useful format as quickly as possible, keeping in mind that if you spend more than 1.8 minutes with each stem following the root, that time must be made up elsewhere.

Some students may wish to highlight or underline the facts. This can either be helpful, or a waste of time. In order to highlight effectively, there must still be some awareness of the relative importance of the material highlighted. You may recall how much material you highlighted in your casebooks during the first weeks of law school. Soon, as you grew more sensitive to the relevant facts and law, less and less was being highlighted. This was a product of learning how to read a case. In much the same way, you will learn how to recognize the vital facts, and disregard the immaterial.

In reading the root of the Archie-Reggie example, above, it may not be as important to note that Archie was running for office as it was to note that the accident occurred in front of the assembled student body, thus increasing the probability that Archie would be humiliated. This is not to completely discount the Archie's purpose for being in the auditorium, or that Reggie was his opponent. The fact that Archie was there to participate in a debate makes it clear that the audience would likely watch Archie's every move. The facts are not clear on Reggie's intent in sticking out his leg; while it might appear that he intended to trip Archie, we have to be careful in making an unwarranted assumption. In this example, we appear to be missing a critical fact, and cannot make up for it with imagination. The resolution of this issue is likely the key to the problem, and will be dealt with in the answer choices.

It is important that you follow the facts and do not fight or respond emotionally to the facts that are given. This means taking the facts at face value, without reading too much into the facts. In this regard, you may need to stifle some of the natural inclinations of an advocate, as arguing or assuming facts may do little except waste time or lead to an incorrect response. Where the facts state that the arresting officer had a valid warrant, do not attempt to challenge the warrant. Where the facts state that the police made a random stop, do not go on to consider the possible exceptions to the warrant requirement. Where the facts state that a deed is valid and has been properly executed, there is no need to ask if the description is sufficient.

Some rules may seem unfair, perhaps even illogical, in applying the facts. For example, Why shouldn't a physician be required to act to render assistance to another who may be seriously injured as a result of the physician's inaction, where there is no risk to the physician, and despite the fact that the victim was placed in peril by another? Why shouldn't a party be allowed to prove up a subsequent remedial measure to prove negligence or culpability, when such remedy is logically connected to the dangerous condition causing injury? The MBE is not the place to argue policy, and attempting to do so will exact a very high toll. Again, do not respond with emotion, but rather a reasoned approach to applying the law to the facts.

If a straight forward interpretation is available, do not over-analyze or seek out an unnecessarily convoluted interpretation. A reasonable, logical inference may, however, be required. Ensure that the inferred fact logically and necessarily follows from the information given. Making assumptions, creating new facts, or working with conclusions that are not warranted by the existing facts will, in most instances, generate an incorrect response.

Constitutional Law, Contracts and Real Property are where the subjects that are more demanding on reading comprehension, given the nature of the subject matter and the tendency that the examiners have to use longer, more complex fact patterns with multiple parties to test in these areas. Fact patterns in these areas will often require greater scrutiny, and therefore require more time.

Testing in Crimes, Evidence and Torts tends to emphasize elements and command of the black letter law. As a result, the fact patterns tend to be shorter, and may require less in the way of reading comprehension, and more in the way of substantive knowledge of the rules of law.

When reading the facts, regardless of the subject, keep in mind that the examiner is testing on lawyering skills. Cases very often turn on details, so an effective reading of the facts will often depend on the examinee's ability to discern the operative from the inoperative, the relevant from the immaterial, and the substantial from the inconsequential. Also, you must be as flexible and as adaptable as conditions may demand. This is known as thinking on one's feet. These are qualities that lead to a successful performance.

As with all the methods and techniques discussed in this introduction, including the following materials on selecting a response, success is dependent on practicing until the approach is virtually unconscious. Techniques must be adjusted to fit each individual's approach, and that only comes through practice. You must sort through each suggestion, and incorporate only that which has produced the greatest result with the practice questions.

Arguably, if the work done in reading the facts and the call of the question has been successful, then there should be little effort expended in reaching your destination, i.e., selecting a correct answer. In the most basic terms, we are usually seeking the best legal basis on which to support a particular or given outcome.

RULE #7 – DON'T GET SIDETRACKED

On occasion, the correct answer may appear obvious. Certainly, if the answer is obvious, do not fight it. In other instances, however, it will seem as though the examiner has taken great pains to hide the ball. The incorrect answers, referred to as distracters by the examiners, are aptly named.

Consider the Archie-Reggie example (Question 1) above. It would appear that Reggie acted intentionally to trip Archie; however, the facts say nothing about Reggie's state of mind, and we cannot afford to guess at what Reggie was thinking. The facts state that Archie was not injured, so the (B) response, based on negligence, is improbable. The (C) response can be ruled out, because an action for battery or intentional infliction of emotional distress can be maintained even in the absence of actual physical harm. The (D) response can also be eliminated, as it limits liability to intent to cause physical harm; however, a cause of action can be based on the offense to Archie's dignity or the intent to cause emotional distress. The (A) response, therefore, is the **key**, or correct response. By using the word know it addresses the missing element of intent.

Typically, the person drafting the question is or has been a law professor. As a result, he or she has ample experience with the phrasings that are likely to lure an examinee into an incorrect response. There must be something attractive in a distracter. It may be an inaccurate or incomplete statement of the law. It may trigger some faint memory of an arcane rule. It may be a concept that has been drilled into you. Or, more likely, the distracter may reflect an incomplete understanding of a rule that has traditionally led to confusion.

In the Archie-Reggie example, the examiner may have been counting on the difficulty some students may have in distinguishing negligence and the intentional torts, or the requirement of physical harm that accompanies a negligence action.

One concept that routinely turns up in distracters is promissory estoppel. Those same people who taught you to love and cherish the concept, law professors, now turn it against you. In the absence of a promise and a reasonable expectation on the part of the promisor that the promise will induce some action or inaction, the doctrine does not apply. Yet students have routinely attempted to use promissory estoppel as an all-purpose substitute for consideration, despite the absence of a promise, or the presence of a more appropriate response that has very real consideration.

In other situations, the distracter may prey on an examinee's confusion as to the identity of the holder of a right, or when the right arises. In a problem where the government is maintaining an action in inverse condemnation, an examinee must realize the action is one properly maintained against the government. In a problem where a defendant seeks to assert the last clear chance doctrine, an examinee must realize that only a plaintiff can assert the doctrine. Where there is a claim of privilege against self-incrimination, be sure that there is a statement in issue, and that the statement is testimonial in nature.

Other distracters may seek to create whole new, incorrect concepts. Only a student with sufficient familiarity with the hearsay exceptions under the Federal Rules will know that there is no exception for a recent sense impression. Bargained-for reliance, a concept that withers in daylight, might get a second glance from the examinee who is unsure of his or her knowledge of Contracts. Keep in mind that after reading outlines in each of the subject areas, and doing thousands of practice questions, if there was such a thing as bargained-for reliance you would recognize the concept.

This is not intended to mean that you will necessarily be familiar with all potential phrasings. In an area such as negligence we cannot expect to see 17 problems that may be answered Liable, if negligent. Some synonyms are in order, such as recklessly, carelessly, unreasonably, without due care, and so on. This does not mean, on the other hand, that new, special duties can be created, e.g., in a negligence action, the defendant owes the highest or an utmost duty of care.

Ultimately, the best cure is a thorough substantive review, followed by judicious amounts of practice questions. Adequate preparation will thwart the intentions of the examiner seeking to trap the unwary examinee.

RULE #8 – REMEMBER TO READ THE TRAFFIC SIGNS

A clear understanding of the language in the stem and the options will be critical to achieving a sense of direction, or, in other words, the objective of the problem and arriving at the correct response.

The language in the stem may cast the examinee in a specific role, which in turn will have a bearing on which response is the most appropriate. For example, a stem that asks for the best basis on which to support a judge's decision is asking you, in essence, to act as that judge's law clerk. A question asking for the strongest or weakest argument is calling for an advocate. On the other hand, a stem seeking the most probable outcome may require a neutral approach in analyzing the most appropriate response.

Consider the following example to determine how much information is contained in the stem:

Question 5 is based on the following facts:

Dennis and Joey operate a private courier service in the city of Metropolis. They entered into a contract with the law firm of Ketcham and Wilson for the delivery of the firm's promotional calendars to clients throughout the city. Prior to commencing the deliveries, Dennis suggested to Joey that the two of them throw away the calendars, pocket the money paid for the deliveries, and spend the rest of day at the local race track. Joey said noth ing. Dennis then proceeded to dispose of the calendars.

5. If Dennis and Joey are charged with conspiracy to commit larceny in a common law jurisdiction, which of the following constitutes Joey's **weakest** defense?

   A. Joey did not have the required intent.

   B. Joey did not form an agreement with Dennis, either explicitly or implicitly, as to a criminal objective.

C. Joey did not act to take the calendars out of Ketcham and Wilson's possession.

D. Joey was feigning agreement.

In the above example, the question stem is identifying the following: (1) the area of law, (2) the specific rule being tested, (3) the law of the jurisdiction, (4) the defendant to focus on in applying the rule, and (5) the role to assume in responding to the question. Actually, very little is needed from the root in this example. The criminal charge has been set out, so in order to respond, apply the rule of conspiracy.

The fact that the question seeks the weakest defense should not dramatically affect your analysis. This question may be more easily solved by working it in reverse; in other words, re-phrase the call to read Which of the following constitutes Joey's **strongest** defenses? In this example, the (A), (B) and (D) responses are all negating an element of conspiracy, i.e., the specific intent to commit larceny or the agreement between two or more actors, and as such, are very strong defenses. Option (C) appears to be dealing with the crime of larceny, and not the inchoate crime of conspiracy, and would not be an adequate defense, is therefore the key in this example. Note that in the areas of Crimes and Torts the strongest, best defenses are those which negate an element of the charge or claim.

The same care must be used in analyzing the options. Consider the following example:

Question 6 is based on the following facts:

Peters was skiing in the exclusive resort of Deer Park, an area which he was not familiar with, and inadvertently skied out of bounds. As he attempted to get back on the ski trail, a blizzard started, making it impossible for him to find his way back. As darkness descended, Peters started to fear that he would suffer from hypothermia unless he found shelter. As he was making his way through the waist-high snow, Peters spotted a ski cabin owned by Denver. Despite seeing a sign which read Private Property – Keep Out!, Peters immediately made his way to the cabin and was able to gain entry by forcing the door open. The cabin was unoccupied.

Once inside the cabin, Peters started a fire in the fire place. Without realizing there was a defect in the fire place screen which allowed sparks to escape, Peters went to sleep. A fire broke out, which destroyed the cabin and caused serious injury to Peters.

6. If Peters asserts a claim against Denver for his injuries, will he be successful?

    A. Yes, **if** Denver was aware of the defective fire place screen.

    B. Yes, **only if** Denver could have discovered the defective fire screen by a reasonable inspection.

    C. No, **unless** Denver had reason to anticipate a skier might break into the cabin.

    D. No, **because** Peters assumed the risk that a fire might break out when he went to sleep.

In this example, notice that each option has a result, followed by a suggested basis on which to support that result. This is the most common formulation of answers on the MBE. Look closer, and you will notice that each outcome is joined to the basis by a conjunction, which can be referred to as the modifier, or operative term. Each different modifier has its own connotation or usage.

The modifier in option (A), **if,** suggests that the outcome **must** follow as a result of the statement of law of fact given, and no other outcome is possible. The determination that must be made is whether the logical connection is sufficient to justify the result. In a problem where there is one missing element in order for the plaintiff to prevail, and that missing element is preceded by an if modifier, then no other result is possible. This would be a very strong choice. The if modifier may be followed by a new fact, in which case the inquiry is whether no other result logically follows the new information. In the above example, we do not need to question whether or not Denver actually knew of the defect. The inquiry is whether or not Denver would necessarily be liable, given this awareness. Your knowledge of Torts will tell you that absent some duty owed, this result does not necessarily follow, and this answer may be rejected.

The **only if** modifier in option (B) suggests that the basis which follows the outcome is the exclusive means of arriving at the outcome, and that there is no other way to logically arrive at the outcome. The word only is a word of restriction or limitation. If there is another way to arrive at the outcome, then this modifier would indicate an incorrect response. In this example, the duty to inspect (owed to invitees) would not be the exclusive basis on which to predicate Denver's liability to Peters, and therefore must be rejected.

Option (C) features the **unless** modifier, which requires a reversal of the analysis of the only if modifier in options (A). In other words, the outcome stated can only be avoided by the statement which follows. The unless modifier should be treated as the logical opposite of only if. Your knowledge of Torts will tell you that Denver will prevail if Peters is unable to satisfy all of the elements of negligence. All of the elements needed to find for Peters have been supplied except one – duty. Another way to view this option is to rephrase it to Peters will recover **only if** Denver had reason to anticipate Peters presence in the cabin. This logically follows, because, based on the facts, duty to the trespassing Peters will only arise where Denver has reason to know or anticipate his presence in the cabin; therefore, this is the key response.

The modifier in option (D), **because**, can be used interchangeably with the conjunctions since and as. Here the inquiry is two-fold. First examine the basis as a correct statement of law or fact. If it is correct, then ask if the outcome stated logically and necessarily follows from the basis. In this example, there is nothing in the facts that indicates Peters voluntarily and unreasonably encountered the known risk of a defective fire place screen. As a result of this, this option must be rejected.

The analysis of the language above may seem awkward, even somewhat convoluted at first. After working through a substantial number of practice questions, you will find that familiarity and comfort with the language increases at a rapid pace.

RULE #9 – BE ALERT FOR CHANGING ROAD CONDITIONS

The three complete examples above followed a fairly standard format. The root was followed by the stem, which in turn was followed by options which each listed an outcome followed by a proposed basis on which to support the outcome. The method used to arrive at the correct response in the explanations above was the process of elimination. Once we eliminated the false statements, whatever remained became our selection.

Another way to view the exam is as a multiple true-false test, rather than multiple choice. That means looking at each option, independently, as a true-false question. It will be helpful to mark a T or an F next to each option as you read through them. Alternately, you might use a system of pluses or minuses, or crossing out the false statements. Selecting the correct option then becomes a function of looking for a T, a plus, or an option which has not been crossed out.

But what about the options with a question mark next to them? What if you can only narrow it down to two choices?

If you are able to narrow it down to two choices, one of which is correct, you are definitely on the right track. You will have increased the odds of getting the problem correct by 100%. This is one reason why you may wish to indicate your second choice as you work through the practice questions. As you read through the explanatory answers, you will seek to develop a sense of why the examiner prefers one choice over another.

Remember that the examiner, at least in the problem types we have reviewed so far, is putting you on the hunt for the **best legal basis** on which to support a given outcome. Consequently, the answer which is narrower or more specific to the result is usually preferred; the same is true when comparing a legal basis with a factual basis. The legal basis is generally preferred. For example, Not guilty, because the facts do not state that Defendant had an improper motive does not present as good a legal basis as Not guilty, because Defendant lacked the intent to steal in exculpating the defendant in an example testing on larceny.

Be on the alert for those answer choices that are underinclusive or overinclusive in stating the basis for the outcome. For example, the option stating Constitutional, because the 1st Amendment only protects words is likely to be wrong in a Constitutional Law problem, because certain acts of expressive conduct may be within the scope of 1st Amendment protection. If you find that the rationale in an option eliminates a right which ought to be included, or encompasses a right or result which does not follow from your understanding of the law, then such option is to be avoided.

The examiners use a number of variations on the problem-types illustrated above, such as where the result is the only thing contained in the option. Consider the following example:

Question 7 is based on the following facts:

During the night, Dexter, a drug addict, broke into Gordon's apartment, a reputed drug dealer, with the intention of stealing Gordon's supply of rock cocaine. Although Dexter did not find any cocaine, he did find some methedrine, an illegal stimulant. Dexter took the methedrine with him when he left the apartment.

7. In a common law jurisdiction, Dexter is guilty of:

    A. Burglary only

    B. Larceny only

    C. Burglary and larceny

    D. No crime

Although the options are not the compound type that we have looked at, the approach is similar, in that we must still go through each possible response and deem it either true or false. We do this by reviewing the elements of each charge, and determining whether or not the facts will support the charge. Where there are multiple charges (or outcomes), deal with the elements of each individual charge.

In this example, we are in a common-law jurisdiction, and the facts state that Dexter broke in to Gordon's apartment at nighttime with the intent to steal drugs. We do not have to struggle with the elements of breaking and entering because they are there in the facts. The examiner is hoping for an emotional response, that somehow stealing illegal drugs is not morally wrong. But the facts make it clear that Dexter had the intent to commit a larceny at the time of breaking and entering, therefore Dexter has committed burglary. He has also taken the drugs, which are the personal property of another, with the intent to steal; therefore Dexter has also committed larceny, and choice (C) is correct. Keep in mind that each crime requires satisfaction of an element the other does not, so there is no double jeopardy prohibition.

Another problem type incorporates the facts into the options themselves, which may be referred to as a **squib-option** format, as in the following example:

8. In which of the following fact situations will the contract most likely be enforceable despite the absence of a written agreement?

   A. Homeowner and Cable Company have a dispute over the placement of Cable's use of the utility poles on Homeowner's land. In an effort to settle the matter, Cable offers to purchase an easement from Homeowner, and Homeowner accepts.

   B. Vendor operates vending machines throughout the city of Sierra Vista. Supplier offers to sell $5,000.00 worth of snack foods to Vendor for only $3,000.00. Vendor accepts.

   C. Agent hears Singer perform in a nightclub and on the spot offers her a two-year recording contract. In reliance on the offer, Singer quits her job at the nightclub, and accepts the offer.

   D. Owner asks Builder to submit a bid for the construction of addition to Owner's house. Builder offers to build the addition for $10,000.00. Owner accepts.

Problems of this type can generally be attacked with a two-step approach. Ask yourself the following: What is the rule being tested (as identified by the stem)? And, How is it to be applied, i.e., what is the task to perform? In this example, the stem indicates that the rule being tested is the Statute of Frauds (requiring a writing in order to enforce certain types of agreements), and the task is to classify each contract to see whether it falls within the Statute. Options (A), (B), and (C) each reflect an agreement that requires a writing under the Statute of Frauds – a contract for the sale of an interest in land, a contract for the sale of goods for the price of $500 or more, and a contract that is not to be performed within one year from the making thereof, respectively. Only (D), involving a construction contract, clearly falls outside of the Statute, and is the key response.

Answer choice (C) may present a problem for some students, as they might want to argue the element of reliance. The examiners are counting on this, expecting some students will waste time wanting to argue. If you have an arguable response, versus a clear cut response, do not waste time. Answer the question, and then completely erase it from your mind. One of the pitfalls of the exam is that certain problems are so challenging that a student will continue to work it in the back of the head long after a response has been marked. Resist this temptation, as it will only slow you down, frustrate you and destroy your effectiveness.

Another problem type the examiners have used is the **tiered** question, as in the following example:

Question 9 is based on the following facts:

Thanatos operates a factory in the city of Olympia which manufactures air conditioners. One of the ingredients used in the manufacturing process is freon gas, which when exposed to the welding torches necessary to the manufacturing process creates the highly toxic phosgene gas. The phosgene gas is pulled out of the inside of the factory by means of large exhaust fans, which are vented directly to the atmosphere. No other means are available to Thanatos for the removal of the phosgene gas. Morpheus, who lives next to the factory, inhaled the fumes and was severely injured.

9. If Morpheus asserts a claim against Thanatos for her injuries, which of the following **must** be established if she is to be successful?

    I. Thanatos operated the factory in a negligent manner.

    II. The factory constituted a public nuisance.

    III. The toxic gas released by Thanatos caused her injuries.

    A. III only

    B. I and III only

    C. II, and III only

    D. I, II, and III

The most efficient, effective way to work this problem is to treat it in the same way that we have already seen, that is, to treat it as a compound true-false question. The stem is asking which of the following is an absolute requirement, regardless of the cause of action. We can cross out or write an F next to statement I and statement II, because Thanatos is involved in an abnormally dangerous activity giving rise to strict liability, i.e., disbursing highly toxic gases into the atmosphere in a popu lated area. Morpheus can therefore prevail even in the absence of proof of negligence or nuisance. Option (A) is therefore correct.

Yet another problem type is the **complex case precedent**. In this problem type, a series of case precedents are set out, with the stems being fact patterns, and the options designating which of the precedents will be controlling, as in the following example:

Questions 10 - 12 are based on the following facts:

Read the summaries in the four cases (A – D) below. Then decide which is the most applicable as a precedent to each of the cases in the questions that follow, and indicate each choice by marking the corresponding space on your answer sheet.

(A) Defendant, while in the process of robbing a liquor store, dropped his revolver. The gun discharged, and the bullet struck and killed a customer in the store. Defendant fled, but is later apprehended and charged with murder. At trial, Defendant testifies that the killing was accidental, and requests that an instruction for manslaughter be given. **Held**: Guilty of murder.

(B) Defendant, angered over not being invited to her next-door neighbor's housewarming party, discharged her gun into their common wall while the party was ongoing. The bullet struck a lighting fixture, and the shards of glass in turn struck and killed a partygoer. Defendant was apprehended and charged with murder. At trial, Defendant testifies that she never intended to harm anyone and requests that an instruction for manslaughter be given. **Held**: Guilty of murder.

(C) Defendant, while in the Mojave Desert region of Southern California, decided to practice target shooting with her new rifle. Taking aim at a cactus, she discharged a round. The bullet struck a rock, ricocheted off of another rock, and struck and killed a person standing 10 yards behind Defendant. Defendant is apprehended and charged with murder. At trial, Defendant testifies that she did not know that the victim was present, and requests that an instruction for manslaughter be given. **Held**: Guilty of manslaughter.

(D) Defendant was away on a two-week lecture tour. On her return home, she discovered her husband having sex with her sister. Defendant then removed a revolver from her briefcase and fired it in the general direction of her husband and sister. The sister is struck by the bullet and dies. Defendant is apprehended and charged with murder. At trial, Defendant testifies that she only intended to shoot her husband, that the shooting of her sister was accidental, and she only discharged the gun because she had lost control and was unable to regain her composure. Defendant also requested an instruction for manslaughter. **Held**: Guilty of manslaughter

10. Defendant, intending to collect on an insurance claim, sets fire to his warehouse. The fire spreads to an adjoining building, which apparently had been abandoned several years earlier. A vagrant who was living in this adjoining building was sleeping at the time and was overcome by the smoke. As a result, the vagrant was unable to escape in time, and was killed in the ensuing blaze. A statute in the jurisdiction defines arson as the malicious burning of any structure.

11. Defendant, while driving his car at the posted speed limit on the Golden State Freeway, began to be perturbed at the close proximity of the car, driven by Victim, immediately behind him. In an effort to send a message to the tailgating driver, Defendant abruptly slammed on his brakes. Victim attempted to avoid the impact by swerving his car, but instead struck the concrete center median barrier and Victim was killed.

12. Defendant and Victim were fellow employees of IDF, a communications software developer. One night the two of them began to argue over which long distance telephone service the company should choose. Victim then reached into her desk drawer, and started to pull out something that appeared metallic. Defendant believed that Victim was pulling out a gun and was about to shoot her, so Defendant reached into her purse and pulled out a gun and shot Victim. Victim, who was merely taking out a letter opener, died.

The temptation will be to match the facts in the stems with the facts in the precedents, which will usually result in confusion and one or more incorrect answers. In the above example, the facts in the question cases did not closely resemble the precedents. The key is to distinguish each precedent as to the legal basis as it relates to the result, use your knowledge of the law to determine the result in each stem, and then match result for result. In the above example, this means identifying the following:

A. Murder/Felony murder rule – robbery

B. Murder/Depraved heart murder

C. Manslaughter/involuntary – act of criminal recklessness

D. Manslaughter/voluntary – adequate provocation

Now, it becomes a task of matching result and basis with each of the ensuing fact patterns. This means that the correct answer to Question 10 is (A), because the accidental killing arose as a foreseeable consequence of the commission of an inherently dangerous felony, arson. Question 11 was an example of involuntary manslaughter involving criminal recklessness, and not depraved heart murder, because the necessary showing of the Defendant's awareness of the high probability of death was not present; thus, option (C) is correct. Finally, Question 12, is an example of voluntary manslaughter because of mistaken justification – Defendant had a mistaken belief in an imminent threat of death or serious bodily injury. The result must be matched with the result in one of the precedents; consequently, option (D) is correct. Thankfully for many students, this question type does not appear with frequency; when it does, usually in Criminal Law/Procedure, you may recognize that with a workable approach, these questions will not seem overly difficult.

In the **supposition stem** problem type, the stem will ask which of the facts contained in the options, if true, will best support a particular result. The goal here is to treat each of the options as true, combine it with the existing facts, and determine if it logically and necessarily leads to the desired outcome, as in the following example:

Question 13 is based on the following fact situation:

On May 28, Pilcher and Dante, a dealer of vintage cars, entered into a written, signed agreement whereby Dante offered to give Pilcher 30 days in which to decide whether or not to purchase Dante's rare BMW 507 automobile for $100,000.00. Only 50 BMW 507s were imported to the United States, and only five are currently known to exist. On June 1, Pilcher tendered a cashier's check for $100,000.00. Dante refused to convey title to the automobile. Pilcher brings an action for specific performance.

13. Which of the following facts, if true, would provide Dante with his **strongest** defense?

    A. Pilcher did not give any form of consideration for the option to purchase the BMW 507.

    B. Pilcher had entered into an agreement with another dealer for the purchase of a different BMW 507 after May 28, and had communicated that fact to Dante.

    C. At the time of commencing the action, Pilcher knew that another BMW 507 was available for $150,000.00.

    D. Both parties thought the agreement was for the purchase of Dante's Maserati Ghibli.

Again, as each option is examined, it is assumed that it is true. Option (A) does not have legal significance, as the facts state that Dante was a dealer in this type of automobile. Under the U.C.C., a merchant who gives assurance in a signed writing that an offer will not be revoked cannot later claim lack of consideration as a defense to an option contract. Option (B) appears to state that Pilcher revoked his offer; however, this does not follow from the facts, as Pilcher is an offeree who has not yet rejected Dante's offer. Option (C) cuts against the remedy of specific performance, yet it is incomplete in that it does not state that the two automobiles were alike in all practical respects. Option (D), although it flies in the face of the facts, is the key response, because if mutual mistake is present, the contract is necessarily voidable at the election of either party. Remember, in this problem type each additional fact must be treated as true.

In the **three-one split** problem type, there will be one option that stands alone as to result. Do not attach any special significance to this, as it probably has a one in four chance of being correct. Work it through as you would any other example, but pay special attention to the modifiers, particularly one that would affect the result such as unless. If one option does not include a basis or rationale, select it only if the facts provide sufficient support for the outcome. Consider the following example:

Question 14 is based on the following fact situation.

Divac, a skater with the Ice Follies, a traveling troupe of ice skaters, stopped into the Fern Bar for a drink after performing one evening. After having several drinks, Divac began to speak with Vlade, who was seated next to him at the bar. The topic turned to the greatest hockey goalkeeper of all time, and the disagreement was so fierce that Divac took a swing at Vlade. The contact was slight, but it was enough to knock Vlade off of his bar stool. Unbeknownst to Divac, Vlade was an undercover officer for the federal Drug Enforcement Agency, and was at the Fern Bar in order to make a drug buy.

Subsequently, Divac was arrested and charged with assaulting a federal officer. At trial, Divac testified that he was unaware that Vlade was a federal officer, and that if he had known, he would have never struck him.

14. If the jury believes Divac, it should find him:

A. Guilty.

B. Not guilty, because he lacked the specific intent to assault a federal officer.

C. Not guilty, unless assault of this type is considered a general intent crime.

D. Not guilty, because Divac was mistaken as to Vlade's identity.

In the above example, the only requirement as to mens rea is that Divac intended the assault. Divac's awareness of Vlade as a federal officer is immaterial. No mental awareness of the jurisdictional element of this type of offense is necessary to convict. Note that option (B) can be eliminated on this basis. Option (C), which has the modifier unless, can be eliminated on the basis that the facts indicate that Divac intended the assault, and so the classification does not have a bearing on guilt. Option (D) is incorrect, because mistake is no defense on these facts. Again, only after eliminating all other choices can we properly arrive at the correct answer, option (A).

Other problem types may appear from time to time. It is the ability to think on your feet and apply the law to the facts in a lawyer-like fashion that will allow you to vanquish each problem, and, ultimately, the MBE.

RULE #10 – ENSURE THAT SPEED IS ADEQUATE TO PASS

Be aware that a number of problems do not appear to test your minimum competency to practice, but rather are designed to screw with your mind. As the exam is a test against time, you cannot afford to get bogged down on any one problem. If the answer proves elusive, mark down a response, and move on. If the facts are lengthy, and there is only one problem, consider skipping it to conserve time, especially if it is testing on arcane or obscure material. For example, if the problem has two full columns of facts, and a single question testing on planned unit developments and the mutuality of equitable servitudes in Real Property, Burby himself might skip it. Before moving on, though, glance at the options to see if any can be eliminated as clear false statements of law, so as to improve the odds of a guess.

Always be sure to mark down an answer so as to avoid skewing the Scantron. If you have skewed the answer grid, say around problem 15, you cannot afford to discover this as the proctor is calling time. You must always be aware of time and speed, so that you do not run into the situation where no time remains, and yet you are still trying to fill in the bubbles.

Avoid changing answers unless you specifically see where you have misread a problem, or later remember the formulation of a rule that applies in a earlier problem; however, if you are still thinking about an earlier problem, the concentration is not there, and speed is likely lagging. If you spend enough time practicing, your first guess will probably be correct anyway.

Remember, no one gets them all, not even the law professors who take the exam. In fact, the examiners will typically throw out two to three questions on each exam due to ambiguity or inconsistency. Of the 200 questions on the bar exam MBE, most examinees will get at least 100 correct. The key to success is getting the next 40 to 60 problems correct.

Always, always remain positive. Indicate to yourself that you are ready to pass by doing the things that you, and only you, know you need to do.

Treat the exam like a game, and do it for the sake of the game. Don't think about the result or the stakes, just enjoy the ride.

THE RULES OF THE MBE ROAD, IN REVIEW:

1. Familiarize Yourself With The MBE Terrain
2. Prepare For The Long Haul
3. Keep Your Eyes On The Road
4. Maximize Your Fuel Efficiency
5. Know Where You Are Headed
6. Use Road Maps
7. Don't Get Sidetracked
8. Remember To Read The Traffic Signs
9. Be Alert For Changing Road Conditions
10. Ensure That Speed Is Adequate To Pass

Good luck on the MBE!

CONTRACTS

CONTRACTS – QUESTION BREAKDOWN

1. Statute of Frauds – Written Confirmation Between Merchants
2. Offer – Meeting of the Minds
3. Consideration – Bargained for Exchange
4. Consideration – Donative Promise
5. Consideration – Reasonable Reliance
6. U.C.C. – Predominant Purpose Test
7. U.C.C. – Firm Offer
8. Consideration – Pre-existing Duty
9. Formation – Additional Different Terms
10. Formation – Additional Terms
11. U.C.C – Place of Delivery
12. Unilateral Contract
13. Offer – Communication to Offeree
14. Anticipatory Repudiation
15. Express Condition
16. U.C.C. – Risk of Loss
17. Defenses – Mistake
18. U.C.C. – Nonconforming Goods
19. Incidental Damages
20. Express Warranty – Sample or Model
21. Third Party Beneficiary – Vesting
22. Contract Liability
23. Third Party Beneficiary – Incidental
24. Excuse – Part Performance/ Substantial Performance
25. Third Party Beneficiary – Vesting
26. Conditions – Implied in Fact
27. Third Party Beneficiary – Detrimental Reliance
28. Third Party Beneficiary
29. Assignments – Non-Assignment Clause
30. Third Party Beneficiary
31. Defenses – Failure to Perform
32. Assignments

33. Assignments – Delegation of Duty
34. Assignment/Third Party Beneficiary
35. Assignment – Delegation of Duty
36. Warranty of Title – Disclaimer
37. Express Warranty
38. U.C.C.– Method of Acceptance
39. U.C.C.– Shipment Of Goods
40. U.C.C. – Firm Offer
41. Acceptance – Additional Terms
42. U.C.C. – Perfect Tender Rule
43. U.C.C. – Acceptance
44. Statue of Frauds – Merchants
45. Express Warranty – Affirmation of Fact
46. Formation
47. Acceptance – Unilateral
48. Revocation
49. Statute of Frauds
50. Divisibility of Contract
51. Parole Evidence Rule
52. U.C.C. – Perfect Tender Rule
53. Liquidated Damages
54. Shipment Contract
55. Risk of Loss
56. Remedies – Rescission
57. Third Party Beneficiary
58. U.C.C. – Perfect Tender Rule
59. U.C.C. – Right to Cure
60. Contract Damages
61. Consideration – Promissory Estoppel
62. Mutual Assent
63. U.C.C. – Firm Offer
64. U.C.C. – Additional Terms
65. U.C.C. – Tender of Goods – Notice of Non-Conformity
66. Repudiation
67. Damages – Loss of Bargain
68. Parol Evidence Rule
69. Leases
70. Breach – Material

71. Third Party beneficiary/Parol Evidence
72. Parol Evidence Rule – Mistake in Integration
73. Consideration
74. Third Party Beneficiary – Detrimental Reliance
75. Unjust Enrichment
76. Statute of Frauds
77. Statute of Frauds – Exception
78. Defenses – Mutual Mistake
79. Contracts with Minors
80. Contracts with Minors
81. Misrepresentation
82. Defenses – Unilateral Mistake
83. U.C.C. – Right to Inspect
84. Non-Conforming Goods – Damages
85. Non-Conforming Goods – Disposal
86. Unilateral Contract
87. Firm Offer
88. Option Contract
89. Option Contract/Counteroffer
90. U.C.C. – Acceptance/Additional Terms
91. Unilateral Contract
92. Statute of Frauds – Sufficient Memo
93. Defenses – Mistake
94. Pre-existing Duty Rule
95. Conditions
96. Acceptance/Rejection
97. Discharge Of Duties
98. Mistake
99. Pre-existing Duty Rule
100. Modification
101. U.C.C. – Service Contracts
102. Illusory Promise
103. Consideration
104. Consideration
105. Consideration
106. Assignment – Defenses
107. Third Party Beneficiary – Vesting

108. Third Party Beneficiary – Donee

109. Assignments

110. Assignments – Defenses

111. Defenses – Ratification

112. Statute of Frauds – Sale of Goods

113. Accord and Satisfaction

114. Novation

115. Remedies – Cover/Specific Performance

116. Consideration – Moral Obligation

117. Offer

118. Measure of Damages

119. U.C.C. – Resale of Non-Conforming Goods

120. Waiver

121. Assignments – Delegation of Duty

122. Assignments – Delegation of Duty – Liability

123. Offer – Advertisement

124. U.C.C. – Freight on Board

125. Risk of Loss

126. Unilateral Mistake

127. Formation

128. Statute of Frauds

129. Consideration

130. Promissory Estoppel

131. Offer

132. Revocation – Detrimental Reliance

133. Unilateral Contract

134. Conditions

135. Revocation

136. Repudiation

137. Breach – Material

138. Damages

139. Does the U.C.C. Apply – Service Contract

140. Rescission

141. Quasi-contract

142. Restitution

143. Adhesion Contract

144. U.C.C. – Acceptance

145. U.C.C. – Method of Acceptance

146. U.C.C. – Sec. 9-313 Security Interest

147. U.C.C. – F.O.B. – Risk of Loss

148. U.C.C. – Security Interest

149. U.C.C. – Sec. 9313 (4) (B) – Perfect Security Interest

150. U.C.C. – Sec. 9313 (4) (A) – Defeat of Pre-Existing Realty Interest

151. U.C.C. – Sec. 9401 (2) – Good Faith Filing

152. Article 9 – Removal of Secured Property

153. Article 9 – Removal of Secured Property

154. Implied Warranty of Merchantability – Disclaimer

155. U.C.C. – Sec. 2-312 – Warranty of Title

CONTRACTS QUESTIONS

1. Henry, a nationwide distributor of stereo equipment, phones Jim and agrees that he will sell twelvehundred stereo systems to Jim, another merchant, for $500 each - if delivery can be made before August 1. Jim states that he will think about it. Jim, then sends a confirmation form to Henry, signed by Jim stating the price of the goods and the quantity of the stereo systems. Henry received this form on July 1. On July 16, Henry informs Jim that he will not perform, due to an increase in production costs. Jim sues Henry for breach of contract. Which of the following statements are most correct?

   A. Given the above facts, the parol evidence rule is applicable, and Jim would win.

   B. If Henry asserts the statute of frauds as a defense, Henry would win

   C. The statute of frauds requires that Jim should have signed the confirmation form.

   D. If Henry asserts the statute of frauds, he will probably be unsuccessful.

Questions 2 – 5 are based on the following facts:

Tammy Fayray had been a hardworking and loyal employee of Staged Entertainment (Staged), an organization that produces puppet shows, for over 28 years. Tammy was the leading puppeteer for Baker and was well known for her work entertaining people of all ages with a puppet she created, named "Jimmy." After receiving Tammy's sudden and unexpected notice of retirement, Mr. Baker, the owner of Staged, promised Tammy $500.00 per month for the rest of her life, in appreciation of Tammy's "28 years of outstanding creative efforts and skills" for Staged. Tammy cried out, "Thank you, this is the biggest surprise I've ever gotten!" Tammy knew, during her employment with Staged, that it never had any retirement plan for any of its employees.

Intending to splurge on herself, Tammy immediately went out and purchased a lynx fur coat. She incurred an installment payment of $600.00 per month for 10 years, after applying her entire savings of $20,000.00 as a down payment. Tammy would never have purchased the coat had Mr. Baker not promised to pay her the money for life. Mr. Baker disapproves of personal indulgence and stopped the payments to Tammy after he discovered Tammy's purchase of the coat. Mr. Baker had sent Tammy the funds for 18 months at the time he discontinued his payments to Tammy.

2. What was the legal effect, if any, of Tammy's statement to Mr. Baker after hearing Mr. Baker's promise of lifetime income?

   A. There was a valid and binding acceptance by Tammy.

   B. At the moment of the statement, there was an objective meeting of the minds.

   C. It created acceptance, only if Tammy expressly promised not to be self-indulgent with the funds.

   D. It has no binding legal effect.

3. Under what legal theory will Tammy least likely recover?

   A. Legally enforceable gratuitous promise.

   B. Moral obligation.

   C. Promissory estoppel.

   D. Legal detriment theory of consideration.

4. In evaluating Mr. Baker's statement, which of the following rules will the court most likely find to be the correct and applicable law to the case:

   A. A gratuitous promise is not enforceable against the promisor in the absence of special circumstances.

   B. An offer without consideration is not enforceable.

   C. A gratuitous promise, coupled with detrimental reliance, is binding upon the promisor where the promise bargains for an exchange.

   D. A party cannot unilaterally change the terms of a gratuitous promise.

5. Tammy contends that she will be successful in enforcing Mr. Baker's promise, under the theory of promissory estoppel. However, Mr. Baker will most likely prevail under which of the following arguments?

   A. Tammy's conduct in reliance on Mr. Baker's statement was unforeseeable.

   B. Mr. Baker did not intend for Tammy to rely upon his promise.

   C. Tammy's conduct was not sufficient legal detriment to support the enforceability of Mr. Baker's promise.

D. Since Mr. Baker was only making a gift to Tammy, promissory estoppel has no application to the facts of this case.

6. Albert purchased a ski boat at a police auction. After one outing, Albert realized the boat had a slow leak and needed to be repaired. Albert took the boat to Sam's Ski and Boat Repair. After Sam had repaired the boat, Albert discovered it still leaked. The repair bill showed that Albert was charged $350 for parts and $400 for labor. A dispute arose over this transaction. Does Article 2 of the U.C.C. apply to this transaction?

   A. Article 2 clearly applies.

   B. Article 2 may apply depending on a determination of whether the predominant factor in the transaction was the sale of goods.

   C. Article 2 does not apply.

   D. Article 2 applies only to the labor.

7. Paul is a merchant who strictly deals in turbo engines. Paul writes to Cam, also a merchant, that Paul will sell Cam two top-notch supreme turbo engines for $6,000.00 each at anytime during the next five months. Cam receives the signed letter the following day. Which of the following is most correct:

   A. The offer does not remain valid because it was not supported by consideration.

   B. Under Article 2 of the U.C.C., the offer will remain irrevocable for five months.

   C. Under Article 2 of the U.C.C., Cam must accept the offer within three months, or the offer will have expired.

   D. Cam must accept the offer by return mail.

8. On August 1, Dee borrowed $600.00 from Mel to enroll in beauty school. Dee had promised to pay Mel on October 1. On October 2, Mel phones Dee and says, "I really need the money you owe me to pay for my bar application which is now due. If you give me $400.00 by Sunday, I will relieve you from payment of the additional $200.00." Dee, noting a bargain, pays Mel the $400.00. Mel does not give Dee a discharge of the debt. Mel then sues Dee for the additional $200.00. The outcome will be for:

   A. Dee, since any pre-existing duty was extinguished.

   B. Mel, since Dee was under a pre-existing duty to pay the original amount of the debt.

C. Dee, because the $400 payment was sufficient consideration.

D. None of the above.

Questions 9 – 10 are based on the following facts:

Andy, a merchant, mailed to Rob (also a merchant), Andy's offer form. The offer form was to sell Rob 12 tons of sunflower seeds, for the total sum of $600.00. Delivery was to be made at Rob's store in Covina, on December 1. Payment was to be due upon delivery. Rob mailed and Andy received Rob's purchase form complying with Andy's terms, but adding that Andy would be liable for damages, if the delivery was delayed and that payment is due within 30 days of delivery. Andy now seeks counsel for legal advice.

9. Which of the following statements are most correct?

   A. A contract was created when Rob mailed the form.

   B. No contract was created until Andy received Rob's form.

   C. No contract was created because the forms varied.

   D. No contract was created because Rob made a counter-offer.

10. For this question only, assume that buyer, Rob, was not a merchant. Therefore, in all probability:

    A. A contract was formed and the contract terms would include those proposed by Rob.

B. No contract was formed, because the addition materially altered the contract.

C. A contract was formed on the terms upon which the parties agreed, and the added terms by Rob would be construed as mere proposals to the contract.

D. None of the above.

11. Jiffy agrees to sell ten tons of peanuts to Dumb. The agreement does not mention the place of delivery. The place of delivery is:

A. A carrier's terminal in the buyer's city.

B. The buyer's place of business.

C. The buyer's loading facility.

D. The seller's place of business, if that is where the peanuts were located.

Questions 12 – 13 are based on the following facts:

Seven-year-old Minnie loved her puppy Fido. Everyday after school, Fido would wait at the front walk way of Minnie's house and greet her. On Friday, Minnie's school class had a special outing and all the children returned from school an hour later than usual. When Minnie came to her front walk, there was no sign of Fido. After several days of sleepless nights and refusing to eat, Minnie's father published, in the local paper, the following notice:

"REWARD" Any person who supplies information leading to the return of puppy Fido will be paid $250.

Annie, an animal lover, without knowing of the reward, secured information which led to the return of Fido. After Fido's return, Annie then learned of the reward and demanded the $250 reward.

12. The reward notice in the newspaper constituted an:

A. Bilateral contract.

B. Offer to negotiate.

C. Unilateral contract.

D. Unilateral contract which became a bilateral contract.

13. If Annie sues to recover the $250 reward, she will:

A. Succeed.

B. Succeed, since a contract implied by law was formed.

C. Not succeed, because there was no bargained for exchange.

D. Not succeed.

Questions 14 – 15 are based on the following facts:

Sam had always wanted a Honda motorcycle. Keith, Sam's friend, had recently restored his 1973 Honda motorcycle. On September 1, Sam approached Keith and promised to pay Keith $2,500 on September 15 for Keith's Honda motorcycle. It was agreed that the motorcycle would be delivered on September 9th. The motorcycle was delivered on September 9th as promised by Keith. On September 10th, Sam repudiated.

14. When will Keith have a cause of action against Sam?

    A. Immediately.

    B. September 10th.

    C. On September 1 only.

    D. September 15, or after.

15. Keith's delivery of the motorcycle on September 9th is:

    A. An express condition.

    B. An implied condition.

    C. A constructive condition precedent.

    D. A concurrent condition.

16. Merry, a merchant who deals in special industrial engines, agrees to construct a special industrial engine grinder for Happy, another merchant. The cost to construct this special grinder is $50,000. Upon completion of the grinder, it was agreed that Merry was to ship the machine to Happy. However, before the engine was completely finished, the warehouse containing the engine burned to the ground, completely destroying the engine. The fire was not the fault of anyone. Which is the most correct statement?

    A. Happy's performance is excused.

    B. Happy must pay damages.

    C. Merry may collect from Happy the loss not covered by the insurance.

    D. Merry may sue for breach of contract.

17. Flint Stone Co., a major constructor, agreed to build a large enclosed shopping mall in Bedrock, for the Rubble Corporation. After long hours of deliberation, the parties agreed on the price of 30 million dollars. The contract was signed on January 1. The completion of the new mall was set for May 1. As Flint started digging, it struck jellystone. Removing this jellystone would increase the cost by one-half million dollars. Other builders who made bids had been aware of the jellystone and had submitted much higher bids. The most probable outcome is:

    A. Flint Stone Co. will be excused from performance.

    B. Flint Stone and Rubble will split the increased costs.

    C. The contract is void due to impracticability.

    D. Flint Stone Co. will be bound to finish the work originally contracted for and will suffer the increased costs.

Questions 18 – 19 are based on the following facts:

Brent, a buyer, contracted with Selma, a seller, to buy 12 dozen roller blades for $1,200. Payment was due 20 days after delivery. When the roller blades arrived they were found to be non-conforming. Brent rejected the shipment of roller blades.

18. Brent still has the roller blades and is required to:

    A. Send the roller blades back to Selma.

    B. Sell the roller blades at a discount and give the proceeds to Selma.

    C. Accept the roller blades and sue for breach of contract.

    D. Hold the roller blades with reasonable care for disposition as Selma instructs.

19. In a general claim for damages, which would not be incidental damages?

    A. An expected profit by the buyer of which the seller was aware at the time the contract was made.

    B. Expenses incurred in inspecting non-conforming goods.

    C. The cost of storing non-conforming goods.

    D. A sales commission paid to accomplish cover.

20. Tess sees a demonstration of a new model curling iron that curls hair in 30 seconds. Tess is interested because she is a model and always has to do her hair in a hurry. The curling iron that Tess purchases takes 2 minutes to curl her hair. Is the curling iron's performance sufficient to create a cause of action for Tess?

    A. No, because she has no privity.

    B. Yes, because there was a warranty of fitness for a particular purpose.

    C. Yes, because there was an express warranty.

    D. None of the above.

Questions 21 – 25 are based on the following facts:

Girkin, the local City Councilman, owns a fast-food restaurant at 1st and Meridian. Because of his special position, he learns the Mayor and the Governor are making the final arrangements to move the state hockey team, the "Knuckleheads," to City. The ten-acre proposed site is very close to 1st and Meridian. Various general contractors are submitting bids to construct the sports complex. Girkin spends a large amount of money hiring marketing consultants and improving the restaurant at 1st and Meridian. After spending nearly all his savings, Girkin is invited to the Governor's mansion. Very late into the evening, he notices the Governor and Mayor engaged in a serious discussion. Girkin gets within earshot to hear, "Well, now that the sport complex deal has been finalized, let's start our downtown renovation program." Girkin gets himself into the conversation and excitedly exclaims, "It's finally going to happen!" Both the Mayor and the Governor nod yes. GK, Inc., one of the general contractors, is awarded the contract to build the sports complex by Mayor. SK Enterprises is an electrical subcontractor who provided a subcontracting bid upon which GK, Inc.'s bid is based.

21. If SK Enterprises fails to perform, can Mayor sue GK, Inc.?

    A. No, because Mayor had no donative intent towards the SK Enterprises.

    B. No, because Mayor would be a creditor beneficiary if she had advanced salary to GK, Inc.

    C. Yes, because Mayor would be a creditor beneficiary.

    D. Yes, because Mayor would have vested rights in the contract between SK Enterprises and GK, Inc.

22. If Mayor sues GK, Inc., can GK, Inc. sue SK Enterprises?

    A. No, Mayor cannot sue GK, Inc., as the general contractor is not responsible for the breach of subcontractors.

    B. Yes, since SK Enterprises, as the subcontractor, is the obligor.

    C. Yes, if Mayor and GK, Inc. have a valid enforceable contract.

    D. Yes, if GK, Inc. and SK Enterprises had a valid enforceable contract.

23. If SK Enterprises' negligence causes a fire, and there is a lack of adequate insurance because of Mayor's negligence, can Girkin sue as a third party beneficiary?

    A. Yes, if the negligence of the two tortfeasors are proven in court.

B. No, because Mayor is an officious intermeddler.

C. No, Girkin did not have the right to receive any duty.

D. No, the agreement of Mayor and GK, Inc. can vitiate any vested rights Girkin had.

24. SK Enterprises completes work according to the sub-contract. Mayor does not pay GK; so GK does not pay SK. SK Enterprises sues Mayor. What is the most likely outcome?

A. Mayor's damages will be offset by any breach of GK, Inc.

B. Mayor's damages will be offset by any breach of SK Enterprises.

C. SK Enterprises has suffered a "legal" detriment.

D. SK Enterprises is an incidental beneficiary to the Mayor/GK, Inc. agreement.

25. Mayor proposes that the business around the sports complex area be painted with a color scheme coordinated to that of the Knucklehead's uniforms. Because this would mean that Girkin's restaurant would have to repaint and change all of the food packaging, Girkin is opposed to the Mayor's renovation plan for the sports complex area. In a 6-to-1 decision, the city council votes in the Mayor's plan. Does Girkin have any rights due to the affirmative nod he received at the party and the reliance upon it?

A. Yes, Girkin has suffered a bargained-for legal detriment.

B. Yes, Girkin has reasonably relied.

C. Yes, mayor should have known by Girkin's exclamation that he would rely.

D. No, the communication between the parties has not yet reached a point where vesting could occur in Girkin.

Questions 26 – 28 are based on the following facts:

Driver injured Ped in an auto accident. Ped hired Axel, an attorney, to represent him. Ped explained to Axel that he was poor and couldn't afford the needed medical treatment. Concerned for his client's health, Axel wrote into their contract that he would promise to "pay from any settlement with Driver, compensation to any physicians who treated Ped for his recently sustained injuries." The contract also stated that Axel's duties were non-assignable. Suit was then filed against Driver. Ped sought medical treatment from Doctor. The total medical costs were $1,500. Ped did not inform Doctor of Axel's promise.

When Doctor asked for payment, Ped told Doctor he was unable to pay and gave Doctor a copy of the contract he had with Axel. Axel then requested a release from his contract. He refers Ped to attorney "Grease." Ped agreed to the release and to representation by Grease. Grease negotiates a settlement with Driver on behalf of Ped, for $1,500. Ped spends the $1,500 paying old bills he owes. Ped does not make payments to Doctor. Ped remains penniless.

26. If Doctor brings an action against Ped to recover the $1,500, what is Doctor's best theory of recovery?

    A. Doctor provided necessary health services.

    B. Doctor has a valid claim based upon an implied-in-fact contract.

    C. Doctor is a creditor beneficiary.

    D. Doctor is a donee beneficiary.

27. If Doctor brings an action against Axel based on the employment contract with Ped, Axel's best defense argument would be:

    A. The Doctor did not change his position in reliance.

    B. The anti-assignment clause is void.

    C. Axel relied to his detriment on Ped's release.

    D. The Doctor is an incidental beneficiary.

28. If Doctor brings an action against Grease, Grease will most likely argue:

    A. There is no evidence supporting that Doctor changed his position in reliance.

    B. There is no evidence supporting a finding that Doctor was either a creditor or donee beneficiary of Grease's promise to Axel.

    C. Grease only made a gratuitous promise.

    D. Doctor is an unidentified beneficiary.

29. Toyco, a recently-established business which manufacture yo-yo's, entered into a written agreement to purchase all of its requirements of hard plastic for 2 years from Plasco. Toyco and Plasco agreed on a unit price and on delivery and payment terms. The agreement also stated that the parties promised not to assign the contract and that the first four months of payments due to Plasco by Toyco would be made to Credo, a creditor of Plasco. Plasco then makes an assignment of the contract to Loanco for security on a loan. In regards to the non-assignment clause, which statement is correct:

   A. The assignment is completely ineffective.

   B. The non-assignment clause has no legal effect.

   C. Plasco's assignment is a breach of contract with Toyco, but there is still an effective transfer to Loanco.

   D. It is void as against public policy.

Questions 30 and 31 are based on the following facts:

Martha owns a small interior decorating business. Because of the record recession, Martha finds herself in financial difficulty. In fact, Martha becomes $10,000 behind in payments to Design Factory, who supplies Martha with her materials. Martha stumbles into a great offer with Swingin Star to redecorate her home. Martha enters into a contract with Swingin Star to redecorate her home and Swingin Star is to pay Martha's fee to Design Factory.

30. Martha's contract with Swingin Star makes Design Factory:

   A. An incidental beneficiary.

   B. A creditor beneficiary.

   C. A donee beneficiary.

   D. An intended beneficiary.

31. If Martha refuses to complete the work for Swingin Star and Design Factory sues Swingin Star for the amount due, Design Factory will most likely:

   A. Lose, because Martha must pay.

   B. Lose, because Design Factory is subject to the defense of the failure of Martha's performance.

   C. Win, because the rights were vested.

D. Win, because no defenses are applicable in this fact situation.

32. Allegro was an unknown struggling songwriter. One evening at a Mozart concert, he meets and falls in love with Soprano. Soprano marvels at the talent of Allegro. In fact, she moves in with him, pays the rent, and cooks and cleans, so he can continue his musical work. Allegro is so grateful that he writes Soprano a beautiful song promising to give her 20% of any future royalties he receives from his music. One day Allegro is humming a new tune walking down Broadway. Because he is not paying any attention, he is hit by a taxi and dies instantly. One week later, his estate enters into a contract with Blast Records and his song, titled "To Soprano", becomes a #2 hit. Also, it is selected as a movie theme for Madonna's new movie. Soprano brings a cause of action against Allegro's estate to recover her 20% of the royalties. What result will most likely happen?

A. She will win because the assignment is enforceable.

B. She will win because her house-keeping constitutes valuable consideration.

C. She will lose because future contract claims are not assignable.

D. She will lose because Allegro made an illusory promise.

Questions 33 – 35 are based on the following facts:

The Van Gogh museum, located in Wyoming, was famous for its collection of rare silver spoons. The museum was very interested in acquiring the spoon used by Henry VIII. Van Gogh enters into a $50,000 contract with Whistler, a world-known dealer, to acquire the spoon. Whistler has an incredible reputation with the museums locally as well as abroad. Fork, who owns the Henry VIII spoon, offers to sell it to Whistler for $60,000. Whistler rejects the offer, explaining that he would lose $10,000 in the deal. Whistler offers to assign his contract with Van Gogh to Fork for $5,000. Fork agrees. Whistler then sends a telegram to Van Gogh explaining the assignment.

33. Fork tenders the spoon to Van Gogh. She then requests payment of $50,000. Van Gogh refuses, stating that there is no obligation. Fork brings a breach of contract action. What will the most likely result be?

A. Fork will lose because the per formance is too personal.

B. Fork will lose because there is no existing privity.

C. Fork will win because she paid valuable consideration for the assignment.

D. Fork will win because the duty was delegable.

34. What if Fork had refused to sell the spoon to Van Gogh and the museum sues for breach of contract?

A. The museum would win because the delegation of duty resulted in a third-party beneficiary contract, giving museum a cause of action.

B. Van Gogh would win because Fork owns the spoon.

C. Van Gogh will lose because there is no privity of contract.

D. Van Gogh will lose because the cause of action is against Whistler.

35. What if Fork refuses to sell the spoon to Van Gogh and Van Gogh sues Whistler for Breach of Contract?

A. Van Gogh will lose because he assigned the contract.

B. Van Gogh will lose because of the doctrine of impossibility.

C. Van Gogh will win because Whistler remains the guarantor for the performance of Fork.

D. Van Gogh will win because Whistler's duty was too personal to delegate.

36. Chairco owned a commercial building, part of which it leased to Sportco. At the time the parties entered into the lease, Chairco also sold some locker room equipment (lockers and saunas) to Sportco. The bill of sale provided that:

"Seller does hereby sell, convey and transfer to Buyer any right, title and interest seller may have in goods. It is expressly understood and agreed seller shall not be obligated, liable or accountable for any warranties on the goods sold to buyer."

Unknown to Sportco, the equipment had been obtained from Franco, a previous lessee who had been unsuccessful in operating his business. After Sportco purchased the equipment, Franco sued Chairco for title and possession of the equipment. Franco prevailed and repossessed the equipment from Sportco. Sportco now sues Chairco for the loss. Who prevails?

A. Sportco, because the warranty of title cannot be disclaimed.

B. Sportco, because Chairco did not specifically disclaim the warranty of title.

C. Chairco, because the language in the bill of sale effectively disclaimed the implied warranty of title.

D. Chairco, provided the disclaimer of warranty was conspicuous.

37. Joe contacted Ed's Marina concerning the purchase of a motorboat. Joe indicated that he needed to use the boat at a water ski show at Marine World, and that the boat would be pulling 10 skiers at a time, at 35 miles per hour.

Ed directed Joe to a used "Starcraft" boat with a 175 horsepower outboard motor. Ed stated, "This baby has a lot of power and you'll be able to pull 20 skiers at 35 miles per hour if you decide to increase the size of your show."

When Joe tried to pull more than 5 skiers, the boat could not muster more than 15 miles per hour. In addition, one week later the motor blew up. Joe contacted Ed about the problems, and was refused a refund. Joe sues Ed for breach of contract. What result?

A. Joe wins because Ed made an express warranty to Joe.

B. Joe wins because of Ed's implied warranty of merchantability, which accompanied the sale to Joe.

C. Joe will lose because he should have tried out the boat before his purchase.

D. Joe will lose because the UCC does not apply to used goods.

Questions 38 – 39 are based on the following facts:

Bill's Boats ("Bill's"), a boat supply store, sent a purchase order to Marine Wholesalers ("Marine") on July 7. Marine wholesales boat engines and parts. The purchase order stated, "Please send immediately two Viking outboard motors at your current list price of $350 each."

Marine received the order on July 9. Since Marine only had one Viking motor in stock, it shipped one Viking motor and one Sputter motor to Bill's. The Sputter motor had comparable features to the Viking motor, but sold for $100 less than the Viking.

38. Was an enforceable contract formed upon Marine's shipment of the motors?

A. Yes, because Marine's shipment constituted an acceptance.

B. Yes, because Marine acted in good faith in shipping the motor.

C. No, since Marine could only accept Bill's offer by a return promise.

D. No, because Marine's shipment of non-conforming goods was not an acceptance, but a counter-offer.

39. What are Bill's rights upon receipt of the motors?

A. Bill's may accept all or part of the shipment without giving notice to Marine.

B. Bill's may either accept or reject all or part of the shipment, upon reasonable notice to Marine.

C. Bill's must either accept all or none of the shipment.

D. Bill's must accept all of the order shipped and sue Marine for breach.

Questions 40 – 41 are based on the following facts:

On August 21, Canco, a vegetable canning company, sent the following letter to Grocer:

"Have 50 cases of canned corn available at $10.50 per case. This offer will remain open for acceptance until October 1. Please reply if interested."

On September 1, Grocer sent a fax to Canco which stated:

"Please be advised that I accept your offer dated August 21. However, I would appreciate delivery of 25 cases in October and 25 cases in November, if possible."

40. According to the facts, could Canco revoke the offer before October 1?

    A. No, because Canco had given Grocer assurance that the offer would remain open.

    B. No, because both parties are merchants.

    C. Yes, because there was no consideration for keeping the offer open.

    D. Yes, since Grocer relied to its detriment.

41. Grocer's fax on September 1 had the following effect:

A. It had no legal effect because the mode of acceptance was not the same as Canco's offer.

B. It operates as a reflection of the offer and creates a counter-offer, since Grocer changed the terms.

C. A contract for 50 cases of corn was formed.

D. A contract for 50 cases of corn was formed for delivery in October and November.

Questions 42 – 43 are based on the following facts:

Shoe Heaven ordered 1000 pairs of children's shoes in specified sizes and styles from Cobbler Distributing. Delivery was requested on May 1, with payment to be due 30 days from delivery. Cobbler found it could only fill the order to the extent of 900 pairs. Without communicating with Shoe Heaven, Cobbler shipped the 900 pairs of shoes. On receipt of the shoes on April 30, Shoe Heaven rejected the shipment.

42. Assuming that Cobbler is now suing Shoe Heaven for breach of contract, which of the following is the most likely outcome?

    A. Judgment will be for Cobbler because he substantially performed.

    B. Judgment will be for Cobbler, but Shoe Heaven will be entitled to set off any damages attributable to the non-delivery of the 100 pairs of shoes.

    C. Judgment will be for Shoe Heaven because Cobbler had not filled the order according to its specified terms.

    D. Judgment will be for Shoe Heaven, but only because a 10% deficiency in the amount delivered would be considered a substantial failure of performance.

43. Assume for this question only, that Shoe Heaven accepted the shipment of 900 pairs of shoes and gave notice to Cobbler that the shipment was incomplete. Upon receiving no reply, Shoe Heaven brought suit against Cobbler for damages caused by Cobbler's failure to deliver the remaining 100 pairs of shoes. Which of the following is the most likely outcome?

    A. Shoe Heaven will recover damages against Cobbler.

    B. Shoe Heaven will recover, but only if Cobbler's failure to deliver the remaining 100 pairs of shoes could be considered a material breach.

    C. Shoe Heaven will not recover because it waived Cobbler's breach by accepting the 900 pairs of shoes.

    D. Shoe Heaven will not recover because Cobbler shipped the shoes it had.

44. Liz, owner of Fabco, and Sally, manager of Silk Creations, had a phone conversation, during which an agreement was reached that Sally would buy 500 yards of silk at $10 per yard from Liz. Liz then sent a signed letter to Sally to confirm the transaction. The letter omitted the price term. A month later, Liz called to confirm the date of delivery, but was told by Sally that she did not need the order. Assuming that Liz sues Sally for a breach of contract, what is the most likely outcome?

    A. There will be judgment for Sally because the written confirmation was not signed by the party to be charged.

    B. There will be judgment for Sally because the confirmation was insufficient since the price was omitted.

    C. There will be judgment for Sally because Liz did not verify the order with Sally within 10 days of sending the confirmation.

    D. There will be judgment for Liz because both parties are merchants.

45. Robin is considering buying a 4-wheel drive truck, but is concerned about rollover safety. She asks Cal about the rollover safety of the new Forge truck. Cal assures Robin that all Forge trucks have always come with an integral rollbar built into the cab structure, as shown in Forge's brochure. The brochure explains that the cab provides complete rollover protection.

    Robin's friend, Martin, rolled an identical Forge truck the prior week when she was off-roading and was seriously injured when the cab was completely crushed. Robin knew of Martin's accident, but purchased the Forge truck, because she thought Cal was a convincing salesman. Robin rolls her truck and is also injured. She sues Forge for her injuries, who prevails?

    A. Robin, since Forge made an express warranty on which she relied.

    B. Robin, since her car was totaled.

    C. Forge, since Robin could not have relied on the affirmation in entering the contract.

    D. Forge, since Cal actually made the representations to Robin.

46. Smith, a commercial real estate broker, traveled quite frequently in order to consummate real estate sales. Late one night, while returning home to California from a business trip, in which Smith had sold a $2.1 billion dollar commercial building, he left his brief case in the baggage claim area at the airport. The next morning, Smith realized that he had left his brief case at the airport. He phoned the airport to see if anyone had turned in his brief case, but the security desk told Smith nobody had turned his brief case in to "Lost and Found." Smith, desperate to get his brief case back, since it had all the legal papers from his $2.1 billion dollar sale, posted flyers all around the airport. The flyers stated:

    > *"Lost - one black brief case, contains the name 'Smith.' Will pay $500.00 to anyone for its return. Call (213) 555-2645."*

    Early that evening, Ethel, who had just arrived to California, read the flyer posted in the arriving area while she was waiting, for some friends to pick her up. After an hour of waiting, she went to the baggage claim area to claim her luggage. Her friends were in the baggage area waiting her arrival. Ethel, retrieved all her bags and noticed the black brief case described on the flyer on the luggage carousel. She picked up the brief case, tore a lost flyer off the wall and left the airport with her friends.

A few days later, Smith realized that he had put those legal papers in his suitcase. Since he had found the papers and the brief case was worth less than $500.00, he decided that he did not need the return of the brief case. As Smith was on his way out the door to go to the airport to take down the posted flyers, Ethel called regarding the brief case that she had found. She asked Smith, "Did you lose a black brief case at the airport?" Before anything else was said by Ethel, Smith replied, "I thought I had left important legal papers in the brief case that I was working on, but I've found the papers." He further stated that he was just leaving to pull all the flyers from the airport in cancellation of the reward offer. If Ethel claims the $500.00 reward from Smith, she will:

A. Recover, because a contract was formed when she called Smith to return his brief case.

B. Recover, because Smith created a unilateral contract upon the posting of the flyers, and once Ethel performed, it became irrevocable.

C. Not recover, because no contract was formed.

D. Not recover, unless she returns the brief case.

Questions 47 – 48 are based on the following facts:

On September 1, X wrote a letter to Y, an acquaintance of his, stating, "I'm in need of a truck for transportation for my business and will buy your 'YO' truck for $10,000, upon you bringing it to my office at 1313 Capitol Street in Anaheim, on or before September 6." On September 3, Y received the letter and immediately replied by mail, "I accept your offer and promise to deliver the truck September 6 before noon." Y mailed the acceptance letter but the letter got lost in the mail and was never received by X.

On September 4, X purchased a truck from Z, for his business transportation needs. Late that night, Z ran into Y, and told him that X had purchased his truck for his business, and that he, Z, was interested in purchasing his truck for $7,000. Y replied to Z that he would think about his offer of purchase and would get back to him in a few days.

On September 6, at 9:00 a.m., Y arrived at X's business, but X was not there. At 11:00 a.m., X arrived and refused to buy Y's truck, because he already purchased a truck and had no need for two trucks. Y sues X for breach of contract.

47. What legal effect did Y's letter have?

    A. The letter dated September 2, bound both parties to a bilateral contract because Y could accept by an act or a promise.

B. The letter dated September 2, bound both parties to a unilateral contract as soon as Y mailed the letter.

C. The letter had no legal effect, allowing X to revoke his offer.

D. The September 2nd letter would only be an acceptance had X received Y's letter.

48. What is the legal effect of Z's conversation with Y?

A. There is no legal effect because X's offer was irrevocable.

B. There is no legal effect because Z was making an offer to purchase Y's truck.

C. Z's conversation with Y terminated X's original offer, and operated as an offer for Z to purchase Y's truck for $7,000.

D. The conversation operated as a termination of Y's power of acceptance of X's offer.

Questions 49 – 50 are based on the following facts:

Jack, a retired Olympic swimmer, decided to follow through with his long-time dream to build a large indoor swimming pool for the purpose of training youngsters for competition. Dan orally contracted with Jack on March 10 to build the pool, spectator bleachers and a parking lot. Bill has already orally agreed to permit the building of a parking lot on his property that is adjacent to Jack's property. Dan agreed to begin work on the project on March 20, and to complete the work by June 15, in time for summer. The total price of the job is $28,000, to be paid in three installments: $13,000 on March 20, $5,000 when the pool and bleachers are completed, and $10,000 when Dan finishes with the parking lot.

49. Assume that Jack tendered the $13,000 on March 20, and that Dan refused to accept it, or perform. If Jack sues Dan for breach of contract, which defense(s) can Dan successfully use?

A. The Jack-Bill agreement was not in writing.

B. The Jack-Dan agreement was not in writing.

C. Both A and B.

D. Neither A nor B.

50. Assume that Jack paid the $13,000 on March 20, and that Dan completed the pool and bleachers, according to specifications. However, Jack then refused to pay the second installment, and repudiates the contract. Which of the following is correct?

    A. Dan has a cause of action against Jack for $5,000 in damages.

    B. Dan can refuse to finish the parking lot, and not be liable for breach of contract.

    C. Both A and B.

    D. Neither A nor B.

51. Bar Candidate orally agreed to sell his bar materials to Student for $1,500. Bar Candidate explained to Student that he was only interested in selling the materials to Student if Bar Candidate passes the bar exam. For that reason, the parties also agreed that the transaction would not take effect unless Bar Candidate passed his bar exam. After two weeks had lapsed, Bar Candidate and Student reduced their agreement into a writing, but no mention was made that the sale would be contingent upon Bar Candidate passing his bar exam.

    In an action by Student against Bar Candidate for breach of contract, how should the court rule on Bar Candidate's offer of proof that he did not pass his bar exam?

    A. The evidence is admissible because Bar Candidate's purpose of the contract was frustrated.

    B. The evidence is admissible because the final writing was not a full integration of the parties oral agreement.

    C. The evidence is barred because of the Statute of Frauds.

    D. The evidence is barred because the oral agreement contradicts the written agreement.

52. Seller, contracted in writing to deliver to Buyer, 10,000 cartons of milk on May 1 at $ 1.00 a carton. Because the farmers who supplied Seller with his milk did not deliver enough milk, Seller only had 9,000 cartons of milk to fulfill his contract with Buyer. If Seller tenders only 9,000 cartons of milk to Buyer on May 1, and Buyer refuses to accept, or pay for any, which is the best statement regarding their contractual relationship?

    A. The doctrine of impossibility of performance excuses Seller from performing the contact.

    B. Seller can sue Buyer since he substantially performed the contract.

    C. Buyer is obligated to give Seller time to cure.

D. Buyer has a cause of action against Seller for Seller's failure to deliver 10,000 cartons of milk.

53. Miller started a car wash in Columbus, Ohio. He leased his equipment from Americo in 1987, under a five-year lease which was renewable for 3 one-year periods. At the end of eight years, Americo would "abandon" the equipment to Miller (he would have paid for it in full). In May 1991, Miller defaulted. Americo repossessed and resold the equipment. Americo claims it is owed $2,000 by Miller, under a lease provision which provides that Americo could collect 10% of the equipment's total cost in the event of any default. Miller claims the liquidated damages clause is invalid. Is the liquidated damages clause valid?

A. Yes, because there was a meeting of the minds.

B. Yes, because it is to determine whether or not Miller would default at the inception of the lease.

C. No, because a 10% liquidated damages clause in any contract is unconscionable as a matter of law.

D. No, because the damages to Americo would not be difficult to ascertain.

Questions 54 – 55 are based on the following facts:

In a written contract, Manufacturer agreed to deliver to Baker, 200 described chairs at $100 each F.O.B., at Manufacturer's place of business. The contract provided that "neither party will assign the contract without written consent of the other." Manufacturer placed the chairs on the carrier on August 31. On September 1, Manufacturer in a signed writing, assigned to Wheeler all his rights under the Manufacturer-Baker contract. On September 3, the chairs were destroyed by fire while in transit.

54. In an action by Wheeler against Baker for breach of contract, Wheeler will recover:

A. $20,000, the contract price.

B. The difference between the contract price and the market value of the chairs.

C. Nothing, because the chairs had not been delivered.

D. Nothing, because the Manufacturer and Baker contract forbid an assignment.

55. In an action by Baker against Manufacturer for breach of contract, Barker will probably:

A. Succeed, since the risk of loss was on Manufacturer.

B. Succeed, since the contract was not assigned.

C. Not succeed, since the risk of loss was on Baker.

D. Not succeed, since the chairs were destroyed making it impossible for Manufacturer to perform.

56. Billy Joe, a disabled veteran, contracted to purchase a certain piece of land from Jermey. The property consisted of a 1.65-acre home site, and an 80-acre tract of land containing the famous tourist attraction, " Blue Lagoon". Billy was excited because he could now be a homeowner and receive income in order to pay the land payments and his living expenses. After BillyJoe purchased the property, he discovered that the home site was on Federal Reserve Land, and that the income from the lagoon was $36,000 rather than $39,000 as represented. Billy Joe sued Jermey. Billy Joe can:

I. Recover money damages only.

II. Rescind the contract.

A. I only.

B. II only.

C. I or II.

D. Neither I nor II.

57. The Bank of Commerce Inc. ("BCI") loaned the Bombay Company $1 million for the manufacture of a new type of computer chip. As a condition of the loan, Wendy Wonder, a majority shareholder in Bombay, agreed in writing to personally guarantee the loan. Thereafter, Bombay defaulted on the loan and entered into a repayment agreement with BCI. This agreement provided that BCI would "use maximum efforts in selling Bombay's assets at the highest possible price." BCI proceeded to sell Bombay's assets, discharging the indebtedness of the Bombay Company.

Later, it was ascertained that BCI did not realize the "highest possible price" in administering the sale of Bombay's assets. Consequently, Wendy was forced into bankruptcy and lost her entire investment in the Bombay Company.

Wendy brings an appropriate action against BCI to recover her investment in Bombay's stock. She will most likely:

A. Not prevail, because Wendy was an incidental beneficiary of the BCI sale of Bombay's assets.

B. Not prevail, because BCI's sale of Bombay's assets discharged whatever contractual relationship existed between Wendy and the bank.

C. Prevail, because BCI did not realize the highest possible price from the sale of Bombay's assets.

D. Prevail, because BCI breached its fiduciary duty to Wendy under the terms of the BCI-Bombay contract.

Questions 58 – 59 are based on the following facts:

On January 5, Prevention Company, a manufacturer of steel security blinds for homes, received the following order from Lion Homes: "Please ship 500 4' x 6' security shutters. Delivery by March 10."

On February 10, Prevention shipped 500 4' x 8' security shutters, which were received by Lion on February 12. The following day Lion's foreman, Dave White, sent the following fax to Prevention's president, John Smallwood, "Be advised that your shipment is rejected. Order stipulated 4' x 6' security shutters." The fax was received by John Smallwood on February 15. Lion, however, did not ship the nonconforming shutters back to Prevention.

On February 16, Mr. Smallwood sent the following telegram to Mr. White: "Will ship conforming security shutters before March 1." This telegram was received by Mr. White on February 17, but he did not respond to it. On March 7, Prevention tendered the 500 shutters of proper size to Lion, which were refused.

58. Did Lion properly refuse the first shipment delivered on February 12?

    A. No, because Lion waived its right to reject the nonconforming goods by not returning them.

B. No, because Prevention could accept Lion's offer by prompt shipment of either conforming or nonconforming goods.

C. Yes, because the security shutters were nonconforming.

D. Yes, because Prevention did not notify Lion that the 4' x 8' security shutters were for accommodation only.

59. Did Lion properly reject the security shutters delivered on March 7?

A. No, because, under the UCC, a contract for the sale of goods can be modified without consideration.

B. No, because Prevention cured the February 10 defective shipment by tender of conforming goods on March 7.

C. Yes, because Prevention's shipping of the 4' x 8' security shutters on February constituted anticipatory breach.

D. Yes, because Prevention's shipping of the 4' x 8' security shutters on February 10 constituted a present breach.

Questions 60 – 61 are based on the following facts:

Tom wanted to have a security system installed in his home. He contacted several companies and had them submit bids for the installation of the system. SecureCo, in turn, requested bids from several wholesalers for prices of burglar alarm components which it planned to use if awarded the job. BurgCo submitted a bid to SecureCo that was used in computing the bid for Tom.

On October 1, SecureCo sent Tom its bid, of $5,000 for the security system and its installation. On October 9, BurgCo notified SecureCo that they would be unable to supply any burglar alarm components to SecureCo. On October 11, Tom sent the following telegram to SecureCo, "I hereby accept your offer to install the security system for $5,000."

SecureCo had to pay another wholesaler $1,000 above the quoted price by BurgCo for the burglar alarm components. As a result, SecureCo advised Tom that the total price for the job would be $6,000. Tom replied that he would hold SecureCo to the price stated in the submitted bid. SecureCo went ahead and installed the security system.

60. In an action by SecureCo against Tom, SecureCo will be able to recover:

A. $5,000, because that was the contract price.

B. $6,000, because of an unanticipated change of circumstances.

C. Only in quantum merit, because SecureCo did not intend to operate at a loss.

D. Only in quantum meruit, because by demanding $6,000 SecureCo repudiated its contract with Tom.

61. What argument best supports the claim for the additional $1,000 by SecureCo against BurgCo?

A. BurgCo had made an offer to SecureCo that was accepted when it submitted its bid.

B. BurgCo had made an offer that SecureCo accepted by using the former's bid in computing the bid it submitted to Tom.

C. BurgCo's bid was an offer that it was obligated to hold open because of the fact that BurgCo and SecureCo were merchants.

D. An option contract was created when SecureCo used BurgCo's bid.

62. Tony, a third year law student at Wazoo Law School, was the captain of the Moot Court team. One evening Tony and a few classmates were drinking beer at Texas Lucky's, a favorite Wazoo Law School hangout. They were worried that the Moot Court team, known as the Litigators, would be forced to disband because the law school had withdrawn its sponsorship. While Ann was discussing the problem with her teammates, Peter, the owner of the bar, approached the group. Peter indicated that he was interested in sponsoring the Moot Court because he felt it would bring in more business from the law school. During their discussion, Peter agreed to sponsor the Moot Court team. They then entered into a written agreement, which provided that Peter would pay for all the "usual sponsoring fees."

Peter had understood the agreement to mean that he would supply the keg of beer following each competition. Conversely, Tony thought that Peter would be reimbursing the team for 1) transportation costs, 2) research and material costs, 3) the keg of beer, and 4) plaques to the competition finalists. Did a contract exist between Tony and Peter?

A. No contract exists.

B. Yes, a contract exists on the terms understood by Tony.

C. Yes, a contract exists on the terms understood by Peter.

D. Yes, a contract exists but only on the consistent terms between the parties.

Questions 63 – 65 are based on the following facts:

On September 1, Oliva Co., an olive wholesaler, sent Mario, the owner of an Italian restaurant in Los Angeles, the following signed letter:

"Have 300 pounds of large fresh olives available at $3.00 per pound for October delivery. This offer will remain open for acceptance until October 1. Please reply if interested."

On September 30, Mario wired the following telegram to Oliva Co., which it received the next day:

"Please be advised that I hereby accept your offer dated September 1. However, I would appreciate your delivering 150 pounds in October and 150 pounds in November if you possibly can."

63. According to the given facts, is it possible that Oliva Co., could have revoked the offer before October 1?

    A. No, because it had given Mario assurance that the offer would be held open until October 1.

    B. No, because Oliva Co. and Mario are merchants.

    C. Yes, because there is no consideration to support an option contract.

D. Yes, unless Mario detrimentally relied on the offer.

64. Mario's telegram of September 30 has which of the following effects?

A. It has no legal effect because the mode of acceptance was not by the same means as the offer.

B. It operates as a rejection of Oliva Co.'s offer, and a proposal of a counteroffer.

C. It creates a contract for 150 pounds of olives for October delivery and 150 pounds of olives for November delivery.

D. It creates a contract for 300 pounds of olives for October delivery.

65. Assume for the purposes of this question only, that Oliva Co. delivered 150 pounds of olives to Mario during October and 150 pounds of olives during November. However, 100 pounds of those delivered in November were not of merchantable quality. If Mario accepts the olives knowing of their defective condition, he probably has:

A. A remedy against Oliva Co., whether or not he gives Oliva Co. notice of the breach.

B. A remedy against Oliva Co., provided he gives Oliva Co. notice of the breach.

C. No remedy against Oliva Co. because he waives whatever claim he may have by accepting the defective olives.

D. No remedy against Oliva Co. because the risk of loss falls on Mario due to the perishable nature of the product.

Questions 66 – 67 are based on the following facts:

On March 1, 1993, Tromp entered into a written contract with Leon wherein the latter agreed to remodel the penthouse suite of Tromp's hotel for $2 million. According to the terms of the agreement, Tromp promised to pay Leon $1 million when work was to commence on May 1, 1993, with the balance payable upon completion of the job.

On April 1, 1993, Leon sent Tromp a letter stating that the cost of building materials had increased from his original estimate. Consequently, Leon indicated that he did not think he could perform the remodeling work unless Tromp agreed to increase the price to $2.5 million. Without notifying Leon, Tromp went ahead and hired Ivan to perform the remodeling for the price of $2.2 million, which was the fair market cost of the work to be done.

Ivan started renovating the penthouse on April 26, 1993. On May 1, 1993, Leon showed up at Tromp's hotel. Leon told Tromp he reconsidered and was ready to begin remodeling the penthouse at the original contract price. Tromp then informed him that he had hired someone else and dismissed Leon from the job.

66. Leon brings suit against Tromp for breach of contract. Judgment will be for?

    A. Leon, because Tromp did not inform him before May 1 that he was hiring someone else to perform the remodeling work.

    B. Leon, because he attempted to perform the remodeling work as contractually agreed.

    C. Tromp, because he hired Ivan for $300,000 less than Leon demanded in his April 1 letter.

    D. Tromp, because Leon's April 1 letter manifested his prospective inability to perform, thereby justifying Tromp treating such as an anticipatory breach.

67. Assume for the purposes of this question only, that Leon is liable for breach of contract in the previous example. In addition, assume that Ivan completed the remodeling of the suite at a profit of $300,000. Tromp went ahead and paid Ivan the contract price of $2.2 million, plus an additional $80,000 so Ivan would not lose any money. In a breach of contract action by Tromp against Leon, Tromp should recover:

    A. $200,000, or the difference between Leon's contract price and Ivan's contract price.

    B. $500,000, or the difference between Leon's original contract price and the amount he demanded in his April 1 letter.

C. $1,000,000, or the difference between Leon's original contract price and the amount Tromp paid Ivan.

D. $280,000, the difference between Tromp's payment to Ivan and Leon's original price.

68. Brown is the owner of Blackacres, a twenty-acre horse ranch. On December 1, Brown and Green both signed an agreement that stated, "In consideration of $1,000, receipt of which is acknowledged, Brown hereby offers to sell Blackacres to Green, for $150,000. This offer is to remain open for thirty days upon the signing by each party. All terms are incorporated."

The property had a fair market value of $165,000. Green failed to pay Brown the $1,000 consideration upon the signing of the agreement. On December 20, Brown sent Green a letter stating:

"Have offer for the purchase of Blackacres from White for $160,000. I hereby withdraw my offer to you for the sale of Blackacres for $150,000, signed Brown."

The next day, Green tendered $151,000 cash to Brown for the purchase of Blackacres (which included the $1,000 unpaid consideration money) and demanded the deed to Blackacres. Brown refused. Green brings an action against Brown for specific performance.

Brown seeks to introduce the fact that Green never paid the $1,000 consideration as required per their written and signed agreement dated December 1. Upon Green's objection, will the trial court permit the testimony?

A. Yes, because the parole evidence doctrine permits contradictory facts in the parties' agreement.

B. Yes, because the parol evidence rule does not operate to exclude evidence of contemporaneous or subsequent oral modifications of the written term.

C. No, because the written instrument is a complete integration of the parties' agreement.

D. No, because the doctrine of promissory estoppel will only apply if Green relied on the Brown-Green agreement to his detriment.

69. Willy owned and operated the Willy's Ice Cream and Sandwich Parlor. The parlor was located at the busy intersection of the Pacific Coast Highway and Dover. Because of its prime location, Willy's was a popular stop for tourists and vacationers. In 1982, Willy leased the Parlor to Dick under a written ten-year lease. During the sixth year of the lease, the city reconstructed the Highway. The city expanded an existing bridge in order to correct the traffic congestion problem. Because of the reconstruction, the highway now went over the parlor. This caused a substantial decline in Dick's business.

    Neither party had knowledge of the city's intent to change that intersection at the time they entered into the lease agreement. Dick contacted Willy and told him of the circumstances. Dick asked Willy to renegotiate the lease agreement, but Willy refused. Because of the decline in the parlor's business, Dick was losing money. He decided to abandon the parlor and refuses to pay Willy any rent. Willy brings an action against Dick to recover the unpaid rent. Who will prevail?

    A. Dick, because of the doctrine of impossibility of performance.

    B. Dick, because the parties inferred, within their agreement, the continued existence of the heavily traveled highway.

    C. Willy, because Dick assumed the risk of any change in circumstances when he entered into the lease.

    D. Willy, because both parties were wrong in their judgment concerning the road change.

70. Tony engaged Dawn, an inexperienced actress, to do a small role in a new Broadway play for a period of six months at a salary of $ 1,000 a week. Dawn turned down another role in a Broadway play, in order to accept this engagement. On the third day of the run, Dawn was hospitalized with bulimia and Betty was hired to do the part. A week later, Dawn recovered, but Tony refuses to accept her services for the remainder of the run. Dawn brings a breach of contract action against Tony. Which of the following is Dawn's best legal theory?

    A. Her acting contract with Tony was legally severable into weekly units.

    B. Her performance of the literal terms of the contract was physically impossible.

    C. She had relied on the engagement with Tony, as shown by declining another acting role.

    D. Her failure to perform for one week was not a material failure.

Questions 71 – 72 are based on the following facts:

On March 5, Seller orally agreed to sell his land, Parcel, to Buyer for $135,000, to be paid on March 31. Buyer orally agreed to pay $35,000 of the purchase price to Creditor in satisfaction of a debt which seller owed to Creditor.

On March 12, Buyer had his attorney, Lawyer, put the agreement into a writing. Lawyer omitted all the terms in reference to the $35,000 payment to Creditor. Lawyer's secretary mistakenly typed $134,000 as the purchase price, rather than $135,000, while preparing the agreement. Neither Seller nor Buyer read the contract carefully before signing it on March 20, and neither Seller nor Buyer noticed the error in the price. Neither Buyer nor Seller raised any question concerning omission of the payment to Creditor.

71. In an action by Creditor against Buyer for $35,000, which of the following is (are) correct?

    I. Buyer could successfully raise the Statute of Frauds as a defense because the Buyer-Seller agreement was to answer for the debt of another.

    II. Buyer could successfully raise the Statute of Frauds as a defense because the Buyer-Seller agreement was for the sale of an interest in land.

    A. I only.

    B. II only.

    C. I and II.

    D. Neither I nor II.

72. If Buyer refused to pay more than $134,000 for Parcel, in an action by Seller against Buyer for the additional $1,000, it would be to Seller's advantage to try to prove that:

    A. The writing was intended only as a sham.

    B. The writing was only a partial integration.

    C. There was a mistake in integration.

    D. There was a misunderstanding between Seller and Buyer concerning the purchase price.

Questions 73 – 75 are based on the following facts:

On Art's twenty-fifth birthday, he drove his father's uninsured motorcycle, which resulted in a crash. The accident happened when Art saw a cute blond and ogled her instead of keeping his eyes upon the road. As a result, Art crashed into Lisa's car. Both Art and Lisa were injured and were rushed to the hospital. Art's father, Allen, while believing that the accident was his son's fault, told Lisa that he would reimburse her for any expenses and losses as a result of the accident. Allen also told Doctor that he would pay Lisa's medical expenses. Art died as a result of his injuries.

73. In an action by Lisa against Allen for lost wages while she was incapacitated as a result of the accident, which of the following would be Allen's best defense?

    A. The Statute of Frauds.

    B. There was a lack of consideration.

    C. Promissory estoppel.

    D. The statement was a mere promise.

74. Which if the following, if true, would be significant in determining whether or not there was a bargained-for-exchange to support Allen's promise to Doctor?

    I. Doctor had not begun treating Lisa before Allen called him.

    II. Allen had a contract with Lisa.

    A. I only.

    B. II only.

    C. I and II.

    D. Neither I nor II.

75. If Doctor is unable to collect his fees from Allen for the medical services provided to Lisa, and he brings an action against Lisa, who will prevail?

    A. Doctor, because Lisa would be unjustly enriched.

    B. Doctor, because a contract existed between Allen and Lisa.

    C. Lisa, because the contract was not in writing.

    D. Lisa, because the contract was not supported by consideration.

Questions 76 – 77 are based on the following facts:

Farmland is a three-acre dairy farm with a small residence upon it. Oliver, the owner of Farmland, entered into a written lease with Terry for the rental of Farmland on a month-to-month basis, at a rate of $1,600 per month. After Terry had been in possession for several years, Terry and Oliver orally agreed that Terry would purchase Farmland for $48,000 payable at a monthly rate of $1,600 (which included principal and interest) for 30 years.

Further, it was agreed that Terry would pay all future property taxes and the expenses for insuring Farmland against fire loss. Oliver agreed that after receiving $24,000 in payments, Oliver would tender the deed to Farmland to Terry, and Terry in exchange, would execute a note secured by a deed of trust for the balance of the unpaid purchase price.

Terry, now being a homeowner, made over $2,000 in improvements on the property. When Terry had tendered $24,000 to Oliver, Oliver, although not denying the oral agreement, refused to tender the deed to Farmland. Terry brought an action against Oliver for specific performance.

76. If Oliver prevails, it is because:

    A. Nothing Terry would have done would have overcome the agreement not being in writing.

    B. The actions and payment of Terry are consistent with her being a tenant.

    C. Oliver has not received any unconscionable benefit, and therefore Terry is not entitled to equitable relief.

    D. The Statute of Frauds controls.

77. If Terry prevails, it will be because of:

    A. The improvements show that Terry detrimentally relied on the oral agreement.

    B. The $24,000 received by Oliver as payment towards the purchase price.

    C. Oliver would receive an unjust benefit if the contract is not enforced.

    D. The contract entered into between Terry and Oliver was supported by consideration.

78. Coiner, a retail coin dealer, purchased a 1916 dime from Investor for $500. The "D" stamped on the coin indicated it had originated at the Denver mint, making it a rare issue. Coiner's owner, Barry, examined the coin before the purchase. Coiner, resold the rare coin to Denny, for $750. Denny later found out that the coin was a counterfeit. Denny sued to rescind its purchase of the 1916 dime from Coiner. The court will:

A. Allow rescission of the contract because of a misrepresentation.

B. Allow rescission of the contract because there was mutual mistake.

C. Not allow the contract to be rescinded because there was no warranty made.

D. Not allow rescission of the contract because buyer assumed the risk upon purchase.

Questions 79 – 80 are based on the following facts:

Ray Rogers Jr. purchased an automobile from a car dealer, Auto, on August 15, 1992. On that date, Rogers was 17 years old and would be 18 on September 25, 1992. Ray executed a purchase money security agreement to finance $4,724, the balance due on the purchase price of the automobile, payable in thirty installments of $198.10 each. Auto subsequently assigned the purchase money agreement to Union Fed Bank.

After making 11 monthly payments, Rogers voluntarily returned the automobile to Auto, and defaulted on his payment obligations. Upon default, Union Fed Bank reassigned the purchase money security agreement to Auto. Auto sold the automobile at public auction for $1,400, leaving a deficiency of over $4,510.

79. Auto now brings suit against Rogers to recover the deficiency. Judgment will be for:

    A. Auto, because Rogers affirmed the contract.

    B. Auto, because a minor cannot disaffirm a contract after reaching the age of majority.

    C. Rogers, because contracts entered into by minors are voidable.

D. Rogers, because by returning the car to Auto, Rogers properly disaffirmed the contract.

80. Assume in this question, that Rogers disaffirmed the contract on September 24, 1992, without making any payments, and failed to return the automobile. After nine months of investigation, Auto finds the car parked in an abandoned lot. Auto takes possession of the car and sells the car at a public action for $1,200, leaving a deficiency. Auto brings suit against Rogers for the amount of the deficiency. Auto will:

A. Prevail, because Rogers did not return the automobile.

B. Prevail, because the automobile was not returned and was found nine months later.

C. Prevail, because the automobile was not found until after Rogers reached the age of majority.

D. Not prevail, because a contract by an infant is voidable.

81. In June 1992, Mrs. Fletcher was transferred by her employer from Denver, Colorado to Lompoc, California. In looking for a house for her family, she consulted a local real estate agency. Mr. Caldwell of that agency showed Mrs. Fletcher several homes, including Mr. Tibbs' home. Mr. Tibbs' property was located a short distance from where Mrs. Fletcher's new office was located. The home obtained its water supply from a well located on the property. Mr. Tibbs received information indicating that the well was contaminated after Mrs. Fletcher had looked at the house. Mrs. Fletcher had Mr. Caldwell write up an offer for Mr. Tibbs' property. Mr. Tibbs accepted the offer, and did not disclose the information about the contaminated well. After escrow closed, Mrs. Fletcher moved into the property and discovered that the well was contaminated. Mrs. Fletcher now brings suit to rescind the contract. The court will find for:

A. Mr. Tibbs, because there was no duty to disclose newly- discovered information.

B. Mr. Tibbs, because escrow closed, releasing him from any further obligations.

C. Mrs. Fletcher, because Mr. Tibbs failed to disclose the contaminated well.

D. Mrs. Fletcher, but she can only recover money damages.

82. Kemper submitted a bid to City to do piping work for a sewer project. The City requires that ten percent of the bid price be posted as a bond, in favor of the City, guaranteeing that the bidder would do the job for the bid price if awarded the contract. Kemper gave a bid at $780,305. Three competing bids were $1,049,592, $1,183,000, and $1,278,895. Kemper discovered a few hours later, after the bids were opened, that there was a $301,769 error in his computations, in which he relied upon in making the bid. Kemper explained the error to City and withdrew his bid, but City accepted the bid anyway.

    Kemper refuses to enter into a contract with City at the mistaken bid price. Kemper sued to rescind the bid. Kemper will:

    A. Prevail, because Kemper made a material mistake.

    B. Prevail, because City would be unjustly enriched if Kemper has to perform.

    C. Not prevail, because City relied on the bid.

    D. Not prevail, because once a bid is submitted, it cannot be withdrawn.

Questions 83 – 85 are based on the following facts:

Bob purchased 100 bolts of lightweight wool fabric of No. 1 quality from Dan. Their contract required Bob to pay for the fabric prior to inspection. The 100 bolts were shipped, and Bob made payment to Dan. Upon his inspection, Bob discovered that the wool was No. 2 quality. Bob tendered back the wool to Dan, and demanded return of his payment. Dan refused on the ground that there is no difference between No. 1 quality wool and No. 2 quality wool.

83. Which of the following statements regarding the contract provision for pre-inspection payment is correct?

    A. It constitutes an acceptance of the goods.

    B. It constitutes a waiver of the buyer's remedy of private sale in the case of nonconforming goods.

    C. It does not impair a buyer's right of inspection or his remedies.

    D. It is invalid.

84. What is Bob's remedy because the wool was nonconforming?

    A. Specific performance.

B. Damages measured by the difference between the value of the goods delivered and the value of conforming goods.

C. Damages measured by the price paid, plus the difference between the contract price and the cost of buying substitute goods.

D. None, since he waived his remedies by agreeing to pay before inspection.

85. Can Bob resell the wool?

A. Yes, in a private sale.

B. Yes, in a private sale- but only after giving Dan reasonable notice of his intention to resell.

C. Yes, but only at a public sale.

D. No, because such an act is inconsistent with the claim such goods were nonconforming.

Questions 86 – 87 are based on the following facts:

Nancy and Melissa, both legal secretaries for the Shiester & Shiester law film, enrolled in the firm's voluntary computer program. This program opted for each to purchase a computer, for daily training during their lunch hours. Nancy bought an inexpensive system. Melissa spent $4,000 for the best system available. After three months, Nancy discovered that she enjoyed working on her computer so much that she would even come in to work on weekends. Melissa really wasn't enthusiastic; in fact, Melissa only worked on her computer about once a week. When Melissa learned of how much Nancy enjoyed working on the computer, she wrote Nancy a memo offering to sell her computer. The memo stated, "I am not a computer buff; if you will pick up the computer at my office before or after work, I will sell it to you for $1,000. I will not revoke this offer."

Nancy knew a deal when she heard one, and sent a letter to Melissa on Tuesday stating, "I accept your offer and will pick up the computer on friday at 7:00 a.m."

The next day, Melissa learns in her employee evaluation conference, that if she becomes competent on the computer, she will receive a large salary increase.

Nancy comes to Melissa's office at 7:00 a.m. on friday. Melissa refuses to sell Nancy the computer.

86. Nancy brings an action for breach of contract against Melissa. What is the legal effect of Nancy's letter accepting Melissa's offer to sell the computer?

    A. It is an ineffective attempt by Nancy to accept Melissa's offer.

    B. A unilateral contract was created, when Nancy mailed the letter.

    C. It constituted notice to Melissa that Nancy would buy the computer.

    D. A bilateral contract was created when Melissa received the letter.

87. What is the effect of Melissa's promise not to revoke the offer?

    A. It prevents Melissa from revoking the offer.

    B. It has no effect because Melissa did not state a date for termination.

    C. It has no effect.

    D. It prevents any implied revocation.

Questions 88 – 90 are based on the following facts:

On April 1, Tim offered to sell his prize mare, Midnight, to Marty for $10,000. Marty handed Tim a $100 bill. In return, Tim handed Marty a written statement which included the offer and also included, that Tim promised not to revoke the offer for a 60-day period. Tim signed the offer. Both Tim and Marty are in the horse breeding business.

On April 5, 1993, Marty wrote a letter to Tim which stated, "I cannot afford to pay more than $8,000 for the mare. If you cannot accept the $8,000, I cannot purchase the horse."

Tim had already sold Midnight to Melinda on April 4, 1993. Marty was unaware of the sale.

On April 15, 1993, Marty discovered he would receive a tax refund. He immediately wrote to Tim. His letter stated, "I accept your offer to purchase Midnight, your prize mare, for $10,000."

88. If Marty sues Tim for damages, the most likely outcome will be:

    A. A contract was formed because Tim was precluded from selling Midnight to another party.

    B. A contract was formed because acceptance any time during the 60 days was effective.

C. Marty's letter of April 5, 1993, prevented a contract from being formed.

D. There was no formation of a contract because Tim's prior sale of Midnight to a third party, revoked his original offer.

89. Assume that Tim did not sell Midnight to another party until April 10, 1993, after receiving Marty's letter of April 5, 1993, and that Marty learned of the sale on April 14, 1993. Marty's power to accept the offer would be:

A. Good for 60 days, because Marty paid $100 for a 60-day option.

B. Terminated on April 14, 1993.

C. Terminated, when Tim received Marty's April 5, 1993 letter.

D. Terminated, when Tim sold Midnight.

90. What if Marty's letter dated April 5, 1993, contained a check for $10,000 and stated "I am going on vacation and will pick the mare up in 30 days. I will pay for any board and necessary care." The letter is:

A. A counter-offer because it changes the terms of the original offer.

B. A counter-offer because it was not definite.

C. An acceptance, and Tim must board the mare.

D. An acceptance, and Tim may refuse to board the mare.

91. Matt began working for Morrocam Food Supply Company in 1969. Matt agreed to work at a pay rate below union scale, in exchange for a promise that Morrocam would employ him "for life." In 1987, Sansabar took over management of Morrocam Food Supply Company. Sansabar assured Morrocam employees that existing employment contracts would be honored. Matt went to a Sansabar supervisor and explained the terms of his employment agreement. The supervisor stated that he would look into the matter, but never got back to Matt. After 18 years of service, Matt was fired by the new owners of the business. Matt brings suit for breach of a contract. Matt will most likely:

A. Win, because if the requirement of consideration is met, there is no additional requirement for enforcing the contract.

B. Win, because Matt agreed to work below scale in exchange for lifetime employment.

C. Lose, because traditional law did not uphold unilateral contracts.

D. Lose, because you cannot promise to employ someone for life.

92. Gil Glass Merchant and Wally Glass Wholesalers had been doing business with each other for 30 years. As was his custom, Gil phoned Wally and placed an order of 1200 glasses to be delivered in sets of 100, one set each month. The glasses were $5 each. After Wally delivered the first set, Gil sent Wally a check for $500 and a letter stating, "$5 a glass is too high; cancel the remainder of my order, Wally." Wally sues Gil for breach of contract. Gil pleads the Statute of Frauds as a defense. The most likely outcome will be that:

   A. Wally prevails, because 100 glasses have been received by Gil.

   B. Wally prevails, because the note constituted a writing sufficient to satisfy the Statute of Frauds.

   C. Gil prevails, because he repudiated the remaining contract.

   D. Gil prevails, because the note does not satisfy the Statute of Frauds.

Questions 93 – 94 are based on the following facts:

Con, a general contractor, was commissioned to build a new motel. Con took bids from several sub-contractors for the plumbing. John submitted a bid for $80,000. The next lowest bid was $85,000. The remaining bids ranged between $86,000 to $87, 500. Con gave the contract to John on March 1, 1993. Work was to begin on April 1, 1993. One week before John was to begin working, he discovered that he had made an error in his calculations. John immediately called Con and told him that he had made a mistake and the bid should have been $84,000, instead of $80,000. John refuses to work, unless Con agrees to pay $84,000.

93. Con refuses to pay the additional amount to John and brings suit for breach of contract. The court will most likely rule for:

   A. Con, because John is bound by a valid contract.

   B. Con, but only if he neither knew nor could have known of the mistake in calculations of the bid.

   C. John, because his obligation is discharged.

   D. John, because time of performance was not due.

94. Assume Con, being in a hurry to get the work started, stated to John he would pay the additional amount. After John completes performance, Con gives John a check for $80,000 and refuses to pay the additional $4,000. The most likely result will be:

A. John will not prevail because of the obligation to perform the work for $80,000.

B. John will not prevail, unless Con never intended to pay the additional $4,000.

C. John will prevail because he intended to work only for the amount of $84,000.

D. John will prevail because the parties mutually agreed to the second contract.

95. Sterling, a merchant, deals in rare coins. Sterling took out an insurance policy from "Gouge Em" Insurance Company, covering the coins Sterling had in stock in his coin shop. There was a written provision in the policy which stated all records describing the coins were to be kept off the store premises in a place where they would not be stolen. Sterling was updating his records, since he had received new inventory. He decided to finish the records the next day. He went home and left the records in the coin shop. The shop was robbed that night. All the coins and the records of the coins were stolen. "Gouge Em" refuses to pay on the policy. Sterling brings suit to recover on the policy. He will most likely:

A. Not prevail, because Sterling breached the contract by leaving the records in the coin shop.

B. Not prevail, because the policy specifically stated the records must be stored in a safe place.

C. Prevail, because the provision in the policy regarding the records has been reasonably satisfied.

D. Prevail, because of the unfairness of the provision.

Questions 96 – 97 are based on the following facts:

Rod and Jim have been friends for many years. Both collect antique cars. Rod had acquired a Model T Ford that Jim felt was the most exquisite Model T he had ever seen. Jim, on several occasions, asked Rod if he could purchase it. Rod did not want to part with the car. Jim then stated, "If you ever decide to sell the car, I want to buy it." On April 1, 1993, Rod realized he was short on cash and would not be able to pay his taxes. He drafted a contract for the sale of his Model T Ford to Jim. He mailed the contract to Jim the same day. Jim received the contract on April 3, 1993. He was so excited that he signed it, and mailed it back the same day. Later that day, Jim's accountant informed him that he was broke. Jim immediately called Rod and told him to ignore the signed contract when he received it, because he was no longer in the financial position to purchase the car. Rod received the signed contract in the mail on April 5, 1993.

96. Can Rod enforce the contract for the sale of his Model T Ford to Jim?

    A. No, because Jim communicated his retraction before Rod received the signed contract in the mail.

    B. No, because the mail is not a reliable source of communication.

    C. Yes, because Jim made his retraction by phone instead of by mail.

    D. Yes, because Jim's act of mailing the signed contract was an effective acceptance.

97. Assume that during the April 3, 1993 telephone conversation, Rod stated, "I'm glad you aren't going to buy my Model T Ford, I really don't want to part with it; I cancel my offer." Does Jim have an enforceable contract to purchase the Model T Ford from Rod?

    A. No, because Jim stated his intent to rescind any contract, and Rod accepted the offer to rescind.

    B. No, because there was no manifestation of contractual intent.

    C. Yes, because you cannot rescind a contract.

    D. Yes, because no valid consideration for rescission occurred.

Questions 98 – 100 are based on the following facts:

Homeowner wanted to have the exterior of his home repainted. He got out the yellow pages, and called a number of established painting firms. He received bids ranging from $6,000 to $7,500. While trying to decide on whom to use, Homeowner received a call from Renoir, who submitted a bid to do the work for $5,500. Homeowner entered into a contract with Renoir to have the exterior of his home painted. The work was to begin on January 1, 1993. On December 30, 1992, Renoir called Homeowner and stated, "My foreman made a mistake in adding the figures. I can't possibly do the work for less than $6,100, or I will lose money."

98. If Homeowner sues Renoir for breach of contract, who prevails?

    A. Renoir, because he had not started painting.

    B. Renoir, because of the defense of mistake.

    C. Homeowner, unless he can still accept the bid of the next lowest bidder.

    D. Homeowner, only if he had no reason to know of Renoir's error.

99. Assume that Homeowner responded to Renoir's statement of an error in his bid by stating, "I'll pay the extra money, but I really think it's unfair." After Renoir finished painting Homeowner's home, Homeowner tenders a check for $5,500 to Renoir. If Renoir brings suit for the additional $600, the court will most likely rule for:

    A. Homeowner, because he did not put his promise to pay the extra $600 in a valid writing.

    B. Homeowner, because Renoir was under a pre-existing duty to paint the house for $5,500.

    C. Renoir, because he detrimentally relied on Homeowner's promise to pay the additional $600.

    D. Renoir, because public policy would mandate enforcing Renoir's promise to pay.

100. Assume that Homeowner responded to Renoir's statement of an error in his bid by stating, "I'll pay the extra money if you also paint the inside of my garage and all the plant boxes in the back yard." Renoir agrees. After Renoir completes the painting of the exterior of the home, the garage and the plant boxes, Homeowner tenders a check for $5,500, refusing to pay the additional $600. If Renoir brings suit for the additional $600, who will prevail?

A. Homeowner, because Renoir was under a pre-existing duty to paint the house for $5,500.

B. Homeowner, because the promise was not in writing.

C. Renoir, because there was a valid modification of the contract.

D. Renoir, because he detrimentally relied on Homeowner's promise.

101. Sub-contractor agrees to install the plumbing in a motel being contracted by Contractor. Three days before Sub-contractor is to begin work, contractor learns that Sub-contractor's employees went on strike. Contractor demands Sub-contractor to explain how he will perform the plumbing work. When Sub-contractor does not explain, contractor withholds an advance payment due to Sub-contractor, under the terms of the contract, and hires a different sub-contractor to perform the plumbing work. Sub-contractor sues contractor for breach of contract. Sub-contractor will most likely:

A. Prevail, because the U.C.C. does not apply to services.

B. Prevail, because he intended to do the work himself.

C. Lose, because another sub-contractor finished the work.

D. Lose, because contractor could demand "assurance of performance."

Questions 102 – 104 are based on the following facts:

Harley allowed his 20 year-old-son, Crash, to drive his motorcycle to school one day. Crash negligently changed lanes, and struck Betty, a cyclist, who was turning the corner. Betty and Crash were both severely injured. Harley believed he was liable for Crash's accident because he was the owner of the motorcycle. Harley went to see Betty in the hospital and assured her that he would pay for her medical expenses and any losses she incurred because of the accident. Harley informed Betty's physician that he would pay for all of Betty's medical expenses. The next day, Harley's son, Crash, died from injuries he sustained in the accident. A week later, Harley received a call from Creditor, stating that Crash owed $250 and he was going to file a claim against the estate. Harley told Creditor that if he did not file the claim, he would pay the $250.

102. Betty now sues Harley for her lost wages. Which is Harley's best defense?

    A. Illusory promise.

    B. Lack of consideration.

    C. Statute of Frauds.

    D. No mutual assent between the parties.

103. Which of the following is significant in whether or not there was consideration to support Harley's promise to Betty's physician is legally enforceable?

    I. The physician had not begun treatment on Betty before his conversation with Harley.

    II. Harley and Betty had a contract.

    A. I only.

    B. II only.

    C. I and II.

    D. Neither I nor II.

104. Assume Harley now refuses to pay Creditor the $250. Will Creditor prevail in an action against Harley?

    A. No, because you cannot sue a deceased person.

    B. No, because there was a lack of consideration.

    C. Yes, because there was detrimental reliance by Creditor.

    D. Yes, because there was consideration.

105. Plumber and Homeowner are neighbors. Homeowner helps Plumber landscape his backyard. Plumber is so excited about his backyard, he decides to throw a barbecue and invite his whole block. At the barbecue, Plumber tells his neighbors how Homeowner helped. He then says to Homeowner, "Because you helped me landscape my backyard and it looks so great, I am going to install your new water heater for you." Subsequently, Plumber refuses to install Homeowner's water heater. Can Homeowner bring a successful suit against Plumber for breach?

   A. Yes, because there was consideration.

   B. Yes, because Plumber owed a duty to perform.

   C. No, because of involuntary servitude.

   D. No, because the consideration was not sufficient to render the party's promise enforceable.

106. Roofer agrees to re-roof Pet Shop's roof for $3,000. The work is to begin on January 1, 1993. Payment of the $3,000 is due upon completion of the work. Roofer began work on January 1, 1993. On January 3, 1993, Roofer sends a letter to Pet Shop, telling them to pay the $3,000 to Mr. Nail, one of Roofer's creditors. A copy of the letter was sent to Mr. Nail. Roofer completed the roof for Pet Shop. Pet Shop now refuses to pay. What is Pet Shop's best defense if Mr. Nail brings suit?

   A. Mr. Nail was incapable of roofing Pet Shop's roof.

   B. Roofer failed to perform his work in a professional manner.

   C. Roofer had promised not to assign the contract on January 1, 1993.

   D. Mr. Nail is not an intended beneficiary.

Questions 107 – 109 are based on the following facts:

In 1980, Isac took out a life insurance policy for $100,000. The policy stated that the insured had power to change the beneficiary and to assign the policy. In 1990, Isac named his wife as the beneficiary. Wife did not know of the insurance policy. In 1991, Isac changed the beneficiary from his wife to his only daughter, from another marriage. Isac wrote the daughter and informed her of the policy. In 1992, Isac borrowed $10,000 and assigned the policy to an assignee as security. Isac died in 1993.

107. Wife learns of the insurance policy and sues insurance company to collect the proceeds. Wife will:

    A. Not prevail, because she was not the intended beneficiary.

    B. Not prevail, because she was not the incidental beneficiary.

    C. Prevail, because public policy would warrant a wife being provided for.

    D. Prevail, because Wife is a donee beneficiary.

108. Daughter sues Insurance Company to collect the proceeds. Daughter will:

    A. Not prevail, because the wife will be entitled to the insurance proceeds.

    B. Not prevail, because Isac borrowed against the policy.

    C. Prevail, because she is his only daughter.

    D. Prevail, as the donee beneficiary.

109. Assignee sues the insured for the $10,000 that Isac borrowed. Daughter intervenes. The court will most likely hold for:

    A. Daughter, because she is the named beneficiary and thus prevails over any assignee.

    B. Daughter, because she is a donee beneficiary; thus, a promisee can not assign any part of the beneficiary's right, once they know of the contract.

    C. Assignee, because Isac reserved the right to change the beneficiary and to assign the policy.

    D. Assignee, because there was consideration given for the assignment.

110. On July 1, 1992, Eva agreed with Elva to plan her August 1, 1992 wedding for a $25,000 payment, to be made upon completion of the performance. On July 20, 1992, while the performance was still incomplete, Eva told Florist Flora that if she would give her the flowers she needed, she would have Elva pay directly the $1,500 she owed for the floral arrangements. Flora agreed, and Eva sent a letter to Elva stating the agreement between Eva and Flora. On August 1, 1992, the wedding took place. Elva refuses to pay Flora any money. Flora brings suit. What is Elva's best defense?

A. Flora was not an intended beneficiary of the contract between Eva and Elva.

B. Flora did not detrimentally rely on the promise.

C. Eva assigned her rights before completion, and an assignment, before personal services are performed, is invalid.

D. The wedding was not performed in a proper manner, if Eva's performance is below accepted standards.

111. On July 1, 1992, Sam fraudulently induced Bud to purchase Seller's Lake Tahoe cabin, by falsely representing that the cabin was in immaculate condition. Payment of $60,000 is due on August 1, 1992. In reality, the cabin was about to slide down the hill into the lake. On July 31, 1992, Bud sees the cabin and is outraged. However, his wife falls in love with the cabin and wants it for their dream home away from home. On August 1, 1992, Bud writes a note stating, "Dear Sam, you lied about the cabin; however, my wife loves it, so I have decided to purchase it. Enclosed is a check for the $60,000." On August 2, 1992, Bud decides he is really being cheated, and puts a stop payment on the check. Can Sam enforce the promise made in the August 1, 1992 note?

A. No, because the original promise was based on fraud.

B. No, because Sam lied to Bud.

C. Yes, because the August 1, 1992 promise was written.

D. Yes, because the promise was a ratification.

Questions 112 – 115 are based on the following facts:

Cathy and Tim operate a foreign car dealership under the name of Cat Imports. In January 1993, Jag orally agreed to supply Jaguar automobiles at 15% below factory cost. Jag immediately sent a written confirmation. Cat Imports never received the written confirmation from Jag. In February 1993, Cathy and Tim had several major disagreements. Tim decided to terminate the business relationship. He executed a document assigning all of his rights in Cat's Imports to Cathy. Cathy, in return, agreed to be solely liable for all of Cat's business obligations. Jag knew of the assignment.

In May 1993, Jag sent Cat Imports an invoice showing a balance owing of $90,000. Cathy sent Jag a check for $76,500, marked "payment in full". Cathy also enclosed a letter stating that Jag had not deducted the 15% discount. Jag sent a letter demanding the additional $13,500, but deposited the $76,500 check into their account. Jag also stated that the 15% agreement was invalid because Tim had left the business.

112. Jag brings suit against Cat Imports for $13,500, asserting the statute of frauds as a defense. Jag will most likely:

    A. Prevail, because Cat never received the written confirmation from Jag.

    B. Prevail, because the sale of goods in excess of $500 must be evidenced by a sufficient writing.

    C. Not prevail, because of the Parol Evidence Rule.

    D. Not prevail, because Cat's protest letter is a sufficient writing.

113. Assume that Jag brings a suit for $13,500. Cat's best argument would be:

    A. Accord and Satisfaction.

    B. Promissory Estoppel.

    C. Novation.

    D. Implied Novation.

114. Assume Jag sues Tim for the contract amount still owing. Tim's best argument would be:

    A. There was a valid accord and satisfaction.

    B. The Statute of Frauds was violated.

    C. There was an implied novation.

    D. None of the above.

115. Assume for this question, that Cat Imports has orders for 10 cars at the discounted price, and the court finds that a valid contract exists, requiring Jag to supply the cars at a 15% discount. What are Cats' remedies:

    I. Damages.

II. Specific performance.

III. Reformation.

A. I only.

B. I and II only.

C. II only.

D. I, II and III.

116. Dr. Othello is attending a Shakespeare play one evening. Playgoer falls out of her balcony seat into the crowd. He hears Playgoer screaming in pain, "Dr. please help me; I'll pay you later." Dr. Othello administers first aid, and then calls the paramedics who take Playgoer to the hospital. One month later, Playgoer receives a bill from Dr. Othello for emergency services in the amount of $375.00. Playgoer refuses to pay. Dr. Othello sues. The court will most likely rule for:

A. Dr. Othello, under the good samaritan rule.

B. Dr. Othello, because Playgoer contracted for his services.

C. Playgoer, because Dr. Othello was under a moral duty to treat her.

D. Playgoer, because there was insufficient consideration.

117. Matt and Eileen are at Matt's house drinking tequila shots. Eileen admires Matt's prize boarhead rug. Matt says, "I'll sell you my rug for $ 1,000." Eileen agrees. Matt scribbles the following note on a tissue: "I'll sell my prize rug to Eileen for $1,000." Both sign this latter note, then pass out from their heavy drinking. The next day, Eileen writes Matt a check and demands the rug. Matt claims that they were both too drunk to know what they were doing and that there is no contract. Eileen sues Matt for breach. What result is most likely?

A. The court will find a contract, and Eileen can seek specific performance if Matt understood the effect of his actions.

B. The court will find a contract, but will not enforce it under the temporary incapacity rule.

C. The court will not find a contract, because both parties lacked the requisite capacity due to intoxication.

D. The court will not find a contract, because Matt made the offer in jest.

Questions 118 – 120 are based on the following facts:

Designer contracted with Clothier to purchase 200 bolts of number one quality fine linen. The contract provided that Designer would make payment prior to shipment and inspection. Upon inspection, Designer discovered that the linen was not number one quality. Designer returned the linen back to Clothier and demanded a refund of his payment. Clothier refuses, contending there is no difference between number one quality linen and number two quality linen.

118. What is Designer's remedy, if the court finds the linen to be non-conforming goods?

    A. Damages, measured by the difference between the price of conforming goods and the contract price.

    B. Damages, measured by the difference in value of conforming goods versus the value of the goods delivered.

    C. There are no remedies because Designer did not inspect the linen prior to payment.

    D. Specific performance.

119. May Clothier resell the linen?

    A. No, unless at a public sale.

    B. Yes, but only at a private sale.

    C. Yes, in a private sale, after Designer gives reasonable notice of Clothier's intent to resell.

    D. No, because the linen is nonconforming.

120. Which is a correct statement, with regard to the contract provision for payment in advance of inspection?

    A. It is invalid.

    B. It waives Designer's remedies.

    C. It constitutes immediate acceptance of the goods.

    D. It does not impair Designer's right to inspect or his remedies.

Questions 121 – 122 are based on the following facts:

Yumi has a fine reputation as a landscaper. He has been landscaping private residences for over 17 years. Candace contracts with Yumi to landscape the backyard of her condominium. The condo has a standard backyard. The contract contains no provisions regarding assignment.

121. Yumi assigns the contract to his son, Tumi, who has worked with him for 10 years. Tumi has a comparable reputation. Which one of the following statements are correct?

    A. A novation has occurred.

    B. Candace must accept performance by Tumi.

    C. Candace may refuse to accept performance by Tumi.

    D. There is a breach of contract.

122. Assume Tumi does not meet the contract specifications. Does Candace have a cause of action?

    A. Yes, against Yumi for damages.

    B. Yes, against Tumi.

    C. Yes, but only against Yumi, after all exhaustion of remedies against Tumi.

    D. No, because when Candace allowed Tumi to perform, she waived any cause of action she had.

123. Yale owns a ski store. Business is slow, so he places an advertisement in the paper. "One set of premium skis-- last one only $250, First come first serve." This is a great deal, since the premium skis usually sell for $800. Mary, seeing the ad in the paper, is the first one at Yale's store in the morning. She asks to purchase the skis, and Yale refuses to sell them to her at $250. Yale claims the advertisement was merely an invitation for offer. Most likely it will be found that the advertisement is:

    A. Only a mere invitation to deal.

    B. A valid offer.

    C. An allowable advertisement gimmick to lure customers.

    D. None of the above.

Questions 124 – 125 are based on the following facts:

Seller agrees to deliver 50 boats at $500 each F.O.B., at Seller's place of business. The contract contains a provision that states neither party will assign, without the consent of the other. Seller ships on June 1. On June 2, Seller assigns to Son all rights under the contract. Buyer was unaware of this assignment. On June 3, the boats were destroyed in transit.

124. If Son brings an action against Buyer, Son will most likely recover:

    A. Nothing, because the boats were never delivered.

    B. Nothing, because the assignment was invalid.

    C. The difference between the contract price and the market value of the boats, if any.

    D. The contract price.

125. If Buyer brings a suit against Seller for breach of contract, he will most likely:

    A. Not succeed, because the risk of loss had shifted.

    B. Not succeed, because of the doctrine of impossibility.

    C. Succeed, because Seller has the risk of loss.

    D. Succeed, because of public policy.

126. Manford, a 77-year-old accomplished musician, decides to retire. He would like to travel the world in his remaining years. He then decides that if he sold his prize possession, his Stradivarius (violin), he could afford to travel. He puts up the following notice in the Musician's Union: "I am selling my Stradivarius for $10,000. I will sell to the first person who offers me the price in cash." Manford signs the notice. Manford had actually intended to ask $100,000, a cheap price for a Stradivarious. Maestro, the orchestra leader, gives Manford $10,000, in cash, and demands the violin. Manford refuses. If Maestro brings suit for specific performance, he will most likely:

    A. Lose, because specific performance is not equitable.

    B. Lose, because there was a unilateral mistake.

    C. Win, because there is a valid offer.

    D. Win, because Manford should have known about the typo.

127. On May 25, Builder wrote Sub, "I will pay you $2,000, if you electrically wire the gymnasium I am building according to the enclosed specifications. I must have your reply by June 1." On May 27, Sub wrote Builder stating, "Can't do the work for less than $2,500." On May 28, Sub wrote again to Builder stating, "Okay," I'll do the work for $2,000." Without hearing from Builder, and without Builder's knowledge, Sub began work on June 1. What is the legal relationship of Builder and Sub on June 1?

   A. There is no contract between the parties.

   B. A contract was formed, when Sub began work on June 1.

   C. A contract was formed, after Builder's receipt of Sub's May 28 letter.

   D. A contract was formed, when Sub mailed his letter of May 28.

Questions 128 – 129 are based on the following facts:

Elly Mae had a rich uncle Jed, who wanted her to pursue a legal career. Uncle Jed gave Elly Mae a signed note stating that if she would attend law school for 3 years, he would pay for her tuition, room and board. In addition, he would give her $2,000 for each 4.0 she earned. Cousin Jethro stated to Elly Mae, "If Uncle Jed does not pay your expenses, I will." Elly Mae enrolled in law school and Uncle Jed paid her tuition, room and board. At the end of the semester, Uncle Jed died. On the same day, Elly Mae received her report card containing three 4.0's. The executor of the estate refuses to pay any tuition, room or board and refuses to give Elly Mae $6,000 for her three 4.0's.

128. Elly Mae wants to enforce cousin Jethro's promise to pay if Jed does not. What is Jethro's best defense?

   A. Uncle Jed's death terminated any possible agreement.

   B. Cousin Jethro was not serious about paying.

   C. Elly Mae and Jethro did not manifestly intend a contract.

   D. The agreement was not in writing.

129. If Elly Mae brought suit against Uncle Jed's estate for payment of $6,000, for the three 4.0's, she will most likely:

A. Not succeed, because there was no consideration.

B. Not succeed, because the $2,000 promise was a gratuitous promise, and thus not enforceable.

C. Succeed, under promissory estoppel.

D. Succeed, because there was a bargained-for exchange.

130. Pete agrees to paint Heather's house for $800. After Pete is over one-third of the way finished painting, Heather learns that Angelo will paint her house for $500. Heather fires Pete. Pete brings suit for breach of contract. Pete will most likely:

A. Succeed, because he has already begun performance.

B. Succeed, because he agreed to perform.

C. Not succeed, because his price was too high.

D. Not succeed, because there had not been substantial performance.

Questions 131 – 135 are based on the following facts:

P.U., a privately owned law school, posted the following notice on February 1: The faculty, seeking to encourage participation in moot court, offers to any student, who wins the current National Moot Court competition, the additional prize of $1,000. All must be submitted to academics by April 20.

Laura law student read the notice, and therefore worked even harder on her brief. She increased the daily hours that she worked on the brief. She also wrote a note to the Dean, stating that she accepted the faculty's offer. The note never was received by the Dean, but was instead inadvertently placed in Laura's file.

On February 28, the above notice was removed and the following notice was put in its place:

P.U. regrets that our offer regarding the Moot Court Competition must be withdrawn.

Laura's paper was submitted to the Dean's office on April 19. On June 1, it was announced that Laura had won the National Competition. P.U. refused to pay Laura the $1,000.

131. If the February 1 notice was placed on the school's main information bulletin board, the notice would constitute:

A. An offer, creating the power of acceptance.

B. An invitation to deal

C. Merely a preliminary invitation, because no offeree is named.

D. A conditional promise.

132. As to Laura, was the offer validly revoked?

A. Yes, because of the posting of the February 28 notice.

B. Yes, because it is a private law school.

C. No, because Laura detrimentally relied, prior to February 28.

D. No, because Laura might not have read the new notice.

133. The offer constitutes a:

A. Bilateral contract, only.

B. Bilateral and/or a unilateral contract.

C. Unilateral contact, only.

D. Unilateral contract, which became a bilateral contract.

134. How will Laura's winning the Moot Court Competition, affect the enforceability of P.U.'s promise?

A. It will act as a condition precedent to P.U.'s performance, and thus make P.U.'s promise enforceable.

B. It will be unenforceable, as a promise to make a gift.

C. P.U.'s promise will be enforceable, under the pre-existing duty rule.

D. None of the above.

135. If Laura dies on April 19 on the way home from submitting her brief, the February 1 promise by P.U. will be found to be:

A. Not enforceable, because Laura was under a pre-existing duty to perform to her best because she had already entered the contest.

B. Not enforceable.

C. Enforceable, because of her detrimental reliance.

D. Enforceable, by the executor of her estate.

Questions 136 – 138 are based on the following facts:

On December 26, Chopin entered into a contract with Bugsy to play piano at his new night club for one year. Chopin was to receive $4,000 per month, beginning January 1. Bugsy's club was to open New Year's Eve. Chopin is very popular, and Bugsy knows he will pack the club with Chopin as the headliner.

136. On December 29, Chopin calls Bugsy and states he may not be ready to start until January 10. Will the court allow Bugsy to bring an immediate suit against Chopin?

   A. No, because a repudiation must be in writing.

   B. No, because there was no repudiation.

   C. Yes, because there was a repudiation.

   D. Yes, because Bugsy will lose money and is entitled to damages.

137. Assume that after the December 26 agreement, no communication between the parties occurred. On January 1, Bugsy receives a telegram from Chopin, stating that he will not start until January 10. May Bugsy cancel the existing contract?

   A. No, because Chopin notified Bugsy.

   B. No, unless there was a material breach.

   C. Yes, because Bugsy will lose money he has counted on.

   D. Yes, because there was a material breach.

138. Assume that Chopin does not appear for the month of January to play at Bugsy's club because he was playing at the Waldorf for $6,000. Bugsy, unaware of why Chopin is not at his appearance, hires Solaire at $5,000 per month for 12 months. Bugsy files suit against Chopin. What is the most likely amount he will recover?

   A. $1,000 damages.

   B. $1,000 damages for the month of January, and present value of the $1,000 per month salary difference, for the remaining 11 months.

   C. Nothing.

   D. The full contract price of the Bugsy - Chopin contract.

139. Builder entered into a contract with Homeowner to build a pool in Homeowner's backyard for $10,000. The price is to include all building materials. The week before performance was to begin, Homeowner called Builder and said, "I've changed my mind, the deal is off." Builder brings a cause of action against Homeowner for breach of contract. Homeowner raises the statute of frauds as a defense. What will the court most likely rule?

I. If the building materials were to exceed $500, the contract is required to be in writing.

II. The building of a pool is a service, thus no writing is required.

A. I only.

B. II only.

C. I and II.

D. Neither I nor II.

140. On November 1, Cam and Ken agreed, in writing, that Cam would purchase Ken's 1990 BMW for $25,000. The sale was to take place November 15. On November 10, Cam tells Ken, "I really can't afford the car, the deal is off." Ken says, "Okay Cam, I'll let you out of the deal." The next day, Ken tells Cam he decided not to let him out of the deal, because he needs the money. If Ken sues Cam for breach of contract, will he recover?

A. Yes, because contracts cannot be rescinded orally.

B. Yes, because on November 1 there was a contract.

C. No, because Cam does not have the money.

D. No, because the contract was rescinded.

Questions 141 – 142 are based on the following facts:

Cal a contractor agrees to build a barn and stable for Mr. Farmer, for $200,000. After finishing 50% of the work, Cal goes broke and is unable to finish the job. Mr. Farmer has to hire another contractor, Kyle, to finish the job.

141. Cal has spent $100,000 in expenses and wants to recover his expenditures. His best theory of recovery will be based on:

   A. Quasi-contract.

   B. Impossibility of performance.

   C. Material breach.

   D. None of the above.

142. What may Cal contractor recover?

   A. No amount, because he is in material breach.

   B. No amount, because he did not complete performance as promised.

   C. Through restitution, he may recover the $100,000 benefit conferred in Farmer, less Farmer's damages from the breach.

   D. Nothing, because the default was willful.

143. Husband buys a car for Wife. Wife is injured when the brakes fail 20 days later. Husband sues Car Dealer and Manufacturer, on an implied warranty theory. Defendants' claim the warranty is disclaimed in fine print on the back of the contract. How will the court rule?

   A. For Husband, because his Wife has been injured.

   B. For Husband, because this is an adhesion contract.

   C. For Defendants, because they have a valid disclaimer.

   D. For Defendants, because there was equality of bargaining position.

Questions 144 – 145 are based on the following facts:

Buyer sends an order for 10,000 #A tennis balls to Manufacturing Company, with instructions to ship immediately.

144. Manufacturer ships immediately, via common carrier. Later that day, Buyer wires a revocation of his order. Is there an enforceable contract?

    A. Yes, under the U.C.C.

    B. Yes, under the "mirror image" rule.

    C. No, because Buyer made a timely revocation.

    D. No, because manufacturer can sell the balls to someone else.

145. Assume Manufacturer was out of #A balls, and shipped #B balls. Is there a contract?

    A. No, because the goods were non-conforming.

    B. No, because the #B balls constitute a breach.

    C. Yes, because it is only an accommodation.

    D. Yes, because shipment is an acceptance.

146. Tom purchases a restaurant, secured by purchase money financing. The restaurant needs a new air conditioning system. Tom, short of cash, purchases the air conditioning system from Earl's Air Systems, on credit. Earl's takes a security interest in the equipment sold to Tom and timely files a security interest under Article 9 of the Uniform Commercial Code.

    Tom fails to pay for the equipment and goes bankrupt. Earl's claims a priority interest in the system over Tom's other creditors. The bankruptcy trustee claims an interest in the system for the benefit of all creditors. Whose interest in the system has priority?

    A. All the general creditors, because they are owed money from Tom for supplies sold to Tom on credit for the restaurant.

    B. Earl's, because any supplier of fixtures sold on credit has a secured interest in the fixture until paid for.

    C. Earl's, because of Earl's perfected security interest in the equipment.

    D. Neither Earl nor the creditors, because once the equipment was installed, it became realty.

147. Sam's Sugar Company ("Sam") sells Bob's Export Foods ("Bob") five thousand 100 pound bags of sugar. Bob placed the order on his own order form by filling in the description and quantity of the goods. In the space for price, Bob wrote: "FOB PLANT PER 100 POUND BAG $15.25."

Because the sugar was being shipped overseas, Sam agreed to load up Bob's shipping container with the sugar. The loaded container was stolen from Sam's plant before Bob's carrier was able to pick it up. Sam sues Bob for the contract price when Bob refuses to pay. Who prevails?

A. Sam, since he had already loaded up the shipping container for overseas transport.

B. Sam, because the parties had "agreed otherwise" to pass the risk of loss at the time and place the shipping container was loaded.

C. Bob, because the risk of loss cannot pass when identified goods have been stolen – although neither party is at fault.

D. Bob, because the term "FOB PLANT" requires delivery to the carrier before the risk of loss passes.

148. John collects antique cars as an investment. In 1992, John purchased a home and assumes the existing mortgage with Bank. Excited about his new home, John purchases lumber on credit from Hardware Store to build a larger garage for his car collection. Hardware's credit application states that it has a secured interest in the lumber until the goods are paid for.

After completing his new garage, John defaults on his debts to Hardware and Bank. Which party's claimed interest in the lumber prevails?

A. Bank, if its secured interest in the realty is first in time.

B. Bank, since the lumber was ordinary building materials.

C. Hardware, if it filed its security interest in the lumber prior to construction of the garage.

D. Hardware, because the lumber became a fixture upon incorporation into the construction of the garage.

Questions 149 – 150 are based on the following facts:

Matt's Motel ("Matt") purchases a new furnace on credit from Furnace R Us ("FRU") which FRU installs the same day. There is a preexisting mortgage on the motel through Intrastate Bank ("Intrastate"). FRU files its security interest in the furnace three weeks after the sale to Matt. Matt then takes out a second mortgage with Continental Bank ("Continental"). Matt defaults on all his debts before they are repaid.

149. Whose interest in the furnace has priority between FRU and Continental?

    A. FRU, because FRU's security interest was filed before Continental recorded its mortgage.

    B. FRU, because its security interest was filed within the 21-day grace period after installation of the fixture.

    C. Continental, since FRU did not file its security interest within the grace period, in order to have priority over a subsequent interest.

    D. Continental, because the furnace became realty which is subject to a mortgagee's claim.

150. Whose security interest prevails between FRU and Intrastate?

    A. FRU, because it filed its security interest within the 21-day grace period.

    B. FRU, because a fixture financier is entitled to a security interest when it extends credit.

    C. Intrastate, due to its pre-existing security interest in the motel.

    D. Intrastate, since FRU failed to file its security interest within the Article 9 grace period.

151. When the medical profession conclusively proved that tanning by artificial lighting is not harmful to humans, tanning salons became the method of choice for that "bronzed look." Hamilton George invested all his money to open up a tanning salon supply store, to profit from the surge in salon business.

    George sold his tanning equipment on credit, which he also installed for his customers. The equipment was affixed to the realty of his customers' businesses.

George attempted to file a secured interest in some tanning equipment sold and installed for Jeff. Because George was unfamiliar with the filing process, he misidentified some of the equipment in the financing statement. He filed the financing statement without discovering his error. Is the filing effective?

A. No, an erroneous filing is never effective.

B. No, because unfamiliarity is no excuse for George's mistake.

C. No, except as to the extent the descriptions were proper.

D. Yes, because George's attempt to file the security interest was in goodfaith, even though he did not pay the filing fee.

Questions 152 – 153 are based on the following facts:

Chuck's Corvette Cafe was constructed on a corner of Pacific Coast Highway, in Malibu. His indoor cafe was known for its authentic Corvette-replica "booths", where customers ordered and were served much like the drive-up restaurants of the 60's. The booths, were purchased from Bob's Booths and were affixed to the restaurant building. Bob properly files his security interest in the booths.

Rock slides along the highway are a constant problem for customers attempting to reach the cafe and the cafe closes for lack of business. Unable to pay his bills, Chuck defaults on his debt to Bob. Bob immediately takes back the booths. Because the cafe doors were too small to permit removal of the booths, Bob smashes a large window to extract the booths.

152. Were Bob's actions proper in repossessing the booths?

A. Yes, he had timely obtained a secured interest in the fixtures prior to repossession.

B. Yes, because Bob had the right to repossession without resort to the judicial process.

C. No, because Bob breached the peace in order to repossess the booths.

D. No, because it was impracticable to remove the booths and Bob should have made them unusable, instead.

153. Assume Bob's conduct was proper in removing the booths, must he reimburse Chuck for the damage to the cafe?

A. Yes, for the diminution in value to the cafe.

B. Yes, for the repair cost for the cafe.

C. Yes, for either the diminution in value or repair cost, whichever is less.

D. No, because Chuck is the debtor.

154. Tina's Toucans sells exotic tropical birds. Pam purchases a toucan, Sam, for $1,000 from Tina. Tina's sales contract with Pam conspicuously states, "HEALTH GUARANTEE FOR 72 HOURS FROM TIME OF PURCHASE. EXCHANGES WILL BE PERMITTED ONLY UPON PRESENTATION OF VETERINARIAN'S REPORT WITHIN THE 72-HOUR PERIOD. NOT RESPONSIBLE FOR INJURY, ACCIDENT OR LOSS AFTER 72 HOURS." Pam had Sam examined the next day by a veterinarian, but no disease or defect was discovered. However, 3 weeks later, Sam died for no apparent reason. An autopsy of the toucan could not identify the cause of death. Pam asks Tina to replace her bird, but Tina refuses. Pam sues Tina to recover her purchase price. What is the most likely result?

A. Tina loses, because she failed to disclaim the implied warranty of merchantability.

B. Tina loses, because the 72 hours is not sufficient time to discover defects or disease in a bird.

C. Pam loses, because she could not prove Sam's cause of death.

D. Pam loses, because the implied warranties of merchantability and fitness for intended use were expressly disclaimed.

155. Tom steals stereo equipment from Vic and later sells the equipment to Paula. Paula, unaware of Tom's wrongdoings, sells the equipment to Tracee through an ad in the Dollarsaver magazine. Vic locates the equipment and repossesses it from Tracee. Tracee sues Paula for breach of warranty of title. What is the most likely outcome?

A. Paula will win, because she was not a merchant.

B. Paula will win, because she was unaware of Tom's wrongdoings.

C. Paula will win, because she was a bona fide purchaser for value of the equipment at the time the sale to Tracee was made.

D. Tracee will win, because, although Paula was unaware of Tom's theft of the equipment, Paula did not have good title at the time of sale to Tracee.

END OF QUESTIONS

CONTRACTS ANSWERS

1. D is the correct answer. A written letter of confirmation, sent by a merchant within a reasonable time after the oral contract is made, will satisfy the statue of frauds, if the receiving party is a merchant and does not object to the contents thereof within 10 days after receipt. A is an incorrect statement because the parol evidence rule is only applicable to alleged conditions of a contract not included in the written contract, itself. Such is not the situation here. B is incorrect because the merchant's exception, as discussed in D, would make the statute of frauds inapplicable. C is an incorrect statement as the merchant's exception does not require Jim's signature on the confirmation form.

2. D is the correct answer. There was no legal effect as to Tammy's exclamation, since Mr. Baker had not made an offer of any kind. A and B are incorrect because no offer was made, and there must be a valid offer for there to be a binding acceptance or "meeting of the minds." C is incorrect because no expressed qualifications were imposed upon Tammy for her to receive the gift.

3. D is the best answer. Tammy encountered no legal detriment; thus, she would not prevail on this theory. A could be an applicable theory for Tammy as modern law holds that if a donative promise induces reliance by the promisee in a manner that the promisor should reasonably have expected, the promise will be legally enforceable. B, although a good choice (the traditional rule holds that a promise based on moral obligation is unenforceable), is not the best answer because the rule is presently, in a growing minority of jurisdictions, modified. C is incorrect because in some circumstances the courts have enforced a gratuitous promise that foreseeably induced reliance.

4. A is the best answer. The general rule is that a donative promise is unenforceable because there is a lack of consideration. B is a correct statement, unless the promise becomes enforceable and is therefore, not the best answer. C is an incorrect statement because there was no bargained for exchange. D is an incorrect statement of the law.

A

CONTRACTS

5. A is the correct answer. Restatement First §90 of Contracts, provides that a promise which the promisor should reasonably expect to induce action or forbearance and which does induce such, is binding if injustice can be avoided only by enforcement of the promise. Here, it can be said that Mr. Baker would have no reason to foresee the action by Tammy; thus, his promise would not be binding. D is incorrect because it is not as concise as answer A. B is incorrect because, whether or not Mr. Baker intended reliance or not, is irrelevant to the applicable rule of law. C is incorrect because it incorrectly states the law. Tammy's conduct was not a legal detriment and there was no bargained for exchange.

6. B is the best answer. When a contract calls for goods and services, the court may apply the Predominant Purpose Test. Under this test, if it is decided that the predominant purpose of the contract was for goods, then the Uniform Commercial Code (U.C.C.) will apply. A is incorrect because services are also included; thus, the U.C.C. does not clearly apply. C is incorrect, as the courts may, under the Predominant Purpose Test, decide that the U.C.C. applies. D is an incorrect statement as the U.C.C. applies to goods, not services.

7. C is the correct answer. A firm offer is irrevocable without consideration for a reasonable time, or for the time specified in the contract; but in no event for a period of time longer than three months. The offer must be made by a merchant and involve the sale of goods. A is incorrect since no consideration is needed. B is incorrect, because the U.C.C. holds firm offers open for three months no longer. D is an incorrect statement of law. Such is not required by the U.C.C.

8. B is the correct answer. Dee's payment of the lesser sum is not consideration as the debt was undisputed. Therefore, Mel's promise to accept the lesser sum as payment in full is not enforceable. A is an incorrect statement of law. C is incorrect, because payment of the $400, which was already owed, is not considered to be legal "consideration". D is an incorrect answer for the same reasons that B is correct.

9. A is the correct answer. When there are dealings between merchants, additional or different terms become part of the contract automatically after a reasonable period of time, unless: 1) the offer expressly limits acceptance to the terms of the offer, 2) the additional or different terms are a material alteration of the offer, or 3) the original offeror notifies the offeree that he objects to the additional or different terms within a commercially reasonable period of time. B is incorrect, as conduct by both parties which recognizes the existence of a contract, is sufficient to establish a contract. C is incorrect for the reasons discussed in answer A. D is incorrect because the additional terms were likely not significant to constitute a counter-offer.

10. C is the correct answer. When a non-merchant offeree proposes additional or different terms in his acceptance, a contract exists consisting of the terms agreed upon, while the additional terms are deemed a proposal for additional or different terms. A is incorrect for the same reasons that C is correct. B is incorrect because the additional terms would merely be considered proposals. D is incorrect, since C is correct.

11. Under the U.C.C., D is the correct answer. Where no place is specified for delivery of the goods, the place of delivery is the seller's place of business, or, if there is none, the seller's residence. Answers A, B, and C are all incorrect for the reason stated in the correct answer D.

12. C is the correct answer. A unilateral contract is one where an offer requires performance of an act as bargained-for consideration. The unilateral contract is formed by doing the required act. A is incorrect since a bilateral contract requires an exchange of promises. B is factually incorrect because the reward was not intended as negotiation. D is an incorrect statement, since a bilateral contract requires an agreement prior to the performance-which was not the case here.

13. D is the correct answer. A reward offer must be accepted by an offeree who knows of the offer. Here, Annie did not learn of the reward until after Fido's return. A and B are incorrect for the reasons discussed in correct answer D. C is not correct because the issue is not consideration, but whether or not the offeree knew of the offer.

14. D is the correct answer. Anticipatory repudiation does not apply in a contract fully performed on the side of the non-repudiating party.

A

CONTRACTS

15. A is the best answer. The agreement expressly stated that the motorcycle was to be delivered on September 9. B is not the best answer, since implied conditions deal with fairness and justice. A is a more concise answer. C is not the best answer, since the delivery was not an event which impliedly had to occur to create an absolute duty to perform. D is incorrect because the performances were not mutually dependent.

16. A is the correct answer. U.C.C. §2-613 states that if the contract involves goods that were identified when the contract was made and the goods are destroyed without fault of either party before the risk of loss passed, the contract is voided. B, C and D are incorrect for the same reasons that A is correct.

17. D is the correct answer. A party bears the risk of a mistake when he is aware at the time that the contract is made, that he has only limited knowledge with respect to the facts to which the mistake relates-but treats his limited knowledge as sufficient. In this case, Flint is obligated to build the mall and pay the increased costs. Flint assumed the risks when it started the job. A is incorrect because Flint's mistake will not excuse its performance. B is incorrect, as Rubble is not obligated to share in the increased costs. C is an incorrect statement. Although it will cut into Flint's profits, the contract is not impracticable to perform.

18. D is the best answer. Brent must notify Selma of the rejection within a reasonable time and must hold the goods with reasonable care for a reasonable time sufficient for Selma to remove the goods. A is incorrect, as Brent is under no obligation to send the roller blades back. Answers B and C are incorrect as Brent only need fulfill the requirements discussed in correct answer D.

19. A is the correct answer. Incidental damages allow the buyer to recover any cost or expense reasonably incurred which are incidental to the seller's delay or delivery of defective goods. Loss of expected profit is not considered to be an incidental damage and is, therefore, not recoverable. Answers B, C and D are all incorrect, as they all constitute incidental damages and could be recovered. (U.C.C. §2-815(1))

20. C is the correct answer. An express warranty can be created by any sample or model which is made part of the basis of the bargain. Here, the demonstration would create an express warranty that the curling iron shall conform to the model used. Thus, the fact that it took 2 minutes to curl her hair instead of the 30 seconds, would be a breach of the express warranty. A is an incorrect statement of law. Under U.C.C. §2-318, direct privity between the manufacturer and the ultimate buyer is not required for there to be a cause of action. B is incorrect because this warranty requires that the seller have reason to know of the particular use of goods contemplated by the buyer, and the seller must also be aware that the buyer is relying on the seller's judgment. The facts do not support the finding of those conclusions. D is incorrect for the same reasons that C is correct.

21. D is the correct answer. The mayor has detrimentally relied. This satisfies the requirement of vesting. A is incorrect (although this answer could possibly make sense if the subcontractor was suing for the loss of use of some gift arguably donated to him). B is incorrect because to be a creditor beneficiary, there must be detrimental reliance or a suit brought on the contract. An advancement of salary is not necessarily detrimental reliance- it is consideration. C is incorrect because it is not the best answer.

22. D is the correct answer. For the general contractor to be able to indemnify himself, there must obviously be a valid contract between himself and the subcontractor. A is incorrect. A general contractor is responsible for the breach of independent contractors. Mayor can sue general contractor. B is incorrect as the subcontractor could be seen as an obligor; however, this bears no relation on whether Mayor can sue the general contractor. C is incorrect, as this bears no relation to the suit between the subcontractor and the general contractor.

23. C is the correct answer. Girkin is an incidental beneficiary. A is incorrect, as Girkin is not an intended beneficiary. B is incorrect. An officious intermeddler is a remedies issue- this answer would make no sense here. D is incorrect. Rights of the third party beneficiary can be cut off up to the time that they have vested. Here, there are no vested rights. Girkin is merely an incidental beneficiary.

24. B is the correct answer. If the subcontractor has made partial performance or a substandard performance, Mayor had the right to offset against any incompleteness to the performance of the contract. Also, Mayor could actually be owed damages, if she has been placed in a position that is worse than before the subcontractor performed the duty under the contract. A is incorrect. The general contractor's actions are not related to the suit between Mayor and the general contractor. C is incorrect as "legal detriment" refers to action of the promisee taken in reliance upon the actions of the promisor. D is an incorrect statement of law.

25. D is the correct answer. The communication between the parties has not yet reached a point where vesting could occur in Girkin. A is incorrect. Girkin has not bargained for legal detriment. None of his actions show that he has offered any consideration. Further, there are no facts to indicate donative intent exists toward Girkin. B is incorrect. There was no promise on which Girkin could reasonably rely. C is incorrect because, if the parties know someone has reasonably relied, there can be an action for restitution, but no facts indicate reliance in this case to be reasonable.

26. B is the correct answer. Ped received medical treatment from the doctor, which implies a promise by Ped to pay for the services received. Answers C and D are incorrect because the status of Doctor as a beneficiary would give him the right to sue Axel, not Ped. C is incorrect because quasi-contractual recovery is not the best recovery, and also is not the best theory of recovery because an implied-in-fact contract exists.

27. A is the correct answer, because Doctor could only proceed against Axel as a third party beneficiary of the Ped-Axel contract. B is an incorrect statement of law. C is incorrect because Axel's detrimental reliance on Ped's release has no relevance to Doctor's right of recovery. D is an incorrect statement of law.

28. B is the correct answer. Grease only promised to represent Ped. This promise did not confer third party beneficiary status on Doctor. A is incorrect because, whether Doctor's rights have vested or not, is irrelevant to this fact-pattern. C is incorrect because there are no facts to support this contention. D is incorrect because Doctor is not a beneficiary of Grease's promise.

29. C is the correct answer. A promise "not to assign" will not prevent an assignment. However, this does constitute a breach of promise not to assign. For the reasoning discussed in correct answer C, A and B are both incorrect. D is incorrect, since it is an incorrect statement of law.

30. D is the correct answer (for Bar Exam purposes). The Restatement II of Contracts is followed where the terms "creditor" and "donee" beneficiary (see Restatement I) have been replaced with the term "intended" beneficiary. (Note that a majority of states still follow the Restatement I, which results in a different answer.) A, B, and C are incorrect for the reasons D is correct.

31. B is the correct answer. Design Factory is a beneficiary and, thus, subject to any defenses which may arise. A is incorrect, as it misstates the law. C is incorrect because vesting is only at issue when the original parties are trying to change the beneficiary rights. D is an incorrect statement of law.

32. C is the correct answer. There was no enforceable rights at the time of the assignment because no enforceable contract existed. Therefore, A and D are incorrect. B is incorrect because this would not justify Soprano's recovery.

33. D is the correct answer. Whistler's assignment to Fork was a delegation of his duty. Thus, when Fork performed, Van Gogh's duty became absolute. A is incorrect under these facts. B is incorrect because the assignment and delegation act as a substitute for privity. C is incorrect because that fact alone is not enough to subject Van Gogh to liability.

34. A is the correct answer. Every delegation gives rise to a third-party beneficiary contract. Therefore, Van Gogh has a cause of action against Fork. B is incorrect only because it is not the best answer. C is incorrect because the facts do not support the answer. D is incorrect because A is correct.

35. C is the correct answer. When a party to a contract delegates their duty, they remain liable as guarantor for the performance of the delegatee. D is incorrect because there are not enough facts to support this choice. A is incorrect because of the rule stated in answer C. B is an incorrect statement of law.

36. B is the correct answer. Under UCC Section 2-312, a warranty of title must be disclaimed by specific language. The provision for sale of "any right, title and interest" is not an exclusion or disclaimer of the warranty of title. Further, the provision disclaiming warranties is ineffective as to title, for its failure to disclaim the warranty of title specifically. A, C and D are incorrect for the reasons stated in correct answer B.

37. A is the best answer. Ed made an express warranty to Joe, regarding specific attributes of the boat that were not true. B is incorrect because A is the better answer. C and D are incorrect for the reasons stated in the explanation to answer A.

38. A is the correct answer. Under UCC section 2-206, an offer may be accepted by any reasonable medium. An offer may be accepted by either a return promise or by specific acts. Marine's act of shipping the motors constituted acceptance of Bill's offer. B and C are incorrect because they are incorrect statements of law. D is incorrect because Marine failed to give notice that the shipment was an accommodation.

39. B is correct. UCC Section 2-608 provides that a buyer may revoke or reject the whole shipment, or accept any commercial unit, and reject the rest. A is incorrect because a buyer must give notice within a reasonable time of rejection. C and D are incorrect statements of law.

40. A is the correct answer. Under UCC section 2-205, an offer by a merchant, in a signed writing which by its terms gives assurances to keep the offer open, is not revocable for a period not to exceed three months. B, C and D are incorrect statements of law.

41. D is the correct answer. Under UCC 2-207(2), where parties to a contract for the sale of goods are both merchants, the proposed additional terms become part of the contract unless: (1) the offer expressly limits acceptance to the terms of the offer; (2) the additional terms would materially alter the contract; or (3) the offeror notifies the offeree within a reasonable period of time that he objects to the additional terms. Because Grocer's response was an inquiry to Canco's offer, the terms will be construed as a proposal and will become part of the contract. A, B and C are incorrect for the reasons stated in correct answer D.

42. C is the correct answer. UCC 2-601 provides where goods or tender of delivery fails in any respect to conform to the contract, the buyer may reject tender (perfect tender rule). A is incorrect because substantial performance does not apply under the UCC. B is incorrect for the same reasons that answer A is incorrect. D is incorrect because of the perfect tender rule.

43. A is correct. UCC 2-601 provides a buyer may accept a non-conforming tender. Under 2 -714, buyer's acceptance of partial tender does not operate as a waiver and buyer can recover damages. B is incorrect because the materiality of seller's breach is not decisive. The buyer is entitled to recover damages for any unexcused failure. C is incorrect because acceptance of partial tender does not operate as a waiver. D is incorrect because a non- conforming shipment constitutes a breach.

44. D is the correct answer. As between merchants, a written confirmation is sufficient to satisfy the statute of frauds, unless written objection is given within 10 days of receipt. A, B and C are incorrect statements of law.

45. C is the correct answer. Section 2-313 provides that any affirmation of fact or promise, relating to the goods in which a buyer could rely, creates an express warranty. Since Robin had actual knowledge of Martin's accident prior to her purchase of the Forge, she could not have relied on the express affirmations by Forge in its brochure. A, B and D are incorrect for the reasons stated in the explanation to answer C.

46. C is the correct answer. An offer of reward is an offer for performance. Since Ethel did not deliver the brief case, and Smith effectively revoked the offer when he informed Ethel that he was canceling the reward, no contract was formed. A is incorrect because Ethel cannot orally accept the reward – a unilateral contract can only be accepted by performance and she has not returned the brief case. B is incorrect for the reasons stated in correct answer C. D is incorrect because Smith effectively revoked the offer.

47. C is the correct answer. X's offer called for acceptance by performance, so the mailing of the letter by Y (a promise to perform) had no legal effect. The mailbox rule only applies to bilateral contracts. When Y learned of X's prior purchase, an indirect revocation took place. Thus, no contract was formed. A is incorrect since X's offer requires acceptance by performance. B and D are incorrect for the same reasons that C is correct

A

CONTRACTS

48. D is the correct answer. An offeree's power of acceptance is terminated when the offeror takes definite action inconsistent with an intention to enter into the proposed contract, and the offeree has reliable information to that effect. When Y learned of X's prior purchase of the truck, Y had notice of X's conduct that was inconsistent with X's intent to subsequently buy Y's truck. A and B are incorrect for reasons stated in correct answer D. C is an incorrect statement of law because only an offeror has the power to terminate his offer.

49. D is the correct answer. Because Dan is not a party, nor an intended beneficiary to the Jack-Bill agreement, Dan cannot raise the argument that the Jack-Bill agreement is not in writing as a defense because he does not have standing to do so. Dan cannot assert the defense that the Jack-Dan agreement is not in writing because such agreement was a construction/building contract that, by its terms, could be completed within one year, and otherwise does not fall within the Statute of Frauds. A, B and C are incorrect for the reasons stated in the explanation to answer D.

50. C is the correct answer. The Jack-Dan agreement calls for performance in separate units making the contract divisible. Upon Dan's performance of completing the pool and bleachers, Jack's performance of paying $5,000 became due. By Jack repudiating the contract, and failing to pay the second installment, Dan may also sue for the damages caused by Jack's repudiation of the remainder of the contract. Dan would be excused from any further obligation under the contract. A, B and D are incorrect for the reasons stated in the explanation to answer C.

51. B is the correct answer. The Parol Evidence Rule provides that when parties have placed their agreement into a writing, which they both agree and assent to as their full and complete integrated agreement, evidence of oral or written terms will not be admitted to change or vary the terms of the writing. However, where the parties reduce their agreement to a writing, without language that the writing is fully integrated, parol evidence is admissible to show there is a condition precedent to the legal effectiveness of the writing. Since the parties orally agreed that the sale would occur only upon Bar candidate passing his bar exam parol evidence of that condition precedent is admissible. A, C and D are incorrect for the stated reasons to answer B.

52. D is the correct answer. UCC §2-508 states that where any tender or delivery by the seller is rejected because of non-conformance, and the time for performance has expired, the buyer may properly reject the non-conforming tender. Here, Buyer properly rejected Seller's tender of the milk, that was short 1,000 cartons, because the time for Seller's performance had expired. A is incorrect because the contract is not objectively impossible to perform. B and C are incorrect statements for the reasons stated in the explanation to answer D.

53. D is the correct answer. A liquidated damages clause will be upheld where the stipulated sum bears a reasonable relation to the actual loss, actual damages are uncertain or difficult to ascertain, and the contract, as a whole ,evidences a conscious intention of the parties to consider and adjust the damages that might flow from the breach. None of these factors are present, particularly since Americo was able to resell the equipment before seeking liquidated damages, and thus was able to ascertain its actual damages. A, B and C are incorrect for the reasons stated above.

54. A is the correct answer. A shipment contract was formed, since the contract required Manufacturer to deliver the chairs. Once Manufacturer placed the chairs upon the carrier, the risk of loss passed to Baker because the contract provided F.O.B. at seller's place of business. Since the risk of loss was on Baker and Manufacturer placed the chairs upon the carrier, he is entitled to the contract price despite the language in the contract, Manufacture could assign its right to collect from Baker. B is incorrect, as stated in correct answer A. C and D are an incorrect statements of law per UCC §2-204.

55. C is the correct answer. The risk of loss passed, once Manufacturer placed the chairs upon the carrier to Baker. Since Baker has the risk, he is unable to recover against Manufacturer. A, B and D are incorrect for the reasons stated in C.

56. C is the correct answer. Billy Joe will not be limited to receive only damages; he can rescind the contract because Jermey misrepresented a fact that relates to an essential part of the bargain. A, B and D are incorrect for the reasons stated in correct answer C.

57. A is the correct answer. In order for a third party beneficiary to recover for a promisor's breach of contract, she must be either a donee or creditor beneficiary. Wendy's guarantee of the loan merely made her an incidental beneficiary of BCI's promise to obtain the higher possible price for the sale of Bombay's assets. B, C and D are incorrect for the reasons stated in the explanation to answer A.

58. C is the best answer. UCC §2-601 requires perfect tender such that if the goods or tender of delivery are nonconforming in any respect, the buyer may reject the whole delivery, accept the whole, or accept part of the delivery and reject the rest. Since the shutters were nonconforming, the shipment was properly refused. A is incorrect because Lion had the right to reject. B is incorrect because Lion has the right to reject nonconforming goods, despite Prevention's acceptance. D is incorrect because Lion still could reject non-conforming goods even if sent as an accommodation.

59. B is the correct answer. Under UCC §2-508, a seller may seasonably notify the buyer of an intention to cure and may make a conforming delivery within the contract time if a non-conforming tender or delivery is rejected. A, C and D are incorrect because of the reasons stated in the explanation to answer B.

60. A is the correct answer. Tom accepted SecureCo's offer at the price of $5,000, creating a contract for that amount. SecureCo bore the risk that his supplier would not be able to provide components at the price bid by the supplier. B, C and D are incorrect for the reason stated above.

61. D is the correct answer. Based on the doctrine of promissory estoppel, when a contractor detrimentally relies on the bid of a subcontractor in making its own bid on a project, the subcontractor is estopped from denying that an option contract was created, to the extent necessary to avoid injustice, when the contractor was induced to rely on the subcontractor's bid. When BurgCo (subcontractor) failed to perform, SecureCo (contractor) may enforce its right to obtain the amount of its loss, based on the reliance when BurgCo would not fulfill its obligation. A, B and C are incorrect for this reason.

62. A is the correct answer. There must be a meeting of the minds (mutual assent) between the parties in order to have a binding contract. Since there was no meeting of the minds in this example, there was no contract. B, C and D are incorrect for this reason.

63. A is the correct answer. The UCC §2-205 "firm offer" rule provides that where a merchant makes a signed, written offer to buy or sell goods that gives assurances that it will be held open, such is irrevocable, absent consideration, during the stated period or, if no time is stated, for a reasonable time (not to exceed three months). B, C and D are incorrect under the above rule.

64. D is the correct answer. UCC §2-207 provides that, between merchants, additional terms become part of the contract, unless they materially alter it. Requesting delivery of 150 pounds of fresh olives that could spoil, in November instead of October, materially altered the terms of the contract. Thus, the court will give effect to the original terms of the offer. A, B and C are incorrect for the reasons stated in the explanation to answer D.

65. B is the correct answer. Under UCC §2-607(3), a buyer who accepts tender of goods from a seller, must notify the seller of any breach within a reasonable time after he discovers or should have discovered the breach, or he is barred from any remedy. Since Mario accepted the non-conforming olives, he must notify Oliva Co. of their non-merchantable quality, in order to have any remedy against the seller. A, C and D are incorrect for the above reasons.

66. B is the correct answer. Where a party expressed a future inability to perform, he has not repudiated the contract. Anticipatory repudiation occurs where one party to an executory bilateral contract repudiates the contract in advance of the time set for performance, by stating unequivocally that he will not perform the contract. Thus, Leon did not breach the contract by repudiation when he stated he did not think he could perform the remodeling work. A, C and D are incorrect for the above reasons.

67. A is the correct answer. Tromp is entitled to the damages he suffered as a result of the loss of his bargain with Leon. Loss of bargain damages are measured by the difference between contract price and market value of the breached performance, at the time and place the contract was to be performed. Since Tromp contracted to pay an additional $200,000 to Ivan to complete the work, this is the difference between the contract price and market value, i.e is the amount recoverable by Tromp. B, C and D are incorrect for the above reasons.

A CONTRACTS

68. C is the correct answer. Green and Brown made a contract that was expressed in a writing, to which they both assented to be a complete and accurate integration. Parol evidence does not allow any terms made prior to or contemporaneously with, to vary or contradict the terms of the writing. A is incorrect for the reasons stated in C. B is an incorrect statement of law. D is irrelevant to the facts as stated.

69. D is the correct answer. Where there is a mutual mistake, such as here, is no defense to a breach of contract that the mistake was one of judgment. Here both parties erroneously thought there would not be any change during the term of the lease. Therefore Dick is liable to Willy for his failure to pay his rent despite the decline in business. A is incorrect, because it is not objectively impossible to pay the rent. B is an incorrect statement of law. C is incorrect, because D is the more precise answer.

70. D is the correct answer. Since Dawn failed to perform first, if the court finds that her failure was not a material breach, Tony's duties would not be excused. A is incorrect because the contract called for performance as a whole. B is incorrect because her performance is not objectively impossible. C is incorrect because D is more precise.

71. D is the correct answer. Answer I is incorrect because Buyer was not answering for Seller's debt. Instead, the Buyer-Seller agreement made Creditor an intended third party beneficiary of the agreement. Such need not be in writing to be enforceable. Answer II is incorrect because, even though a contract for the sale of an interest in land must be in writing to be enforceable, parol evidence is admissible to correct a mistake in the contract. A, B and C are incorrect for the reasons stated in the correct answer D.

72. C is the correct answer. The parol evidence rule provides when a written contract is entered into between parties where the writing is intended to be the full and complete integration of their agreement, evidence of prior or written terms will not be permitted for the purpose of changing or altering the written terms. However, there are exceptions to the rule: fraud, duress, mistake, illegality and lack of consideration. Here, the secretary mistakenly put in the term \$134,000 instead of \$135,000. Thus, parol evidence could be introduced to show the actual price for Parcel because of the mistake. A, B and D are incorrect for the above reasons stated in C.

73. B is the correct answer. A contract is not enforceable, unless it is supported by consideration. Since the facts do not indicate that Lisa gave any consideration, no contract based upon the above facts was formed. A and D are incorrect because B is the more precise answer. C is incorrect because this would not be the best defense. Rather, this would hinder Allen's claim that the contract is unenforceable.

74. C is the correct answer. Statement I is correct because Allen told the doctor he would pay his fees before Doctor treated Lisa for her injuries resulting in Doctor's reliance (i.e., this is a valid substitute for consideration). Further, statement II is correct because if Allen had a contract with Lisa, Doctor would be a third party beneficiary to the Allen-Lisa contract. Upon Allen telling Doctor he would pay, Doctor's rights vested. A, B and D are incorrect for the same reasons that C is correct.

75. A is the correct answer. Since Doctor performed his services to Lisa for her injuries, she received a benefit. To allow her to not pay would be contrary to public policy. B is incorrect because it is irrelevant. C and D are incorrect for the reasons that A is correct.

76. B is the best answer. The Statute of Frauds requires contracts be in writing: (1) for the transfer of an interest in land or, (2) which cannot be completed within one year of the date of contracting. While Terry will argue that her payments and improvements are part performance of the contract, thereby taking it out of the Statute of Frauds, her actions are also consistent with her prior relationship with Oliver, as a month-to-month tenant. A and D are incorrect for this reason. C is an incorrect statement of law.

77. B is the correct answer. The Statute of Frauds requires a contract for the sale of land to be in writing. However, partial payments by Terry takes the oral agreement outside the statute. A is incorrect because it does not fall within an exception to the Statute of Frauds. C and D are incorrect for the reasons stated in correct answer B.

78. B is the correct answer. Where parties enter into a transaction under a mistake regarding a fact assumed by each party which is the basis of the bargain for which they enter into the contact, it is voidable by either party, if enforcement would materially alter that which was bargained for. Here, Denny bargained for a 1916 "D" dime that turned out to be counterfeit. Thus, the contract can be rescinded. A, C and D are incorrect for the reasons stated in correct answer B.

79. A is the correct answer. A contract entered into by a minor, except for necessities, are voidable at the election of the minor, and may be disaffirmed by the minor during minority or within a reasonable time after reaching majority. The continuing payments and use of the car by Rodgers after reaching the age of majority constituted affirmation of the contract. B is incorrect for the reasons stated in correct answer A. C is incorrect because not all contracts entered into by minors are voidable (e.g., necessities). D is incorrect because, under the majority rule, a minor does not have to return the merchandise to have a valid disaffirmance.

80. D is the correct answer. A contract entered into by a minor is voidable and can be disaffirmed up until majority, or a reasonable time thereafter. A is incorrect because the majority rule does not require the minor to return the merchandise. B and C are incorrect for the reasons stated in correct answer D.

81. C is correct because a seller has a duty to disclose any information involving latent dangerous conditions on the property. Mr. Tibbs had knowledge of the contaminated well, and failed to disclose. This amounted to a fraudulent misrepresentation. A and B are incorrect because it incorrectly states the law. D is incorrect because fraudulent misrepresentation is a basis to rescind a contract.

82. A is the correct answer. Kemper's omission of the $301,769 price from the company's bid was a material, unilateral mistake. A unilateral mistake is grounds for rescission. B is incorrect because it is an incorrect statement of law. C is incorrect because it assumes facts not given in the question. D is incorrect because a submitted bid can be withdrawn- prior to its acceptance, as here.

83. C is the correct answer. Under the UCC, when the contract requires buyer's payment before he receives the goods, such payment is not an acceptance of the goods. Therefore, Bob has retained his right to inspect the wool despite his payment for the goods. A, B and D are incorrect for this reason.

84. C is the correct answer because it is a correct statement of the amount of damages recoverable to a buyer when the seller has tendered nonconforming goods. Bob will seek damages in the amount of the price paid, plus an amount for reimbursement of the price to purchase substitute (No. 1 quality) goods. A, B and D are incorrect for the same reasons that C is correct.

85. B is the correct answer. Under the UCC, if a seller does not give the buyer instructions on how to dispose of non-conforming goods, a buyer may resell the goods, store the goods, or reship the goods back to seller. If the buyer intends to resell the goods at a private sale, he must give the seller reasonable notice of his intention to do so. A, C and D are incorrect for the reasons stated above.

86. A is the correct answer. Melissa's offer was for a unilateral contract, which can only be accepted by the doing of the act requested in the offer and not by a return promise. B is incorrect because a unilateral contract would only be formed when Nancy performed the required act of coming to the office before or after work, not by mailing an acceptance. C is incorrect because it is an untrue statement of fact. D is incorrect because Melissa's offer was for a unilateral contract.

87. C is the correct answer. Under U.C.C. §2-205, a firm offer applies only to an offer made by a merchant. A, B and D are incorrect because the common law rule is that a promise of irrevocability must be supported by consideration.

88. B is the correct answer. Marty had an option for 60 days. His counter-offer of April 5, 1993, did not terminate that option. A is incorrect because it is not the best answer. Although a contract was formed, it was breached because of Tim selling Midnight to an innocent third party. C is incorrect because Marty's counter-offer does not terminate his option. D is incorrect because it is an incorrect statement of law.

89. D is the correct answer. Although the counter-offer, in an option contract, does not terminate the power to accept the offer, if the optionor (Tim) detrimentally relies upon the rejection, the power to accept terminates at the time of reliance. Here, the time of reliance would have been when Tim sold the mare. A is incorrect because of the reasoning stated in correct answer D. B is not the best answer, although Marty was aware of the sale of Midnight on this date. C is incorrect because the option to accept was for 60 days. The counter-offer would not terminate the option contract.

90. C is the correct answer. Under U.C.C. §2- 207, proposed new terms in a contract between merchants do not terminate the offer and become part of that contract, unless: (1) the offer is limited to its own terms; (2) the terms materially alter the contract; and (3) the offeror objects within a reasonable time. These three conditions were not met. A and B are incorrect because Tim and Marty are both merchants; thus, U.C.C. §2-207 would apply. D, although a correct answer, is not the best answer because D, without justification, assumes that Tim objects to the terms.

91. B is the correct answer. A bilateral contract consists of a promise in exchange for a promise. Here, Morrocam Company agreed to give Matt lifetime employment in exchange for a reduced wage. A, although a correct statement of law, is not the best answer. C and D are incorrect, because they misstate the common law.

92. B is the correct answer. All of the necessary terms needed to satisfy the requirement of a sufficient memorandum, under the U.C.C., are contained in Gil's note. A is incorrect because, without the memo, Gil is only liable for the glasses he has accepted. C is incorrect because a repudiation by one party, does not terminate a valid contract. D is incorrect because the note does satisfy the Statute of Frauds.

93. B is the correct answer. For Con to win, it must be shown that he neither had actual nor constructive knowledge of the miscalculation. A is incorrect because John would not be bound by the contract if Con knew of the miscalculation. C is an incorrect statement of law. D is incorrect because there was an anticipatory breach of contract.

94. A is the correct answer. John was under a pre-existing duty to do the work for $80,000. There is no consideration to support Con promising to pay the additional $4,000. B is incorrect because whether or not Con intended to pay the additional amount is irrelevant. C is incorrect because of the pre-existing duty. D is an incorrect statement of fact.

95. C is the correct answer. Sterling had essentially complied with the provision, and only had the records at the store for inventory purposes. Thus, he reasonably satisfied the insurance provision. A is incorrect because Sterling had attempted to fulfill his performance under the contract. B is incorrect because the facts do not indicate that the provision was an express condition. D is an incorrect statement of law.

96. D is the correct answer. When the offeree dispatches an acceptance and changes his mind and dispatches a repudiation, when such repudiation reaches the offeror first, there is, nevertheless, a valid contract - unless the offeror relies to his detriment on the rejection. A is incorrect because of the reasoning in correct answer D. B is an incorrect statement of law. C is incorrect because the telephone is a reasonable method of communication, under these circumstances.

97. A is the correct answer. The parties to a valid bilateral contract, which is partly unperformed on each side, may agree to a discharge of all remaining duties. The consideration is provided by each party's discharge of the other's duties. B is incorrect because there was mutual assent when Jim accepted Rod's offer. C and D are incorrect for the same reason that A is correct.

98. D is the correct answer. Only if Homeowner had known that Renoir's bid was made through error, could he not recover. A is legally irrelevant. B and C are incorrect statements of law.

99. B is the correct answer. Renoir was under a pre-existing duty to paint Homeowner's home for $5,500. Further, Homeowner's promise to pay an additional $600 was not supported by consideration. A is incorrect because there is no reason that the promise to pay additional money be in writing. C is incorrect because the detrimental reliance does not cure the lack of consideration. D is incorrect because it is an untrue statement of law.

100. C is the correct answer. Traditionally, the pre-existing duty rule, and the promise for increased performance, could not be enforced, due to lack of consideration. Modernly, courts permit the modification, where it is fair and equitable. A is incorrect for the reasons stated in correct answer C. B is incorrect because the promise did not need to be in writing. D is incorrect because "detrimental reliance" is used where a substitute for consideration is required. Here, there was a valid modification supported by consideration.

101. A is the best answer. The U.C.C. would not apply to this contract, since it involves services. B is incorrect, because it is irrelevant. C is an incorrect application of law to fact. D is incorrect. Although U.C.C. §2-609 permits a party to a sales contract to demand "assurance of performance," the U.C.C. would not apply to this fact pattern.

102. B is the best answer. In a bilateral contract, each party's promise supplies consideration. Thus, if one party's promise does not subject him to a legal detriment, it does not supply the requisite consideration, and the other party's promise is not enforceable. A is incorrect because an illusory promise generally arises where one party makes a promise in exchange for a promise that does not limit the other's future options. Here, Betty made no promise in exchange for Harley's promise so no issue of illusory promise arises. C is incorrect because the Statute of Frauds is not applicable to this fact pattern. D is a correct statement of fact but B is the better answer.

103. C is the correct answer. Statement I is correct because Harley's promise in advance of the doctor's performance would give rise to detrimental reliance. Statement II is correct because the Harley-Betty contract could make the doctor an intended third party beneficiary

104. D is the correct answer. There is a bargaine-for-exchange under these facts. Harley will pay, if Creditor will not file a claim. A is incorrect because one can bring a claim against the estate of a deceased person. B is incorrect because there was consideration. C is incorrect because promissory estoppel is not applicable to these facts.

105. D is the correct answer. Where the inducement of a party's promise is a past event or benefit, the past consideration is not sufficient to render the party's promise enforceable. A is incorrect because the consideration was past consideration. B is an incorrect statement of fact. C is an incorrect statement, as applied to these facts.

106. B is the correct answer. An assignee takes a contract subject to defenses against his assignor. If Roofer has not properly performed, this defense could be used by Pet Shop. A is incorrect because it is irrelevant whether or not Mr. Nail is capable of applying a roof. C is incorrect because an agreement not to assign destroys the right, but not the power to assign, e.g. the right to receive payment. D is incorrect, because Mr. Nail is not claiming to be a third party beneficiary, but rather is claiming to be an assignee.

107. A is the correct answer. Wife had no vested rights under the policy, since any rights were expressly subject to Isac's power to change beneficiaries. B is an incorrect application of the facts to the law. C is an incorrect statement of law. D is incorrect because, although at one time she was a donee beneficiary, Isac used his power to change beneficiaries and made his daughter the sole beneficiary.

108. D is the correct answer. Isac named his daughter as a donee beneficiary. A is an incorrect statement of law. B is incorrect because borrowing against the policy would not extinguish the daughter's rights as a donee beneficiary. C is incorrect because public policy, as presently interpreted, does not so mandate.

109. C is the correct answer. The assignment would be viewed as an exercise of the power inherent in the contract. A and B are incorrect statements of law. D is incorrect since, even if the assignment were gratuitous, the outcome would be the same.

110. D is the correct answer. The general rule is that the assignee is subject to the same defenses that the obligor has against the assignee. If Eva had not performed properly, Elva would have a defense against her, and could use this defense against Flora. Although the facts do not stipulate this dereliction in performance, the answer does. As a general strategy with multistate questions, it is better that all of the facts appear in the fact pattern. Nevertheless, when the three remaining options are clearly incorrect, as here, this kind of answer is correct. A is incorrect because Flora is an assignee, not a beneficiary. B is incorrect because it is legally immaterial to these facts. C is a correct statement of law; however, furnishing the flowers would not be deemed to be a personal service, and thus the special services rule would not be applicable. That is, C is an irrelevant statement of law.

111. D is the correct answer. A new promise to perform an obligation which is voidable, will be enforced so long as the new promise is not voidable for the same reasons. The new promise is called a ratification. A and B are incorrect for the same reasons that D is correct. C is incorrect because the writing itself is not at issue based upon these facts.

112. D is the correct answer. The U.C.C. Statute of Frauds requires that the sale of goods priced at $500 or more to be in writing to be enforceable. Although the original agreement was oral, a written confirmation between merchants may be binding on the party to be charged, without signing, if the receiving party fails to object within 10 days of receipt. While, the first written confirmation was not received, Cat will assert that the protest letter, a second confirmation, identifies the existence of a contract, and therefore is sufficient. A and B are incorrect for the reasoning stated in correct answer D. C, although a correct answer, is not the best answer, under the prevailing interpretations given to the U.C.C.

113. A is the correct answer. When a check marked "payment in full" is cashed for a disputed debt, the courts generally regard it as evidencing an accord and satisfaction with the debtor. Therefore, no further rights to additional payment exist. Answers B, C and D are nonsensical and irrelevant, when applied to these specific facts.

114. C is the correct answer. An implied novation occurs where: there has been (1) an effective delegation; (2) the obligor repudiates liability to obligee (Jag); and (3) the obligee accepts performance of the delegatee (Cathy), without reserving rights against the obligor. All of the above elements have been satisfied, under the given facts. A is an incorrect application of law. B is incorrect because it is not a good argument for Tim, but a good argument for Jag. D is incorrect for the same reasons that C is correct.

115. B is the correct answer because only Choices I and II are correct. Cat Imports will be entitled to "cover" damages. Thus, it can purchase substitute automobiles from another dealer, and recover the difference in price from Jag. Therefore, Choice I is correct. Cat may also request specific performance, Choice II. The U.C.C. provides that a buyer may receive specific performance, where the goods are unique (or in other proper circumstances). If Cat Imports is unable to locate the cars, Jag may be required to deliver. Choice III is incorrect because reformation is clearly not an appropriate remedy when a court has found that a valid contract exists - as here stipulated. A, C, and D are incorrect for the same reasons that B is correct.

116. B is the correct answer. There was an agreement between Playgoer and Dr. Othello based on the offer to pay later for help from Doctor. A is an irrelevant statement of law, because there was no need to look for an implied contract based on the rationale for answer B. C and D are incorrect statements of law.

117. A is the correct answer because it presumes Matt was not incapacitated by his drinking. A reasonable person would have found Matt's statement to be an offer, whether or not he made it in jest. Therefore, the court will find a valid contract, and Eileen can most likely sue for specific performance. B is incorrect because the court will enforce the contract- most likely through specific performance and A is the better answer. C is incorrect because being drunk will not automatically act as a defense. D is incorrect because whether or not Matt's statement was made in jest, a reasonable person would find his statement to be an offer and such is the correct legal standard.

118. A is the correct answer. The buyer's remedy for non-conforming goods is: damages measured by the contract price differential, or by cover price. B is incorrect, since it misstates the law, regarding the measure of damage. C is incorrect, since it is a misstatement of law. D is incorrect because specific performance would only be applicable where the goods were unique or where damages would be inadequate.

I19. C is the correct answer. U.C.C. §§2-711(3) and 2-706(2), (3), state that when a buyer has paid for goods, which are nonconforming and buyer demands repayment, seller may resell the goods either at a private or public sale. However, if it is a private sale, reasonable advance notice must be given to the original buyer. A and B are incorrect since they are incomplete answers. D is an incorrect statement of the law of the U.C.C.

120. D is the correct answer. Under U.C.C. §2-512(2), pre-inspection payment does not act as a waiver of inspection or remedies. Answers A, B and C are incorrect statements of law.

121. B is the correct answer. The personal services appear to be routine, rather than unique - thus, the duty will be found delegable. A is incorrect since it is unsupported by any facts. C and D are incorrect applications of the given facts to the law.

122. A is the best answer. Although a delegatee may be also be liable to the obligor/delegator, he is personally liable for the performance to the obligee (here, Candace), who is a creditor beneficary of Tumi's promise. Answers B and C are therefore incorrect, because they are incomplete. D is a misstatement of the law.

123. B is the correct answer. The offer was a manifestation of an intent to be bound. It was very specific. It described the subject matter (skis) the amount ($250), and was directed to a specific group, (first come first serve.) A is incorrect, since it is an offer – not merely an invitation to deal. C is an incorrect statement of law. D is incorrect, for the same reasons that B is correct.

124. D is the correct answer. The contract stipulated F.O.B., Seller's place of business. Thus, the risk of loss passed to Buyer. Seller would be entitled to the contract price. Therefore, Son, as the assignee, would be entitled to the contract price. A is incorrect, because the contract stated F.O.B. Seller's place of business. B is incorrect because most contractual provisions, stating that rights may not be assigned, is ineffective. C is incorrect, since it misstates the law which is appropriate to this fact pattern.

125. A is the correct answer. The risk of loss had shifted to Buyer. B is incorrect, because Seller had already delivered the boats to the carrier. C and D are incorrect statements of law.

126. B is the correct answer. The typo was a unilateral mistake. Further, Maestro would have known of the mistake, since he is an accomplished musician and would know that a Stradivarius is worth over a million dollars. A is incorrect since it is not the best answer. Specific performance is equitable in certain situations; however, it is not in this situation. C and D are incorrect for the reasons stated in correct answer B.

127. A is the correct answer. A valid contract was not formed because Sub gave Builder a counter-offer rather than an acceptance. B is incorrect because acceptance must be made by a reply, not conduct. C is incorrect because if the writing had been an acceptance, the mailbox rule would apply. D is incorrect because at that stipulated time, Sub no longer had the power to accept the original offer.

128. D is the best defense. The Statute of Frauds is applicable since the agreement, by its terms, could not be performed within one year of the making thereof. A is incorrect since Uncle Jed's death is irrelevant to any agreement between Elly Mae and Jethro. B is likely factually incorrect and is also incorrect because D is a better answer. C is factually incorrect because arguably some manifestation of intent could be found between the parties.

129. D is the correct answer. Elly Mae's academic hard work would constitute valid consideration. A is incorrect because there is consideration, as discussed in correct answer D. B is an incorrect application of law. C is incorrect because promissory estoppel is a more appropriate argument when there is a lack of consideration.

130. B is the correct answer. Pete is entitled to sue on the basis of his bilateral contract with Heather. A, although a correct statement, is not the best answer because it fails to give legally appropriate reasons. C is incorrect because it is irrelevant. There was a bargained-for-exchange; and there are no issues of fraud, etc. relevant here. D is an irrelevant statement of law, under the given facts. There was an enforceable contract

131. A is the correct answer. The offer was an offer for an act (a unilateral contract). B and C are incorrect because the notice constituted contractual intent. D is incorrect because the faculty was, in fact, bargaining- by trying to encourage moot court participation.

132. C is the correct answer. Laura increased her efforts in reliance of P.U.'s offer. Her intensified efforts would constitute sufficient part performance. A is incorrect because of the reasoning in correct answer C. B and D are incorrect and legally irrelevant statements.

133. C is the correct answer. The offer constituted a unilateral contract, since only the act of winning the competition would constitute the acceptance. A, B and D are incorrect because of the reasoning in correct answer C.

134. A is the correct answer. P.U.'s promise was conditioned on the occurrence of Laura winning. B and C are misstatements of law. D is incorrect for the same reasons that A is correct.

135. D is the correct answer. Laura's death would not terminate the offer because she has already performed (turned in the winning brief). A and B are incorrect legal statements. C is incorrect because it misses the mark – there is no reason to rely on promissory estoppel principles.

136. B is the correct answer. Chopin's statement that he might not be ready to start, would not constitute an "unequivocal" repudiation. A is incorrect because a repudiation does not have to be in writing. C is incorrect because there was not a definite repudiation. D is an incorrect statement of law, as applied to these facts.

137. B is the correct answer. An aggrieved party is relieved of his obligation, only where a material breach occurs. A 10-day delay would likely not constitute a material breach. A is incorrect because notification, under these facts, does not constitute an anticipatory repudiation. C is incorrect because such is not a justifiable legal reason, standing alone, by which a contract is permitted to be canceled. D is incorrect because it is most likely that there was no material breach, under their contract and these facts.

138. B is the correct answer. Bugsy is entitled to be placed in the position he would have been in, had Chopin followed through with the contract. A is incorrect because it does not account for the other 11 months. C is incorrect for the reasons stated in correct answer B. D is incorrect because the damages are $1,000 a month, not $4,000.

139. B is the correct answer because only Choice II is correct. The Statute of Frauds requires contract for the sale of goods for $500 or more to be in writing. Choice I is incorrect because the Statute of Frauds does not apply to a contract for services, unless performance cannot be completed within one year of the making thereof. That is not the situation here. A, C and D are incorrect because they either do not contain correct Choice II, or contain incorrect Choice I.

140. D is the correct answer. Under modern law, a contract can be rescinded orally. A is incorrect for the reasons stated in correct answer D. B is an irrelevant factual statement, based on the above law. C is incorrect because it is legally irrelevant.

141. A is the correct answer. Although Cal is in material breach, he may recover in quasi-contract. B is an incorrect application of the doctrine of impossibility. This doctrine requires there be more than a mere shortage of funds. C is incorrect because it is Cal who is in material breach. D is incorrect for the same reasons that A is the correct answer.

142. C is the correct answer. Although Cal is in material breach, he may recover in quasi-contract. His recovery will be based on restitution. A and B are incorrect because of the analysis stated in correct answer C. D is incorrect because Cal's breach was not willful.

143. B is the correct answer. Public policy finds adhesion contracts unenforceable, since they represent gross inequality of bargaining position. A, although a correct statement of fact, is not a legal reason for recovery. C and D are incorrect for the same reason that B is correct.

144. A is the correct answer. Under U.C.C. §2-206(1)(b), an offer to buy goods for prompt shipment can be acceptable by notice or by actual shipment. B is an inapplicable statement of law. C is factually incorrect because the shipment had already occurred before revocation. D is incorrect because it is legally irrelevant.

145. D is the correct answer. Under U.C.C. §2-206(1)(b), shipment is a legal acceptance, even if the goods shipped are non-conforming. However, the shipment of non-conforming goods is a breach of contract. Thus, Buyer can reject the goods. Answers A and B are incorrect for the reasoning stated in correct answer D. C is incorrect because Manufacturer did not state that the non-conforming goods were only accommodations.

146. C is the correct answer because Uniform Commercial Code (UCC) section 9-313 allows Earl's to prevail over any person becoming a lien creditor, after the security interest became perfected by Earl's timely filing of the security interest in the air conditioning system. A is an incorrect statement of law. B is incorrect because a secured interest is not automatically perfected, absent a filing. D is incorrect because, upon a proper filing of a secured interest in fixtures, that party is protected from other creditors claiming an interest in the fixture.

147. D is the correct answer. The FOB term is a delivery term - even if only used in conjunction with the price; thus, requiring delivery from the seller to the buyer's carrier to shift the risk of loss. The risk of loss did not pass because the container was merely loaded, not delivered, at the time it was stolen. A is incorrect because Sam did not deliver the goods by merely loading Bob's shipping container. B is incorrect because there are not facts to support this contention. C is an incorrect statement of law.

148. B is the best answer. UCC section 9-313(2) provides that no security interest exists in ordinary building materials incorporated into an improvement on land. Once John used the lumber to construct the garage, Hardware was prevented from having a security interest in the goods. A is incorrect because it is not as concise as B. C is incorrect because of the reasons stated for answer B. D is an incorrect statement of law, as it applies to ordinary building materials such as lumber, drywall or window glass.

A

CONTRACTS

149. A is the correct answer. UCC section 9-313(4)(b) provides that, between a fixture financier ("FRU") and a subsequent real estate interest ("Continental"), the first secured party to file or record prevails. Because FRU filed its interest before Continental, FRU prevails. B is incorrect because it is an incorrect statement of the law. C is an incorrect statement of the law as applied to a subsequent realty interest. D is incorrect because Article 9 permits fixture financiers to have a secured interest in chattels affixed to realty.

150. D is the correct answer. UCC section 9-313(4)(a) permits a fixture financier to defeat a pre-existing realty interest when: (1) the fixture security interest is a purchase money security interest, (2) the fixture security interest is perfected by a fixture filing, (3) the filing is made before the goods become fixtures or within twenty days thereafter, and (4) the debtor has a recorded interest or possession of the realty. Since element 3 is missing, FRU's priority claim against Intrastate is defeated. A is incorrect because the grace period is only 20 days. B and C are incorrect because of the rule stated in the explanation to answer D.

151. C is the best answer. UCC section 9-401(2) provides that an improper filing which is made in good faith is effective: (1) to the extent of the collateral for which the filing was proper and (2) against any person who actually knows the contents of the financing statement. Since part of George's description was proper, the filing is effective as to the properly-described collateral. A, B and D each are incorrect statements of law.

152. C is the best answer. Although a secured party may remove his collateral upon default without resort to the judicial process, unless otherwise agreed, he must do so without a breach of the peace. Bob's smashing of the cafe window was a breach of the peace which is not permitted under Article 9. A, B and D are incorrect for the same reasons that C is correct.

153. D is the correct answer. A secured creditor of fixtures may remove his collateral upon default, but he must reimburse any party, except the debtor, for the cost of repair for the physical damage caused by the fixture removal. A, B and C are incorrect for the reasons stated in the explanation to answer D.

154. A is the best answer. The implied warranty of merchantability must be disclaimed by use of the term "merchantability." The language in Tina's contract made no mention of disclaiming the implied warranty of merchantability. B and C are incorrect because they neglect to consider the attempted disclaimer of warranty. D is incorrect for the reason stated in the explanation to answer A.

155. D is the correct answer. Under UCC 2-312, a seller of goods warrants that she is conveying good title, that her title is rightful, and that the goods will be delivered free of security interest or other liens. Paula did not have good title at the time she sold the stereo to Tracee, so she breached the warranty of title to Tracee. A, B and C are incorrect for the reasons stated in the explanation to answer D.

END OF ANSWERS

CRIMINAL LAW

CRIMINAL LAW – QUESTION BREAKDOWN

1. Status Crimes
2. Malum in Se Crime – Mens Rea
3. Inchoate Crimes – Solicitation
4. Theft Crimes
5. Burglary – Modern Law vs. Common Law
6. Larceny
7. Felony Murder Rule
8. Defenses – Necessity
9. Attempt – Substantial Step
10. Burglary – Common Law
11. Defenses – Infancy
12. Involuntary Manslaughter
13. Involuntary Manslaughter
14. Accomplice Liability
15. Defenses – Insanity
16. Misdemeanor – Battery
17. Assault/Battery
18. Murder
19. Murder/Mitigation
20. Burglary
21. Attempted Rape
22. Defenses – Crime by Arresting Officer
23. Larceny/Embezzlement
24. Defense – Claim of Right
25. Protection of Property – Deadly Force
26. Malicious Mischief
27. Mistake of Fact
28. Battery
29. Defenses – Infancy
30. Statutory Rape – Defense
31. Inchoate Crimes – Solicitation
32. Actus Reus
33. Inchoate Crimes
34. Defenses/Year and a Day Rule

35. Voluntary Manslaughter
36. Embezzlement
37. Theft Crimes
38. Misprision
39. Assault/Battery
40. Inchoate Crimes – Conspiracy
41. Conspiracy/lst Degree Murder
42. Conspiracy/Murder
43. Theft Crimes
44. Larceny/Malicious Mischief
45. Larceny
46. Theft Crimes/Burglary
47. Mayhem
48. Defenses – Intoxication
49. Miscellaneous Crimes
50. Burglary/Larceny
51. Battery
52. Involuntary Manslaughter
53. Attempt/Habitation Crimes
54. Arson
55. Year and a Day Rule
56. Defenses
57. Larceny
58. Larceny
59. Burglary – Mens Rea
60. Murder
61. Malice Mischief – Personal Property Element
62. Malice Mischief
63. Assault/Voluntary Manslaughter
64. Battery – Mens Rea
65. Involuntary Manslaughter
66. False Imprisonment
67. Battery
68. Malicious Mischief
69. Uttering/Larceny
70. Embezzlement
71. Burglary
72. Burglary – Breaking & Entering
73. False Pretenses

74. False Pretenses
75. Embezzlement
76. Involuntary Manslaughter
77. Murder
78. Common Law Crimes
79. Vandalism
80. Rape – Defense of Consent
81. Malicious Mischief
82. Voluntary Manslaughter
83. Actus Reus/Mens Rea
84. Malicious Mischief
85. Larceny
86. Murder
87. Insanity
88. Defenses – Diminished Capacity
89. Mens Rea
90. False Pretenses
91. Theft
92. Theft
93. Involuntary Manslaughter
94. Murder – Causation
95. Conspiracy – Wharton's Rule
96. Mens Rea
97. Defenses – Necessity
98. Forcible Entry & Detainer
99. Defenses – Defense of Property
100. Defenses – Necessity

CRIMINAL LAW QUESTIONS

1. The state of Columbia has made it a crime to "be addicted to any illegal substance." The crime is a felony. The crime is violative of due process because:

    A. It is a "status" crime which has insufficient actus reus.

    B. Involuntary intoxication should be a defense.

    C. It is void for vagueness.

    D. It is fundamentally unfair.

2. Josey was convicted of false pretenses. The judge instructed the jury as follows: "The burden of proof is on the prosecution, to prove each and every element of the crime beyond a reasonable doubt. Here, the prosecution must prove that the defendant obtained title to property of another by means of misstatement of past or existing fact. If you find each element proven by the facts, then the defendant is guilty." The defendant was convicted. His best ground of appeal, based on the preceding, is:

    A. The evidence was insufficient, as a matter of law.

    B. He has no grounds of appeal, since the instruction was perfect.

    C. The mens rea element was left out of "false pretenses," and since this is a malum en se crime, such omission violates due process.

    D. The instruction does not require the obtaining of documentary title.

Questions 3 – 7 are based on the following fact situation:

Ready and Randy came over to visit Able one fateful morning and did their utmost to get Able to agree to join them in a burglary. Able would not agree; however, Randy and Ready then pretended to need Able's car to buy groceries. Instead, they drove to a certain warehouse, broke in and stole the rare painting they had told Able about. They then drove home without incident, having had the car for only two hours and, as prearranged, left the keys in Able's mailbox. Randy, tucking the small painting under his left arm, proceeded to walk with Ready to his apartment. The police stopped them on their walk, to ask some questions. Randy pulled a gun and fired, killing an officer. The other police officer then drew and fired, killing Ready and accidentally killing a young school girl on a nearby porch.

3. After Randy, Ready and Able first spoke with one another about the burglary:

   A. They were all guilty of conspiracy to commit burglary.

   B. Ready and Randy were guilty of solicitation to commit burglary.

   C. Ready and Randy were guilty of attempted burglary.

   D. No crimes were committed, since there was no actus reus.

4. When Ready and Randy borrowed Able's car and used it for an unstated purpose, at common law:

   A. They were guilty of embezzlement.

   B. They were guilty of obtaining property by false pretenses.

   C. They were guilty of malicious trespass.

   D. They were guilty of larceny by trick.

5. When Ready and Randy broke into the warehouse to steal the painting:

   A. At common law, they were guilty of burglary.

   B. Under most modern statutes, they were guilty of burglary.

   C. Under both modern and common law, they were not guilty of burglary.

   D. None of the above.

6. When Ready and Randy stole the painting:

   A. They were guilty of embezzlement, because they used no trick or force in the taking.

B. They were guilty of false pretenses, because they obtained both title and possession.

C. They were guilty of larceny, because there was a trespassory taking.

D. None of the above.

7. When the exchange of gunfire was complete, Randy was guilty of:

A. False pretenses and involuntary manslaughter.

B. Burglary at common law.

C. Voluntary manslaughter, because there was a heat of passion.

D. Murder, at common law, of the girl.

Questions 8 – 10 are based on the following fact situation:

One evening in December, Sam came to the unoccupied summer home of a wealthy banker who used it only during the months of July and August. Sam found the back door completely open. He walked in, looking for something to eat. Sam had no money and was dying of starvation.

After finding something to eat, Sam noticed a beautiful diamond ring on the dining room table. He tried it on just to see how it would look. After admiring it for some time, he removed the ring and placed it back on the table. As he settled down on the living room couch to take a nap, he resolved that following his nap he would take the ring and leave.

While asleep, the police, on their regular security patrol, discovered Sam and arrested him. He was charged with common law burglary and larceny.

8. Which of the following is the best defense to the charge of larceny of the food:

A. There was no concurrence of mens rea and actus reus.

B. Sam's taking the food was out of necessity.

C. The back door was wide open, he walked in without touching a tangible thing and he did not take the ring.

D. It would violate due process to punish in this instance.

9. Which of the following is the best defense to a charge of attempted larceny of the ring:

A. He had not taken a substantial step to commit larceny.

B. Larceny is a crime against possession and nobody was in possession of the ring at the time.

C. Since he never left the house with the food, there was no "asportation" as defined by the common law.

D. The ring was abandoned property.

10. Which of the following would be the best common law defense to the charge of burglary:

A. Sam had diminished capacity.

B. Burglary is a crime against habitation, and nobody lived in the house at the time.

C. There was no "breaking."

D. Sam was under compulsion.

Questions 11 – 13 are based on the following fact situation:

Frank, 6 years old, and Jesse, 16 years old, decided it would be great fun to "scare the pants off " Lionel Hart, the neighborhood grouch. Their idea was to gain entry to Hart's home and leap out at him as he was about to enter upon returning home from work.

One evening about 9:00 p.m., Jesse drove to Hart's house and, pushing open the already slightly-opened ground floor window, they entered. While waiting for the moment to arrive, Frank's eyes were attracted to a small gold figurine standing on a bookcase. Without Jesse's knowledge, Frank put it in his pocket.

When Hart arrived home, the boys leaped out at him. Startled by their actions, Hart stepped backward, falling down the stairs. The fall resulted in Hart's death.

11. Frank's best defense at common law to a charge of burglary would be:

A. That there was no breaking, since the window was already open.

B. There was no felonious intent at the time of the breaking and entering.

C. Since the boys were neighborhood kids known to Mr. Hart, they impliedly had consent to go into the premises.

D. He was under seven years old, and thus as an infant, he had a complete defense.

12. Jesse's best defense at common law to a charge of conspiracy to commit involuntary manslaughter would be:

    A. The crime of manslaughter merges with the greater crime of burglary.

    B. There was no such crime at common law.

    C. Jesse was guilty of another crime instead.

    D. There was no specific intent to do this particular action.

13. If apprehended and charged with the death of Hart, Jesse would most probably be found:

    A. Guilty of involuntary manslaughter.

    B. Guilty of second degree murder, based on the malicious intent of the boys.

    C. Guilty of voluntary manslaughter, based on the Misdemeanor Manslaughter Rule.

    D. Not guilty of homicide, based on the accidental manner of Hart's death.

14. Ace and Don commit a bank robbery. Don goes to his mother's and tells her, "I am in trouble with the law. Hide me." Ace is arrested and implicates Don. The police go to Don's mother's house where they inquire if Don is there, as he is wanted for investigation of a bank robbery. Don's mother states that she does not know where Don is, despite the fact that Don, at the moment, is hiding in the closet. Modernly, Don's mother may be guilty:

    A. Of conspiracy.

    B. Of obstruction of justice.

    C. As a principal, in the second degree.

    D. As an accessory before the fact.

15. Dugan has suffered from chronic alcoholism for twenty years. One night while sober, Dugan shot and killed a man he claimed had been sent by the devil. At Dugan's trial for murder, a psychiatrist testified Dugan knew what he was doing, but because of chronic alcohol-induced mental illness, he did not know it was wrong. Dugan should be found:

    A. Guilty, because voluntary intoxication is no excuse.

    B. Guilty, because he knew the nature and quality of his acts.

C. Not guilty, because he was legally insane.

D. Not guilty, because of a good faith unreasonable mistake of fact.

Question 16 – 19 are based on the following facts:

On December 5, 1990, Lori Vieux went to the Wastooni Night Club for a few drinks. Before she could enter, however, Bouncer asked for identification. Vieux was 35 and proceeded to show Bouncer, an enormous weightlifter, her driver's license indicating the same. For no apparent reason, Bouncer shoved her. Vieux, a skinny bespectacled woman, fell hard. As she was getting back to her feet, Bouncer shoved her again and slapped her face. Vieux's nose began to bleed profusely.

Vieux crawled away. As she was leaving Bouncer yelled: "Hey, baby, stick to the (expletive deleted) law books. If I see you again, I'll leave nothing."

The following evening Vieux returned to Wastooni and shot Bouncer from point-blank range, instantly killing him.

At trial, Vieux testified she thought Bouncer was going to kill her. A battery of both prosecution and defense expert medical witnesses corroborated this belief, but all, too, testified Vieux was not legally insane.

16. When Bouncer shoved Vieux, the least serious crime he committed was:

    A. False imprisonment.

    B. Battery.

    C. Kidnapping

D. Negligent infliction of emotional distress.

17. Bouncer committed which of the following crimes:

I. Battery - one count.

II. Battery - two counts.

III. Assault.

A. I and III only.

B. II and III only.

C. I and II only.

D. III only.

18. At common law, Vieux's killing of Bouncer would be:

A. Murder.

B. First degree murder.

C. Voluntary manslaughter.

D. Involuntary manslaughter.

19. In a jurisdiction following modern rules, Vieux's best argument in mitigation would be:

A. Self-defense.

B. Insanity.

C. Imperfect right of self-defense.

D. None of the above.

Questions 20 – 22 are based on the following facts:

One hour after sunset, Cyrus Sinner set out to enjoy himself. He had two fine Canadian beers at a local bar, then decided he would like a date. No one was interested. He then bragged to several men that he would have a woman that night one way or another, even if it had to be by force.

Cyrus decided to "create" a date with a woman he had admired for months. He went to Wanda's house and pushed her front window open with a crow bar. He put one foot through and alarms went off. While running away he was apprehended by Officer Tough, who, while on patrol, was ordered by his superior to investigate the alarms.

Tough placed Sinner under arrest, pursuant to all legal requirements, but then, for good measure, punched him in the stomach.

At trial, Sinner's attorney offered expert medical testimony that Sinner was impotent. Further, it was shown that Wanda was not home that evening.

At trial, several instructions were given to the jury, only one of which, the following, however, has been appealed:

"Jury Instruction #7: I am now going to instruct you on the requirement of intent necessary for the crime of burglary. Such requires an intent to commit a felony. No one can truly know what goes on in another man's mind. However, the subjective intent required may be proven from an individual's actions and from the other circumstances of the case. If you find, beyond a reasonable doubt, that the defendant intended to commit a larceny, or an arson, or a rape, or any felony, then you should find that this element has been met."

20. Sinner's worst argument in defense of burglary is:

    A. He lacked the mens rea necessary.

    B. He did not intend to rape.

    C. The entry element was lacking.

    D. The jury instruction was prejudicial.

21. The prosecution will likely convict Sinner of attempted rape because:

    I. He took a substantial step toward commission of rape.

    II. He intended to rape.

    III. His impotence was merely a factual impossibility.

    IV. His impotence was merely a legal impossibility.

    A. I and II only.

    B. I and III only.

C. I, II and III only.

D. I, II and IV only.

22. Tough's punching of Sinner is:

A. A defense to a charge of burglary.

B. A defense to the charge of attempted rape.

C. A mitigation only.

D. Irrelevant to the prosecution of Sinner.

Questions 23 – 26 are based on the following facts:

Chance Chewer, having an insatiable lust for gourmet chewing tobacco, walked into Tarno Brothers Tobacconist. Having chosen his blend, he handed Mr. Smoak, the manager, a $100.00 bill. The cost of the tobacco was $3.12, only. Smoak handed Chewer $6.88 from the cash register and said "thank you, sir." Chewer left.

Smoak then placed the $100.00 bill into his own wallet. Smoak chuckled to himself and muttered that the drooling, slobbering customer deserved to lose more than a few bucks for his vile habit.

Later in the day, Chewer realized he was missing that $100 bill. He retraced his steps and decided he must have overpaid Tarno Brothers. He returned to the store, deciding to even up the score. He walked in and pocketed a $100.00 gold inlaid tobacco pouch. Smoak saw this and said "stop" to Chewer. Chewer kept going. Smoak then shot Chewer in the back of the leg.

The police came. On his way out, Chewer purposefully bashed in two glass display cases. Repairs cost $75.00.

23. When Smoak pocketed Chewer's $100 bill he committed which of the following crimes?

I. Embezzlement against Tarno of $10 only.

II. Embezzlement against Tarno of $6.88 only.

III. Larceny against Chewer of $100.

IV. Larceny against Chewer of $93.12.

A. I and III only.

B. II and IV only.

C. I only.

D. II only.

24. Chewer's pocketing of the tobacco pouch was:

A. Robbery.

B. Burglary.

C. Larceny.

D. None of the above.

25. Smoak's shooting of Chewer was:

A. An aggravated battery because it was all Smoak's fault.

B. Not an aggravated battery because Chewer was only entitled to $93.12.

C. Not an aggravated battery because of the guilt of the victim.

D. An aggravated battery because deadly force, in this situation, is impermissible.

26. When Chewer bashed in the display cases he committed:

A. Mayhem.

B. Malicious mischief.

C. Larceny.

D. Robbery.

Questions 27 – 30 are based on the following facts:

Jan was a sexually promiscuous 17 year old. She decided to have an affair with Ted, who was married. Ted refused her invitation. However, one night she broke into Ted's house and secreted herself in Ted's bed.

Ted's wife was out. Ted went to bed and had sex with Jan, thinking her to be his wife. Just prior to the time of the liaison, Ted had ten stiff vodkas.

27. Ted's best defense to a charge of statutory rape would be:

    A. Consent.

    B. Infancy.

    C. Mistake of fact.

    D. Mistake of law.

28. Jan can be successfully prosecuted for which of the following crimes at common law:

    I. Rape.

    II. Battery.

    III. Burglary.

    A. I only.

    B. II only.

    C. III only.

    D. I and III only.

29. Modernly, Jan's best defense to a prosecution for sexual assault is:

    A. Infancy.

    B. Public Policy.

    C. Consent.

    D. Equal Protection.

30. The following arguments would be unsuccessful if Ted is charged with statutory rape:

    I. Jan instigated the liaison.

    II. Jan was guilty by breaking and entering.

    III. Jan consented.

    IV. He was drunk.

    A. I and III only.

    B. I and II only.

    C. I, II and III only.

    D. I, II, III and IV.

Questions 31 – 35 are based on the following facts:

Jo's twin sister, Fawn, was terminally ill with a painful variety of cancer. She was being artificially sustained by respirator and other medical equipment. Jo hated to see her sister suffer so.

One afternoon at the hospital, Fawn implored Jo to kill her. Jo refused and left.

Dr. Donna, however, had heard Fawn's request and decided to "pull the plug" on Fawn's life-sustaining equipment in one week, if her condition did not improve. She believed Fawn would die as a result.

Nurse Ned also heard the request and decided to help the family by immediately taking Fawn's life by lethal injection of poison. Ned prepared a syringe and went to Fawn's room. Unable to proceed, he "nerved" himself by taking several tranquilizers. Not truly then understanding what he was doing, he injected Fawn with the poison.

Fawn's condition worsened, but she did not die.

The hospital called Jo and told her that Dr. Donna tried to poison Fawn, but that Fawn would be all right. Jo became immediately enraged. She took out her Uzi machine gun, packed it in a gym bag, and drove to the hospital. Because of heavy traffic, it took Jo almost one hour to arrive at the hospital. Dr. Donna was in the front lobby. Jo spotted Donna and took out the Uzi. She shot Donna repeatedly and yelled, "You deserve to die more than poor Fawn! You shouldn't have poisoned her!" Donna died ten months later from the bullet wounds Jo inflicted.

31. Fawn can be successfully prosecuted for which of the following crimes?

    A. Solicitation.

    B. Attempt.

    C. Conspiracy.

    D. None of the above.

32. Dr. Donna, if she survived, could be successfully prosecuted for which of the following crimes:

    A. Solicitation.

    B. Attempt.

    C. Conspiracy.

    D. None of the above.

33. Ned can successfully be prosecuted for which of the following crimes?

    I. Battery.

    II. Attempted murder.

    III. Larceny.

    A. I only.

    B. I and II only.

C. I, II and III.

D. III only.

34. If Jo is charged with second degree murder, she should not make which of the following arguments in defense or partial defense:

I. The Year and a Day rule.

II. Mistake of Fact.

III. Provocation.

IV. Defense of others.

A. I and II only.

B. I, II and III only.

C. I, II and IV only.

D. III only.

35. Jo's best argument in mitigation is:

A. Diminished capacity.

B. Insanity.

C. Provocation.

D. Mistake of Fact.

Questions 36 – 38 are based on the following facts:

Joe Money worked for a large marketing firm. In the ordinary course of business, Joe Money was exposed to enormous sums of money. Ordinarily, he would deposit checks he received into his company, "Walls," accounts. However, Joe developed a dislike for his employer, and a belief that he was being underpaid.

Thus, on occasion, Joe would simply pocket cash accounts received. Inadvertently, the Internal Revenue Service discovered discrepancies between Joe's stated earnings and his bank deposits.

In order to avoid tax fraud charges, Joe struck a deal with his employer "Walls," to repay all sums misappropriated and "Walls" would indicate that Joe's "extra" deposits were simply advances on expenses soon to be incurred.

36. Which crime has Joe committed at common law?

A. Larceny.

B. Embezzlement.

C. Theft.

D. False pretenses.

37. Which crime has Joe committed modernly?

A. Receiving stolen property.

B. Fraud.

C. Petty theft.

D. Grand theft.

38. Assume Walls is charged with misprision.

A. Walls will be found guilty.

B. Walls will not be found guilty, because it is a corporation.

C. Walls will not be found guilty, because Joe did not commit a crime.

D. None of the above.

Questions 39 – 42 are based on the following facts:

Jay Mean managed a chain of restaurants. Whenever any other employee showed signs of dissatisfaction, Mean would find some excuse and fire them.

Mean would most often discover such dissent via the "tattling" of William Plomat, his personal "gofor."

Shark, on one occasion, called Mean a power-crazed despot. Shark was promptly fired.

Shark, quite angry at this turn of events, hired Kerr to kill Mean. Kerr devised an ingenious plan wherein he would poison Mean over a course of several days via dispensing a poisonous gas in Mean's office. The effect of the gas would mimic first simple breathing difficulties and then paralysis.

In order to plant the gas dispenser, Kerr broke into Mean's office one night.

Mean dies via the poison.

39. Had Mean survived he would have been guilty of which of the following crimes?

I. Assault.

II. Battery.

III. Wrongful termination.

IV. Intentional infliction of emotional distress.

A. I and II only.

B. III and IV only.

C. I only.

D. None of the above.

40. When Shark hired Kerr, which of the following crimes were committed?

A. Solicitation.

B. Conspiracy.

C. Attempt.

D. Murder.

41. Under the modern law, Shark is guilty of which crimes?

A. First degree murder and conspiracy.

B. Second degree murder and conspiracy.

C. First degree murder only.

D. Second degree murder only.

42. At modern law, Kerr committed which of the following crimes?

I. Conspiracy to commit murder in the first degree.

II. Murder in the first degree.

III. Burglary.

A. I only.

B. II only.

C. I, II and III.

D. I and II only.

Questions 43 – 46 are based on the following facts:

Lott Ri was feeling quite unlucky. He had, sadly, spent his last dollar, and was pondering his fate while walking on the beach. He reached down and let his fingers run through the sand. To his surprise, he found a two-carat diamond ring!

Although he wanted to keep the ring, his conscience demanded he surrender it to the local police. Lott filled out some forms, left the ring at the police station and walked out. Little did Lott know, but the police soon learned the ring had been abandoned, thrown away, by a local millionaire, and Lott was to be the owner after the 48 hours waiting period.

Lott sat on the beach and watched the sun set. He sat for hours, and slowly realized he should have kept the ring. He decided to regain the ring. It was 3:00 a.m. and the small town police station was unoccupied and closed up. Lott broke a window, entered, turned on the lights, found the ring and fled. Lott figured that some rich actress lost the ring and that some rich insurance company would pay her back. He felt no guilt.

43. When Lott initially picked up the ring, he committed which of the following crimes?

    A. Larceny.

    B. Embezzlement.

    C. Trespass.

    D. None of the above.

44. When Lott took the ring from the police station, which of the following common law crimes were committed?

    I. Larceny.

    II. Malicious mischief.

    III. Burglary.

    A. I only.

    B. II only.

    C. I and II only.

    D. I, II and III only.

45. Lott's worst argument against a charge of larceny is:

    A. The property was lost.

    B. The property was not owned by the police.

    C. The property was abandoned.

    D. The owner consented.

46. Were this jurisdiction to follow the modern law, which crimes has Lott committed?

    I. Larceny.

    II. Grand theft.

III. Vandalism.

IV. Burglary.

A. I and II only.

B. II and III only.

C. I, III and IV only.

D. II, III and IV only.

Questions 47 – 48 are based on the following facts:

Todd the Snake is a professional wrestler. During the wrestling match he puts his famous "sleeper" hold on his opponent John the Giant. Snake and Giant had actually rehearsed this move prior, but Snake decides to do it for real. Snake wins the match, but Giant is hospitalized with neck injuries and permanent partial paralysis.

After the match is over, a fan accosts Snake and calls him a cheater. Because Snake has been under a lot of pressure lately: he didn't get the title fight he wanted with Howard the Animal; and because he is feeling extremely aggressive from the doctor-prescribed hormones he is taking; the fan's taunt snaps the Snake's delicate ego. Snake picks up the fan and throws him down, instantly killing him.

47. Todd's use of the sleeper hold on John is:

    A. Battery.

    B. Not battery because John consented.

    C. Mayhem.

    D. Not mayhem because John consented.

48. Snake's killing of the fan is:

    A. Murder.

B. Not murder, because of involuntary intoxication.

C. Voluntary manslaughter.

D. Not voluntary manslaughter, because of self-defense.

Questions 49 – 56 are based on the following facts:

Otto was a "survivalist." He purchased a semi-automatic Uzi machine gun at the local gun shop. Even though he knew it to be illegal, he modified the gun to be fully automatic. The gun thus, at just one continuous pull of the trigger, would keep on shooting bullets.

Otto slept with the gun under his pillow. One night, after Otto had anesthetized himself to sleep (with a fifth of bourbon), Philip Panther broke into Otto's house. Although Panther was usually quite good at this kind of thing, in this particular instance, he made a tremendous racket entering. Otto's big 18 x 7 foot picture window overlooking the Pacific was smashed.

Waking from his apocalyptical dream, Otto grabbed his gun and ran to the scene of the tumultuous entry. Panther was busily gathering Otto's valuable cross-bow and arrow collection. Otto, still legally intoxicated, and in a blood rage, pulled the trigger. Otto believed he had to kill Panther to protect himself from Panther who had one cross-bow (a deadly weapon) loaded and ready to fire. Further, Otto wanted to kill Panther out of the sheer joy of the kill. At Otto's one pull of the trigger, fifteen bullets issued forth. Thirteen of these entered the abdomen of Panther.

One bullet, however, ricocheted off of Otto's foosball table and flew through the smashed window, through his next door neighbor's open window, into the heart of his next door neighbor, Sylvester. Houses in this neighborhood were built very close together. Sylvester died instantly.

Otto put down his gun and called the police. Mrs. Sylvester called an ambulance. Before the ambulance or police came, she lit up a torch, ran over to Otto's house, confronted him through the smashed window, and screamed, "I'll kill you, you crazy survivalist nut! You killed my husband!"

Dumbfounded, Otto just stared at Mrs. Sylvester. He then said, "Relax." Mrs. Sylvester threw a makeshift torch at Otto. The torch chipped a piece of glass away on its way into the house. Otto ducked out of the way. She fled. The torch ignited Otto's home.

Otto called the fire department and waited outside. Captain Ignite arrived in the city firetruck. He knew Otto, and hated him. He therefore purposely took his time in setting up the hoses. His willful delay, in fact, caused Otto's house to burn down.

Panther remains in a coma, at the State West Hospital. Assume the law of this jurisdiction to include the following statute:

The willful modification of a semi-automatic weapon so that it is fully automatic, absent state permit, is a misdemeanor. Any unnecessary death or injury caused by this weapon shall not be excused by the uncontrollable nature of the weapon.

49. At the common law, Otto's modification of the gun was:

    A. Malicious mischief.

    B. Statutory rape.

    C. Treason.

    D. None of the above.

50. Panther committed which of the following common law crimes?

    A. Burglary.

    B. Larceny.

    C. Burglary and larceny.

    D. None of the above.

51. Otto's use of deadly force on Panther was, under the law of this jurisdiction:

    A. Reasonable and thus justifiable.

    B. Unreasonable and thus a battery.

    C. Reasonable and thus a battery.

    D. Unreasonable and thus a second degree murder.

52. At common law, Otto's stray bullet, which struck Sylvester, amounted to:

    A. Burglary and involuntary manslaughter.

    B. Burglary and murder.

    C. Involuntary manslaughter.

D. Burglary.

53. Mrs. Sylvester committed which of the following crimes?

I. Arson.

II. Burglary.

III. Attempted murder.

A. I, II and III.

B. I and II only.

C. II and III only.

D. II only.

54. Ignite committed which of the following crimes?

A. Willful delay.

B. Culpable omission.

C. Negative omission.

D. Arson.

55. At the common law, if Panther stays in a coma for two years then dies, the worst crime Otto can be convicted of, regarding Panther's death, is:

A. First degree murder.

B. Second degree murder.

C. Manslaughter.

D. None of the above.

56. Otto asks you, his attorney, to interpret the statute's effect on his prosecution. Your best explanation will include which of the following points?

I. The statute is irrelevant.

II. He is guilty of this statutory misdemeanor.

III. The statute may prevent his use of the defense of habitation defense.

IV. The statute may prevent his use of the self-defense defense.

V. The statute may prevent a successful defense regarding Sylvester's death.

A. I, II, III, IV and V.

B. II, III, IV and V only.

C. III, IV and V only.

D. II and IV only.

Questions 57 – 58 are based on the following facts:

Layla borrowed Eric's Lamborghini automobile without Eric's consent. Once on the road, she decided to keep it. She drove 200 miles and then decided to rest. It was 10:00 p.m. Since there were no motels open, Layla broke into Cindy's house, which was empty and went to sleep. When Layla awoke, she decided to pack a breakfast "to go", helping herself to Cindy's food. Cindy reported the above to the police the following day when she had returned.

57. Layla's theft of the car will be based on which of the following theories?

    A. Larceny.

    B. Larceny by trick.

    C. Embezzlement.

    D. False pretenses.

58. At the common law, which crimes has Layla committed?

    I. Burglary.

    II. Larceny.

    III. Embezzlement.

    A. I only.

    B. I and II only.

    C. I and III only.

    D. II only.

Questions 59 – 62 are based on the following facts:

It was a dark and stormy New Year's Eve and Mike decided to shoot his .44 magnum firearm into the sky. The bullet fell through the roof of Arnold's house, killing both Arnold and Arnold's dog Laddy. Mike was aware that someone could get hurt, but thought nevertheless "it was the right thing to do to celebrate New Year's Eve."

59. At common law:

    A. There was a burglary, by way of instrumentality used to consummate the crime.

    B. There was a burglary, because a felony was committed therein.

    C. There was not a burglary, because there was no entry.

    D. There was not a burglary, because there was no specific intent.

60. At the common law, Mike's killing of Arnold is:

    A. Second degree murder.

    B. Reckless homicide.

    C. Murder.

    D. Involuntary manslaughter.

61. At the common law, Mike's killing of Laddy was:

    A. Malicious mischief.

    B. Cruelty to dogs.

    C. Canine homicide.

    D. None of the above.

62. Which of the following other common law crimes were committed?

    I. Malicious mischief.

    II. Unlawful assembly.

    III. Rout.

    IV. Riot.

    A. I and II only.

    B. II and IV only.

    C. I only.

    D. II only.

Question 63 is based on the following facts:

On Sunday, March 17, 1991, Charles went to Newport Beach with his girlfriend, Denise. While Charles was surfing, Denise rested in the sun, and read a book. This was their typical Sunday afternoon behavior. Charles and Denise had been dating for about three years and planned to marry in June. They were going to open their own specialty surf shop.

While Charles was searching for the perfect wave, about 100 feet from Denise, Edward walked up to Denise and struck up a conversation. Denise had dated Edward before she met Charles. Bored with Charles, and remembering the good times she had with Edward, Denise offered Edward a seat beside her. Remembering how much they cared for each other, they talked, and soon began to kiss.

Shortly thereafter Charles returned to discover their intimacy. Denise was startled and said, "I'm sorry Charles, it's not what you think."

Charles said, "It's cool Denise" and walked off. However, as he walked away he, became angrier and angrier. He turned around and approached Denise and Edward. Edward said, "Beat it wimp."

Charles grabbed Edward by the neck and applied pressure to the carotid artery. Edward died from strangulation. Charles let go of Edward and turned to Denise. He made a threatening gesture to her and said, "I ought to strangle you, too." Denise screamed and ran away. Charles chased her, but was apprehended by several other surfers.

63. Charles has committed which of the following crimes?

    I. Murder in the second degree of Edward.

    II. Voluntary manslaughter of Edward.

    III. Assault of Denise.

    IV. Battery of Denise.

    A. I and III only.

    B. II and IV only.

    C. II and III only.

    D. I and IV only.

Questions 64 – 65 are based on the following facts:

On Saturday, March 16, 1991, Arnold entered the Redondo Bar. He ordered an Australian Red Back Wheat Beer and a sandwich. Betty sat beside Arnold and asked if she could have a taste of his beer. Arnold replied, "Yes," and Betty reached for the bottle. Mostly out of shyness but also evidencing her klutzy nature, she inadvertently spilled the beer on Arnold.

Arnold became incensed. Betty apologized. Arnold slapped her. Betty fell down, banging her head and died as a result of the fall.

Arnold was so upset and completely surprised at Betty's death, that he forgot to pay for the sandwich and beer.

64. Had Betty survived, she committed which of the following crimes?

    A. Assault.

    B. Battery.

    C. Malicious mischief.

    D. None of the above.

65. Arnold has committed which of the following crimes?

    I. Involuntary manslaughter.

    II. Second degree murder.

    III. Embezzlement.

    IV. Larceny.

    A. I only.

    B. I and III only.

    C. II only.

    D. II and IV only.

66. Hannah invites Greg out to a picnic in the open fields. Hannah brings all sorts of foods, beverages and condiments. Greg, expecting a sexual encounter in the country, brings wine, condoms and a gun – just in case some intruder hassles them. Lunch is served and Greg requests Hannah for the expected sexual favor. Hannah says "Greg, I appreciate your feelings; but not today. Sorry." Greg then pulls out his gun and tells Hannah, "Stay put and think that over." Hannah glares at him, Greg apologizes, then takes her home. Which of the following crimes has Greg committed?

    A. Rape.

    B. False imprisonment.

    C. Battery.

    D. He has committed no crime – Hannah led him on.

Questions 67 – 70 are based on the following facts:

Grunch was a law student convinced that most of his time in law school was wasted. He sat behind Betty, who he found to be very attractive. As his own little game, he would play with Betty's long pretty hair. Betty told him to stop.

One day, during Grunch's Torts class, he left early. He noticed the car of the Torts professor, Phil, and no one else in the lot. Grunch took out his own car keys, then "keyed" the poor Prof's car. It left a nasty scratch.

Grunch then opened his own car. He had not paid his law school for a gate card, but did have several Chuck E. Cheese tokens, which worked well in opening the gate. They were the same size as the school's "guest" tokens. He placed one in the gate-exit slot, the gate pulled up, and he drove off.

67. When Grunch touched Betty's hair, assuming that Betty did not notice, what, if any crimes at common law did Grunch commit?

    A. He committed no crime, because the touching was not offensive.

    B. He committed no crime, because this was the tort of battery.

    C. He committed battery, because there was no consent.

    D. None of the above, but it would be a crime modernly.

68. When Grunch "keyed" the car of his Torts professor, Phil, what if any crimes did he commit?

    A. He committed no crimes, because the car could be repaired.

    B. He committed the intentional infliction of emotional distress.

    C. He committed a theft of movables.

    D. He committed malicious mischief.

69. When Grunch used the counterfeit token, which, if any modern crimes did he commit?

    I. Forgery.

    II. Uttering.

    III. Theft by false pretenses.

    IV. Theft by larceny.

    V. Theft by embezzlement.

    A. I and III, only.

    B. II and IV, only.

    C. V only.

    D. I and V, only.

70. Assuming, Chuck E. Cheese did not consent to Grunch taking the tokens out of the restaurant, that Grunch did so accidentally, then Grunch decided to keep them, which, if any common law crimes did he commit against Chuck E. Cheese?

    A. Larceny.

    B. Embezzlement.

    C. False pretenses.

    D. None of the above.

Questions 71 – 77 are based on the following facts:

With the intent to steal all the belongings in what appeared to be a fine beachfront house, Jennifer picked the front door lock and walked in. She was nervous, because it was a full moon and she thought someone might notice. However, there was nothing whatsoever in the house. Evidently, due to the recent rain and landslides, the occupants had moved out. The house was to be torn down – as it was deemed to be on highly unstable ground. Jennifer left.

Instead of driving home, however, she went to a liquor store and picked out a $175 bottle of Single Malt Scotch. While no one was looking, she scraped off the price tag and put on a price tag from a bottle of cheap Scotch. That price tag read $7.99. Jennifer paid the clerk $7.99 for the Scotch, put the receipt in her purse and left.

She had a few quick gulps of the Scotch in the car, felt a little "unsteady" from the alcohol, then drove home. It was a short drive home, so Jennifer thought that there would be no danger to herself or anyone. On her way home, however, she missed seeing a pedestrian (because of her intoxication) and hit him. The pedestrian, Robert, was badly injured and died from his wounds two weeks later.

71. If Jennifer is charged with common law burglary, what is her worst argument?

    A. The house was abandoned.

B. It was not a "dwelling."

C. There was no one there.

D. None of the above.

72. Did Jennifer commit any common law crime when she entered the beachfront house?

A. No, because there was no burglary.

B. No, because trespass was only a tort.

C. Yes, there was a trespass.

D. Yes, there was a forcible entry.

73. At the common law, did Jennifer commit a crime when obtaining the Scotch?

A. Yes, it was a larceny.

B. Yes, it was a larceny by trick.

C. Yes, it was a false pretenses.

D. Yes, it was an embezzlement.

74. Assume for this question only, that the liquor store clerk thought Jennifer was cute, and decided to let her get away with the price-tag switch. Does this relieve Jennifer of criminal liability?

A. Yes, because there was consent.

B. Yes, because there was condonation.

C. Yes, because there was no trespass.

D. No.

75. If the liquor store clerk let Jennifer get away with the price-tag switch, has he committed any crime against his employer?

A. Yes – embezzlement.

B. Yes – larceny.

C. Yes – conversion.

D. No – it was good business – no one would have bought it anyway.

76. Under the common law, when Jennifer killed Robert, what crime did she most likely commit?

A. Vehicular manslaughter.

B. Murder.

C. Involuntary manslaughter.

D. Driving Under the Influence.

77. Assume for this question only, that Robert died from being hit by Jennifer's car 13 months later. At the common law, is Jennifer guilty of his criminal homicide?

A. Yes, because it is stipulated she was the proximate cause.

B. No, because she was not the proximate cause.

C. Yes, because of the year and a day rule.

D. No, because of the year and a day rule.

Questions 78 – 81 are based on the following facts:

Miranda was prone to jealousy anyway, but her new boyfriend, Stone, brought out the worst in her. Although they supposedly had a one-on-one relationship, Stone dated several other women contemporaneously. Miranda queried Stone about this, but he was adamant and somewhat convincing in his denials.

As a result of the above, Miranda decided to "get Stone in a way that really hurt." One late evening, Miranda called Stone up and relayed to him the following ever-so-brief conversation: "Come right over, Stone. I really want to make love."

Stone replied, "On my way." Stone jumped into his car and made it to Miranda's apartment in record time. He couldn't find the key which Miranda had given him, so he forced the front door open. He went to Miranda's bedroom, found her naked in bed and proceeded to have sexual relations with her. However, soon after genital penetration, Miranda said, "Stop. You're a heel and I'm done with you. Get out of my house...now!"

Stone did not stop having sex. Three minutes later, after Miranda again told him to leave, he did. After quickly dressing, he smashed the picture Miranda had of the two of them together.

78. Under the common law, has Miranda committed any of the following crimes?

    A. Yes, cruelty to animals.

B. Yes, fornication.

C. Yes, intentional infliction of emotional distress.

D. No.

79. When Stone forced open Miranda's front door, modernly, what crime, if any, did he commit?

A. Vandalism.

B. Malicious mischief.

C. Burglary.

D. Forcible entry and detainer.

80. If Stone is charged with rape, he will:

A. Be convicted, since consent was withdrawn.

B. Be convicted, since Miranda was not his wife.

C. Be acquitted, since Miranda's consent was binding.

D. Be acquitted, because there was not complete carnal knowledge.

81. At common law, when Stone smashed the picture, he committed which common law crime?

A. Malicious larceny.

B. Malicious mischief.

C. Vandalism.

D. Uttering.

Questions 82 – 88 are based on the following facts:

Cereal had just had a big fight with his girlfriend, Melody. He caught her in bed with his best friend, Kello. Immediately after discovering their betrayal, Cereal walked off and got out his gun. It was unloaded. He felt the cold unforgiving metal in his hands... and at once realized shooting people was not the way to handle the problem. He put the gun back, and went out for a walk.

He pondered going back to kill Melody and Kello, but instead decided to "walk it off." A police horse walked in front of him. Cereal kicked the horse, breaking one of its ribs. Cereal laughed, as he ran off.

Cereal then saw a hot new red Mazda Miata. Cereal pried off one of the car's mirrors and threw it in the gutter, feeling better all the while.

Cereal then walked into a bar. He saw a woman who looked remarkably like Melody. He approached her, said, "enough is enough," and struck her with a bar stool. The woman, Jane, immediately expired from the wound. Cereal started crying and begged all of those who were present for understanding and forgiveness. He said, "My girlfriend looks a lot like her. I feel so bad. I didn't even know this lady... What can I do now; it's too late..."

82. Assume for this question only, that Cereal killed Melody immediately upon discovery of her sexual betrayal, what crime did he commit?

    A. Murder.

    B. Voluntary manslaughter.

    C. Involuntary manslaughter.

    D. No crime – she had it coming.

83. Under the facts as given, when Cereal picked up the gun, what crime, if any, did he commit?

    A. Battery.

    B. Assault.

    C. Illegal firearms possession.

    D. None of the above.

84. When Cereal kicked and hurt the horse, what crime, if any, did he commit at common law?

    A. Malicious mischief.

    B. Cruelty to animals.

    C. Resisting a police officer.

    D. Treason.

85. Cereal's damage to the Miata was a:

    A. Good way to "vent."

    B. No crime at the common law.

    C. Receiving stolen property.

D. Larceny.

86. When Cereal killed Jane, what crime is he most likely to have committed?

A. First-degree murder.

B. Second-degree murder.

C. Voluntary manslaughter.

D. Involuntary manslaughter.

87. What is Cereal's best complete common law defense to the killing of Jane?

A. Insanity.

B. The Rule of Provocation.

C. Mistake of fact.

D. Diminished capacity.

88. What is Cereal's best modern partial defense to the killing of Jane?

A. The Rule of Provocation.

B. Insanity.

C. Imperfect self-defense.

D. Diminished capacity.

Questions 89 – 94 are based on the following facts:

It was raining quite hard in Los Angeles, but Mason desired to try out his new Jaguar sedan, with special anti-lock brakes. Mason was aware that in the rain it was more dangerous to drive, but felt, "Why buy an expensive car, if you can't try it out?"

So Mason went driving. In order not to get a chill, Mason had a couple of drinks of fine Perestroyka Brand Vodka (made in New Jersey). Mason was a big man, so there was no way he was at all intoxicated.

Mason observed many interesting things. On the side of the road, he saw an old man limping. He drove on.

Mason then went to a restaurant. Carelessly, he left the car unlocked and the keys in the ignition. He sat in a cozy booth and ordered a sandwich and a soft drink. The waiter miscalculated the amount owed. The food should have totaled $4.88; but the waiter totaled it as $3.59. The waiter gave Mason the bill along with the food. Mason at once observed that the bill was too low, and pondered whether he would bother to correct it with the waiter. While sipping the soft drink and munching on the "Double Bypass" sandwich, Mason decided that he wouldn't bother to correct the error. Mason paid the $3.59 and left a dollar tip.

Mason left, and was shocked to note that his car had been stolen. Teena was the thief. While driving off with the Jaguar, she inadvertently killed a pedestrian after getting into a rain-induced skid. Although Teena did not have a driver's license, she was driving quite safely.

89. Mason's not giving aid to the old man was:

    A. Battery.

    B. Assault.

    C. Misprision.

    D. No crime.

90. Mason's under-payment to the restaurant of the food bill was which crime?

    A. Larceny.

    B. Larceny by trick.

    C. Embezzlement.

    D. False pretenses.

91. Under the modern law, Mason's non-payment of the food bill was which, if any, crime:

    A. Theft.

    B. Petty theft.

    C. Grand theft.

    D. None of the above.

92. Teena's taking of Mason's car, modernly, was which, if any crime?

    A. Grand theft.

    B. Petty theft.

    C. Vandalism.

    D. No crime, because she had constructive consent.

93. If Teena is convicted of involuntary manslaughter, which theory will, most likely, have been utilized by the prosecution?

    A. Malum in se unlawful act.

    B. Criminal negligence.

    C. Sufficiency of the evidence.

    D. Depraved heart.

94. Is there any theory by which Mason could be charged with the criminal homicide of the pedestrian?

    A. Yes, he was a substantial factor.

    B. Unclean hands.

    C. Depraved heart.

    D. None of the above.

95. Assume that Breach of the Peace is defined as follows:

The purposeful assembly of four or more individuals in public, with the intent or with reckless disregard for the tranquillity of others present.

If Al, Betty, Chuck and Denise light off firecrackers in Central Park, their best defense to charges of Conspiracy to Breach the Peace and Breach of the Peace is:

A. There was no proof that anyone else was present.

B. This crime has multiple intent requirements – and these have not been proven.

C. Wharton's Rule.

D. Firecrackers in Central Park are no big deal.

96. Finn is an ex-hippie, now yuppie, living in suburbia. One of Finn's neighbors, Nasty, is very jealous of Finn for his success in trading stocks. One Saturday night, Nasty rings Finn's doorbell and asks whether he can come in. Finn says "Sure." Nasty then offers Finn a marijuana cigarette. Finn exclaims "Whoa, baby – that stuff is illegal – but it was fun and it has been years." Nasty responds, "Keep it my friend." Nasty then calls the police and tells them Finn is in illegal possession of marijuana. The police arrive 10 minutes later, with a fully proper telephonic search warrant, and find the marijuana in Finn's home. What is Finn's best defense to a charge of "Knowing possession of marijuana ?"

A. He lacked knowledge or scienter.

B. He was entrapped, as a matter of law.

C. He was not in true possession.

D. He lacked evil motives, and was a creature of circumstance.

Questions 97 – 100 are based on the following facts.

Dick was homeless and decided to camp out in the back yard of Marcia. Marcia had quite a big back yard, so at first Dick was not noticed. Then one night, Marcia saw Dick and, with gun in hand, threatened to shoot Dick immediately – if he did not leave. Dick said, "Madam, I mean no harm; I just need a place to sleep."

Marcia replied, "Two minutes, or you're dead." Dick did not leave, and instead, said to Marcia, "If you shoot that gun at me and miss, believe me, you'll be sorry." Marcia shot the gun at Dick and missed. Dick then raced toward Marcia, forcibly grabbed the gun, waved a fist at her and left. He threw Marcia's gun in her garbage pail (which was by the side of the house).

97. Under modern majority rules, if Dick is charged with "Criminal Trespass," what is his best defense?

    A. Necessity.

    B. Duress.

    C. Guilt of the Opposing Party.

    D. Unclean hands.

98. Under the common law, if Dick is charged with Forcible Entry and Detainer, will he be guilty?

    A. Yes, because he trespassed onto Marcia's land.

    B. No, because Marcia used excessive force.

    C. No, because he used no force in the trespass.

    D. No, because such was not a common law crime.

99. Under the modern law, if Marcia is charged with aggravated assault, she will most likely:

    A. Be found guilty, since deadly force cannot be used to protect property.

    B. Be found guilty, since she fired a shot.

    C. Be found not guilty, based on the defense of habitation defense.

    D. Be found not guilty, because Dick was unlawfully present.

100. If Dick is charged with battery of Marcia and robbery of her gun, his best affirmative defense will be:

    A. Marcia was the aggressor.

    B. Necessity.

    C. He did not intend to permanently deprive.

    D. Diminished capacity.

END OF QUESTIONS

CRIMINAL LAW ANSWERS

1. A is the "best" answer but it is not the only correct answer. The Columbia statute punishes for substance addiction. But, although the addict likely often has a guilty mental state (the desire to have the drug), he need not necessarily have done any action whatsoever. Crimes which so punish often violate due process. They are called "status" crimes – because they punish guilty status only. Our system of justice requires that status not be punished unless there also occurs a guilty action (actus reus) and guilty mental state (mens rea). Answer A correctly, though briefly, states the above reasoning. B is incorrect because substance addiction, as a matter of law, is considered to be voluntary intoxication only. Such is based on public policy (to deter drug use) and because the first use of the drug was voluntary. C is the second best answer. This statutory crime probably does not have a mens rea, is therefore strict liability and strict liability crimes are not preferred. However, answer A gives a more precise description of the problem. D, although arguably correct, is again far less precise than A.

2. C is correct. The jury instruction defined a basic crime (false pretenses) but left out any mens rea requirement. As a general rule, true crimes should include a mens rea and if they do not, there is a possible due process violation. A is incorrect because no facts whatsoever were set out. Thus, one cannot reasonably conclude whether the evidence was sufficient or insufficient. B is incorrect for the same reason that C is correct. D is incorrect because false pretenses requires obtaining title, not "documentary title." Documentary title is, in fact, not a legal term of significance.

3. B is the correct answer. Solicitation to commit burglary is enticing another to commit burglary with the intent that the other commit burglary. (Modernly, burglary is the entry of the structure of another with the intent to commit a felony or petty larceny.) The facts stipulate that Randy and Ready tried to get Able to commit burglary and that Able declined. Since there was a serious request to do burglary, both elements of solicitation are established. A is incorrect because conspiracy requires that there be a meeting of the minds and actual intent to do a crime. Here, since Able declined, there was no meeting of the minds and no intent on the part of Able. C is incorrect because attempt requires that there be a substantial step (dangerous proximity to success), and here at the time of the enticement the parties were not nearly close enough to commission of the crime. D is incorrect for the same reason that B is correct – solicitation is a crime and the enticement is a sufficient actus reus (guilty action).

4. A is the best answer. Ready and Randy had permission to borrow Able's car to buy groceries – but not to commit a burglary. This fraudulent misuse is an embezzlement. Since they did not obtain title to the car, Choice B is wrong. There was no "false pretenses." Choice C is wrong because there is no such crime as "malicious trespass." Since Ready and Randy did not have an intent to permanently deprive Able of his car (the last element of larceny by trick) there is no larceny by trick. Therefore, D is incorrect.

5. B is correct. Ready and Randy entered into a warehouse (walled structure) intending to and committing a larceny. Thus, all of the elements of modern burglary have been satisfied. A is incorrect because common law burglary requires the breaking and entry occur at night and to a dwelling house. Those two elements are lacking here. C and D are incorrect for the same reason that B is correct.

6. C is correct. Larceny is the trespassory (here, stealing) taking (stealing) and carrying away (stolen from warehouse) of the personal property of another (here the painting) with the intent to permanently deprive. The facts indicate that all of the elements are present. Thus, a larceny has been committed. A is incorrect because for there to be an embezzlement, the defendant must be in lawful possession of the property. Here, Randy and Ready did not have lawful possession of the painting. B is incorrect because false pretenses requires that the defendant obtain title to the property. Here, Ready and Randy did not get title. D is incorrect for the same reason that C is correct.

7. D is the best answer. Since Randy and Ready were still in the process of hiding the painting they were, arguably, still in perpetration of the burglary. Use of the felony murder rule, requires the defendant to be in perpetration (including, as here, flight from) of an inherently dangerous felony (like burglary) and that a death be the result. Use of the felony-murder rule, at common law, did not require that the defendant do or even initiate the killing. Thus, Randy can be found guilty of Ready's death, even though it was a police officer who did the killing. The killing was the result of the warehouse burglary. Thus, D is the best answer. A is incorrect because, although the homicide could be argued to be an involuntary manslaughter, there was absolutely no false pretenses. That is, Randy did not obtain title to the painting. B is incorrect because common law burglary requires the breaking and entry occur at night and to a dwelling. C is incorrect because voluntary manslaughter also requires there be "legally adequate provocation." Being upset because of resistance to your burglary is objectively quite inadequate.

8. B is the best answer. Necessity or choice of evils is a complete defense to all crimes except murder and rape. Necessity allows doing a criminal act in order to avoid a greater calamity. Here, since Sam was starving, stealing some food (larceny) was better than his own death. This, in fact, is a paraphrasing of Sir Francis Bacon's famous maxim. A is incorrect because when Sam took the food (the actus reus), he intended to steal it (the mens rea). Thus, the mens rea and actus reus of larceny did concur. C simply misreads the question. The issue is not burglary here, but larceny of the ring. D is incorrect only because it is imprecise. Due process or "fundamental fairness" would be violated by punishing here, but the defense of necessity is the more accurate legal explanation.

9. A is correct. Attempt requires there be a substantial step and that intent to do the crime be present. Here, the facts stipulate Sam did have the requisite intent. However, after he formed the intent he took no action – he simply took a nap! Thus, there was not a substantial step and the first element of attempt was lacking. B is factually incorrect. Larceny is a crime against possession. Here, however, the ring was not abandoned. It was still in possession of the owner. It need not be on the victim's person for there to be a larceny. Such confuse the requirements of larceny with those of robbery. C misreads the question. The issue here is larceny of the ring, not larceny of the food. Moreover, C is also incorrect because any movement satisfies the carrying away/asportation element. D is factually incorrect. It is absurd to conclude that all chattels in a summer home are "abandoned."

10. C is correct. Burglary, at common law, requires there be a breaking. This element is satisfied when there is any movement of the structure. Here, the facts stipulate that the back door (where Sam entered) was completely open. Thus, there was no breaking. A is incorrect because diminished capacity was not a common law defense. B is incorrect. Burglary is a crime against habitation, but this was a habitation. Having slept there and intending to sleep there again is all that is required. Since it was a summer home with quite a few effects in it (food, ring, couch, etc.), we can certainly infer the dwelling requirements have been satisfied. D is incorrect because the defense of compulsion (or duress) requires that another human threaten the defendant with imminent violence, so that the defendant will commit a crime. There was no compulsion here. This option confuses compulsion with necessity.

11. D is the best answer. Frank, at 6 years old, was irrebuttably presumed incapable of committing a crime at common law under the infancy defense. A is incorrect because any movement of the structure satisfies the breaking element, and here the window was pushed open wider. B is incorrect only because D is a better answer. The boys' intent was to assault, which was not a common law felony. However, since B requires weighing of facts and making inferences, whereas D is obviously right because Frank's age is given, D is the better answer. C is incorrect because it creates facts. No consent to enter was stipulated or even implied.

12. B is the best answer. Conspiracy requires there be an actual intent to do the target crime. Involuntary manslaughter requires there be an unintentional killing. There can, therefore, be no conspiracy to do this crime. It is a contradiction in terms. A is incorrect because manslaughter does not merge (is not a lesser included offense) of burglary. They are distinct crimes. C is incorrect because guilt of "another crime" does not relieve guilt. This statement is silly. D is correct – there was no intent to kill. However, B which dismisses the validity of the whole charge, is a better answer.

13. A is the correct answer. Involuntary manslaughter is the unintentional unlawful killing of a human with criminal negligence or when done in the perpetration of a malum in se unlawful act. Here, Jesse unintentionally killed Hart by assaulting him. This action evidenced criminal negligence (Jesse should have known of the risk) and also satisfied the unlawful act-manslaughter rule (assault is a malum in se unlawful act). B is incorrect. Second degree murder requires the presence of malice aforethought. Here, there was no express malice (no intent to kill). Likewise, there was no intent to cause serious bodily injury and no conscious, reckless disregard of the risk. Since malice aforethought was lacking, there was no murder in the second degree. C is incorrect, factually and legally. This was not an intentional/heat of passion killing. It was an accidental killing. Therefore, voluntary manslaughter is incorrect, factually. Furthermore, it is involuntary manslaughter and not voluntary manslaughter which is linked up with the unlawful act-manslaughter rule. C is, therefore, also legally incorrect. D is incorrect because accidental killings certainly can lead to criminal homicide convictions. Felony-murder and involuntary manslaughter are two such examples.

14. B is the best answer. An accessory after the fact or obstruction of justice, with knowledge of the existence of a completed crime, helps hinder the arrest of the perpetrator. Modernly, close relatives, like the perpetrator's mother, are often not prosecuted. Nevertheless, B is the best answer, since the others are entirely incorrect. A is incorrect because Don's mother did not agree with another to commit a crime. C is incorrect because Don's mother was not a perpetrator of the robbery. D is incorrect because Don's mother was not involved in the planning of the robbery.

15. C is correct. If a defendant commits a crime while under the influence of drugs or alcohol, even if the drugs make him delusional, insanity is not available. Only voluntary intoxication is relevant. However, if the defendant has caused himself brain damage by chronic use of drugs – and is not then under the influence, insanity is relevant. Such is the stipulated situation in this question. Under the prevailing majority and common law M'Naghten insanity test, Dugan had mental illness, a defect of reason (the devil message) and did not know this killing was wrong. Therefore, M'Naghten is satisfied and Dugan is legally insane. A is incorrect because Dugan was not here intoxicated and is also incorrect because voluntary intoxication cannot be a defense to a malice crime like murder. B is incorrect. Although Dugan did know what he was doing (the nature and quality of his acts), this element is only an option in the M'Naghten test. M'Naghten can also be satisfied if the defendant does not know what he is doing to be wrong – as here. D is incorrect because the mistake of fact defense, for a malice crime like common law murder, requires the mistake to be objectively reasonable. D is incorrect because it misstates the relevant law.

16. B is the correct answer. Battery is generally a low-grade misdemeanor. There was certainly a battery here, as evidenced by the slaps. A and C are each incorrect for two reasons. First, false imprisonment and kidnapping are more serious crimes. Second, it does not appear that there was a confinement – thus, neither crime was committed. D is incorrect because the negligent infliction of emotional distress is not a crime. It is a tort.

17. B is the correct answer. Although it is a close call, it appears that Bouncer committed two batteries: the initial shove and the secondary slap. Thus, II is a better choice. Moreover, since assault is a lesser included offense of battery and since there was an intentional scaring (by way of the threat), III is also correct. Only answer B includes both II and III.

18. A is the correct answer. The malice aforethought element of murder can be shown by an intent to kill. Vieux obviously possessed such. Since the other elements of murder are present, such is the correct crime. B is incorrect because first degree murder was not a crime at the common law. C is incorrect because a requirement of voluntary manslaughter is that the killing follow immediately upon the passion-provoking incident. A day's wait is too long. D is incorrect because involuntary manslaughter covers only unintentional killings, and this killing was on purpose.

19. C is the correct answer. Vieux had a good faith but unreasonable belief that the killing was necessary to protect herself– the exact requirement of this partial defense. A is incorrect because Vieux was the aggressor the following evening -thus, self-defense is not available. B is incorrect because it was stipulated that Vieux was legally sane. D is incorrect because C is correct.

20. C is the correct answer. The entry element of burglary is satisfied when any part of the perpetrator's body penetrates the dwelling. Since Sinner's foot penetrated, C is a bad choice. A and B are incorrect because Sinner did intend to rape, as stipulated in the facts. D is incorrect because the jury instruction correctly defined the mens rea necessary and correctly discussed whose burden it was to prove such.

21. C is the correct answer. Attempted rape requires that Sinner took a substantial step toward rape (shown here by the breaking and entering) and that he had the intent to rape (shown here by the facts). Thus, I and II are correct. Since Sinner, in fact, intended to rape, and rape is a crime, there was merely a factual impossibility – which is not a defense. Thus, III is correct and IV is incorrect. Only C offers I, II and III.

22. D is the correct answer. After a crime has been committed, a crime by an officer does not retroactively limit the guilt of the original perpetrator. Thus, Tough's battery of Sinner is irrelevant. A, B and C are incorrect for the same reason that D is correct.

23. A is the correct answer. This is a very tricky question. Since Smoak was the manager, he was in more than mere custody and, thus, was capable of embezzling Tarno. Since he did not put Chewer's money into the register, the $6.88 he took out was Tarno's. Further, he deprived Tarno of the $3.12. Thus, he embezzled a total of $10. I is correct and II is incorrect. Since it appears that Smoak intended to steal Chewer's $100 before obtaining possession, the crime is larceny (not embezzlement). Thus, III is correct. II and IV are incorrect for the same reasons that I and III are correct. Only choice A offers I and III.

24. D is the correct answer. In a slim majority of jurisdictions, an honest claim of right negates the intent element of the theft crimes. For that reason A, B and C are incorrect.

25 . D is the correct answer. Deadly force is never permissible when used merely to protect property. Chewer's action was larceny and Smoak used deadly force. D, alone, states this relevant legal rule. The guilt of the victim is irrelevant to this question – thus, B and C are incorrect. Furthermore, A is incorrect because the earlier guilt of the perpetrator is not relevant in this case.

26. B is the correct answer. Malicious mischief covers the damaging of property. A is incorrect because there was no dismembering. C and D are incorrect because there was no "taking" (control) of any property.

27. C is the best answer. Often statutory rape is considered to be strict liability; thus, there are no defenses. However, since such is not an option, we must choose the "best" answer given. Certainly A is incorrect because consent is not an element of this crime. Actually, the alleviation of consent is the gravamen of this offense. B is also totally incorrect – Ted is obviously of age, so the infancy defense is unavailable to him. Since Ted in no way misunderstood the law, D is also incorrect. Thus, we are left with C as the best choice. Ted thought Jan was his wife and this was a reasonable mistake under the circumstances.

28. B is the correct answer. Choice I is incorrect because rape, at common law, could not be committed by females. Choice III is incorrect because for there to be a burglary there must be "the intent to commit a felony." Jan's intent was, at worst, to commit the misdemeanor of battery. Since Jan "offensively" touched Ted, there is a battery. Only II (and B) are correct.

29. A is the best answer. Modernly, infancy can be defined as under 18 years of age. Jan is 17, so she might have such a defense. B is incorrect since, literally, public policy is not a defense. C is incorrect because Ted's consent was gained by gross fraud/impersonation. Fraud in the factum invalidates consent. D is incorrect because in no way would the equal protection clause mandate preferential treatment of young women.

30. D is the correct answer. The sexual aggressiveness of an underage female is irrelevant to a charge of statutory rape. Thus, choices I and III are incorrect. Choice II is incorrect because the guilt of the "victim" is not a defense at criminal law. Choice IV is incorrect because voluntary intoxication is not a defense to a strict liability crime.

31. A is the correct answer. When Fawn asked Jo to kill her, she was enticing Jo to commit a murder. Thus, there was a solicitation. Consent of the victim is no defense to murder. Since Fawn did not take a substantial step, there is no attempt, and, thus, B is incorrect. Since Jo did not agree, there is no conspiracy and C is incorrect. D is incorrect for the same reasons that A is correct.

32. D is the correct answer. Since Dr. Donna only thought about killing Fawn: only intended to kill. Thus, there was no crime. Mens rea alone cannot be punished. Thus, A, B and C are incorrect.

33. C is the correct answer. When Ned used the syringe on Fawn, there was an unlawful application of force – thus, I is correct. When he decided to kill Fawn and took the syringe and drugs, there was a substantial step – and at that instant there was the intent to kill. The taking of the hospital's drugs and syringe was trespassory – thus, there was a larceny. Only choice C includes I, II and III.

34. C is the correct answer. Note: the call of this question is phrased in the negative. Since Donna died within a year of the attack and from the attack, the "year and a day" rule is inapplicable. So Jo should not argue I (but I is correct because of the negative call of the question). Although Jo was misinformed as to who tried to kill her sister (it was actually Ned), use of the mistake of fact defense requires that: were the facts as the defendant believed them to be the conduct would not be criminal. But, here, Jo's attack would still be unjustified. Jo should not make this argument – thus, II is also correct. Since Fawn was in no further danger, the imminence element of defense of others is lacking, so the argument in IV also should not be made. Only choice C includes all of these poor arguments. Since Jo was acting under reasonable provocation, option III would be a viable argument.

35. C is the best answer. When an individual is reasonably provoked (here by the attempt on her sister's life), is actually upset (stipulated in the facts), and has insufficient time to "cool down" (the attack occurred soon after the passion-provoking incident) the rule of provocation will mitigate murder to voluntary manslaughter. Although A, diminished capacity, is also a mitigation defense, because it is such an extreme minority position, C is a better choice. B and D are incorrect because they are not mitigating factors. Rather, they are complete defenses, excuses.

36. B is the correct answer. Since Joe was in a managerial position, he had "lawful possession" of the money – not mere custody. Since the other elements of embezzlement are present, that is the correct choice. A is incorrect for the same reasons that B is correct, i.e., there was no trespass in the taking. C is incorrect because, when there is a lawful possession, there is no trespass – which is a requirement of larceny by trick. Although there was a "trick," there was no trespass – and, thus, no larceny by trick. D is incorrect because title did not pass, and such is a necessary element of false pretenses.

37. D is the best answer. Clearly Joe committed a theft (based on embezzlement) of Walls' accounts. Grand versus petty theft is determined by fair market value of what is stolen. A typical cut-off figure is $400. Although the facts are unclear as to the amount stolen, a reasonable inference is that it was an "enormous sum." Thus, D is better than C. A is incorrect because no facts indicate Joe received stolen property. B is incorrect because fraud is not a crime.

38. A is the correct answer. Misprision is the knowing concealment of the felony of another. Walls' cover-up appears to be such. B is incorrect because corporations can be found guilty of crimes. C is incorrect because Joe likely committed a grand theft. D is incorrect for the same reasons that A is correct.

39. D is the correct answer. I is incorrect, since Mean neither threatened nor attempted a battery. II is incorrect, since Mean applied force to no one. III and IV are incorrect, since they are torts, not crimes. Thus, A, B and C, which include I, II, III or IV, are incorrect.

40. B is the best answer. Since Shark and Kerr reached a criminal agreement, there was a conspiracy. Although Shark also solicited Kerr, such merges in the conspiracy. Therefore, A is not the best answer. Since, at the time of hiring, no substantial step was taken, there is no attempt . C is incorrect. Similarly, at the time of the hiring, no killing had occurred – so there is no murder. D is incorrect.

41. A is the correct answer. Since Shark hired Kerr to kill Mean, such evidences the premeditation and deliberation necessary for first degree murder. Moreover, since Shark and Kerr were in criminal combination, there was a conspiracy. Since only choice A includes both of these crimes, it is the correct answer.

42. C is the correct answer. Kerr and Shark were in criminal combination, thus, choice I is correct. When Kerr killed Mean, there was a premeditated intent to kill, thus, satisfying the mens rea element of murder in the first degree. Thus, choice II is correct. Modern law burglary does not require the breaking of a dwelling. Kerr broke into Mean's office. Only choice C offers choices I, II and III.

43. D is the best answer. Since when Lott picked up the ring initially his intent was neither to steal (larceny) nor to defraud (embezzlement), A and B are incorrect. C is incorrect for two reasons: first, trespass is not a crime; and second, even if it were, there is no trespass when finding lost property provided one's intent is to turn it in.

44. C is the correct answer. Choice I is correct because all of the elements of larceny are present (Lott took ring with intent to keep it). Although one might argue the "of another" element was lacking, it was present. This element refers to whether the "victim" (here the police) had, at the time of the taking, a lawful possession. They did. One can commit larceny on property owned by oneself. Choice II is also correct, because there was damage to the property of another (the window) and, thus, there was a malicious mischief. Since the breaking and entering was not of a dwelling, choice III (burglary) is not present. Only choice C offers I and II.

45. B is the best answer. Note: The call of this question is phrased in the negative. We are looking for the worst argument. Since ownership is not a requirement of larceny, this choice is truly poor. Although this is a difficult, hair-splitting question, it is somewhat typical of multiple choice exams. A is incorrect because the fact that property is lost can sometimes preclude a conviction of larceny (if the intent to steal forms after the taking), but sometimes is irrelevant (if the intent forms prior to or at the time of the taking). Thus, A is a mediocre argument. C is incorrect because sometimes abandonment is a defense to larceny. Similarly, choice D is incorrect because consent by the lawful possession is a defense to larceny.

46. D is the correct answer. Lott's taking of the ring, which was then in lawful possession, would amount to a grand theft modernly (not a larceny – the common law term). Thus, II is correct and I is incorrect. III is correct because a damage to another's property is often, modernly, called "vandalism." Choice IV is correct because, modernly, burglary only requires an entry into a structure with felonious intent. Only choice D offers II, III and IV.

47. C is the best answer. Mayhem includes not only disfigurement; but also any permanent damage to the body interfering with self-defense abilities. Paralysis qualifies as such. Since the most serious crime is always to be chosen (unless the call of the question directs otherwise), although there was a battery, such is not the best answer. Therefore, A is incorrect. Choices B and D are incorrect because John gave a conditional consent – only and such is limited to the condition allowed. John did not consent to the sleeper hold – he consented to faking the sleeper hold.

48. B is the correct answer. Although this is a close one, the involuntary intoxication defense would alleviate Snake's guilt -since it was stipulated the hormones were doctor-prescribed and that they created a mental disorder (aggressiveness). A is incorrect for the same reasons that B is correct. Although it can be argued that Snake committed a manslaughter, since his response to the fan was based on words alone, the provocation was insufficient. C is therefore incorrect. D is incorrect because in order to utilize self-defense, there must be an imminent attack and only reasonable force may be used. Neither situation here existed.

49. D is the best answer, because A, B and C are incorrect. A is incorrect because the gun was not "the property of another" – an element of malicious mischief. B is incorrect because there was no sexual activity. C is incorrect because no aid was given to the enemies of the state.

50. C is the correct answer. Panther fulfilled all the elements of burglary. Moreover, since Panther obtained control of at least a cross-bow there was a larceny, as well. Only choice C offers both burglary and larceny.

51. B is the best answer. Otto used excessive force per the statute. Thus, he is responsible for Panther's injury. Although the injury is likely more than a battery, such is the best option listed. A and C are incorrect for the same reason that B is correct. D is incorrect because Panther is still alive.

52. C is the correct answer. Either under the misdemeanor-manslaughter rule, or under the criminal negligence method, Otto is responsible for the death of Sylvester. Since the killing was unintentional, all of the elements of involuntary manslaughter have been satisfied. There is no burglary at common law, since there was no "breaking" and no "intent to commit a felony." Thus, A, B and D are incorrect. Additionally, B is incorrect because there was no malice, a requirement of murder.

A

CRIMINAL LAW

53. A is the correct answer. Choice I is correct because there was a burning of Otto's dwelling. Choice II is correct because the torch not only broke the window, but was also used to try to complete the intended felony (murder). Thus, legally there was an entry - even though Mrs. Sylvester did not personally enter Otto's home. Choice III is correct because Mrs. Sylvester took a substantial step toward completion of murder with the intent to kill. Since Mr. Sylvester was not then in danger, defense of others is unavailable. Only A offers I, II, and III.

54. D is the correct answer. This is a difficult question. More than one party can be guilty of a single crime - even if they were acting independently – provided that both perpetrators were substantial factors (causation), as here. Moreover, if there is a legal duty to act and no act is performed, the perpetrator is criminally liable under an omission theory. Such was our situation. A is incorrect because "willful delay" is not a crime. B is incorrect because "culpable omission" is not a crime – it is merely a method of proving causation. C is incorrect because such is not a crime.

55. D is the correct answer. At the common law, the inflicted wound must result in death within "a year and a day." As stipulated, the death here took two years. Thus, all of the homicides: A, B and C are incorrect. At worst, under these facts, there would be a battery or mayhem. These options were not offered.

56. B is the correct answer. Choice I is incorrect because the statute was highly relevant, as shown by the following. Choice II is correct because Otto did willfully modify the gun. Choices III, IV and V are correct because, by definition, use of such a weapon precludes use of defenses which would otherwise be available. Use of such a weapon is a, per se, unreasonable use of force. Only B includes choices II, III, IV and V.

57. A is the correct answer. Since there was a trespass in the taking of the car, and the intent to permanently deprive formed during the taking, there is a continuing trespass larceny. B is incorrect since no facts indicate that Layla got possession by trick. C is incorrect since no facts indicate that Layla was entrusted (lawful possession of Eric's car). D is incorrect because title to Eric's car did not pass; thus, there can be no false pretenses.

58. D is the correct answer. Since the mens rea of burglary (intent to commit a felony) must concur with the actus reus (breaking and entering, etc.), and at the time of the breaking there was no felonious intent, there can be no burglary. Thus, choice I is incorrect. Since Cindy stole the food, there was a simple larceny; and choice II is correct. Since Cindy was not entrusted in lawful possession, of the food, there is no embezzlement and, thus, choice III is incorrect. Only D offers choice II alone.

59. D is the correct answer. For there to be a burglary, there must be intent to commit a felony in the dwelling. Mike did not have the required intent. Thus, D is correct. A is incorrect because it misses this fundamental requirement. B is incorrect because the issue is not whether a felony was actually committed, but rather was the intent felonious. C is incorrect because entry by instrumentality is valid if, as here, the instrumentality is used to complete the felony. In this case, the bullet was used to kill.

60. C is the correct answer. The killing was a classic "depraved heart" killing. Mike was aware of the substantial risk to human life, and ignored such. A and B are incorrect because they are modern crimes. D is incorrect for the same reason that C is correct.

61. D is the best answer. A correct answer requires knowledge of a hairline distinction. Dogs were not personal property at the common law, so technically this was not a malicious mischief. Both B and C were not common law crimes, so D is the best answer.

62. C is the best answer. When the bullet penetrated the roof, it probably damaged something in Arnold's home – thus, there was probably a malicious mischief. Although this is not a "correct" answer, it is the "least worst" of the alternatives. As such, this is a very tricky question. Choices II, III and IV are all incorrect because these crimes required three perpetrator participants.

63. C is the correct answer. The killing was a classic heat of passion killing. There was provocation (the betrayal), passion (Charles' anger), and insufficient time to cool. Thus, II is correct and I is incorrect. When Charles threatened and chased Denise there was an assault; but, since there was no application of force, there was not a battery. Thus, III is correct and IV is incorrect. Only C offers the above.

64. D is the best answer. Since an accidental spilling of beer on a person evidences no mens rea whatsoever, Choices A, B and C are incorrect; and D is the best answer.

65. A is the correct answer. This is a classic involuntary manslaughter, based on the misdemeanor (unlawful act) theory, Arnold committed a battery and Beth died accidentally as a result of such. Thus, choice I is correct and II is incorrect. Since Arnold was upset and simply "forgot" to pay for his food, there was no specific intent to defraud or deprive; thus, choices III and IV are incorrect. A, alone, includes only choice I.

66. B is the correct answer. False Imprisonment occurs when another is confined without consent. Confinement does not require there be a room. Thus, in this fact pattern, Hannah's movement was confined in the open fields – by way of gun threat. A is incorrect because Rape requires sexual penetration. C is incorrect because Battery requires there to be an application of force and none was shown here. D is incorrect for the same reasons that B is correct.

67. C is the correct answer. Battery is an unlawful application of force to the person of another. Grunch's touching of Betty's hair was purposeful and certainly unapproved or "offensive." Betty, in the facts, did say to stop. Of course, had Betty consented, there would have been no Battery. Therefore, although C could have been more legally precise, it is a correct answer – and, as it turns out, the best of the group. A misreads the facts – Betty told Grunch to stop – therefore, it was offensive. B is legally incorrect because a given act can be both a tort and a crime. Such are entirely separate issues. D is incorrect for the same reason that C is correct.

68. D is the correct answer. Malicious mischief is the malicious damaging of another's property. Since Grunch scratched (damaged) the car, since it was Phil's and since he did it purposely (thereby satisfying the malice element), all the elements are met. A is incorrect because nothing in the common law crime of malicious mischief requires the vandalism to be irreparable. B is incorrect because such is a tort, not a crime. C is incorrect because there was no taking, carrying away... or for that matter – there were few elements of theft proven by the facts.

69. B is the correct answer. This is a very difficult question. Choice I is incorrect because forgery requires the making of a false document. Although it is arguable the Grunch's token constituted a document; it is quite clear, he did not make it. Therefore, since one element is missing, this crime is lacking. Choice II, however, is probably correct. Uttering only requires the using of a forged instrument knowing it to be such. Although a Chuck E. Cheese token, in the context of going to Chuck E. Cheese, is not false; using it as a token of value somewhere else probably is. Moreover, it was used to defraud the law school. Thus, there probably was an uttering. Choice III is incorrect, for two reasons. First, false pretenses require the defendant obtain title fraudulently. No facts indicate Grunch to have obtained title to the token, itself, fraudulently. Secondly, and more to the point, Grunch received no title to anything of the victim law school. He simply borrowed a parking space without paying. If the intent to steal (defraud) forms prior to obtaining possession, then the possession is not lawful and there can be no embezzlement. In that instance, the crime is larceny. Although the facts are not perfectly clear, it appears that since Grunch had the false token, he probably intended to use it prior to entering the lot – so his possession of the parking space was not in good faith. Therefore, the crime is Larceny (choice IV), not embezzlement (choice V). Since only B includes just II and IV, it is the correct answer.

70. B is the correct answer. Conversion with fraudulent intent, by one with lawful possession, constitutes the crime of embezzlement. Since Grunch accidentally took the tokens outside the restaurant, and since they were presumably lent to him by the restaurant, he had the requisite lawful possession. A is incorrect because for there to be a larceny there must be an initial "trespass" – here, there was none. C is incorrect because false pretenses requires there be a passing of title; and there was none here. D is incorrect for the same reasons that B is correct.

71. C is the best answer. Note: the call asked, which was the worst legal argument. Since no one has to be home, provided the house is a dwelling and the perpetrator has felonious intent, choice C is factually irrelevant. Choices A and B, however, are actually good arguments. Under the common law, abandoned houses are not considered to be dwellings. So, there can be no common law burglary of this stipulated-to-be abandoned house. D is incorrect, for the same reason that C is correct.

A CRIMINAL LAW

72. D is the correct answer. Forcible entry entails the willful trespass onto the land of another by force. The force required is not necessarily destructive force. Thus, Jennifer's picking of the lock satisfies this element. Moreover, she was clearly trespassing onto land – so all of the elements are met. A is incorrect because an abandoned dwelling is not a "dwelling" for common law burglary purposes. B is incorrect for the same reasons that D is correct. C, though a correct statement, is not as precise a definition of the common law crime here committed.

73. C is the correct answer. When title is obtained fraudulently, the crime is false pretenses. Here, the lie was in the act of changing price-tags and title passed with the passing of the receipt. A and B are incorrect because there was no trespass in the taking. D is incorrect because Jennifer was in bad faith, not "lawful possession" of the Scotch – and such is a requirement of embezzlement.

74. D is the correct answer. Jennifer committed the crime of false pretenses, because she obtained title fraudulently. The fact that the clerk was an accomplice, does not alleviate Jennifer's guilt. Of course, the answer would differ had the owner known and consented to Jennifer's actions. A is incorrect because the consent needed was of the store owner – and no facts indicate such. B is incorrect because condonation is not a defense to a crime, once it is completed. Although C is a correct statement of law, it is irrelevant because trespass is not an element of false pretenses.

75. A is the correct answer. There is an embezzlement when a trusted employee, in lawful possession of a chattel, fraudulently converts it. That was the situation here. B is incorrect because there was no trespass by the clerk; and this is an element of larceny. C is incorrect because conversion is not a crime. It is a tort, only. D is incorrect because the clerk's actions satisfied all of the elements of embezzlement. It is irrelevant whether it was good business.

76. C is the correct answer. Involuntary manslaughter is essentially a criminally negligent, accidental killing. Jennifer's driving under the influence was such a deviation from the reasonable standard of care owed. Choices A and D are incorrect because they were not crimes at common law (which is the stipulated jurisdiction). Choice B is incorrect because murder requires malice aforethought. This mens rea can be proven by an intent to kill (not present here), intent to cause serious bodily injury (also not present here), reckless/depraved heart (not present here because Jennifer was unaware of the risk to life), or felony-murder (not present here, because she was not in perpetration of a dangerous felony).

77. D is the correct answer. At the common law, the inflicted wound must produce death within 12 months. This specific rule of causation was called the "year and a day" rule. Here, the death occurred 13 months later. Choice A is incorrect for the very same reasons that D is correct. Choice B, though correct analysis at common law, is far less specific than choice D. Thus, D is the better answer. C is incorrect for the same reasons that D is correct.

78. D is the correct answer. This is the case, because A, B, and C were not crimes at common law.

79. A is the best answer. Vandalism entails the damaging of another's property. Since the lockpicking was likely not consented to, damage to the door is a reasonable possibility. B and D are clearly incorrect because they were crimes only at common law – and the call stipulated [only] modern law crimes. C is clearly incorrect because no felonious intent (as required by burglary) is indicated by a reasonable interpretation of the facts.

80. A is correct. Under both the modern and common law, the consent to engage in sex can be withdrawn at any time – even after sexual intercourse has commenced. B is a correct statement of fact, but is irrelevant. C is incorrect for the same reasons that A is correct. D is incorrect, legally, because sexual penetration is all that is required for carnal knowledge.

81. B is the correct answer. Malicious mischief is the malicious damaging of the property of another. Stone demonstrated the requisite intent, and the smashing certainly appears to be damage. Moreover, it was Miranda's picture. A and C are incorrect because they were not crimes at the common law. D is incorrect because uttering entails offering a forged instrument- facts totally irrelevant here.

82. B is the correct answer. A killing, following a sexual betrayal, is the classic voluntary manslaughter scenario. With such, there is actual provocation, anger and an immediate killing. A is incorrect because when the elements of voluntary manslaughter are present, as here, it takes precedence over murder. C is incorrect because this crime requires the killing to be unintentional. D is incorrect both legally and ethically.

83. D is the correct answer. A is incorrect because there was no touching. B is incorrect because there was neither a substantial step toward battery (there was only "preparation"), nor was there an intent to scare anyone. C is incorrect because it requires reading in an essential fact not even hinted at, i.e., that it was not his gun.

84. A is the correct answer. At common law, malicious mischief included the damaging of another's horse. B and C are incorrect because they were not common law crimes. D is incorrect because treason requires giving aid to the enemies of the state, and no facts suggest this.

85. D is the best answer. There is a larceny, provided the defendant intends to abandon the property in such a way that the owner is unlikely to recover it. Although these facts are amorphous on this point, it is the best of the choices given. A is an incorrect answer-many crimes involve emotional outbursts – and such is not a defense. B is incorrect because, under the facts given, there was certainly a malicious mischief (vandalism) and quite possibly a larceny. C is incorrect because Cereal was the "taker," not the "receiver" of stolen property.

86. B is the correct answer. Cereal demonstrated malice aforethought – by his intent to either kill or seriously injure Jane. Therefore, there was a second-degree murder. A is incorrect because there was no premeditation and deliberation regarding the killing of Jane – and these are required elements of first-degree murder. The anger Cereal felt for Melody cannot be transferred to reduce his crime on Jane. Thus, C, voluntary manslaughter, is incorrect. D is incorrect because the most reasonable interpretation of the facts is that Cereal either intended to kill or hurt Jane seriously – thus, the more serious crime of second-degree murder is present. (The most serious homicide committed will be the correct answer.)

87. A is the correct answer. At the time of the killing, Cereal was likely mentally deranged and may not have known right from wrong. B is incorrect for two reasons: Killing an uninvolved third party is not legally adequate provocation; and this Rule is not a complete defense. C is incorrect because it misreads the facts – Cereal admitted he had not mistaken Jane for Melody. D is incorrect because this was not a common law defense, and also because it is only a partial defense.

88. D is the best answer. Cereal's mental faculties were diminished because of the earlier betrayal. Although diminished capacity is a minority position, it is the best of the choices given. A is incorrect because killing an innocent third party who simply has a resemblance to your ex-lover, is not legally (objectively) valid provocation. B is incorrect because Insanity is not a partial defense. C is incorrect, because Cereal did not have the belief that he was in imminent physical danger.

89. D is the correct answer. The criminal law does not require good behavior. It simply prohibits bad conduct. Mason's leaving alone the old man was unethical, but not illegal in any way. Thus, the crimes offered in choices A, B and C are incorrect answers.

90. D is the correct answer. When Mason paid up, he received title to the food, fraudulently. There was false pretenses. A is incorrect because larceny requires a trespass in the taking- and Mason received the food consensually. B is incorrect because larceny by trick requires tricking the victim into giving the chattel – since Mason did not trick the waiter into producing the food, this crime was not present. C is a more difficult analysis. For there to be an embezzlement, the perpetrator must be in lawful possession prior to his misappropriation. Therefore, D is the better answer. Mason probably did not have "lawful possession," as required for there to be an embezzlement.

91. B is the correct answer. Petty theft is the fraudulent misappropriation of property worth, as a general rule, under $400. The food fell within this fair market value, and Mason had the requisite intent to underpay. A is correct, but less specific than B, and, therefore, B is the better answer. C is incorrect because grand theft entails misappropriation of property over $400 - certainly not the case here. D is incorrect for the same reasons that B is correct.

A
CRIMINAL LAW

92. A is the correct answer. Grand theft is the fraudulent misappropriation of property valued at, as a general rule, over $400. Mason's car certainly exceeded that amount and Teena's conduct gives rise to the inference that not only did she misappropriate the car – but also that she intended to defraud. B is incorrect because petty theft covers stealing property of value under $400 - and the car here was worth much more than that. C is incorrect because no facts indicate damage to the car (and such is required for there to be a vandalism). D misreads the facts: Neither actual nor constructive consent was given.

93. A is the correct answer. Involuntary manslaughter can be proven by showing that the defendant's killing occurred while perpetrating a "malum in se" (bad in itself) crime. Here, Teena was in perpetration of a larceny (car theft) and this will allow use of the so-called "misdemeanor-manslaughter" rule. B is incorrect because no facts indicate Teena's driving to be a gross deviation from the reasonable standard of care owed. C is incorrect because sufficiency of the evidence is an appellate or post-trial procedural defense. The call of the question asked for prosecution arguments. D is incorrect because "depraved heart" is a method of proving malice aforethought. It is not an element of involuntary manslaughter, and, thus, is irrelevant to this question.

94. D is the correct answer. There is no theory in which Mason could be held criminally responsible for the death of the pedestrian. A is incorrect because he was not a substantial factor. B is incorrect because it is a tort doctrine; and irrelevant in any case. C is incorrect because it goes to the mental state of taking a reckless risk to human life. Mason did not possess such.

95. C is the correct answer. Wharton's Rule indicates that if a crime requires a set and necessary number of perpetrators, if only that minimum number is involved, then the perpetrators cannot be convicted of both the conspiracy and the target crime. The definition which was given for Breach of the Peace requires four individuals. That was the number involved – so there cannot be conviction for both the Breach and the conspiracy. A is a possibly correct answer – but it requires reading in facts – so C is better. Like A, B requires reading in unlikely facts; so choice C is a better answer. D is a misinterpretation of obvious social mores, and is therefore incorrect.

96. C offers the best choice in a series of poor answers. Although it does appear Finn was in possession of the marijuana, perhaps it can be argued that Nasty simply left it at Finn's home, and Finn had not exerted dominion and control over it. A is incorrect because Finn clearly knew the substance to be marijuana. B is legally incorrect because the inducement to commit a crime must be from a government agent – not a private party, as here. D is also legally incorrect because evil motives are not a requirement for conviction of crimes.

97. A is the correct answer. Necessity, or "choice of evils," is a defense when a criminal act is performed, so as to avoid a greater harm to the perpetrator. Although, here, there may not have been a legitimate necessity, of the given choices, it is the best. B is incorrect because Duress is only relevant when one performs a crime at the imminent threat of another. Both choices C and D are incorrect because neither are defenses at Criminal law.

98. C is the correct answer. Forcible Entry requires there be force used in the trespass. No force was evident here. A is incorrect for the same reason that C is correct. B is incorrect because the guilt of the victim is not a criminal law defense. D is legally incorrect – this was a crime at common law.

99. A is the correct answer. On the facts given, it appeared that in no way was Dick attempting a burglary, arson or a crime against Marcia's person. Thus, Marcia utilized deadly force just to protect her property. The criminal law does not allow this. [Note: The mere threat of physical force is, however, allowed.] B is a correct statement, but choice A is a better answer, because it is more specific – it gives the legal reason. C is incorrect for the same reasons that A is correct – Marcia was not defending her habitation. D is incorrect because the guilt of the victim does not allow an excessive use of force against that victim.

100. B is the best answer. The question did not ask for reasons; instead it asked for "affirmative defenses." Of the choices given, only B is a true affirmative defense. Moreover, B is a fairly good choice, because one is permitted to do an otherwise criminal act to avoid a greater harm. Here, Marcia's deadly assault was averted by Dick. Although Dick ordinarily would have had no right to take her gun, under these circumstances, it was acceptable. The weakness with Dick's position is that he was trespassing – and Necessity requires substantial "innocence" on the part of the defendant. It should also be noted that Necessity requires ceasing the necessary criminal ("evil") act, as soon as the necessity ceases. In throwing the gun in Marcia's garbage pail and fleeing, Dick met most, if not all, of the requirements of Necessity. A offers an element of Self-Defense- but it does not state that such is the relevant defense. Therefore, B is a better answer. Moreover, Self-Defense may not be available – since Dick's presence was illegal (i.e., he was not "innocent" as required by Self-Defense). C is a correct statement, which disproves the last element of robbery. However, it has nothing to say about the battery – and most importantly, it is not an "affirmative defense" – as the call of the question demands. D is incorrect because, not only is Diminished Capacity not a true affirmative defense; it is also incorrect because no facts whatsoever indicate that Dick's mental clarity was significantly impaired.

END OF ANSWERS

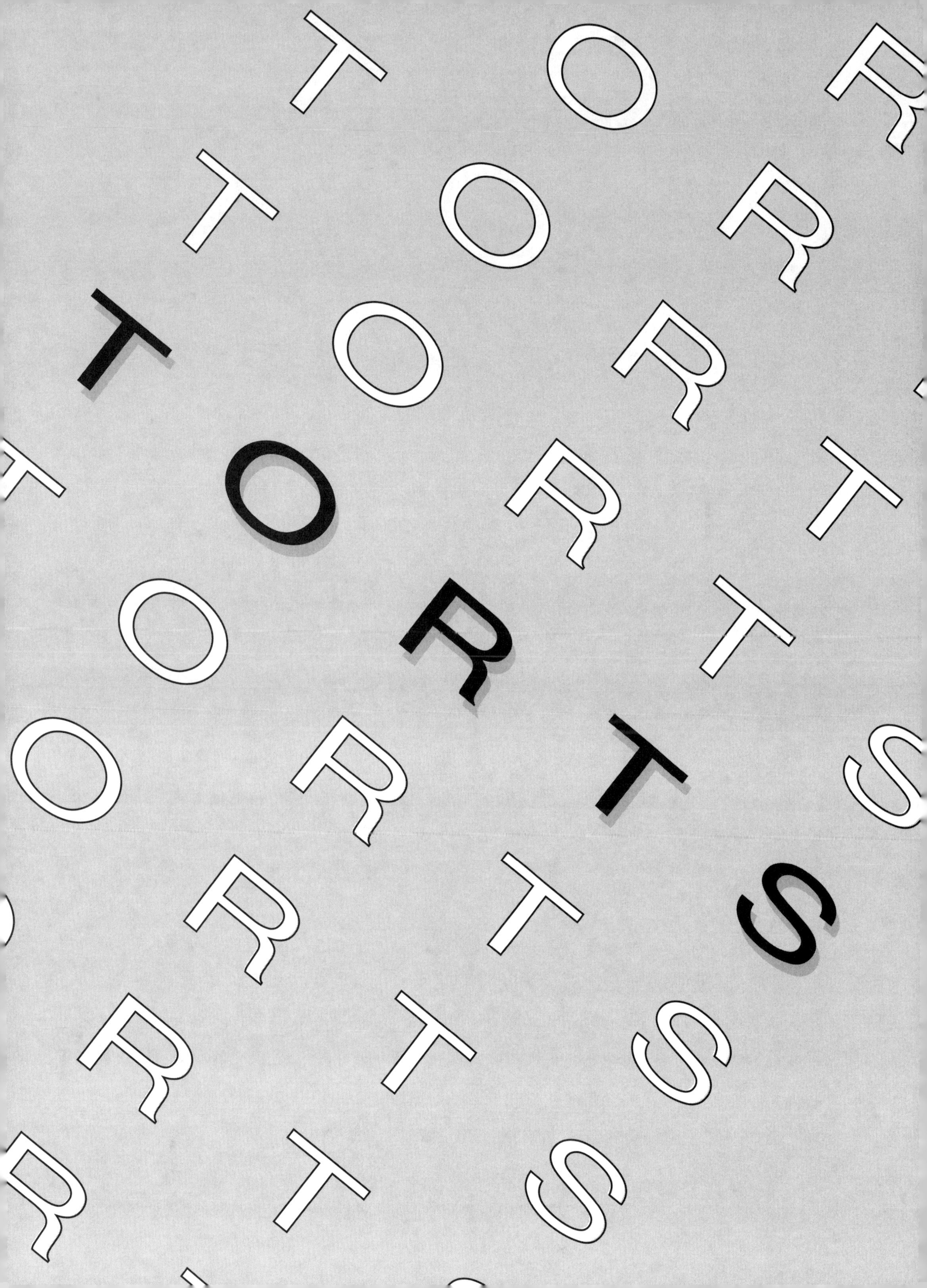
TORTS

TORTS – QUESTION BREAKDOWN

1. Nuisance – Private
2. Nuisance – Private
3. Nuisance
4. Deceit
5. Deceit – Reliance
6. Negligent Misrepresentation
7. Negligent Misrepresentation – Liability
8. Deceit – Reliance
9. Deceit – Concealment
10. Trade Libel
11. Trade Libel – Special Damages
12. Invasion of Privacy – Misappropriation
13. Abuse of Process
14. Abuse of Process
15. Interference with Contract
16. Negative Covenant
17. Assault
18. Transferred Intent
19. Trespass to Land
20. Defense of Property
21. Negligence Per Se
22. Causation
23. Negligence – Duty
24. Duty – Cardozo's View
25. Joint and Several Liability
26. Duty – Licensee
27. Licensee – Duty Owed
28. Contributory Negligence
29. Last Clear Chance
30. Comparative Negligence
31. Strict Liability
32. Strict Liability
33. Strict Liability – Defenses
34. Strict Liability – Causation
35. Duty Owed to Rescuer

36. Duty Invitee
37. Res Ipsa Loquitur
38. Res Ipsa Loquitur
39. Respondeat Superior
40. Negligence – Attractive Nuisance Doctrine
41. Negligence – Attractive Nuisance Doctrine
42. Causation
43. Battery
44. Battery – Social Standards
45. Shopkeepers Privilege
46. Products Liability
47. Pre-existing Condition
48. Strict Liability
49. Assault – Apprehension
50. Trespass to Chattels
51. Battery
52. Res Ipsa Loquitur
53. Duty – National Standard of Care
54. Negligence – Omission to Act
55. Intentional Infliction of Emotional Distress
56. Intentional Infliction of Emotional Distress
57. Intentional Infliction of Emotional Distress- Damages
58. Negligence Per Se
59. Causation
60. Causation
61. Joint & Several Liability
62. Contribution
63. Guest Statute
64. Battery
65. Implied Consent
66. Negligence – Duty
67. Negligence – Duty
68. Intervening Acts
69. Thin Skull Plaintiff
70. Survival Action – Common Law
71. Wrongful Death
72. Respondeat Superior

73. Vicarious Liability – Course and Scope of Employment
74. Federal Torts Claims Act
75. Defamation – Libel
76. Defamation – Common Law
77. Defamation – Libel
78. Defamation – Slander v. Libel
79. Defamation – Republication
80. Defamation - Malice
81. Defamation – Burden of Proof
82. Defamation – Slander Per Quod
83. Defamation – Falsity
84. Privileges
85. Defamation – Republication
86. Strict Liability in Tort
87. Strict Liability – Foreseeable Bystanders
88. Strict Liability in Tort
89. Products Liability
90. Strict Liability in Tort – Warning
91. Negligence
92. Vicarious Liability
93. Products Liability
94. Products Liability
95. Duty to Act
96. Good Samaritan Statute
97. Wrongful Life
98. Wrongful Life – Defenses
99. Wrongful Birth – Damages
100. Professional Negligence – Privity Requirements
101. Strict Liability in Tort
102. Products Liability – Design Defect
103. Products Liability – Defenses
104. Concurrent Tortfeasors
105. Strict Liability in Tort – Damages
106. Implied Warranty of Merchantability
107. Products Liability – Causation
108. Products Liability – Recoverable Damages
109. Landowner Occupier Rule
110. Indemnity

111. Warning Defect

112. Causation

113. Causation

114. Negligence

115. Causation – Substantial Factor

116. Causation – Substantial Factor

117. Implied Warranty

118. Warranty

119. Express Warranty

120. Strict Liability in Tort

121. Strict Liability in Tort

TORTS QUESTIONS

Questions 1 – 3 are based on the following facts:

Oil Company owns an oil refinery in a sparsely-populated area. Although the refinery is a "state of the art" operation, it occasionally releases noxious, but harmless, gas into the atmosphere.

Stan recently leased land adjoining Oil Company's refinery and occupies a home on the property. Stan complains that the gas released by the refinery sometimes makes him nauseous.

1. If Stan sues oil company over the gas, his best theory of recovery will be for:

   A. Strict liability for abnormally dangerous activities.

   B. Private nuisance.

   C. Public nuisance.

   D. Negligence.

2. If Stan sues Oil Company and Oil Company challenges Stan's standing to sue, the court should:

   A. Dismiss the action, because Stan, as lessee, has no standing to sue over a private nuisance.

   B. Dismiss the action, because a private citizen never has standing to sue over a public nuisance.

   C. Allow the action, because Stan is a resident of the area.

   D. Allow the action, because Stan is lessee of the land.

3. Oil Company's best defense to a suit by Stan to enjoin the refinery's operation is:

   A. Stan moved to the nuisance and, thus, cannot complain.

   B. The refinery is a social necessity, which is operated in a proper place and in a proper manner.

   C. No one else has ever complained about the gas.

   D. Stan's cause of action is against his landlord, not Oil Company.

Questions 4 – 5 are based on the following facts:

Stockbroker was responsible for the portfolio of Aaron, a personal friend. Stockbroker believed that shares in Micra Company would be a good investment for Aaron. In his enthusiasm to convince Aaron to purchase Micra Company shares, Stockbroker told Aaron that the stock was a good buy because Micra had received an unannounced major government contract. Stockbroker knew this statement was untrue when he made it. Aaron purchased 100 shares of stock for $10 each. Aaron recently learned that Micra Company is now insolvent.

4. If Aaron sues Stockbroker for common law deceit:

   A. Aaron will recover, even though Stockbroker had his best interest in mind when he made the statement about Micra Company.

   B. Aaron will recover, because Stockbroker's negligence caused Aaron's actual injury.

   C. Aaron will not recover, because the malicious intent element required for common law deceit is absent.

   D. Aaron will not recover, because he assumed the risk that the stock would fall in value.

5. Stockbroker's best defense to a suit by Aaron for common law deceit based on Stockbroker's statement would be:

   A. That Stockbroker acted in good faith when he made the statement.

   B. That Aaron was going to purchase the stock anyway.

   C. That Aaron has suffered no out-of-pocket damages.

   D. That the insolvency of Micra Company was not reasonably foreseeable when he made the statement.

Questions 6 – 7 are based on the following facts:

In the course of conducting an audit for Brown Company, Accountant carelessly computed asset totals. As a result, the audit report stated that Brown Company was substantially stronger financially than it was. Federal Bank relied on the audit when it approved a $1 million loan to Brown Company. Brown Company is now insolvent and unable to repay the $1 million loan to Federal Bank.

6. If Federal Bank decides to sue Accountant, its most promising cause of action is for:

   A. Common law deceit.

   B. Negligent misrepresentation.

   C. Innocent misrepresentation.

   D. None of the above.

7. In the majority of American jurisdictions, if Federal Bank sues Accountant for misrepresentation:

   A. Federal Bank will not recover because Accountant did not owe a duty of care to Federal Bank.

   B. Federal Bank will not recover, because it did not justifiably rely on the audit report.

   C. Federal Bank will recover because it is a reasonably foreseeable plaintiff.

   D. Federal Bank will recover, but only if it can establish gross negligence on Accountant's part.

Questions 8 – 9 are based on the following facts:

Rhonda went to Clay's Cars to purchase a used car. Clay's salesman, Harry, showed Rhonda a 1985 Crevet. Harry stated that the Crevet was "a honey of a car, a one of a kind steal for the money." Rhonda relied on Harry's statements and purchased the vehicle from Clay's Cars "as is." The Crevet's engine failed soon after Rhonda purchased it.

8. If Rhonda sues Clay's Cars for common law deceit, the result will be:

   A. Rhonda will recover because Clay's Cars is vicariously liable for the fraud of Harry.

   B. Rhonda will recover because it is fraud to sell a car "as is."

   C. Rhonda will not recover because she could not justifiably rely on Harry's opinion.

   D. Rhonda will not recover because the "as is" clause in the contract insulates Clay's Cars from liability for a deceit action.

9. Assume, for purposes of this question only, that the car's engine failed because it had a cracked engine block, that Clay's Cars knew about the defect before the sale to Rhonda, and had painted over the crack to conceal it from any potential purchaser. In an action by Rhonda against Clay's Cars:

   A. Rhonda will have no cause of action for common law deceit, since the element of a false statement of fact has not been met.

   B. Rhonda will have no cause of action, since she should have taken the car to a mechanic who could have discovered the defect.

   C. Rhonda will have a cause of action, since active concealment constitutes common law deceit.

   D. Rhonda will not have a cause of action for deceit because of the "as is" clause.

Questions 10 – 11 are based on the following facts:

Brakeco is a manufacturer of hydraulic brake systems. Its chief competitor is Stopco. In an effort to cut into Stopco's sales, Brakeco distributed a brochure to potential Stopco customers in which Brakeco favorably compared its product to Stopco's. The brochure contained numerous false and derogatory statements of fact about Stopco's hydraulic brake systems. Six months after the brochure was distributed, Stopco began experiencing a drop in profits.

10. If Stopco decides to sue Brakeco, the most appropriate cause of action would be for:

    A. Libel.

    B. Trade libel.

    C. Trade slander.

    D. Common law deceit.

11. Under common law rules, the likely outcome of Stopco's suit against Brakeco will be:

    A. Stopco will recover because it has sustained a loss in profits.

    B. Stopco will recover for general lost profits, plus punitive damages.

    C. Stopco will not recover, unless it can show loss of specific customers as special damages.

    D. Stopco will not recover because Brakeco's activity is an accepted business practice.

12. Grey is a major league baseball player. Clay, a manufacturer of sports equipment, used Grey's photograph in a newspaper advertisement for his products. While Clay's products are of high quality, he did not have Grey's permission to use the picture. In an action by Grey against Clay, Grey will have a cause of action for invasion of privacy under which of the following theories:

    A. Public disclosure of private facts.

    B. Misappropriation.

    C. Intrusion on seclusion.

    D. False light.

Questions 13 – 14 are based on the following facts:

Clement had a civil judgment against Lake for $100. Lake refused to pay the award. In an effort to "teach Lake a lesson," Clement had writs of attachment issued against Lake's real property, personal property, and bank accounts which had a total value of $500,000. As a result of Clement's actions, Lake suffered financial loss and considerable embarrassment.

13. Lake is most likely to succeed against Clement under which of the following theories?

    A. Malicious civil prosecution.

    B. Malicious criminal prosecution.

    C. Abuse of process.

    D. Conversion.

14. In order for Lake to recover against Clement, which of the following is Lake not required to establish.

    A. The prior proceeding was terminated in Lake's favor.

    B. Clement had an ulterior motive for bringing the multiple attachments.

    C. Lake suffered damages as a result of Clement's actions.

    D. Lake's excessive attachments was intentional.

Questions 15 – 16 are based on the following facts:

Laura, a famous diplomat, entered into a contract with X College, in which she agreed to teach international relations for one year. Because of her special expertise, the contract provided a large salary. Under the contract's terms, Laura agreed she would not teach at another college in the same city during the contract term.

Y College, which is located in the same city as X College, learned about the contract and decided to offer Laura more money to teach the same courses. Laura decided to accept Y College's offer. When Y College made public the fact that Laura would be teaching there, enrollments at X College's international relations program dropped dramatically.

15. If X College sues Y College for damages resulting from Y College's actions:

    A. X College will not recover because Laura has the right to an efficient breach of the contract.

    B. X College will not recover because Y College did not breach any agreement.

    C. X College will recover, but only if Y College intentionally interfered with the contract between Laura and X College.

    D. X College will recover, whether Y College acted intentionally or otherwise when it interfered with the contract between X College and Laura.

16. If X College brings an action against Laura based on the contract, the most likely result will be:

    A. Laura will be forced to work for X College.

    B. Laura can work for Y College.

    C. The negative covenant will be found unenforceable because it is unreasonable.

    D. The court will enforce the negative covenant.

Questions 17 – 18 are based on the following facts:

Logan and Adam were students in Professor Smith's Physics class. Much to Professor Smith's disgust, the students were conversing loudly during his lecture. Professor Smith decided to "get Logan's and Adam's attention" by throwing a pen over their heads. The students saw the pen coming toward them and ducked to avoid being hit by it. Unfortunately, the pen struck Davey, a student seated behind Logan. Davey suffered a serious eye injury as a result.

17. If Logan and Adam sue Professor Smith, the most likely outcome will be:

    A. Logan and Adam will recover for intentional infliction of emotional distress.

    B. Logan and Adam will recover for assault.

    C. Logan and Adam will not recover because the pen did not strike them.

    D. Logan and Adam will not recover because Professor Smith did not intend to hit them with the pen.

18. If Davey sues Professor Smith for the injury to his eye:

    A. Davey will not recover because Professor Smith did not intend to hit him.

    B. Davey will not recover because the extent of the injury was not reasonably foreseeable.

    C. Davey will not recover because the transferred intent doctrine does not apply where an actor attempts to assault one individual and commits a battery on another.

    D. Davey will recover.

Questions 19 – 20 are based on the following facts:

Eunice owns a tract of undeveloped land in Madison County. Every autumn, she has had a problem with hunters who enter her land without permission to shoot geese. In an effort to discourage hunters, she posted large "no trespassing" signs in conspicuous places along the property's boundary. She also dug a number of deep holes, which she covered with brush to catch any intruders.

Calvin, a local land surveyor, was retained to survey the parcel of land adjoining Eunice's. While conducting the survey, Calvin inadvertently walked onto Eunice's property. He fell into one of the holes and was seriously injured.

19. In an action by Eunice against Calvin for trespass to land, the likely outcome will be:

    A. Eunice will recover because Calvin is a licensee who has exceeded the scope of his license.

    B. Eunice will recover, even if the land was not damaged.

    C. Eunice will not recover because Calvin did not intend to trespass.

    D. Eunice will not recover, unless she can prove some actual damage.

20. If Calvin countersues for injuries he suffered from falling into the hole:

    A. Calvin will not recover because he was a trespasser and the land was properly posted.

    B. Calvin will not recover because he exceeded the scope of his license.

    C. Calvin will not recover because Eunice was justified in protecting her property.

    D. Calvin will recover.

Questions 21 – 23 are based on the following facts:

The State of Columbia has a statute that makes it a misdemeanor to leave the key in the ignition of an unattended motor vehicle. Sherry needed to pick up a dress at the dry cleaners and left her unattended car idling while she ran into the store. Peter, a twelve-year-old boy, jumped into the car, put it in gear, and drove away. Within a mile of the dry cleaners, Peter lost control of the vehicle. The car jumped the curb and struck Alfred, a pedestrian. Alfred suffered extensive injuries.

21. In a negligence suit against Sherry, if Alfred raises the claim of negligence per se, the court should:

    A. Apply the doctrine because the thing speaks for itself.

    B. Apply the doctrine because Alfred was within the class of persons the statute was designed to protect.

    C. Reject the doctrine because the reasonably prudent person test is the universal standard of care in negligence cases.

    D. Reject the doctrine because Peter was contributorily negligent.

22. Sherry's best defense to a negligence action by Alfred is:

    A. Alfred had the last clear chance to avoid being hit by the car.

    B. Peter's actions were a superseding cause of Alfred's injuries.

    C. The acts of an intentional tortfeasor always break the chain of causation.

    D. Sherry's liability insurance policy does not cover injuries committed by a negligent car thief.

23. If Alfred sues Peter for his injuries, the likely result will be:

    A. Peter will be liable because the injuries were suffered while Peter was stealing the car.

    B. Peter will be liable, if he failed to exercise the care expected of a reasonable, prudent twelve-year-old when he drove the car.

    C. Peter will be liable, if he failed to exercise the care expected of a reasonable, prudent person when he drove the car.

    D. Peter will not be liable because a twelve-year-old does not have the capacity to be negligent.

24. Dieter was walking across the street in a crosswalk with a friend, Sue, when a car, driven by Eddie, approached. Eddie accidentally stepped on the accelerator instead of the brake pedal, causing his vehicle to lurch forward. The car struck Sue and she sustained serious physical injuries. As a result of witnessing the accident, Dieter went into shock and suffered serious emotional distress. He has incurred substantial expenses for psychiatric treatment.

    In most jurisdictions, if Dieter sues Eddie for negligent infliction of emotional distress:

    A. Dieter will recover because he was within the zone of danger.

    B. Dieter will not recover because he did not sustain a physical impact.

    C. Dieter will not recover because he is not closely related to Sue.

    D. Dieter will not recover because his injuries were not reasonably foreseeable.

25. Glenda, a bicyclist, was injured when John lost control of his automobile while rounding a curve on a local highway. In a single lawsuit, Glenda sued John for negligently operating his automobile and also sued State Highway Department for negligent design of the curve. In a special verdict, the jury found John to be 75% responsible for Glenda's injuries and State Highway Department 25% responsible. State Highway Department is not immune from a damages judgment.

    In a state that follows common law principles, if John is insolvent:

    A. Glenda can recover the entire judgment from State Highway Department.

    B. Glenda can recover only 25% of the judgment from State Highway Department because of the rule of indemnification.

    C. Glenda can recover only 25% of the judgment from State Highway Department because of the rule of contribution.

    D. Glenda cannot recover anything from State Highway Department on the judgment.

Questions 26 – 27 are based on the following facts:

Miller recently purchased a 100-acre farm in the State of Columbia. Power Company has an easement across Miller's property, which includes the authority to trim trees that might interfere with Power Company's electrical lines. Denton, an employee of Power Company, entered Miller's property to check the electrical lines. Denton fell into an abandoned well and suffered numerous injuries. The well had been over grown with brush, so that Denton could not see it. Miller was not aware of the existence of the abandoned well.

26. While on Miller's land, the law would characterize Denton as a:

    A. Trespasser.

    B. Business invitee.

    C. Social guest.

    D. Licensee.

27. If Denton sues Miller for negligence, a court applying common law rules will find:

    A. Miller owes no duty of care to Denton.

    B. Miller's duty of care is limited to warning Denton of dangers known by Miller.

    C. Miller's duty of care is to warn Denton of dangers known by Miller and to inspect his property for unknown dangers.

    D. Miller's duty of care is that of the reasonable, prudent landowner in the circumstances.

Questions 28 – 29 are based on the following facts:

Arlen was driving his van on Route 12 when he noticed he was running out of gas. He stopped and parked the van on the shoulder of the highway. The van's rear bumper extended one-half foot into the highway. Betty, who was driving an automobile in the same direction on Route 12, approached Arlen's van from the rear. Betty was traveling at an excessive rate of speed and was not paying attention to her driving. Betty's vehicle struck the rear of Arlen's van and he was severely injured.

Arlen sued Betty for negligence. The jury returned a special verdict, wherein it found that Betty was 95% responsible for the accident, while Arlen was 5% at fault in failing to park his van entirely off the highway. The jury also found that Arlen's total damages were $100,000.

28. In a jurisdiction that has not adopted comparative fault and still follows common law principles, Arlen will:

    A. Recover $100,000 from Betty.

    B. Recover $95,000 from Betty.

    C. Not recover anything from Betty because Arlen was contributorily negligent.

    D. Not recover anything from Betty because Arlen assumed the risk.

29. In a jurisdiction that has not adopted comparative fault and still follows common law principles, if Arlen can show that Betty had the "last clear chance" to avoid the accident, the result will be:

    A. Arlen will recover $100,000 from Betty.

    B. Arlen will recover $95,000 from Betty.

    C. Arlen will recover nothing from Betty.

    D. None of the above.

30. The State of Columbia has enacted a comparative negligence statute which provides: "The negligence of the injured party will not bar recovery against another person, so long as the injured party's negligence was not greater than the negligence of the person against whom recovery is sought. Any damages shall be diminished in proportion to the amount of negligence attributable to the injured party." Tom and Wanda were involved in an automobile accident, in which Wanda sustained personal injury damages totaling $100,000. The jury returned a special verdict wherein it found Tom 40% and Wanda 60% at fault, respectively, for the accident. Under Columbia's comparative negligence statute, Wanda will recover from Tom:

    A. $100,000.

B. $60,000.

C. $40,000.

D. Nothing.

Questions 31 – 35 are based on the following fact situation:

Gasco stores and manufactures acid gas on its premises. Early one morning a leak developed in the connecting lines between the tanks. The leak was not the fault of Gasco. The escaping gas forms a greenish cloud. Before the greenish cloud of acid gas reached the point of dispersal it made contact with a cable repairman who was repairing a cable atop a telephone pole. The repairman did not see the cloud and he inhaled the gas which caused him to black out and fall from the pole, sustaining severe injuries.

31. In a suit by cable repairman against Gasco, which of the following legal theories should he base his cause of action?

    A. Battery

    B. Private nuisance.

    C. Strict liability.

    D. Negligence.

32. Gasco took every possible precaution to prevent this type of accident. Will Gasco be free from liability to repairman?

    A. Yes, because the exercise of extreme care was used.

    B. Yes, because there is no fault.

C. No, because the gas was negligently stored.

D. No, because this was an activity involving a serious degree of danger.

33. Gasco asserts the defense of contributory negligence for failure of repairman to see the greenish cloud. Gasco will:

A. Win, because repairman assumed the risk.

B. Win, because repairman was negligent.

C. Lose, because contributory negligence is not a defense to strict liability.

D. Lose, because repairman was not negligent.

34. Assume, for this question, that some of the gas settled on an antique car in a Beverly Hills antique car lot. The car was damaged beyond repair. Will the car lot have an action against Gasco?

A. No, if this type of damage is unforeseeable from the activity conducted by Gasco.

B. No, because only the original market value of the cars are protected.

C. Yes, because the car lot was only one block from the Gasco manufacturing plant.

D. No, because strict liability does not compensate for loss to property.

35. Assume that Neighbor sees the greenish cloud approaching repairman, and, knowing that it is acid gas, runs out to assist repairman who had fallen to the ground. As Neighbor is running to repairman, she trips in a gopher hole and breaks her leg. Will Neighbor prevail in an action against Gasco?

A. No, because neighbor assumed the risk.

B. No, because Neighbor's conduct was unforeseeable.

C. Yes, because Gasco was engaging in abnormally dangerous activities.

D. Yes, since Gasco put repairman in peril, they are responsible to any foreseeable rescuer.

36. Mrs. Shopper went into Happytime Yogurt Shoppe to get change for her parking meter. As Mrs. Shopper entered the shop, the door closer snapped and struck Mrs. Shopper on the head and rendered her unconscious. In a cause of action for negligence, Mrs. Shopper's best theory would be?

A. Res Ipsa Loquitur.

B. She was owed a duty of care as a business invitee.

C. She was owed a duty of care as a licensee.

D. None of the above.

Questions 37 – 38 are based on the following facts:

Pete was a passenger in a car driven by Kent. Kent suddenly lost control of the car and swerved off the shoulder of the road. The car then overturned and rolled down the embankment. Pete was killed on impact. Kent stated that the loose rocks and gravel on the road might have caused him to lose control of the car, but he could not be definite.

37. The best theory of recovery for Pete is?

    A. Res Ipsa Loquitur.

    B. Wrongful death.

    C. Survival statute.

    D. Substantial factor.

38. If the court finds Res Ipsa Loquitur, the result would be?

    A. Binding on the jury.

    B. Kent would win.

    C. Pete would win.

    D. An inference of negligence is created.

Questions 39 – 41 are based on the following facts:

Otis is the owner of a small paint and hardware store. One of Otis' clerks had negligently stacked a number of rolled window shades behind the customer service counter. The area behind the customer service counter was not open to the public. Mrs. Patron entered the store one afternoon looking for some vinyl tile, accompanied by Martha, her 6-year-old daughter. Martha walked unseen behind the counter and tried to climb atop of the pile of rolled window shades. Because of how the window shades were stacked, they fell. Several of the heavy shades landed on Martha, causing serious injuries to her.

39. In order for Martha to recover for her injuries, an appropriate action would be:

    A. Negligence.

    B. Doctrine of Respondeat Superior.

    C. Strict Liability.

    D. There is no appropriate action because Otis was not negligent.

40. Martha's best theory in holding Otis liable for her injuries is:

    A. She was a business invitee.

    B. She was owed a duty as a child trespasser.

    C. Attractive Nuisance Doctrine.

    D. Inspection would have revealed a patent defect.

41. If Otis asserts the defense of contributory negligence, he will:

    A. Win, because Martha assumed the risk.

    B. Win, because Martha caused her own injuries.

    C. Lose, because the attractive nuisance doctrine negates contributory negligence.

    D. Lose, because store owners are strictly liable for foreseeable injuries.

42. A and B are hunting in the forest. Each, at the same time, fires his shotgun. A pellet from one of the shotguns strikes C in the leg. What is C's best theory of recovery?

    A. Substantial factor.

    B. Alternative liability.

    C. "But For."

    D. None of the above.

43. Sue loved to play practical jokes on her classmates. One morning, as her classmate Mary was about to sit in her chair, Sue pulled the chair from under her. Surprised by Sue's conduct, Mary fell down and was humiliated by the incident. Mary can most likely make a claim against Sue for:

    A. Battery.

    B. Assault.

    C. Assault and battery.

    D. Infliction of emotional distress.

44. While Jogging down a crowded street, Jogger noticed a beautiful brunette ahead. At that moment, Jogger was not watching where he was going. He stepped in a pot hole and lost his balance. In order to keep from falling, Jogger grabbed Brunette by the arm. If Brunette brings a cause of action, jogger will most likely be found:

    A. Not liable, because Brunette was not hurt.

    B. Not liable, because jogger's conduct was acceptable under the circumstances.

    C. Liable for battery.

    D. Liable for assault.

45. Two teenage girls went into the ABC department store. The security guard, who was always suspicious of teenage shoppers, asked the girls to remove their coats and to empty their purses. After about 10 minutes, the guard, convinced that the girls had not taken anything, apologized and let the girls leave. If the girls bring a cause of action for false imprisonment, the department store will most likely:

    A. Win, since the store had a privilege to detain them.

    B. Win, because the girls were, at all times, free to leave.

    C. Not win, since they took nothing.

    D. Not win, since the guard had no reasonable grounds for suspicion.

46. Janice saw a demonstration of a hair dryer made by Hairco, that dried hair in 3 minutes. Janice purchased the dryer. After several uses, Janice noticed that the dryer took longer than 3 minutes to dry her hair and that the dryer made a loud noise. Janice called Hairco who assured her that some dryers were just louder than others. Several days later, while using the dryer, Janice received a severe shock which caused her physical injury. In an action against Hairco, Janice will most likely:

A. Prevail, because the dryer was defective.

B. Prevail, because Hairco should have warned Janice of the danger when she called.

C. Not prevail, because an intelligent person would not have continued to use the dryer.

D. None of the above.

47. Al was hit by an automobile negligently driven by Robert. Al was immediately taken to the hospital for treatment. At the hospital, he developed severe uncontrolled internal bleeding, as a result of pre-existing hemophilia. He died the next day from the bleeding. What effect will Al's pre-existing hemophilia have on recovery of his estate's recovery of damages?

A. Robert is liable for all damages resulting from his negligent conduct.

B. Al's hemophilia is an intervening independent cause of death, therefore Robert is only responsible for those damages that would had occurred if Al was not a hemophiliac.

C. Al's estate will not recover any damages from Robert.

D. None of the above.

48. Dee decides to have a garage sale at her home. She buys signs from Signco to advertise her garage sale. The signs are made of thin sheet metal and have rough edges. She places the signs in her front yard. Cal is skateboarding in the street when Driver, driving his pickup truck, fails to see Cal and collides his front bumper with him. Cal goes flying through the air and lands on the garage sale signs which cut him severely. In an action by Cal against Signco, his best theory of recovery is?

A. Strict liability.

B. Battery.

C. Negligence.

D. Breach of warranty.

49. Sam, a large 6'2" man, was at a sports bar watching the USC Trojans pummel the UCLA Bruins. Sam was excitedly cheering as USC completed another touchdown. George, a wee bit of a man who was a Bruin fan, became enraged at Sam's exuberance. George raised his fist and shouted to Sam, "If you weren't such a large pig, I would knock you down." Sam brings a suit against George for assault. Sam will most likely:

A. Win, since he felt apprehension when George was shaking his fist at him.

B. Win, since George was shaking his fist.

C. Lose, since in light of George's statement, his conduct was not sufficient to create immediate apprehension in Sam.

D. Lose, because George is not big enough to assault Sam.

50. Bob and Mary lived in a remote area of town. One evening, Bob heard a noise outside. He grabbed his gun and proceeded to look around his front yard. Thinking he saw a wolf, he fired a shot and killed the animal. It turned out that the animal was the neighbor's dog Spot. Which of the following propositions is most correct?

A. Neighbor will have a cause of action for trespass to chattel.

B. Bob will not be liable to neighbor because he made a reasonable mistake.

C. Neighbor will have a cause of action for battery.

D. Bob will be found guilty of cruelty to animals.

Questions 51 – 54 are based on the following facts:

Marvin was dissatisfied with his facial features, especially the large "bags" under his eyes. He finally decided to consider elective plastic surgery. Marvin visited the office of Doctor, a certified licensed plastic surgeon. Doctor advised Marvin that if he surgically removed the bags, Marvin would "look years younger." Marvin agreed to undergo the surgery, at Doctor's office as an out-patient.

Doctor administered a general anesthetic and performed the surgery around Marvin's eyes. While Marvin was still unconscious, Doctor decided to remove a mole on Marvin's chin that Doctor thought was unsightly. When Marvin awoke, he found that he had no sensation on the left side of his face. He was also upset to learn that Doctor had removed the mole.

51. If Marvin sues Doctor for removing the mole:

A. Marvin will not recover, so long as Doctor performed the surgery as would a reasonable, prudent plastic surgeon.

B. Marvin will not recover because he impliedly consented to Doctor's removal of the mole.

C. Marvin will recover because Doctor has committed the tort of battery.

D. Marvin will recover because Doctor was negligent.

52. If Marvin contends that Doctor was responsible for Marvin's loss of sensation in his face, the likely outcome will be:

A. Marvin will recover, if he can show that Doctor had exclusive control of his person during the surgery and that the injury suffered usually would not occur in the absence of negligence.

B. Marvin will recover because a surgeon is always responsible for a patient's injuries during surgery.

C. Marvin will not recover, unless a percipient witness testifies that Doctor's negligence was the cause in fact of the injury.

D. None of the above.

53. The standard of care that the court should apply in Marvin's negligence action against Doctor is that of:

A. The reasonable, prudent physician.

B. The reasonable, prudent plastic surgeon in Doctor's locality.

C. The reasonable, prudent plastic surgeon as determined by national standards.

D. The reasonable, prudent plastic surgeon with education and experience similar to Doctor's.

54. Assume, for purposes of this question only, that Marvin's loss of sensation in his face resulted from the operation around his eyes, but that Doctor was not negligent in performing the surgery. In a suit by Marvin against Doctor:

A. Marvin will recover because a surgeon is responsible for all injuries a patient sustains during an operation.

B. Marvin will recover under a negligence theory, if Doctor failed to inform him that loss of facial sensation is a common side effect of surgery around the eyes.

C. Marvin will recover because of the rule of post hoc ergo propter hoc.

D. Marvin will not recover.

Questions 55 – 57 are based on the following facts:

Nancy owns a collection agency. She prides herself on collecting debts where other collection agencies have failed. Nancy attempted to collect a debt that Darren owed one of her clients. She made numerous telephone calls to Darren's home between the hours of 11:00 P.M. and 6:00 A.M., to induce him to pay the debt. She continued this practice for over two months. Finally, Nancy visited Darren's home and told him in the presence of his wife, Anne, that Darren would suffer "serious consequences to his health" if he did not pay the debt within 24 hours. Darren paid the debt later that day.

Darren and Anne claim that Nancy's collection tactics caused them serious emotional disturbance. Both are being treated by psychologists and wish to recover from Nancy for their mental distress and doctor bills.

55. Darren is most likely to recover from Nancy for his injuries under which of the following theories:

    A. Intentional infliction of emotional distress.

    B. Assault.

    C. Negligence.

    D. False light invasion of privacy.

56. If Anne sues Nancy for intentional infliction of emotional distress:

    A. Anne will not recover because Nancy had no intent to cause her emotional distress.

    B. Anne will recover because the doctrine of transferred intent applies.

    C. Anne will not recover because she has not suffered pecuniary loss.

    D. Anne will recover, if she can show that Nancy should have reasonably foreseen that Anne would suffer emotional distress.

57. To recover for intentional infliction of emotional distress, most jurisdictions require a plaintiff to prove, in addition to an intentional and outrageous act, that the act has caused:

    A. Plaintiff a physical impact that caused the emotional distress.

    B. Plaintiff physical consequences from the emotional distress.

    C. Plaintiff severe emotional distress only.

    D. Plaintiff's emotional distress by an assault, battery, or false imprisonment by defendant.

Questions 58 – 60 are based on the following facts:

Nellie operates a restaurant in a part of the city that is notorious as a high-crime area. The restaurant opens every day at 11:00 A.M. and closes at midnight. Customers park their automobiles in a lot, which Nellie owns, that is adjacent to the restaurant. A city ordinance requires that each restaurant owner maintain a parking facility that "is continuously lighted for the hours beginning with dusk and ending one hour after said restaurant has closed for business."

One evening, Nellie's parking lot lighting system malfunctioned and failed to operate. Otis, a customer, was beaten and robbed in the lot by an unknown assailant at 10:00 P.M. This was the first time that anyone had been the victim of a crime in the lot. The same evening, Willard, an intoxicated customer, fainted in the parking lot and struck his head on a parking space divider that was not visible in the darkness.

58. If Otis and Willard sue Nellie for negligence, the judge should instruct the jury that the city ordinance:

    A. Establishes the duty of care.

    B. Is a factor that the jury can accept or reject when it determines the duty of care.

    C. Is of no relevance in establishing the duty of care.

    D. Sets the duty of care under the theory of res ipsa loquitur.

59. Assume, for this question, that Nellie breached her duty of care by failing to keep the parking lot lighted. If Otis sues Nellie in negligence for injuries caused by the robber:

    A. Nellie should prevail because the intentional act of a felon is always a superseding cause.

    B . Nellie should prevail because no one had ever been beaten or robbed in her parking lot before.

    C. Otis should prevail if, given the fact that Nellie's establishment is in a high-crime area, he can prove that it was reasonably foreseeable that he might be robbed in the unlighted parking lot.

    D. Otis should prevail because the owner of a restaurant owes a higher duty of care to a patron that results in strict liability.

60. Assume, for this question, that Nellie breached her duty of care by failing to keep the parking lot lighted. If Willard sues Nellie for injuries he suffered in his fall:

    A. Willard will prevail, because Nellie was negligent per se.

B. Willard will prevail because his fall was a reasonably foreseeable result of Nellie's negligence.

C. Nellie will prevail because her breach of the duty of care was not the cause in fact of Willard's injury.

D. Nellie will prevail because Willard had the last clear chance of preventing the injury.

Questions 61 – 63 are based on the following facts:

Irene was a passenger in Hank's automobile. As Hank drove the car through the mountains, a heavy snow storm suddenly came up. Hank, who was driving too fast for the conditions, failed to see a tractor trailer that was blocking the road. Trucker, the owner of the tractor trailer, had stopped his vehicle to install snow chains, but had carelessly failed to pull off the road. Hank was unable to stop his car and it struck the tractor trailer. Irene was injured in the accident.

61. If Irene sues Hank and Trucker in negligence to recover damages for her injuries:

    A. Irene will recover only those damages which she can prove each defendant caused.

    B. Hank and Trucker will each be liable to Irene for the full amount of her damages.

    C. Hank and Trucker will each be liable for fifty percent of Irene's damages.

    D. Irene will recover nothing because she assumed the risk.

62. Assume, for this question, that a jury determined that Hank and Trucker were both responsible for Irene's damages and that Hank paid Irene the full amount. Hank's best recourse against Trucker would be under the theory of:

A. Satisfaction.

B. Indemnification.

C. Release.

D. Contribution.

63. Assume, for this question, that Hank's negligence was the sole cause of the accident and that the jurisdiction has an automobile guest statute. If Irene sues Hank for damages:

    A. Irene will recover because Hank was negligent.

    B. Irene will recover only if she can show Hank's conduct amounted to gross negligence.

    C. Irene will recover only if she can show Hank's conduct amounted to an intentional act.

    D. Irene will recover nothing.

Questions 64 – 65 are based on the following facts:

Paul was a member of a professional baseball team that was involved in a heated competition for the league championship. His team was playing its arch rival in an important late-season game. With his team down by one run with one out in the final inning, Paul was on first base. When a ground ball was hit to the second baseman, Paul decided he would "break up" a potential double play by making a hard, but legal, slide into Tom, the shortstop. Paul prevented the double play, but also broke Tom's ankle in the process.

64. If Tom sues Paul for the injury to his ankle, his most likely cause of action will be for:

    A. Assault.

    B. Battery.

    C. Intentional infliction of emotional distress.

    D. Strict liability.

65. Paul's best defense to Tom's suit for injury to his ankle would be:

    A. Contributory negligence.

    B. Justification.

    C. Implied consent.

    D. Private necessity.

Questions 66 – 69 are based on the following facts:

Scott owns a furniture store in the town of Smallville. Scott advertises his location by means of a large neon sign attached to the building. The sign, which extends out over a public sidewalk approximately 15 feet from the ground, is anchored by two large cables.

Scott had not checked the condition of the cables in years, so he was unaware that they were severely corroded. During an unusually violent windstorm, the cables broke and the sign fell, striking Pam, a pedestrian. Pam, who suffers from a rare bone disease, suffered injuries much more severe than would the average person when the sign struck her.

66. At common law, most courts would classify Pam as:

    A. A trespasser.

    B. A licensee.

    C. An invitee.

    D. None of the above.

67. If Pam sues Scott in negligence for her injuries, a court will likely find that Scott:

    A. Had a duty of care to keep the cables in good repair.

    B. Had a duty of care to warn Pam only of known, latent defects.

    C. Had a duty of care to warn Pam only of dangerous active operations on his property.

    D. Had no duty of care to Pam.

68. The effect of the unusually violent windstorm on Pam's negligence suit will likely be to:

    A. Prevent Pam from recovering from Scott, because the storm was an intervening act of God.

    B. Prevent Pam from recovering from Scott, because a violent storm is not a reasonably foreseeable event.

    C. Not adversely affect Pam's suit, as a defendant is liable for all injuries directly caused by him.

    D. Not adversely affect Pam's suit, because the storm was a reasonably foreseeable intervening act of God.

69. Assume, for this question, that Scott's negligence caused the sign to strike Pam. Pam will be able to recover:

    A. Only those damages which Scott could have reasonably foreseen under the circumstances.

B. Only those damages which an ordinary person would have suffered, because Scott is not responsible for Pam's preexisting condition.

C. All damages sustained in the accident, even though Pam has a rare bone disease that makes her more susceptible to injury.

D. None of the above.

Questions 70 – 74 are based on the following facts:

Grover, a civilian employee of the United States Army, was responsible for delivering packages between military bases. He drove a small government-owned van when making his deliveries. One day, Grover was driving on a public highway and, because he was careless, he lost control of the van. The vehicle jumped the curb and struck Inge, a pedestrian.

Inge was seriously injured in the accident. She lingered in the hospital for almost two months before she died of her injuries. Inge is survived by her husband and two minor children.

70. At common law, if Inge's estate sued Grover to recover for medical expenses incurred between the date of the accident and the date of her death, the result would be:

    A. Inge's estate would recover medical expenses in a wrongful death action.

    B. Inge's estate would recover medical expenses in a survival action.

    C. Inge's estate would recover nothing because her right of action against Grover ended with her death.

    D. None of the above.

71. In most states today, if Inge's husband and minor children wish to recover for lost financial support, services, and society suffered as a result of her death, their claim against Grover will be:

   A. A wrongful death action.

   B. A survival action.

   C. A negligent infliction of emotional distress action.

   D. A simple negligence action.

72. Assume, for this question, that Inge's husband and children have a valid negligence claim against Grover. If they wish to hold the Army responsible for Grover's negligence, they should raise the doctrine of:

   A. Negligent hiring.

   B. Respondeat superior.

   C. Nondelegable duty.

   D. Independent contractor.

73. Assume, for this question, that, at the time of the accident, Grover was on a personal errand totally unrelated to Army business. If Inge's husband and children sue the Army for Grover's negligence, the Army's best defense will be:

   A. Grover was acting within the scope of his employment.

   B. Grover's actions were a superseding cause.

   C. Grover was engaged in a frolic and detour.

   D. The Army's duty was nondelegable.

74. Assume, for this question, that Grover was negligent and that the Army was vicariously liable. If the Army raises the defense of sovereign immunity, the result will be:

   A. The Army will be liable because sovereign immunity violates the Equal Protection Clause of the Fourteenth Amendment.

   B. The Army will be liable because Congress waived sovereign immunity in negligence cases through the Federal Tort Claims Act.

   C. The Army will be liable because agencies of the United States government have never enjoyed sovereign immunity.

   D. The Army will not be liable.

Questions 75 – 77 are based on the following facts:

The Smalltown Sentinel is a local weekly newspaper. Each issue includes a column detailing births, deaths, marriages and other events of interest in the community. In a recent issue, the Sentinel ran an item stating: "Local resident Sally Smith, age 21, gave birth to twins last week." There is one Smalltown resident named Sally Smith and she is 21, but she is not married and has never had a child. Smith suffered ridicule and embarrassment because of the news item. When informed of its mistake, the Sentinel printed a retraction and apology.

75. At common law, if Sally Smith sued the Sentinel for libel based on the news item:

    A. She would recover because the statement is libel per se.

    B. She would not recover because there has been no publication.

    C. She would not recover because she has not established the colloquium.

    D. She would recover, so long as she produced sufficient evidence to show reasonable innuendo.

76. If the Sentinel can prove that the item was published as a result of an innocent mistake, at common law the effect on Sally Smith's libel suit would be:

    A. Her suit would fail because libel required malicious intent at common law.

    B. Her suit would fail because libel required at least reckless conduct at common law.

    C. Her suit would fail because libel required at least negligence at common law.

    D. Her suit would succeed.

77. Assume, for this question, that Sally Smith has proven a prima facie case for libel. The effect of the Sentinel's retraction and apology would be:

    A. To limit damages the Sentinel must pay, because of the mitigation rule.

    B. To limit damages the Sentinel must pay, because of the collateral source rule.

    C. To limit damages the Sentinel must pay, because of the offsetting benefit rule.

    D. To prevent Sally Smith from recovering any damages from the Sentinel.

Questions 78 – 81 are based on the following facts:

Roman is the host of a nationally-syndicated radio show. Roman is very controversial and specializes in exposing unsavory details about the lives of politicians and celebrities. Roman decided to exploit his notoriety by marketing a series of cassette tapes entitled, "Lifestyles of the Sick and Sleazy." The information on the tapes had never been revealed or published before. The tapes were distributed to bookstores nationwide for sale. Cleo, a bookseller, sold a number of the tapes but never listened to them himself.

On one of the tapes, Roman alleged that Linda, a United States Senator, had worked as a dancer in a topless bar while in college. Roman heard this "rumor" from an ex-convict with a very poor reputation for the truth, but he did no further investigation before recording the story. In fact, the story was a complete fabrication. Linda, a very conservative individual, was distressed and embarrassed when she learned of the story.

78. Modernly, if Linda sues Roman for defamation, the most appropriate cause of action would be:

    A. Slander.

    B. Libel.

    C. Slander per se.

    D. Libel per quod.

79. If Linda brings a defamation action against Cleo, the result will be:

    A. Cleo will be liable for republishing the defamatory statement.

    B. Cleo will be vicariously liable.

    C. Cleo will not be liable because he is a secondary publisher.

    D. Cleo will be liable, but he may have indemnification from Roman.

80. If Linda sues Roman for libel, the rulings of the United States Supreme Court require that she must prove:

    A. "Actual malice," meaning that Roman acted willfully and wantonly in publishing the defamatory statement.

    B. "Actual malice," meaning that Roman acted with knowledge that the defamatory statement was false or with reckless disregard for the truth.

    C. Roman was at least negligent and she suffered "actual injury."

    D. Roman intended to make the defamatory statement.

81. Under rulings of the United States Supreme Court, Linda's burden of proof in her libel action against Roman is:

A. Preponderance of the evidence.

B. Clear and convincing evidence.

C. Beyond a reasonable doubt.

D. None of the above.

Questions 82 – 85 are based on the following facts:

Harriet and Jenny were once general partners in the same law firm. Harriet and Jenny had numerous disagreements which led them to dissolve the firm. After the breakup, Harriet learned that Jenny was telling other lawyers that Harriet was facing disciplinary action by the state bar for commingling client trust fund monies with her personal assets. This allegation was untrue in all respects. She also learned that Jenny told other acquaintances that Harriet "was a real clown, who wouldn't recognize a lawbook if one fell on her head."

82. At common law, if Harriet sues Jenny for defamation with respect to the statements about commingling client trust funds, the appropriate cause of action would be:

    A. Slander per se.

    B. Slander per quod.

    C. Simple slander.

    D. Intentional interference with prospective business advantage.

83. Modernly, if Harriet sues Jenny for defamation with respect to the statement about her being a clown, the likely result would be:

A. Harriet will not recover because the statement is Jenny's opinion and all opinions are constitutionally protected under the Gertz v. Welch decision.

B. Harriet will not recover because lawyers are always public figures under New York Times v. Sullivan.

C. Harriet will not recover because Jenny's statement is an opinion that does not appear to be founded on underlying false facts.

D. Harriet will recover.

84. Assume, for this question, that Harriet sued Jenny for defamation and that during the trial Jenny falsely stated on the witness stand that Harriet had commingled client funds with her personal assets on other occasions. If Harriet sues Jenny for defamation for the in-court false statement, Jenny's best defense will be:

A. Harriet assumed the risk of the in-court statement when she filed the first suit.

B. Jenny's statement is protected by a conditional privilege.

C. Jenny's statement is protected by an absolute privilege.

D. One is never liable for damages for statements made on the witness stand in a civil suit.

85. Assume, for this question, that Aaron, a courtroom spectator, heard Jenny's false statement on the witness stand. When Aaron returned to his office, he repeated Jenny's statements to Clyde, a co-worker, but Clyde did not believe the statement. If Harriet sues Aaron for defamation, the result will be:

A. Aaron will prevail because he is protected by the reporter's privilege.

B. Harriet will prevail because Aaron has republished the defamatory statement.

C. Harriet will prevail because Aaron has exceeded the scope of his conditional privilege.

D. Aaron will prevail because Clyde did not believe the statement.

Questions 86 – 88 are based on the following facts:

Snowco is a manufacturer of snowmobiles. Ski-Fun, an independent retailer, sells a number of snowmobiles from Snowco's line. Marlene purchased a Snowco snowmobile from Ski-Fun. The very first time she operated the vehicle, the steering mechanism malfunctioned, causing the snowmobile to overturn. The snowmobile struck Harold, a bystander. Marlene and Harold both suffered serious injuries. Accident investigators determined that a critical bolt in the steering mechanism was missing and that the accident resulted from this defect.

86. If Marlene sues Snowco for injuries suffered in the accident, the likely result will be:

    A. Marlene will not recover because she is not in privity of contract with Snowco.

    B. Marlene will not recover, unless she can prove Snowco was negligent.

    C. Marlene will recover, under a strict liability in tort theory, because Snowco is responsible for the design defect.

    D. Marlene will recover, under a strict liability in tort theory, because Snowco is responsible for the manufacturing defect.

87. Assume, for this question, that Ski-Fun did not inspect the snowmobile's steering mechanism before it sold the vehicle to Marlene. If Harold sues Ski-Fun for his injuries under a strict liability in tort theory, in most jurisdictions today:

    A. Harold will not recover because Ski-Fun did not cause the manufacturing defect.

    B. Harold will recover, so long as he was a reasonably foreseeable bystander.

    C. Harold will not recover because he was not in privity with Ski-Fun or Snowco.

    D. Harold will recover, but only if he was related to Marlene.

88. Which of the following statements would constitute Snowco's best defense to a strict liability in tort action by Marlene?

    A. The evidence shows that Marlene tampered with the steering mechanism before she drove the snowmobile.

    B. A snowmobile is an inherently dangerous instrument, and Marlene assumed the risk when she operated it.

    C. Marlene had never driven a snowmobile before the accident.

D. In the snowmobile industry, Snowco has the most elaborate quality control checks during the manufacturing process.

Questions 89 – 90 are based on the following facts:

Moribundia is a rare tropical disease that causes death to 98% of humans who contract it. There has been no known cure for the disease. Recently, Pharmco developed a new drug to counteract Moribundia. Laboratory tests revealed, however, that a side effect of the drug is deafness in 1% of patients who were treated with the medication. Despite diligent efforts, Pharmo's scientists have been unable to eliminate the deafness side effect associated with the drug. Elmer contracted Moribundia and his physician prescribed Pharmco's new drug. While the drug saved Elmer's life, it also left him profoundly deaf.

89. If Elmer sues Pharmco under a strict liability in tort theory for his deafness, the likely result will be:

    A. Elmer will recover because Pharmco is responsible for the manufacturing defect.

    B. Elmer will recover because Pharmco is responsible for the design defect.

    C. Elmer will not recover because the drug was unavoidably unsafe.

    D. Elmer will not recover because drug manufacturers are exempt from strict liability rules.

90. Assume, for this question, that Pharmco's new drug is available only by prescription and that the package contains a conspicuous warning of the possible deafness side-effect. Assume, also, that Elmer's doctor administered the drug, but that he failed to tell Elmer of the risk of deafness. If Elmer sues Pharmco under a strict liability in tort theory for his deafness, the result will be:

A. Elmer will recover because Pharmco failed to warn him of the deafness side effect.

B. Elmer will recover because Pharmco is responsible for all personal injuries caused by its drug.

C. Elmer will not recover because Pharmco's warning to Elmer's doctor constitutes a warning to Elmer.

D. Elmer will not recover because drug manufacturers are exempt from strict liability rules.

Questions 91 – 92 are based on the following facts:

Blaster Co. is a manufacturer of dynamite, nitroglycerin and other volatile products. The management at Blaster Co. takes pride in its excellent safety record. It runs a state-of-the-art training program for employees, and constantly demands that employees act with the utmost care. Careless employees are summarily dismissed.

Rudy, a Blaster Co. employee, carelessly left a container of liquid nitroglycerin in the aisle of an unlighted section of Blaster Co.'s warehouse. Susan, an inspector from the state Department of Safety, tripped over the container. Fortunately, it did not explode, but Susan broke her arm when she fell.

91. If Susan sues Blaster Co. for injuries she suffered when she broke her arm:

A. Blaster Co. should be held strictly liable because it is engaged in abnormally dangerous activity.

B. Blaster Co. should be held liable because its employee was negligent.

C. Blaster Co. should not be liable because the injury was not reasonably foreseeable.

D. Blaster Co. should not be liable because Susan's injury is covered by worker's compensation.

92. Blaster Co.'s safety controls and its policy of summarily dismissing careless employees will:

    A. Prevent Susan from recovering from Blaster Co., because Rudy was engaged in a frolic and detour.

    B. Prevent Susan from recovering from Blaster Co., because Rudy was acting beyond the scope of his employment.

    C. Not prevent Susan from recovering from Rudy only.

    D. Not prevent Susan from recovering from both Rudy and Blaster Co.

Questions 93 – 94 are based on the following facts:

Arlene purchased a toaster which was manufactured by Crispco. The first time she used the toaster, a wire shorted and caused a fire. Arlene's kitchen was destroyed and she received minor burns in attempting to extinguish the blaze. An investigation revealed that the type of wire in question, which was used in all Crispco toasters, was inadequate to safely conduct normal household electrical current.

93. If Arlene sues Crispco for injuries to her kitchen and person, the most appropriate cause of action would be:

    A. A suit for strict liability in tort, because the toaster had a manufacturing defect.

    B. A suit for strict liability in tort, because the toaster had a design defect.

    C. A suit for strict liability in tort, because Crispco failed to warn of the danger.

    D. A negligence action, provided Arlene can show that Crispco and she were in privity.

94. Assume, for this question, that the inadequate wire caused the toaster to be destroyed, but that Arlene and her kitchen were not harmed. If Arlene sues Crispco in tort to recover the cost of a replacement toaster, the result will be:

A. Arlene will recover because the toaster had a manufacturing defect.

B. Arlene will recover because the toaster had a design defect.

C. Arlene will recover because Crispco breached its implied warranty of merchantability.

D. Arlene will not recover.

Questions 95 – 96 are based on the following facts:

Sandra, a physician, was driving to the ballet with a friend. A car driven by Don had overturned on the road ahead and Don was severely injured. Emergency paramedics had not arrived on the scene, and Sandra could see that Don was bleeding. Although Sandra believed she could stop the bleeding, she decided to continue on her journey to the ballet so that she would not miss the first act. Don died from loss of blood. He left a wife and two minor children.

95. If Don's wife and children sue Sandra for wrongful death:

    A. They will recover because a physician has a common law duty to stop and assist an accident victim.

    B. They will recover because most states modernly require physicians to stop and assist an accident victim.

    C. They will recover because the American Medical Association's Principles of Medical Ethics require physicians to render emergency medical services to the best of their ability.

    D. They will not recover.

96. Assume, for this question, that Sandra stopped to assist Don, but that her treatment was below the professional standard of care and Don died. If Don's wife and children sue Sandra for wrongful death, in a state that has a Good Samaritan statute:

   A. They will recover because Sandra undertook a duty and performed it negligently.

   B. They will recover because Good Samaritan statutes provide physician liability for negligent acts.

   C. They will recover, assuming they can prove Sandra acted recklessly in the circumstances.

   D. They will recover, but only to the extent that Sandra was negligent and aggravated Don's injuries.

Questions 97 – 99 are based on the following facts:

Clara learned she was pregnant with her first child. Clara's family had a history of congenital birth defects, so she went to her doctor, Anna, for tests to determine if her fetus would likely be born in an impaired state. Anna performed amniocentesis, a procedure that can detect chromosomal abnormalities. Anna negligently misread the test results and informed Clara that the fetus was normal. Clara carried the fetus to term. Her child, Randolph, has severe birth defects. Randolph will require expensive medical care and special education for his entire life.

97. If Randolph sues Anna for damages, in most jurisdictions, his cause of action would be called a suit for:

   A. Wrongful birth.

   B. Wrongful life.

   C. Wrongful death.

   D. None of the above.

98. Anna would prevail in Randolph's suit against her, if she could prove:

   A. When Anna performed the amniocentesis procedure, she did not actually injure the fetus.

   B. Clara's religion forbade abortion and Clara would have given birth to Randolph anyway.

C. Anna could not have reasonably foreseen the extent of Randolph's medical and educational expenses.

D. Clara signed a form agreeing not to sue Anna for negligence.

99. In most states that recognize Randolph's claim against Anna, his recovery would include:

I. General damages.

II. Special damages.

III. Punitive damages.

A. I only.

B. II only.

C. I and II only.

D. I, II and III.

100. Clancy retained Wanda, an attorney, to write his will. They entered into a standard written attorney-client contract and Clancy paid the fee Wanda charged. Clancy instructed Wanda that he wished to leave his real property to Fred, his favorite nephew. Wanda prepared the will, but carelessly overlooked a relevant section of the Probate Act.

When Clancy died and the will was offered for probate, Fred and the other heirs learned of Wanda's error. As a direct result of the error, the devise to Fred was adeemed and Fred received nothing from Clancy's estate.

If Fred sues Wanda for professional negligence in the preparation of Clancy's will, in most jurisdictions today the likely outcome will be:

A. Fred will not recover because he was not in privity of contract with Wanda.

B. Fred will not recover because an attorney does not owe a duty of care to anyone but his client.

C. Fred will recover because he is a third party beneficiary of the contract between Wanda and Clancy.

D. Fred will recover, but his damages will be limited to the fee Clancy paid Wanda.

Questions 101 – 104 are based on the following facts:

Peter was driving his Tetra car down the highway at the legal speed limit when traffic suddenly stopped ahead of him. Because he was driving cautiously, Peter was able to come to a smooth stop about ten feet from the car ahead of him. Denny was driving behind Peter and had taken his eyes off of the road for a second or two to adjust his radio. During that short period of time that Denny's attention was distracted, the traffic stopped and Denny was unable to stop before hitting Peter's car in the rear. When Denny hit Peter's car, it was pushed forward quickly and the back of Peter's head hit the head rest. The headrest was built of padding around a central metal core. The metal core was shaped like the cross section of an airplane wing, with a rounded point in front and a sharper point to the rear, giving the head rest an aerodynamic shape. As Peter's head hit the rest, the padding compressed and allowed the front portion of the metal core to focus and concentrate the pressure on the back of Peter's head to a small area, causing a fracture to his skull and first vertebra. Had the metal core been broader and flat, it would have spread the pressure over a wider area and caused no damage to Peter. Peter is paralyzed from the neck down as a result. Peter has sued the car maker, Tetra, under Restatement Torts 2d 402A.

101. In a suit under 402A, Peter would have the burden of proving:

   A. The manufacturer was unreasonable.

   B. The product was defective.

   C. That he has privity with the Manufacturer.

   D. He received the product as a result of a technical sale.

102. On the facts set forth above, the product has the following defect:

   A. A design defect, because it creates an avoidable hazard.

   B. A manufacturing defect, because it was made as intended.

   C. A marketing defect, because it was advertised as a safe car.

   D. A fabrication defect, because the core was too thin.

103. The best defense that Tetra could offer is:

   A. That this was the first time this had happened and Tetra☐was not aware of the danger.

   B. That the car was sold with a legally effective disclaimer of liability.

   C. That Peter was contributorily negligent.

   D. That the car was designed to be driven and wrecking it was☐a form of misuse.

104. Tetra contends that it should only be liable for the enhanced damages caused by the defective head rest, and that Danny should be liable for all other damages. This argument is:

A. Incorrect because Tetra was a substantial factor in causing Peter's damages.

B. Correct because some damage to Pete would have occurred even if the head rest was properly designed.

C. Correct, but Tetra has the burden of apportioning the damages.

D. Correct, and Peter must prove what portion of his damages were caused by Tetra in order to recover.

Questions 105 – 109 are based on the following facts:

Questa Corp manufactured carpets. One of its carpets was a thick plush, advertised and promoted mainly as a good carpet for hotels and motels because of its long wearing qualities. It's trade name was Royal Plush. Prince Hotel purchased the Royal Plush carpet and had it installed in the halls and lobby, having to close the hotel down in order to rip up the old carpet and install the new. This job was accomplished just prior to the opening of the summer season, a time during which Prince Hotel could expect full occupancy and make a good profit. Before reopening, the hotel had to get a certificate from the local fire inspector. The fire inspector tested a sample of the carpet and found it was highly flammable, so refused to certify the hotel for occupancy.

Prince Hotel had to remain closed, rip up the carpet and install new, fire retardant carpet, and lost all profits from the first month of the summer season.

105. If Prince Hotel sues Questa Corp on a theory of negligence and 402A, it will probably:

A. Not recover for lost profit, because this is pure economic□loss.

B. Recover for expense of replacing the carpets.

C. Recover for profits lost while the hotel was closed.

D. Both B and C.

106. On these facts the best theory of recovery for Prince Hotel is:

A. Negligence.

B. 402A.

C. Express warranty.

D. Implied warranty of merchantability.

107. In addition to the above facts, assume that a fire retardant is available that would make the Royal Plush carpet safe at a reasonable cost, and that this retardant is generally used in the carpet industry. Questa made a practice of not using the fire retardant because it enabled Questa to make an additional 1% profit on its carpet sales. After the carpet is installed Prince Hotel opens to the public and is fully occupied when a disgruntled employee deliberately starts a fire to express his anger at the hotel. Patricia, a guest, is severely burned over most of her body in the fire because of the high flammability of the carpet. She is permanently scarred and disabled as a result. On these facts, Questa's best defense in a suit by Patricia would be:

A. Patricia lacks privity and cannot sue Questa.

B. Prince Hotel was negligent in not discovering the flammable quality of the carpet.

C. The arsonist was a superseding cause of Patricia's injury.

D. Patricia is an unforeseeable plaintiff and barred under□the rule enunciated by Justice Cardozo in Palsgraff.

108. Patricia seeks to recover the following damages:

I. Compensation for her medical expenses.

II. Compensation for her lost wages and earning capacity.

III. Compensation for pain and suffering.

IV. Punitive damages against Questa.

She will probably recover the following:

A. I and II only.

B. I and III only.

C. I, II and III, but not IV.

D. All four.

109. If Patricia seeks recovery from the hotel by joining it as a party defendant in her lawsuit against the carpet maker, her best theory for recovery is:

   A. A suit under Rest. Torts 2d 402A.

   B. A suit as a business invitee.

   C. A suit under Rest. Torts 2d 402B.

   D. A suit under some form of warranty.

110. If Patricia obtains a substantial judgment against both Questa and Prince Hotel, and Prince Hotel satisfies the judgment, it will be entitled to sue Questa for:

   A. Indemnity.

   B. Contribution.

   C. Equitable Apportionment.

   D. None of the above.

Questions 111 – 114 are based on the following facts:

Ajax Corp made a drug called Alphacin used to treat Multiple Sclerosis, a degenerative and usually fatal disease. Alphacin was effective in treating MS and prevented further degeneration as long as the drug was taken, but contained a component part, a compound called Chlorofin, which caused a deterioration of the optic nerve and consequent blindness in a small percentage of patients who used the drug over a long period of time. Ajax marketed the drug from 1980 through 1985, at which time the side effect was discovered. Ajax stopped marketing the drug after discovering the side effect. Baxter Drug Co also made a drug call Betacin, used for the treatment of MS, which also contained the ingredient Chlorofin. Chlorofin is the ingredient in the medication that causes it to be effective in treating MS. Baxter Drug Co continued to market Betacin through 1990 without a warning of the side effect, even though Baxter knew or could have known of the side effect as early as 1986. In 1991, Baxter Drug Co began publishing a warning of the side effect in the Physician's Desk Reference and also in package inserts. Pauline had been taking Alphacin through a prescription from her physician, Dr. Smith, since 1980. When Alphacin was discontinued in 1985, Dr. Smith began prescribing Betacin and Pauline continued taking Betacin until 1993 when she went blind. She has sued Baxter Drug Co on a theory of strict products liability under Rest. Torts 2d 402A.

111. On these facts, Pauline will probably be able to prove that the drug Betacin marketed by Baxter Drug Co is defective under a theory of:

A. Manufacturing defect.

B. Design Defect.

C. Warning Defect.

D. She can't prove defectiveness.

112. At trial of the case against Baxter Drug Co., all the expert witnesses agree that Pauline would probably have gone blind from the effects of taking Alphacin for five years, even if she had never taken Betacin; they also agree that Betacin would have caused the blindness as a result of taking the drug for more than five years. In attempting to prove that Baxter Drug Co.'s actions were the cause in fact of her injury, Pauline must rely on:

A. The Sine Qua Non test.

B. The Substantial Factor test.

C. Alternative Liability under Summers v. Tice.

D. Market Share Liability under the Sindell case.

113. In order to rebut Pauline's evidence of actual causation, Baxter Drug Co. may successfully argue the following:

A. Pauline had no choice but to take the drug.

B. The degenerative effect of untreated MS was much more severe than the side effect.

C. Pauline would have died from the disease but for the drug.

D. Dr. Smith's continued prescribing of the drug shows the lack of warning was not the cause of her injury.

114. If Pauline sues Dr. Smith for prescribing the drug without warning her, she may prevail under the following theory:

A. Negligent failure to obtain her informed consent.

B. Strict liability of section 402A of Rest. Torts 2d.

C. Breach of implied warranty of merchantability.

D. Negligent prescribing of a drug with side effects.

Questions 115 – 117 are based on the following facts:

Pete worked for many years as an installer of asbestos insulation. He became ill at age 55 and was diagnosed as suffering from Asbestosis, a disease caused by exposure to small asbestos spicules that lodge in the lungs and, after a long incubation period of 10 to 20 years, result in asbestosis. Pete was never warned of the danger of breathing asbestos dust, and had he been warned he could have worn a simple protective mask to prevent the asbestos spicules from entering his lungs. Pete is barred from suing his employer by the worker's compensation act of the state. He wants to sue the manufacturer of the asbestos insulation sold to his employer and installed by the workers, including Pete. Although the asbestos industry had been aware of the hazards of asbestos dust and particles to workers using insulation for more than 50 years, no warnings had ever been issued by the asbestos manufacturers. Pete knows that his employer has purchased asbestos insulation from Ajax Asbestos Co during Pete's tenure, and knows also that his employer has purchased insulation from at least 10 other manufacturers while Pete worked there. He is unable to discover the identity of the other asbestos suppliers.

115. In order to get a complete recovery for his damages in the case, Pete should use:

    A. The Sine qua non test for causation in fact.

    B. The Substantial Factor test for causation in fact.

    C. Alternative liability under Summers v. Tice.

    D. Market Share Liability under the Sindell case.

116. Ajax Asbestos Co had only been in the asbestos business for five years and claims it did not have access to early studies that showed the danger of asbestos to workers installing insulation. These facts may provide an arguable defense based on:

    A. The State of the Art.

    B. The claim that there is no design defect.

    C. Ajax was not the cause in fact of Pete's injury.

    D. All of the above.

117. If Pete sues Ajax for breach of implied warranty, the best defense available on these facts for Ajax is:

    A. There is no warranty because no representation concerning□the product were made by Ajax.

    B. All warranties were disclaimed by Ajax.

    C. Pete lacks vertical privity.

    D. Pete lacks horizontal privity.

Questions 118 – 121 are based on the following facts:

Patricia watched, with interest, a series of television ads for a vehicle called “the Outlaw” produced by Wily Car Co. These ads showed the four-wheel drive Outlaw going up and down extremely steep hills, bouncing over large rocks, and generally giving the impression that it was a remarkably rugged and powerful machine. Patricia went to the local dealer for Wily Car Co, Jim’s Off Road Shoppe, and purchased an Outlaw. She immediately took her new vehicle up into the rugged mountains near her home and, as she was driving up a steep dirt road, decided to put the vehicle into four-wheel drive. The Outlaw climbed the steep slope in the four wheel drive, but when Patricia started down the equally-steep reverse slope, the transmission did not slow the vehicle down, she lost control and wrecked the vehicle on a large boulder at the bottom of the hill. Patricia miraculously escaped injury. She hired a mechanical engineer to look at the vehicle, to determine what happened. Because the transmission and the linkage were destroyed in the crash, he was unable to determine if there was any kind of defect, but he said it was possible that a spring was not fastened that would have permitted the transmission to slip out of gear and free wheel down the slope, although it would have worked fine when going up hill.

118. On these facts, Patricia’s best chance for a full recovery would be a suit based on:

    A. Rest. Torts 2d 402A.

    B. Negligence.

    C. Warranty.

    D. All of the above.

119. If Patricia sues Jim’s Off Road Shoppe for breach of Express Warranty, Jim’s best defense would be:

    A. Jim made no warranty.

    B. Patricia lacks vertical privity.

    C. Patricia lacks horizontal privity.

    D. Patricia can’t prove a defect.

120. If Patricia sues Wily Car Co for 402a and Negligence, the best way she can prove the vehicle was defective is by use of:

    A. Res Ipsa Loquitor.

    B. Her expert’s testimony that a missing spring was the possible cause of the transmission failure.

    C. The fact that it was a new vehicle, she had not damaged it□or had it serviced improperly.

    D. Circumstantial evidence.

121. Just before trial of her case against Wily Car Co., Patricia discovers that Wily Car Co. has discontinued using cast aluminum gear boxes on the Outlaw transmission, and has instead substituted cast iron gear boxes; a much stronger material. She wishes to introduce evidence of this fact to the jury. A motion in limine made by Wily Car Co. to exclude this evidence will likely be:

A. Denied, because fault is not at issue.

B. Granted, because the evidence is irrelevant.

C. Granted, because of the public policy to encourage safety.

D. Denied, because it shows that Wily Car Co. has a consciousness of guilt.

END OF QUESTIONS

TORTS ANSWERS

1. B is the correct answer, since a private nuisance action will protect Stan's right to use and enjoy his property. A is incorrect because the facts show that the gas is harmless. C is incorrect, since the facts do not state that other members of the public are affected by the gas. D is incorrect because there is no statement that Oil Company was careless.

2. D is the correct answer, since a person in lawful possession of land has standing to bring suit to abate a private nuisance. A is incorrect because one need not be an owner to sue for private nuisance. B is incorrect, since a private citizen can bring suit to abate a public nuisance when he has an injury different in kind from the general public. C is incorrect because mere residency in the area does not confer standing.

3. B is the correct answer. Since an equity court, when considering whether to abate a nuisance, will balance the hardships and find that the value of the refinery as operated outweighs Stan's occasional inconvenience. Stan, of course, can still recover damages. A is incorrect because coming to the nuisance is not a complete defense, but rather one factor the court will consider on the abatement issue. C is incorrect because it is not relevant to Stan's individual claim for private nuisance. D is an incorrect statement of law.

4. A is the correct answer because one who intentionally deceives another, even for a good motive, is liable for common law deceit. B is incorrect, since Stockbroker's act was intentional, not negligent. C is incorrect because malice is not an element for common law deceit. D is incorrect because Aaron was justified in relying on the statement of a trusted financial advisor.

5. B is the correct answer because Aaron must show that he was induced by Stockbroker's statement when he bought the stock as an element of common law deceit. If he intended to purchase the stock anyway, he has not met this element. A is incorrect because Stockbroker made a false statement of fact, even if in good faith. C is incorrect because the facts show Aaron has out-of-pocket damages. D is incorrect because it is reasonably foreseeable to a broker that a company might become insolvent.

6. B is the correct answer, since Accountant's carelessness in preparing the audit was a negligent misrepresentation to one relying on it. A is incorrect because Accountant did not intend to deceive anyone. C is incorrect because Accountant was negligent according to the facts. D is incorrect because B is correct.

7. A is the correct answer. Under the majority rule of Ultramares v. Touche, one making a negligent misrepresentation is liable only to third parties in situations approaching privity of contract. Since Accountant did not know of the existence of Federal Bank or that it would be making a loan, the privity-like requirement is not met. B is incorrect because Federal Bank did rely on the audit report. C is incorrect because it states the minority rule. D is incorrect because it states a spurious legal principle.

8. C is the correct answer because one cannot justifiably rely on statements of opinion of quality and value when entering into a contract. A is incorrect, since Harry did not commit fraud, Clay's Cars cannot be vicariously liable. B is an incorrect statement of law. D is also a plainly incorrect statement of law, as deceit is a tort action and is not based on contract. Any contractual waiver of fraud liability would violate public policy.

9. C is the correct answer, since courts have long recognized that active concealment constitutes common law deceit. A is incorrect because a false statement is not necessary in concealment cases. B is incorrect because the concealment was designed to cover the crack and to discourage Rhonda from making further inspection. D is incorrect because an "as is" clause does not insulate one from liability for fraud.

10. B is the correct answer, since when one disparages the product of another through false statements of fact, a cause of action for trade libel arises. A is incorrect, since the honesty and ethical integrity of Stopco has not been challenged. C is incorrect, since this tort does not exist. D is incorrect, as Stopco has not been injured by relying on any misrepresentation made to it.

11. C is the correct answer, since the common law required a trade libel plaintiff to show special damages in the form of particular lost customers or profits. A is not correct because a general loss of profits is not enough to meet the special damages rule. B is incorrect, for basically the same reason. D is a false statement of law, as Brakeco's actions exceed the bounds of legal business competition.

12. B is the correct answer, since Clay has misappropriated Grey's image for Clay's commercial benefit. A is incorrect, since there has been no disclosure of private facts about Grey. C is incorrect, since publication of the picture did not invade on Grey's seclusion. D is incorrect, since picturing Grey in a reputable sporting goods ad did not place him in a false light.

13. C is the correct answer, because Clement has used an appropriate civil process for an unlawful purpose. He is not merely collecting on a valid judgment, but is attempting to punish Lake through his excessive executions. A is incorrect because Clement had probable cause to bring the execution and is entitled to attach property valued at $100. B is incorrect because this is not a criminal case. D is plainly incorrect, as there has been no conversion.

14. A is the correct answer, since it is not a prerequisite for an abuse of process action that the proceeding be terminated in plaintiff's favor. B is incorrect because Lake must show that Clement had an ulterior motive for his actions. C is not correct because a plaintiff must show some damage, be it financial or otherwise. D is not correct because abuse of process is an intentional tort.

15. C is the correct answer because the tort of intentional interference with contractual relations requires intentional, purposeful conduct. A is incorrect because it misstates contract law. B is incorrect, since the suit is based on tort, not on breach of any agreement between the colleges. D is incorrect in that it indicates a tort action would lie if the conduct was not intentional.

16. D is the correct answer because the negative covenant is reasonable in geographical location (the city) and in time (one year). A is incorrect because a court will not order a person to perform a personal services contract. B is incorrect because an injunction based on the negative covenant will issue. C is incorrect because the covenant's terms are not unreasonable.

17. B is the correct answer because Professor Smith committed an assault. An actor is liable for assault if he intends to cause a harmful or offensive contact, or creates a reasonable apprehension of contact, and the victim believes that the contact is imminent. A is incorrect because the facts do not show that Logan and Adam suffered any emotional distress. C is incorrect because contact is a requirement for battery, not assault. D is incorrect because Professor Smith should have known that his act was substantially certain to cause an apprehension of an imminent harmful or offensive contact.

18. D is the correct answer, since, under the doctrine of transferred intent, Professor Smith is held to have intended to commit the battery against Davey. A is not correct because the transferred intent rule is a legal fiction that does impute intent. B is incorrect, since a defendant is responsible for all personal injuries resulting from a tort. C is an incorrect statement of the transferred intent doctrine. If one intends to commit an assault on one person and batters another, transferred intent applies.

19. B is the correct answer, because damages are presumed in trespass cases. Even if Eunice cannot show actual damage, the law will allow nominal damages. A is incorrect because the facts show Calvin was a trespasser, not a licensee. C is incorrect because the only intent necessary for trespass is to walk on the land, an intent that Calvin had. D is incorrect for the same reason stated in B.

20. D is the correct answer because Eunice (as a land owner/occupier) owes a duty to an undiscovered trespasser not to set traps for him. A is incorrect for the reason stated above. The fact that the land was posted is irrelevant. B is incorrect because Calvin is not a licensee. C is incorrect because Eunice cannot protect her property by use of a trap.

21. B is the correct answer because the negligence per se rule provides that a statute sets the duty of care when the plaintiff is within the protected class and the statute was designed to prevent against the type of injury which occurred. A is incorrect because it states the res ipsa loquitor rule. C is incorrect because a statute, not the jury, determines the duty of care in a negligence per se case. D is incorrect because the negligence of Peter has no bearing on the application of the negligence per se standard.

22. B is the best answer, since Sherry can argue that it was not reasonably foreseeable that a person would steal her car and drive it negligently. If the court finds Peter's actions to be a superseding cause, Sherry will not be liable. A is incorrect because the last clear chance doctrine is a rule designed to save the plaintiff's case when he is contributorily negligent. The facts here do not show any negligence on the part of Alfred. C is incorrect because it overstates the effect of an intentional tortfeasor in a negligence case. Intentional acts are not always unforeseeable. D is incorrect because Sherry's insurance coverage is irrelevant.

23. C is the correct answer because a child who engages in adult activity, such as driving a car, is held to the adult standard of the reasonable prudent person. A is incorrect, since Peter will not be liable in the absence of fault. B is incorrect because the subjective standard for children does not apply when a minor is engaged in adult activity. D is incorrect because a twelve-year-old can be negligent.

24. A is the correct answer because most jurisdictions follow the zone of danger rule. Dieter was a reasonably foreseeable plaintiff because Eddie was aware of his presence and it is unlikely that Dieter will be feigning his injuries. B is incorrect, since most jurisdictions do not require a physical impact. C is incorrect, since the close relationship requirement applies only when a witness is outside the zone of danger. D is incorrect for the reasons stated in A.

25. A is the correct answer because the common law recognized joint and several liability for joint tortfeasors. B is incorrect because indemnification involves a claim for payment that one tortfeasor has against another. C is incorrect because contribution involves a claim by one tortfeasor against another for a fair sharing of damage liability. D is an incorrect statement of law.

26. D is the correct answer, as Denton has lawfully come onto Miller's property primarily for his own purposes as an employee of Power Company. A is incorrect because Denton's entry was lawful in light of the easement. B is incorrect, as Denton did not enter Miller's land at the express or implied invitation of Miller. C is incorrect, since the facts do not show that Denton was Miller's social guest.

27. B is the correct answer because the duty of care owed by a landowner to a licensee is only to warn of dangers known by the landowner. A is incorrect because since Denton is not an undiscovered trespasser, Miller does owe him a duty of care. C is incorrect, since a landowner owes this more extensive duty to an invitee. D is incorrect because the common law recognized a more limited duty for landowners than the reasonable prudent person test.

28. C is the correct answer because plaintiff's contributory negligence, even if slight, totally barred recovery against a defendant at common law. A is incorrect; even under comparative fault principles, Arlen would not recover the full $100,000. B is incorrect, since this is the result under a comparative negligence scheme. D is incorrect because the facts do not show that Arlen voluntarily assumed the risk of a known danger.

29. A is the correct answer, since the last clear chance rule "saves" the contributorily negligent plaintiff's case and puts the entire burden of loss on defendant. B is incorrect, since the last clear chance rule does not apportion damages according to degree of fault. C is incorrect for the reason stated in A. D is incorrect for the same reason that A is correct.

30. D is the correct answer because under Columbia's modified comparative negligence statute, Wanda will recover nothing because her negligence was greater than Tom's. A is incorrect because Wanda is given the full amount of her damages without consideration of her fault. B is incorrect because of the statutory language; it would be an incorrect calculation even under a pure comparative negligence scheme. C is incorrect because of the statutory language. If Columbia had a pure comparative fault system like California's, this would be the correct answer.

31. C is the correct answer. The Restatement Second of Torts establishes that one who carries on an abnormally dangerous activity is subject to liability for harm to the person, land or chattels of another resulting from the activity, although he has exercised the utmost care to prevent the harm. Here, in these facts Gasco, through the escaping gas, causes harm to repairman. Even though the escaping gas was not caused by any fault on Gasco's part, they will be subject to liability. A is incorrect as there was no intentional touching (a requirement of battery). B is incorrect because there was no invasion of the repairman's use and enjoyment of his land. D is incorrect because Gasco was not negligent.

32. D is the correct answer. Where strict liability is applied, evidence that Gasco is without fault is of no consequence. A and B are incorrect because the justification for strict liability is that, "useful but dangerous activities must pay their own way." The fact that extreme care was used will not matter. C is incorrect because the gas was not negligently stored.

33. C is the correct answer. The general rule is that contributory negligence is not a defense to strict liability. The only exception is where the plaintiff knows of the danger and his negligence is the cause of the activity creating harm. A is incorrect because the repairman did not know of the risk much less assume it. B is incorrect because the repairman was not negligent. D, although a correct statement, is not the best answer since it fails to spot the issue of the general relevance of contributory negligence to strict liability.

34. A is the best answer. Liability only extends to foreseeable hazards. Although it is arguable whether this type of damage was foreseeable, because the answer choice indicates that the damages claimed by the car lot were unforeseeable, this is the best alternative. B is an incorrect statement because the fair market value is protected. C is arguably factually correct, but A remains the better answer because it is a correct statement of the law. D is an incorrect statement of law.

35. D is the correct answer. Where one is responsible for putting another in peril then a duty is owed to one who attempts a rescue as long as the rescuer is acting reasonably under the circumstances. Here, neighbor was acting reasonably in trying to assist repairman. The haste in the rescue attempt is what caused neighbor to trip in the gopher hole and Gasco will be liable. A is incorrect as neighbor did not assume the risk. B is incorrect because neighbor's conduct does not have to be foreseeable, just reasonable under the circumstances. C is not a complete statement as to why Gasco would owe liability, and, therefore, D is the better answer.

36. B is the best answer. Shopper will argue that she was a potential customer since she may come back later and make a purchase. Courts have held that one who enters a store open to the public is a potential customer. Here, Shopper, a business invitee, is owed a duty by Happytime to inspect and remedy any defect on the premises. Res ipsa loquitur is relevant when there is a reasonable presumption that the defendant is the negligent actor. A is incorrect because the door could be defective without negligence. C is not the best theory because if Shopper was only a licensee, Happytime would only owe a duty to warn of known defects. The facts do not indicate that Happytime knew of the defective door. D is incorrect because B is a viable theory for recovery.

37. A is the best answer. Because there is absence of evidence as to the breach of duty owed by Kent, the best theory is Res Ipsa Loquitur. Under the Restatement Second of Torts, it may be inferred that harm suffered by the plaintiff is caused by the negligence of the defendant when: 1) The event is of a kind which ordinarily does not occur in the absence of negligence; 2) The negligence must be within the scope of a duty that the defendant owes plaintiff; 3) Plaintiff must not have contributed to his own injury. Therefore, the elements of Res Ipsa have been satisfied and would be Pete's best theory of recovery. B and C are not correct answers because they would and could not establish fault on Kent's part. Rather, they are causes of action brought by the surviving spouse or the estate. D is an incorrect and irrelevant statement of law as applied to these facts. Causation is only one element of the required proof of a tort.

38. D is the correct answer. In most courts, Res Ipsa warrants an inference that the defendant is negligent. A is incorrect. The jury may or may not agree on the inference that the defendant is negligent. B is an incorrect statement as it would be up to the jury to decide whether they find Kent negligent or not. C is incorrect because even if Res Ipsa is established the jury may find that the defendant has sufficient evidence to rebut the presumption. If this were the case, Pete would not win.

39. B is the best answer. The Doctrine of Respondeat Superior would cause Otis to be liable for the negligence of his employee, which occurred during the course and scope of employment. A is not the best answer because Otis was not negligent – his employee was. Martha would have a better chance of recovery against Otis (deep pocket theory) than the employee. C is incorrect, as strict liability is not applicable to this fact pattern involving non-inherently-dangerous-activity. D is incorrect because, although Otis was not negligent, he can still be held liable under Respondeat Superior.

40. C is the best answer. Martha could establish the Attractive Nuisance Doctrine since: 1) Martha is only 6 years of age, and could not appreciate the dangerous condition of the pile of rolled window shades. 2) Since the pile of shades was an artificial condition created by Otis' employee, it could be said that the pile would be attractive to children of Martha's age. 3) The pile of shades could have been made safe with little effort on Otis or his employee's part. 4) It can also be said that the pile of shades was the cause of Martha's trespass. 5) Otis should have been aware of the risk, as he should know of the inquisitive nature of children and the likelihood that children will go behind counters. A is incorrect as it is not the best theory of recovery. B is incorrect because it is not a complete answer or the best answer. D is incorrect because it relies on negligence, which is not the best theory of law for this case.

41. C is the correct answer. Otis would be unsuccessful asserting the defense of contributory negligence, since a finding of Attractive Nuisance would negate such a possibility. Further, Martha, being so young, is considered incapable of contributory negligence. A is incorrect because, Martha being of such a young age, is considered incapable of assuming any risks. B is incorrect, as the successful application of the Attractive Nuisance Doctrine would find Otis responsible for her injuries. D is an incorrect statement of law.

42. B is the correct answer. Each of the defendants has the burden of proving that it was not his gun which fired the damaging pellet. Since this burden is equally impossible for each defendant, the effect is to make them jointly and severally liable. A is incorrect because this test is used where each of the defendant's acts were a substantial factor in causing the damage. Here, one of the defendant's acts was not a substantial factor. C is incorrect because not only is the "but for" test not the preferable test of causation; but also because C will be unable to prove complete responsibility of either A or B. D is incorrect for the same reason that B is correct.

A

TORTS

43. A is the correct answer. Battery is the intentional harmful or offensive touching of another without consent or privilege. Battery extends to any part of the body or anything attached to it. Thus, when Mary's body contacted the floor, a "touching" occurred. This touching was offensive to Mary, and Sue will be liable to her for battery. B is incorrect, as assault requires the intentional placing of another in reasonable apprehension of a harmful or offensive touching without consent or privilege. The facts indicate that Mary was surprised by Sue pulling out the chair. Therefore, no apprehension could have been created. C is incorrect because assault does not exist in this fact pattern, and Choice C requires both battery and assault. D is incorrect, as the facts do not imply that Sue's conduct was extreme and outrageous and calculated to cause severe emotional distress.

44. B is the best answer. Under Restatement Second of Torts, "a bodily contact is offensive if it offends a reasonable sense of personal dignity." Here, Jogger's conduct would be acceptable under the circumstances. A is incorrect because whether harm was caused to Brunette or not is not at issue. C is incorrect because, under the circumstances, the touching would not be considered harmful, or offensive. D is incorrect because the facts do not indicate that Brunette felt any apprehension by Jogger's conduct.

45. D is the correct answer. The security guard had no reasonable grounds for suspicion. Shopkeepers privilege would not apply in this situation. A is incorrect, since the store had no privilege to detain the girls. No reasonable suspicion existed. B is incorrect because, under the facts, the girls were not free to leave. C is incorrect because the suspicion need not be correct -it need only be reasonable. Therefore, although C's conclusion is correct, its reasoning is incorrect.

46. A is the best answer. Restatement Second of Torts. sec. 402A holds that one who sells any product in a defective condition unreasonably dangerous to the user or consumer or to his property is subject to liability for physical harm thereby caused to the ultimate user or consumer. Here, A is the best answer because Hairco was engaged in the selling of the product and the product was defective. Although B is a factually correct answer, it is not the best answer because Hairco can be liable even if it was unaware (and therefore could not warn) of the product defect. A is a more concise answer. C is incorrect as it is legally irrelevant and possibly factually incorrect. D is incorrect for the same reasons that A is correct.

47. A is the correct answer. Under the "thin skull" plaintiff doctrine, which is recognized in all jurisdictions, a person injured by the negligent conduct of defendant may recover damages to the full extent of his injuries where his injuries are more severe (even if resulting in death) because of a pre-existing condition such a hemophilia. Note that damages in a wrongful death case may be reduced because of the decedent's lowered life expectancy due to the pre-existing condition. B, C and D are incorrect for the reasons supporting Choice A.

48. A is the best answer because the burden of proof is easier than the other two choices. B is incorrect as the intentional element is missing and would be needed to establish battery. C is not the best answer as the elements of negligence would be harder to establish. D is not the best answer as a warranty theory would be harder to prove than strict liability.

49. C is the correct answer. Although the shaking of one's fist under the nose of another person can constitute an assault, where the fist shaking is accompanied by a statement that reasonably would remove the assaultive effect of the physical act, there is no assault (as in this fact situation). A is incorrect for the reasons discussed above. B is incorrect because the statement of George removed the assaultive effect of the fist shaking. D is incorrect because a small person can certainly assault a big person .

50. A is the best answer. Here, Bob can be liable for trespass to chattel, even though he did not intend to interfere with neighbor's property. It is necessary only that the defendant intended to deal with the chattel in the manner in which he did. B is incorrect because, for this tort, a reasonable good faith mistake is no defense. C is incorrect because you cannot have a battery against an animal. D is not the best answer. Although Bob could be charged with cruelty to animals, his good faith mistake would probably relieve him of liability.

51. C is the correct answer, since Doctor committed an offensive, unconsented touching of Marvin when he removed the mole. Marvin's express consent to eye surgery does not extend to the non-emergency surgery on the mole. A is incorrect because, while the surgery's success might limit Marvin's damages, it is not a defense to a battery action. B is incorrect because the facts do not reveal any consent beyond the eye surgery. D is incorrect because the facts do not show that Doctor was negligent.

52. A is the correct answer because this is a classic case of res ipsa loquitur. B is incorrect because a surgeon is not responsible for an injury unless he is negligent. C is incorrect because the doctrine of res ipsa loquitur creates an inference of negligence, even if there are no percipient witnesses. D is incorrect for the same reasons that A is correct.

53. C is the correct answer because, modernly, there is a national standard for most medical specialties. A is incorrect because it does not take into account that Doctor is a plastic surgeon. B is incorrect because the national standard has replaced the local standard. D is incorrect because it focuses on Doctor's subjective qualifications rather than on those expected of all practitioners of plastic surgery.

54. B is the correct answer, because the informed consent doctrine provides that a physician may be liable for an injury, even if not caused by negligence, if he fails to inform a patient of material risks associated with a medical procedure. A is incorrect because it overstates the extent of the surgeon's potential liability. C is incorrect because post hoc ergo propter hoc (because an event happened, a preceding event must have been the cause) is not a correct legal maxim. D is incorrect for the reasons that B is correct.

55. A is the correct answer because Darren may have a cause of action for intentional infliction of emotional distress. Nancy's conduct appears to be intentional, extreme and outrageous; and it may have caused extreme emotional distress. It is the best answer of the four. B is incorrect because a threat of future action is not an assault. C is incorrect because Nancy's acts are intentional, not negligent. D is incorrect because Darren has not been placed in a false light by Nancy.

56. D is the correct answer because the tort of intentional infliction of emotional distress encompasses reckless conduct, which might cause emotional distress to a reasonably foreseeable bystander. A is incorrect because intent is not always required. B is incorrect because transferred intent does not apply in intentional infliction of emotional distress cases. C is incorrect because it is inconsistent with the facts.

57. C is the correct answer, because the modern rule, as reflected in the Restatement of Torts (Second), allows for recovery of severe emotional distress without any physical injury. A is not correct because a physical impact is not required. B is incorrect because most states do not require a showing of physical consequences as a prerequisite for recovery. D is incorrect because a plaintiff need not show another underlying intentional tort to recover for intentional infliction of emotional distress.

58. A is the correct answer because the negligence per se rule provides that where a law, ordinance, or administrative regulation is intended to protect a class of persons from a particular type of harm, the legislative body has impliedly established the duty of care. B is incorrect because the general rule is that the jury cannot deviate from the negligence per se standard. C is incorrect because the ordinance obviously is relevant. D is incorrect because negligence per se, not res ipsa loquitur, is at issue.

59. C is the correct answer because Otis will recover if he shows the beating and robbery were reasonably foreseeable. This is the best of the four answers. A is incorrect because courts have found proprietors liable where the intentional acts of third parties are reasonably foreseeable. B is incorrect because an act may be reasonably foreseeable, even if it has yet to occur. D is incorrect because strict liability does not apply.

60. C is the correct answer because the facts show that Nellie's negligence was not the cause in fact of Willard's injury. Willard fainted and fell due to his intoxication, not because he could not see where he was going. A is incorrect because negligence per se relates to the duty and breach elements which are already conceded in the question. B is incorrect because the element in contention is causation in fact, not proximate cause. D is an incorrect statement and application of the last clear chance rule.

61. B is the correct answer because when the concurrent negligence of two or more tortfeasors results in an indivisible injury, they are jointly and severally liable for plaintiff's entire loss. A is incorrect because the law does not require Irene to prove proportionate liability under the circumstances. C is incorrect because each defendant is liable for the entire amount. D is incorrect because there is no evidence that Irene voluntarily assumed any risk.

62. D is the correct answer because modern law allows contribution among joint tortfeasors. A is incorrect because the satisfaction doctrine limits recovery by a plaintiff who has already recovered against another joint tortfeasor. B is incorrect because Hank is not entitled to indemnification, but only to having Trucker share in paying the judgment. C is incorrect because release is not an issue raised by the facts.

63. B is correct because automobile guest statutes require a higher standard of culpability on a defendant's part – such as gross negligence or reckless conduct. A is incorrect because ordinary negligence is not actionable if there is a guest statute. C is incorrect because the culpable conduct need not be intentional. D is incorrect because Irene can have a recovery, as stated in B.

64. B is the correct answer because Paul's intentional harmful contact with Tom is a battery. A is incorrect because the facts do not reveal that Tom was in apprehension of the contact before it occurred. C is incorrect because the facts do not show that Paul intended to cause emotional distress or that Tom suffered any distress. D is incorrect because this activity does not give rise to a strict liability tort.

65. C is the correct answer because by playing baseball, Tom impliedly consented to possible harmful contact that is within the rules of the game. A is incorrect because contributory negligence is not a defense to an intentional tort, and also because there is no evidence that Tom was negligent in any case. B is incorrect because justification is not a defense raised by the facts. D is incorrect for the same reason.

66. D is the correct answer, since Pam has not entered Scott's property. A, B and C are incorrect because they relate to categories of persons who are on a landowner's property for different reasons.

67. A is the correct answer because a landowner owes a person off the premises a duty of ordinary care with respect to artificial conditions the landowner maintains. B is incorrect because this is the duty owed a licensee. C is incorrect because this is the duty owed a discovered trespasser. D is incorrect for the same reasons that A is correct.

68. D is the correct answer because it was reasonably foreseeable that an act of God could cause the corroded cables to give way. A is incorrect because an intervening act of God does not automatically relieve one of liability for negligence. B, which is really a rephrasing of A, is incorrect for the same reason. C is incorrect because it overstates the potential liability of a defendant by not taking foreseeability into account at all.

69. C is the correct answer. In personal injury cases, the adage "you take the plaintiff as you find her" is still the majority rule. A is incorrect because personal injury damages are not limited to what the defendant might reasonably foresee. B is incorrect because this is not a preexisting injury case. D is incorrect for the same reasons that C is correct.

70. C is the correct answer because at common law a cause of action personal to a plaintiff terminated when the person died. A is incorrect because wrongful death actions were not recognized at common law and, also, because, modernly, this is a survival claim. B is incorrect because survival claims were not recognized at common law. D is incorrect for the same reasons that C is correct.

71. A is the correct answer because lost financial support, services and society are available to designated beneficiaries under a statutorily-created wrongful death action. B is incorrect because survival statutes typically allow an estate to recover for injuries sustained by the decedent only until the time of death. C is incorrect because the husband and children do not qualify for a negligent infliction of emotional distress claim and could not recover the damages mentioned in the question in this type of action, in any case. D is incorrect because, without the wrongful death statute, Grover would not have negligence liability to the husband and children.

72. B is the correct answer because an employer is responsible for the negligence of an employee, so long as the employee was acting within the scope of his employment. A is incorrect, as the facts do not state the Army was negligent in hiring Grover. C is incorrect because the nondelegable duty rule applies to independent contractor cases. D is incorrect because the facts show Grover was not an independent contractor and Inge's family certainly would not argue that he was.

73. C is the correct answer because the Army will not be vicariously liable for Grover's negligence if his activity, when the accident occurred, was totally unrelated to Army business. A is incorrect because the Army would be liable if Grover were acting within the scope of his employment. B is incorrect because superseding cause is not an issue. D is incorrect because the nondelegable duty rule applies in the independent contractor setting.

74. B is the correct answer because Congress waived sovereign immunity in numerous cases, including negligence, under the Federal Tort Claims Act of 1946. A is incorrect because sovereign immunity has never been held to violate the Equal Protection Clause. C is incorrect because until 1946, United States government agencies did enjoy sovereign immunity. D is incorrect because Congress has waived the immunity in negligence cases.

75. D is the correct answer. Since the statement is not libelous on its face, Sally Smith must show facts that make the otherwise innocent statement actionable. (This fact would be that she is unmarried.) This is called a reasonable innuendo. A is incorrect because the statement is not libelous on its face. B is incorrect because there has been publication to others who read the newspaper. C is incorrect because the statement clearly related to the only person named Sally Smith in the community.

76. D is the correct answer because libel was a strict liability tort at common law. Defendants were liable for unintended and innocent defamation. A, B and C are incorrect because they all state that some degree of fault was required in a common law libel action.

77. A is the correct answer because retraction and apology are steps a libel defendant can take to limit the damages caused by a libelous statement. B is incorrect because the collateral source rule relates to payments made to a plaintiff from a source independent of the defendant. This doctrine is not raised by the facts. C is incorrect because the facts do not show Sally Smith received any benefit from the libel. D is incorrect because retraction and apology only mitigate damages and do not completely relieve a defendant of liability.

78. B is the correct answer because, although the defamatory statement was "spoken" on the tape, it has been reduced to permanent physical form through the taping and, thus, would be libel. A and C are incorrect because they relate to spoken defamation that is transitory. D is incorrect because the statement is libelous on its face, without need to refer to extrinsic evidence.

79. C is the correct answer because a bookseller who sells libelous matter without knowledge is not liable under the secondary publisher rule. A is incorrect because it does not take into account the exception stated in C. B is incorrect because Cleo and Roman did not have a relationship that would give rise to vicarious liability. D is incorrect because, since Cleo is not liable, an indemnification issue would not arise.

80. B is the correct answer. When a public official or figure sues for libel related to a matter of public concern, "actual malice" as defined in New York Times v. Sullivan becomes part of the plaintiff's prima facie case. A is incorrect because this definition is typically used for punitive damages by state courts. C is incorrect, since this is the rule established in Gertz v. Robert Welch Co. for private persons defamed on matters of public concern. D is incorrect because it embodies the common law rule, before the Supreme Court decisions beginning with New York Times.

81. B is the correct answer, as the Supreme Court held, in New York Times, that the burden of proof for "actual malice" is clear and convincing evidence. Therefore, A, C and D are incorrect.

82. A is the correct answer because Jenny has defamed Harriet by accusing her of unethical business practices and perhaps, also, the commission of a crime. Thus, the statement is slander per se for two reasons. B is incorrect because there is no slander per quod theory of recovery. C is incorrect because the statement goes beyond simple slander. D is incorrect because this tort does not protect a plaintiff's reputation interest.

83. C is correct, since Jenny's statement is an opinion that does not appear to be premised on false underlying facts. A is incorrect because the Gertz holding, regarding opinion, has subsequently been interpreted in Malkovich as not protecting all opinions under a First Amendment umbrella. B is incorrect because it does not address the opinion issue, and also because lawyers are not always public figures. D is incorrect because, modernly, an opinion not based on underlying false facts is not defamation.

84. C is the correct answer. A witness testifying in a court proceeding has absolute immunity from defamation liability, provided the statements relate to issues in the trial. A is incorrect because assumption of risk does not apply in defamation actions. B is incorrect because this is not a conditional privilege case. D is incorrect because it overstates the breadth of the absolute immunity.

85. B is the correct answer. Aaron is a republisher. The fact that Clyde did not believe the statement is not required. It is sufficient that the person understand the words as accusing plaintiff of some disgrace. A is incorrect because Aaron is not protected by the reporter's privilege. C is incorrect because no conditional privilege is raised by the facts. D is incorrect for the same reason B is correct.

86. D is the correct answer. Modernly, a manufacturer is strictly liable for a manufacturing defect. A is incorrect because privity of contract between a manufacturer and a purchaser is no longer required. B is incorrect because a purchaser need not prove negligence to recover for a personal injury caused by a dangerously defective product. C is incorrect because a manufacturing defect, not a design defect, caused the injury.

87. B is the correct answer. Most states today allow bystanders to recover for personal injuries caused by dangerously defective products, so long as they were reasonably foreseeable bystanders. A is incorrect because every party in the manufacturing/marketing chain is liable for injuries caused by a dangerously defective product. C is incorrect because privity is not required. D is incorrect because a bystander need not be a family member to recover for personal injuries.

88. A is the best answer because a plaintiff may not recover in strict liability in tort, if the manufacturer can show that the product has been altered after it leaves the manufacturer's hands. B is incorrect because snowmobiles are not inherently dangerous products, and because Marlene did not assume the risk that the product would be defective. C is incorrect because the facts do not show that Marlene's inexperience caused the accident. D is incorrect because a manufacturer is strictly liable, even though it took all possible care to avoid manufacturing defects.

89. C is the correct answer. The Restatement of Torts and the courts recognize that, although some products pose a risk of injury, where their utility outweighs the risk, they are not unreasonably dangerous. Many new drugs fall within this category. A is incorrect because there is no manufacturing defect. B is incorrect because the design defect is not unreasonably dangerous. D is incorrect because drug manufacturers do not have a blanket exemption from strict liability rules.

90. C is the correct answer. An adequate warning to a "learned intermediary" (here the doctor) is generally held to be a warning to the patient. A is incorrect because in the case of prescription drugs, the warning need not be directly to the consumer. B is incorrect because it overstates the liability of a drug manufacturer. D is incorrect because drug manufacturers do not have a blanket exemption from strict liability rules.

91. B is the correct answer. The injury was caused by the carelessness of Blaster Co.'s employee. A is incorrect because Susan was not injured as a result of activity that was abnormally dangerous. (Had the container exploded, the result would be different.) C is incorrect because injuries caused when a person falls over a container in a dark aisle are reasonably foreseeable. D is incorrect because the facts do not mention a worker's compensation statute, and also because these laws usually affect only those in employer-employee relationships.

92. D is the correct answer. Susan can recover from Rudy because he was negligent and from Blaster Co. because it is vicariously liable for the negligence of its employee. A is incorrect because Rudy was acting within the scope of his employment when he was negligent. B is incorrect for the same reason. C is incorrect because it states Susan can recover from Rudy only.

93. B is the correct answer. Since Crispco used an inadequate wire in all its toasters, this is a design defect that created an unreasonable risk of danger. A is incorrect because this is not a manufacturing defect. C is incorrect because whether Crispco warned Arlene or not is irrelevant. D is incorrect because negligence might be more difficult to prove, and because the statement about privity is incorrect.

94 D is the correct answer. A tort suit is not an appropriate means of insuring the quality of a product. A, B and C are all incorrect because Arlene cannot recover for loss of the product itself under a tort theory. If Arlene wants to recover for pure economic loss, including loss of the product, she may recover under a warranty theory, which may include a suit for breach of implied or express warranties.

95. D is the correct answer. Generally, a person has no duty to come to the aid of one in distress. A is incorrect because the common law did not recognize a duty to rescue. B is incorrect because most states have not changed the common law rule. C is incorrect because although the AMA rule is correctly stated, it has not been applied in tort cases.

96. C is the correct answer. In a jurisdiction with a Good Samaritan statute, a physician who administers aid in an emergency is not liable for mere negligence, but instead must have acted recklessly or willfully and wantonly in causing an injury. A is incorrect because Good Samaritan statutes insulate physicians from liability for negligence in emergencies. B is incorrect because it misstates the effect of Good Samaritan statutes. D is incorrect because Sandra will not be liable for negligence, as stated above.

97. B is the correct answer. When a child sues a health care provider for damages caused when the provider negligently failed to discover a possible birth defect in a fetus, the claim is called a wrongful life claim. A is incorrect because wrongful birth is the term used when a parent sues for damages in the same circumstances. C is incorrect because this is plainly not a wrongful death claim. D is incorrect for the same reason that B is correct.

98. B is the correct answer. If Clara intended to give birth to Randolph in any case, Anna was not the cause in fact of Randolph's birth. A is incorrect because a health care provider does not cause the injury in a wrongful life case, but rather deprives the mother of an opportunity to end the pregnancy. C is incorrect because most courts would find these special damages reasonably foreseeable. D is incorrect because a waiver of liability in a medical malpractice case would not be enforced —it violates public policy.

99. B is the correct answer. Most jurisdictions that recognize a wrongful life claim limit, recovery to special damages. A is incorrect because general damages are not usually allowed. (This is because a jury cannot determine damages based on the difference between non-life and life in an impaired state.) C is incorrect because it includes general damages. D is incorrect because it includes general damages and punitive damages, which are generally not available in negligence cases.

100. C is the correct answer. Although an attorney usually does not owe a duty of care to a non-client, an exception has been recognized in cases where a specific person is an intended beneficiary of a will. A and B are incorrect because privity is not universally required in attorney malpractice cases. D is incorrect because Fred's recovery will not be limited to the amount of the fee. He may recover all proximately caused damages from Wanda for her negligence.

101. B is the correct answer. A is incorrect, since it states one of the elements of negligence which is not necessary, in strict liability, under 402A. C is incorrect because 402A expressly excludes any requirement of privity. D is incorrect because 402A is equally applicable to a lease transaction, although warranty theories do require a technical sale.

102. A is the correct answer. A design defect is found when the product is made as the maker intended but causes an avoidable hazard to the user. The essence of design defect is the concept of unreasonably dangerous, and an avoidable danger is an unreasonable danger. B is incorrect because it is a nonsense statement. A manufacturing defect is found when the product is not made as intended. C is incorrect because a marketing defect is found when the maker has failed to warn the user of a danger known to the maker. D is also a nonsense statement because fabrication means the same as manufacturing, and if the product was as intended it is not a fabrication or manufacturing defect.

103. D is the correct answer. There is a line of cases which would support the defense; however, none of the defenses will succeed. A is clearly irrelevant because knowledge of the hazard is important to negligence but not necessary for liability under 402A. B is clearly erroneous because it is not possible to disclaim liability under 402A. C is clearly wrong both factually and legally because Peter was not unreasonable in driving in traffic and contributory negligence is not a defense to strict liability. The theory of D, that the precipitating cause of the injury was the negligence of another driver and that the maker has no duty to create a crash proof car, has been rejected by a majority of the courts, but at one time was a supportable and arguable defense, so it is the best defense offered.

104. C is the correct answer. Concurrent tortfeasors always bear the burden of apportioning loss or they are jointly and severally liable for the entire loss. Tera can obviously apportion the property damage, but will probably be jointly and severally liable for all of Peter's personal injury, at least the paralysis. A is incorrect because technically Tetra is liable only for the enhanced damages. The question is who has the burden of apportionment. B is incorrect because, under the facts, apportionment will be virtually impossible. D is incorrect because Peter does not have the burden of apportioning damages caused by joint and concurrent tortfeasors at modern law.

A

TORTS

105. A is the correct answer. The courts have consistently drawn a line at what type of damages may be recovered under negligence and 402A. Damage caused to persons or property other than the defective product itself may be recovered, but any damages other than that are deemed part of the loss of the benefit of the bargain. Here, lost profits clearly are a pure economic loss, and the cost of replacing the carpet is probably also not recoverable under either of these two theories. B is wrong because it does not fit within the concept of damages to persons or property, other than the defective product. C is incorrect because lost profits from the defective product are clearly a pure economic loss.

106. D is the correct answer. Since any warranty would permit recovery based on the "benefit of the bargain", lost profits and expenses of replacing the defective product fit within this concept. A and B are incorrect for the reasons expressed in the analysis of question 105. C would permit recovery if it could be proven, but on these facts there is no Express Warranty shown.

107. C is the correct answer because an intentional or criminal intervening act is normally unforeseeable as a matter of law; however, the defense will fail in this case, since the arsonist is within the risk created by the sale of the defective carpet. A is not an arguable defense, since lack of privity is no longer a defense in any of the theories, including horizontal privity, since Patricia would be covered by all of the alternatives set forth in the Uniform Commercial Code. B is not even an arguable defense, since Prince Hotel's intervening passive negligence would not protect Questa. D is not arguable, since a guest at a hotel is clearly foreseeably at risk from the defective product.

108. D is the correct answer, even though punitive damages are not normally available in products cases, because Questa exhibited a callous disregard for the high probability of injury to hotel guests and chose to expose them to the risk to make a little extra profit. This would be the equivalent of implied Malice and subject Questa to punitive damages. All other answers are incorrect because they do not include punitive damages.

109. B is the correct answer. The hotel would owe Patricia a duty of inspection to discover defects in the premises. A is not correct, since 402A is applicable only to a commercial seller of products. C is incorrect, since 402B requires a representation and a sale of a product, neither of which is present here. D is also incorrect, since it requires a technical sale of a product, although some courts have constructed a 'hybrid' form of warranty called "warranty of habitability", which could conceivably fit this situation, but only a few courts have adopted it.

110. A is the correct answer. The parties are not in pari delicto, Prince Hotel being, at most, only passively negligent. Also, Questa has breached its implied warranty of merchantability to Prince Hotel. B is not correct, since Prince would be entitled to indemnity on these facts. C is not correct, since the doctrine of equitable apportionment is found in only a few states.

111. C is the correct answer because Baxter was aware of the side effect of the drug in 1986 and marketed the drug without a warning of the hazard after 1986. A is not correct, since there is no indication of mismanufacturing. B is not correct, since the drug clearly passes the cost/benefit and risk/benefit analyses and is unavoidably hazardous.

112. B is the correct answer. Since A, the sine qua non test, will not find causation, according to the experts. She probably would have gone blind, even if she had not taken the Betacin. However, since long term use of the Betacin would also have caused blindness, most courts would hold that Betacin was a substantial factor in causing her injury and would hold Baxter liable. Neither C nor D can be correct, since Pauline does not find it impossible to prove cause in fact. Both Alternative liability and Market Share are substitutes for causation when Pauline cannot prove that the defendant's act caused the injury, although it could have.

113. D is the correct answer. Dr. Smith continued to prescribe the drug even after the warning was given, and we can infer that he would have done the same thing had the warning been given earlier. If a warning would not have changed the plaintiff's actions, then the warning cannot be the cause in fact. The other options all contain good arguments why Pauline should have taken the drug, but in the final analysis whether she exposes herself to the hazard of the drug, rather than the hazard of the disease, has to be her choice and she is deprived of this choice by not being given a warning.

114. A is the correct answer because Pauline has the right to decide for herself whether to accept the risk of medical treatment. B and C are clearly wrong, since they both require sales of products, which medical doctors do not engage in. D is incorrect, since balancing the risks against the benefits will show that Dr. Smith was not unreasonable in subjecting her to the risk of the drug to avoid the disease.

115. B is the correct answer. Exposure to any asbestos provided by any of the many suppliers over the years could be sufficient to produce asbestosis. Thus, A is incorrect because, if Ajax's conduct is removed from the factual equation, the damage will probably still occur. C is incorrect, since Pete can prove that Ajax's conduct was the cause of his injury, and D is not correct, since he can identify at least one of the suppliers. D is also incorrect, since it would not give him a complete recovery. Each maker would only have to pay its percentage of the injury coincident with its market share. In the many decades of exposure, many of the suppliers will have gone out of business and can't be held liable for their percentage.

116. C is the correct answer. Since long term exposure to asbestos is necessary for the onset of asbestosis, the fact that Ajax has only been in the business for five years may be sufficient to convince a jury that Ajax could not have been even a substantial factor in Pete's damage. A is incorrect, since it refers to D's knowledge of the hazard as a prerequisite to its duty to warn. A seller of a product is held to be aware of all knowledge available in the industry and the facts indicate that the industry has been aware of the hazard for several decades. B is irrelevant. P is suing for failure to warn, and D is incorrect because A and B are incorrect.

117. D is the correct answer. The UCC has provided three alternatives for states to adopt to permit recovery for consumers who are not in vertical privity with the manufacturer. The first of these alternatives would permit recovery by natural persons for personal injury who were members of the purchaser's family or his guests. Under this alternative, Pete would lack the requisite horizontal privity for recovery under breach of implied warranty. A is not correct, since a representation is not necessary to create an implied warranty of merchantability. B is not correct, since, although warranties are still subject to disclaimer, a disclaimer for personal injury to a consumer is prima facie unconscionable. C is not correct, since vertical privity is no longer necessary since the decision in Henningsen.

118. C is the correct answer because her only damages are to the defective product itself and would be deemed pure economic loss or loss of the benefit of the bargain. A and B are not correct, since both 402A and Negligence would permit recover only for personal injury and damage to property other than the defective product.

119. A is the correct answer because, on these facts, the only express warranty was made by Wily Car Co in its television ads, and there are no facts showing that Jim adopted the express warranty. B and C are incorrect, since Patricia has both vertical and horizontal privity with Jim's Offroad Shoppe. D is incorrect, since Patricia can easily show a defect under a warranty theory by showing that the product did not perform as intended.

120. D is the correct answer. It can be inferred that the transmission was defective because it did not perform as it should have. A is not correct, since res ipsa is limited to proving breach of duty in a negligence case and here she is suing in 402A. B is not correct, since her expert's opinion, that a missing spring was "possibly" the cause, does not meet the minimum standard for the plaintiff's burden of proof by a preponderance of the evidence. The mechanical engineer would have to testify that the missing spring was "more likely than not" the cause, or that it was "probably" the cause. C comes close to being correct, but it is merely a statement of the various facts she would adduce to bolster a circumstantial evidence case by negating other possible causes of the accident.

121. C is the correct answer. The Evidence Code specifically excludes such evidence for the reason stated, although a few courts, including California, have ruled otherwise with respect to Strict Liability actions. A is incorrect, since the facts indicate that Patricia is suing for negligence in addition to 402A, so fault is at issue. B is incorrect because the fact that the evidence would tend to show that Wily Car Co. felt that the cast aluminum was not strong enough for the rigors expected and this would certainly be relevant to Patricia's claim that her vehicle failed because of a defective design. D is not correct, since consciousness of guilt is not a part of a civil case, and would be barred by the public policy to encourage safety measures in any event.

END OF ANSWERS

SIMULATED BAR

SIMULATED BAR QUESTIONS

Questions 1 – 6 are based on the following facts:

Art Kittect was a very successful designer and builder of custom-made homes in Southern California. After lengthy discussions with Bob and numerous revisions of the plans, Art agreed to build a home for Bob. Art and Bob signed a contract providing that Bob's duty to pay would not arise unless the home was constructed according to the construction plans, except to the extent of construction changes approved in writing.

1. Assume that Art began construction of the home but determined that there was a shortage of roofing tile because of recent large-scale efforts to rebuild many local homes destroyed in seasonal fires. When contacted on the telephone, Bob agreed with Art to the construction of a "shake" roof because of the tile shortage. After a week, Bob decided that his "dream home" must be completed as he originally planned and told Art he wanted the tile roof. Art refused because he knew the tiles would be difficult to obtain, although he had not purchased the shake roof materials. If Bob brings an action against Art for breach of contract, the court will most likely find for:

    A. Art, because Bob waived his rights to have the tile roof installed.

    B. Art, because Bob agreed to modify the contract.

    C. Bob, because of Art's pre-existing duty to use the roofing tiles.

    D. Bob, because the modification must be expressly agreed upon.

2. Assume that while Art was constructing Bob's home, the IRS notified Art of its intent to audit him. When Bob, a tax accountant, heard Art grumbling to himself about the upcoming audit, Bob volunteered to meet with the IRS to resolve Art's problem. Fearing the worse, Art was ecstatic to learn that Bob was able to reach a favorable resolution on his behalf. Knowing that Bob had wanted an automatic garage door opener, but did not include one within the plans because of financial reasons, Art stated to Bob, "The Genie door raiser we talked about is yours. I'll pull one off another job and install it on Monday." On Monday, Art's generosity fizzles and he refuses to supply the door opener. Bob sues. The court will find for:

    A. Art, since Bob's gratuitous services were insufficient consideration for Art's promise.

B. Art, since the parole evidence rule bars oral testimony of Art's promise.

C. Bob, since Art's statement constituted an enforceable moral obligation.

D. Bob, since the doctrine of promissory estoppel is a substitute for Bob's otherwise gratuitous services.

3. Assume that the contract provides for the installation of an automatic garage door opener, but does not mention the type of door opener to be used. Art has installed a 1/2 horsepower motor for the door opener. Garage doors of similar size and type to Bob's reasonably require a 1 horsepower motor. Bob has noticed the 1/2 horsepower motor and states, "You'll never get paid." If Art files a lawsuit to obtain payment, Art will recover:

   A. Full price, because he substantially performed the contract.

   B. Full price, because neither the contract nor plans specified the type of motor to be used.

   C. Nothing, because there was no meeting of the minds due to the failure of Art and Bob to set forth each material term in the written contract.

   D. Full price, but less any damages for Art's breach of the implied duty to install a motor with the reasonably required amount of power.

4. Assume for this question, that Art has agreed to complete Bob's home by August 1. On July 15, when construction of Bob's home is about 80% complete, the home is accidentally destroyed by fire, without fault of either Art or Bob. Art seeks to recover for the work previously performed. Will Art prevail?

   A. Yes, for the reasonable value of his services less cost of completion of the home.

   B Yes, for 80% of the contract price less Bob's damages.

   C. No, because no benefit was conferred upon Bob because of the destruction of the home.

   D. No, if Art cannot complete the home by August 1.

5. Assume for this question, that the contract between Art and Bob provided that Bob would pay Art only upon receipt of an "architect's certificate," which certifies that the house was built in accordance with the Architect's Code of Standards. Bob hired Conrad, a highly reputable architect, to inspect the house and to issue the certification. Conrad inspected the home, but refuses to issue the certification because the house was not constructed in a workmanlike manner pursuant to the Standards. Bob refuses to pay the contract price. If Art brings suit against Bob for the contract price, the court will most likely find for:

   A. Art, if Conrad has made a gross mistake in his decision.

   B. Art, unless Bob proves the home was not constructed in a workmanlike manner.

   C. Bob, because both Art and Bob agreed to the condition that performance must be to the satisfaction of a third person.

   D. Bob, unless Art can prove another architect would have issued an architect's certificate.

6. Assume that Art assigned his rights under the Art/Bob contract to University for the outstanding college tuition bills of Art's daughter, Gloria. University notifies Bob of the assignment, but Art only completes 50% of the home before deciding to obtain a Bachelor's Degree in Business Administration, at College. College caters to older students seeking to change careers. Art refuses to complete the home. What result if University files an action against Bob to recover the contract price?

   A. Bob will prevail, because the contract is not assignable.

   B. Bob will prevail, but only because Art did not complete the job.

   C. University will prevail, but will only receive the reasonable value of the services performed, less damages caused by Art's failure to complete the home.

   D. University will prevail, but only the contract price, less the cost of completion of the contract.

7. Milton was taking a weekend retreat to his cabin in the local mountains during the week before Christmas. He had neglected to bring along snow chains, even though there was the possibility of snow and ice on the roadway. Although Milton was driving slowly through the icy areas, he lost control of his car and crashed, making his car inoperable. Milton fractured his arm in the accident, but was able to walk back to a small cabin 10 miles from where he had crashed.

   Florence, a retired nurse, lived at the cabin and was able to provide medical treatment to mend Milton's arm. Florence was also starved for companionship and decided to keep Milton from leaving by locking the door to the room where she had placed him. Exhausted from his injuries and the 10-mile walk, Milton had fallen fast asleep before Florence had locked him in the room. After a night's sleep, Florence realized what she was doing was wrong and unlocked the door. When Milton later awoke, he asked Florence to telephone a relative for transportation home, and Florence complied. Is Florence liable to Milton for false imprisonment?

   A. Yes, because Milton was actually confined with no reasonable means of escape.

   B. Yes, because Florence intended to confine Milton within the room.

   C. No, because Florence did not threaten or force Milton into confinement.

   D. No, because Milton was unaware of his confinement.

Questions 8 – 9 are based on the following facts:

Robin and Mark were married last week and set off for a honeymoon in Florida. The state of Florida has been having a serious problem with people being robbed in front of automatic teller machines. Florida has just imposed a statute to protect their citizens and tourists. The statute makes it a law that every facility where people may obtain money from an automatic teller machine, must have a security guard posted during the period the machine is operative, or in the alternative a 4' x 4' sign must be posted at the facility warning the consumer of the potential risk of robbery.

Despite the new law, Bank de Monies ("Bank") did not provide a security guard, nor did they post a sign at its automatic teller. On her first evening in Florida, Robin wasn't feeling very well and decided to stay in the room to get some extra rest. Mark decided to go to Disney World and play the arcade games. Mark made a stop at Bank to withdraw some money from the automatic teller. Several hours later, Robin was awakened by a police officer. She learned that her husband, Mark, was robbed and killed at the automatic teller machine at Bank. Robin brings a wrongful death action against Bank.

8. Bank is most likely to prevail under which of the following theories?

    A. The failure to comply with the statute was not the actual cause of Mark's death.

    B. None of Bank's customers had ever been killed before at any of its automatic teller machines.

    C. Mark was negligent for using an automatic teller in an unfamiliar city.

    D. The statute is an ex post facto law.

9. Assume for this question, that Robin, upon hearing of her husband's death, goes into severe emotional distress, requiring a two-week hospitalization before she recovered. If Robin brings an action against Bank de Monies based upon the theory of negligent infliction of emotional distress, Robin will:

    A. Prevail, because Bank de Monies violated the state statute.

    B. Prevail, but only because she suffered emotional distress.

    C. Not prevail, because Robin was not present at the scene when Mark was killed.

    D. Not prevail, because Robin was not a foreseeable plaintiff.

Questions 10 – 12 are based on the following facts:

Siegfried "convinces" Max to rob Savings R Us Bank by handcuffing a locked briefcase to Max's wrist, telling him it is full of plastic explosives that will be detonated by a remote control unit in Siegfried's possession if Max fails to follow Siegfried's request. Unknown to Max, the briefcase is actually full of Play Doh. Max obtains $100,000.00. from Savings R Us after threatening the bank teller with a loaded gun. State's penal code makes it a crime to "obtain bank funds by use of a weapon or threat of injury." Max was arrested before he could flee the bank.

10. State prosecutor Buck charges Max and Siegfried with conspiracy to violate the penal code section. Max and Siegfried will most likely be found:

    A. Guilty, because the general rule is that withdrawal is not a defense to the crime of conspiracy.

    B. Guilty, because Max failed to thwart the completion of the crime.

    C. Not guilty, because Max was an unwilling participant to the crime.

    D. Not guilty, because Siegfried never agreed to the details of Max's plan to carry out the crime.

11. Max is charged with violating the penal code section. Is it likely he will be convicted?

    A. Yes, because there is no defense of duress since there was only Play Doh in the briefcase.

    B. No, because he robbed the bank under the duress of Siegfried's threats.

    C. Yes, because he threatened the bank teller with injury if the money was not given to him.

    D. No, because he never intended to keep the money.

12. Can Siegfried be convicted of the penal code section even though Max is acquitted?

    A. No, because only the party performing the prohibited act may be convicted under the penal code section given.

    B. No, because Max did not successfully complete the crime.

    C. Yes, because all parties to a conspiracy will be found guilty of the underlying crime.

    D. Yes, because Siegfried can commit the crime through an innocent agent.

13. Gloria, the buyer for Lost Adolescence ("Lost"), a retailer of sophisticated adult toys, faxes an order to CompuPlay, the nation's leading manufacturer of video games. Gloria requests prompt shipment of 5,000 of CompuPlay's most popular game, "Res Gestae," which pits an escaped convict (the player) against a crack police force (the game), awarding points to the convict for each successive crime committed while continuing to elude capture by the police.

    CompuPlay tenders the 5,000 games to Lost one week later, payment in full due in 30 days. Unknown to Lost, CompuPlay's programmer had secretly reprogrammed Res Gestae to be "politically correct" by always having the convict immediately captured at the beginning of the game. This change was not apparent without actually playing the game. When Gloria tested one of the games the day after delivery, the change was discovered. She immediately contacted CompuPlay to return the video games, but CompuPlay refused. Who will prevail if Lost sues CompuPlay for breach of contract?

    A. Lost, because CompuPlay accepted Gloria's offer to buy when it shipped the non-conforming games.

    B. Lost, because it has the option of either accepting or rejecting the non-conforming goods.

    C. CompuPlay, because it had the option of shipping non-conforming goods as an accommodation to Lost.

    D. CompuPlay, because Lost failed to inspect the goods at time of tender.

14. Phil owned a home on 5 acres of land, in an oil rich region of his home state. Continental Petroleum ("Continental") owned and operated a pipeline delivering oil to its refineries which, in part, passed across Phil's property. Continental is the state's largest employer. After two years of operation, the pipeline cracked, with oil from the pipeline flooding Phil's property with a black gooey mess. This did not present any danger to Phil, but caused substantial damage to his property. If Phil brings an action against Continental, under what theory will he most likely prevail?

    A. Strict liability, because the operation of a pipeline is an inherently dangerous activity.

    B. Strict liability in tort, if the pipeline was defective.

    C. Nuisance, because Phil's use and enjoyment of his property was interfered with.

    D. Negligence, if the pipeline was improperly maintained.

15. Buck, the owner of a 100-acre cattle ranch, raises cattle for show. Buck's ranch is directly in the middle of an amusement park, which is located on the west side of his property, and the amusement park's parking lot, which is on the east side of his property. The amusement park offers a tram service to shuttle people to and from the park. However, people still walk across Buck's property, and to prevent the trespassing, Buck installs an electrical fence around his ranch. When the fence is touched, a mild shock is given. Billy, an amusement park visitor, boarded the tram. While the tram was traveling from the parking lot to the amusement park facility, Billy's hat blew off and landed against Buck's fence. Billy hopped off the tram to retrieve it. When Billy reached for his hat, he received a shock. Although the shock would not ordinarily harm a person, Billy died from the shock. The medical examiners determined that Billy's pacemaker malfunctioned as a result of the shock. If Billy's estate brings suit against Buck for wrongful death, Billy's estate will:

   A. Prevail, because Buck's electrical fence was the cause in fact of Billy's death.

   B. Prevail, because Buck cannot use deadly force to protect his property.

   C. Not prevail, because Billy was a trespasser.

   D. Not prevail, because Buck was not using unreasonably excessive force to protect his property.

16. Jeff experienced some difficulty when his washer broke while doing his laundry, flooding his basement. Jeff went to his neighbor, Sue, and borrowed her water pump to clean up the mess. Although Jeff pumped out all the water in his basement, he failed to return Sue's pump. Several months later, a heavy rainstorm hit and flooded Sue's garage. After several hours of looking for the pump, Sue remembered that she had loaned her pump to Jeff. By the time she went to Jeff's home, it was after dusk. Sue then remembered that Jeff was on a weekend gambling junket to Las Vegas and was not at home. Not wanting to wait until Jeff returned home, she forced Jeff's back door open and went into his house. Sue promptly left upon finding her pump. Did Sue commit a common law burglary?

   A. Yes, because she forced Jeff's back door open.

   B. Yes, because Jeff had legal possession of the pump until he returned it.

   C. No, because Jeff did not return the pump.

   D. No, because Sue entered to retrieve her own property.

17. Armor, an armored truck carrier service, was hired to pick up and deliver the Royal Crown Jewels to the Metropolitan Museum for an upcoming exhibition. Armor has been experiencing some difficulties within the last month. Its trucks have been ambushed and robbed several times, causing Armor to lose business. Armor hired Clint Westwood, a retired detective, to ride in the truck when the Royal Crown Jewels are being transported. Westwood is instructed to "shoot to kill" if necessary, to prevent a robbery. Armor picked up the Jewels and, while in transit, Felon forced the truck off the road and approached the truck with an automatic rifle. When Westwood saw Felon aim the rifle at him, he fired at Felon, killing him. Westwood is charged with homicide. Westwood will be found:

    A. Guilty of murder in the first degree, because he deliberately shot Felon.

    B. Guilty of murder in the second degree, because Westwood believed the killing was necessary.

    C. Guilty of involuntary manslaughter, because deadly force was used to protect personal property.

    D. Not guilty, if Westwood reasonably believed deadly force was necessary to prevent the robbery.

18. Amy, a sixteen-year-old student, wanted to make extra money for the upcoming school year. Amy decided to walk dogs after school and prepared flyers to advertise her services in the neighborhood. While passing out flyers door-to-door, advertising her new services, Amy met Wilbur. After talking with Amy for a few minutes, Wilbur decided to hire her to exercise his talking horse, Mr. Ed, every weekend afternoon. After a few weeks, Wilbur asked Amy if she could take care of Mr. Ed for an entire week, until the following Friday when he returned home from an unexpected business trip. Amy secretly decided to keep Mr. Ed for herself before agreeing to Wilbur's proposal. When Wilbur returned on Friday, he discovered that Amy had not returned Mr. Ed. Amy was later arrested when Mr. Ed telephoned authorities to report his whereabouts. If Amy is charged with larceny, she will most likely be found:

    A. Guilty, because Amy never returned Mr. Ed to Wilbur.

    B. Guilty, because Amy had a secret intent to keep Mr. Ed when she took the horse from Wilbur.

    C. Not Guilty, because Amy had legal possession.

    D. Not Guilty, because Amy was given possession of Mr. Ed without any fraudulent act or inducement.

Questions 19 – 23 are based on the following facts:

Bugs, the owner of Roach Coach, a mobile catering van, entered into a contract with Bart, the owner of Fresh Foods. Bugs and Bart signed a written contract on December 28. The contract provided that Roach Coach would purchase all their sandwich requirements from Fresh Foods for the following calendar year. The contract further provided that no specific purchase quantity was required, but only the daily requirements needed by Roach Coach at a fixed price of $20.00 per dozen, cash on delivery. During the first year, Fresh Foods had supplied Roach Coach with approximately seven dozen sandwiches per week.

19. On January 15 of the second year, Fresh Foods was notified of a rise in cost in production. Bart decided not to supply Roach Coach with any more sandwiches. Roach Coach brings a breach of contract action against Fresh Foods. If Fresh Foods argues that the contract is not binding because it lacks consideration, the court will find for:

    A. Fresh Foods, because all contracts must be supported by consideration

    B. Fresh Foods, because the contract is illusory.

    C. Roach Coach, because no consideration is needed for a requirements contract.

    D. Roach Coach, because Roach Coach's agreement to buy all the sandwiches that they required, and Fresh Foods' agreement to supply the same quantity, is sufficient consideration.

20. Assume for this question, that on January 30 of the second year, Bugs purchased two new mobile catering vans. This caused Roach Coach's sandwich requirements to escalate to 20 dozen sandwiches per week. Fresh has refused to supply Roach Coach with any more than seven dozen sandwiches per week. Roach Coach brings a breach of contract action against Fresh Foods. The court will find for:

    A. Fresh Foods, if the normal requirements of the original contract are seven dozen sandwiches a week.

    B. Fresh Foods, because Bug's increase in his requirements was not contemplated by the parties at the time of contracting.

    C. Roach Coach, because a valid requirements contract was formed.

    D. Roach Coach, because the purchase of the two mobile catering vans is a normal expansion.

21. Assume for this question, that in April, upon doing his taxes, Bugs realized that he was only netting $12,000.00 a year. This was primarily because he was only making a $.10 profit per sandwich. Bugs decided that the contract price for the sandwiches was too high and notified Bart, asking if Bart would lower the price to $17.00 a dozen. Bart refused. Bugs then decided to sell hot food only and stop selling sandwiches altogether. Fresh Foods brings a breach of contract action against Roach Coach. The court will find for:

    A. Fresh Foods, because Bugs' action of not selling sandwiches was not in good faith.

    B. Fresh Foods, because under the contract an agreement of seven dozen sandwiches a week was formed.

    C. Roach Coach, because Fresh Foods refused to lower the price to $17.00 a dozen when asked.

    D. Roach Coach, because a buyer, under a requirements contract, can eliminate his requirements for any reason.

22. Assume that Bugs sells his Roach Coach business to Ken and, as part of the sale, assigns all his rights and delegates his duties under the Roach Coach/Fresh Foods agreement to Ken. Fresh Foods is notified of the sale and assignment. Fresh Foods refuses to supply Ken with any sandwiches. If Ken brings an action against Fresh Foods seeking to be supplied with sandwiches, what result?

    A. Ken will be able to enforce the Roach Coach/Fresh Food agreement.

    B. Fresh Foods must supply Ken's requirements in an amount not unreasonably disproportionate to Bugs' requirements prior to the business sale.

    C. Fresh Foods has no obligation to supply Ken with sandwiches.

    D. Ken is entitled to be supplied with an increased number of sandwiches he requires as a con templated result of the anticipated improvement in management of the business.

23. Assume the same facts in question 22, except that when Bugs sold his Roach Coach business, Bugs, Bart and Ken all mutually agree to substitute Ken for Bugs in the Roach Coach/Fresh Foods agreement. Ken does not buy all the sandwich requirements through Fresh Foods, but rather buys half of his requirements through another sandwich maker. If Fresh Foods brings an action against Bugs, the court will find for:

    A. Fresh Foods, because it was a third party beneficiary to the Bugs/Ken sale agreement.

    B. Fresh Foods, because Bugs, the assignor, is still liable under the original contract.

    C. Bugs, because the sale of Roach Coach terminated any further obligations to purchase sandwiches from Fresh Foods.

    D. Bugs, because there was a novation.

Questions 24 – 27 are based on the following facts:

While in vacation in Colorado, Donald bought his daughter, Tiffany, a Slick Sled at Schwartz' Supplies ("Schwartz"). The sled was manufactured by Hemsley.

Tiffany and her friends took the sled to a large hill next to Donald's vacation home, where Tiffany and her friends rode the sled down the hill many times. Christopher, the older brother of Tiffany's friend, Suzy, asked if he could ride the sled down the mountain and show Tiffany how to maneuver between the trees. Tiffany handed the sled to Christopher who got onto the sled and started down the mountain. As he was whipping in and out between the trees, the metal runner on the sled snapped, causing Christopher to fall off the sled and strike his head on a rock. Christopher suffered severe head injuries from the accident. Tina, one of Tiffany's friends, saw the whole incident and became very ill and severely upset when she witnessed what happened to Christopher.

It was determined that although most sled manufacturers used steel runners, which is a much stronger metal than that used by Hemsley, the use of steel would increase the manufacturing cost of each sled by about $2.25.

24. If Christopher brings an action against Hemsley based on the theory of strict liability to recover for his injuries:

A. Christopher will recover, because most sled manufacturers used a different metal to make the ski on the sled.

B. Christopher will recover, if use of the weaker metal used by Hemsley resulted in the sled being unreasonably dangerous.

C. Christopher will not recover, because he was not the purchaser of the sled.

D. Christopher will not recover, because he was contributorily negligent.

25. If Christopher brings an action against Schwartz based on the theory of strict liability, Christopher will:

A. Not Prevail, because Schwartz was not the manufacturer of the product.

B. Not prevail, because Christopher was not in privity of contract with Schwartz.

C. Prevail, only if the sled was defective.

D. Prevail, but only if Schwartz could have discovered the defect.

26. If Christopher brings an action against Schwartz based on the theory of negligence, Christopher will:

A. Prevail, because the sled was defective and unreasonably dangerous.

B. Prevail, but only if Schwartz could have discovered the defect by a reasonable inspection.

C. Not prevail, because Christopher was not an intended user of the sled.

D. Not Prevail, because Schwartz owed no duty of care to Christopher.

27. If Tina asserts a claim against Hemsley based on strict liability in tort, Tina will:

A. Prevail, because she witnessed the accident.

B. Prevail, but only if the sled was defective and unreasonably dangerous.

C. Not prevail, because Tina was not using the sled.

D. Not Prevail, if she suffered no harm other than becoming very ill and severely upset.

Questions 28 – 30 are based on the following facts:

Al Bundy, a shoe salesman, was tired of his wife Peggy. Peggy would sit around the house all day, eat bonbons, and watch soap operas. When Al would arrive home from work, he would come home to an uncooked meal and the nagging of "Peg." Overhearing plans to kill Peggy between Marcey, a neighbor who also hated Peggy, and her friend, Jefferson, Al left open the bedroom window that Marcey and Jefferson had planned to use to enter the Bundy home, then stab Peggy. The murder was to take place while Al was at the car dealer getting his Dodge repaired. Later that evening, Jefferson went to the Bundy house. Jefferson was extremely nervous because it was his first murder and he could not stand the sight of blood. Instead of stabbing Peggy, he took a broom laying outside the Bundy home, soaked it in gasoline, ignited it and threw it through the open window. Peggy died while in panic trying to escape from the fire to her bed coverings that were ignited by the broom. After the fire was extinguished, the only damage to the structure was smoke discoloration to the walls in the bedroom.

28. If Al is prosecuted for the murder of Peggy, he should be found:

    A. Guilty, because he opened the window to permit access to the Bundy home.

    B. Guilty, because the actus reus was performed by Jefferson.

    C. Not guilty, because Peggy was not killed as originally planned.

    D. Not guilty, because the agreement to kill Peggy was between Jefferson and Marcey.

29. If Jefferson is prosecuted for common law burglary, he should be found:

    A. Guilty, because he committed a felony therein.

    B. Guilty, because he threw a flaming broom through the open window and set Peggy's bed coverings on fire.

    C. Not guilty, because he never entered the house.

    D. Not guilty, because he did not commit a breaking.

30. If Jefferson is prosecuted for arson, he should be found:

    A. Guilty, since he inserted the flaming broom into the house.

    B. Guilty, since he had the specific intent to commit a felony therein.

    C. Not guilty, because there was no burning to the structure.

    D. Not guilty, because arson is a specific intent crime.

31. Eric telephones Lovejoy Antiques to determine whether his 15th Century wooden table can be refurbished to its original condition. Lovejoy asks Eric to bring it by his shop for inspection. When Eric does, Lovejoy recognizes the table as part of some antique furniture stolen from the inventory of a local auction warehouse. After telling Eric that he knows the table is stolen, he agrees to refurbish the table for $500.00, payable upon the sale of the table. This is twice his regular price for similar work. Eric and Lovejoy were arrested after an undercover police officer "bought" the table at Eric's garage sale for $2,000.00. If Lovejoy is charged with the crime of conspiracy to sell stolen goods, the verdict will be:

   A. Not guilty, because only Eric had the table for sale.

   B. Not guilty, because Lovejoy's business of refurbishing furniture is not illegal.

   C. Guilty, because Lovejoy had knowledge the table he was refurbishing was stolen.

   D. Guilty, because he agreed to be paid $500.00 for the refurbishing of the table upon its sale.

Questions 32 – 33 are based on the following facts:

Hugo and George were two of the top students at a nationally-acclaimed drama school, each vying for the lead male role in the school's version of West Side Story. Hugo succeeds in being nominated for the lead role, while George is given a much lesser role. George physically confronts Hugo in the Drama School parking lot between scenes and a fight ensues between them. Hugo strikes George over the head with a copy of the script during the fight, resulting in a concussion and loss of consciousness to George. George's attorney files a lawsuit against Hugo and Drama School to recover for George's injuries.

32. Will George be successful in his claim against Hugo?

   A. Yes, if Hugo intended to strike George with the script.

   B. Yes, because Hugo failed to retreat.

   C. No, unless Hugo used unreasonably excessive force.

   D. No, if George was unusually susceptible to concussions.

33. Who will prevail in George's lawsuit against Drama School?

   A. Drama School, if George actually started the fight.

B. Drama School, unless it did not use reasonable care in supervising the school's premises.

C. George, because he was injured at Drama School's premises.

D. George, because the fight took place between scenes.

Questions 34 – 35 are based on the following facts:

Phil, a paparazzi photographer, photographs Gear Grind, a famous car racer, driving a Nogo convertible one sunny weekend. Because the top is down, Gear can be seen wearing a broad smile and appears to be enjoying himself. Phil sells the photograph to Pleasure Journal ("Pleasure"), a publication devoted to photographs of famous people having fun, and the photograph appears in the next edition.

Nogo obtains a copy of the photograph and enlarges it for a national billboard advertising campaign. The billboard advertisement states, "The fun goes where you go in a Nogo!" Many of the billboard advertisements are erected before Gear discovers the use of his picture. He immediately contacts Nogo and demands that the ad campaign be terminated.

34. Gear sues Nogo for its use of his photograph on the billboard advertisements. Who will prevail?

    A. Gear, if he did not agree to the use of his picture for the advertisements.

    B. Gear, if his picture was taken without consent.

    C. Nogo, because Gear was already a public figure.

D. Nogo, because the photograph of Gear had already been published in Pleasure Journal.

35. Who will prevail in Gear's lawsuit against Pleasure Journal?

A. Gear, if his picture was published without consent.

B. Gear, because Pleasure Journal profited from publishing the photograph of Gear.

C. Pleasure Journal, because Gear was photographed in a public place.

D. Pleasure Journal, if Gear benefited from receiving commercial endorsements as a result of his photograph appearing in the publication.

36. While Julia was taking her daily walk in her neighborhood, she found the original Diary of Anne Frank, with a bookmark between the pages containing the name and address of the book's owner. Julia threw away the bookmark, but kept the book because she remembered hearing about it at school and believed that she would make a lot of money selling the original version. What crime, if any, did Julia commit?

A. No crime, because Julia obtained possession of the diary in a lawful manner.

B. Uttering, because Julia did not believe the book was actually the original version, but instead was a forgery.

C. Larceny, because Julia intentionally kept the book instead of returning it to the owner.

D. Embezzlement, because Julia's possession was lawful at the time she formed the intent to keep the diary.

37. Wayne was an avid long-distance bicycle racer who had entered a grueling 100-mile race to be held the following weekend in a neighboring state. On his way home from having the local bicycle shop perform a pre-race "tune-up" to his bicycle, Wayne's bicycle became dislodged from the rack on his car, allowing the bicycle to fall to the roadway. Several cars ran it over before he was able to remove it from the roadway, resulting in severe damage to the bicycle.

Upon his return home, he called his friend, Chuck, and asked Chuck to loan his bicycle to him for "a little exercise" on the weekend. Knowing that he could not return the bicycle until Monday, Wayne told Chuck that he would return the bicycle on Sunday. Wayne never returned Chuck's bicycle and never contacted Chuck again for any reason. If Wayne is arrested and charged with larceny of Chuck's bicycle, will he be convicted?

A. Yes, because Wayne first lawfully obtained possession of property, then later converted it unlawfully.

B. Yes, because Wayne never returned the bicycle.

C. No, because Chuck gave possession of the bicycle to Wayne voluntarily.

D. No, because the actus reus and mens rea did not concur at the same time.

Questions 38 – 41 are based on the following facts:

Dave was a famous comedian who was best known for his impressions of historical public figures that were spiced up by acting out the characters in humorous situations. His most famous character was a cross-dressing J. Edgar Hoover. Dave was booked for five weeks at The Comedy Stop by Conan, the owner of the club. Three days before he was scheduled to appear at Comedy Stop on Monday, Dave was struck on the head and suffered amnesia. Dave's doctor advised Conan that Dave would not be able to perform because he had forgotten his entire act.

Conan immediately overnight mails identical letters to Arsenio and Jay, two nationally known stand-up comedians, stating:

> *"Dave cannot perform at my club as scheduled because he has amnesia. His act is scheduled to start in three days and I have nobody to replace him. I need a comedy act right away and will pay your normal appearance fee. Be here by Sunday so that I can see a dry run of your act before opening curtain.*
>
> *signed . . . Conan"*

Jay receives the letter at his Burbank offices and sends Conan a reply by way of telegram stating: "Thanks, I've just ended an appearance at Las Vegas and currently have no other commitments, but I hope you provide me limousine service during my stay this time. Will arrive at the club Saturday morning. Sincerely, Jay." After Conan had sent the letter, but before he received Jay's reply, Dave called Conan and told Conan that his memory had returned and would be performing his act as scheduled. Conan then telephoned Jay and told him that Jay would not have to fill in for Dave because Dave's memory had returned.

38. Jay brings an action against Conan and Conan raises the defense that there was no valid acceptance of Conan's offer. Will Jay prevail?

    A. Yes, because Conan did not revoke his offer by the same method he communicated the offer.

    B. Yes, because Jay sent a telegram stating his acceptance prior to Conan's attempt to revoke the offer.

    C. No, because there was uncertainty in the salary term.

    D. No, because Jay's request for a limousine constituted a counteroffer which Conan was free to reject.

39. Because Conan sent the identical letter to Jay and Arsenio, and he only needed one act in place of Dave, Conan claims that the letter cannot be construed by Jay to be an offer. Will he prevail on this argument?

    A. No, if Jay was unaware of Conan's mailing of the letter to Arsenio.

    B. No, if Jay and Arsenio insist on working for the Comedy Stop.

    C. Yes, because Conan's intent was to hire only one act to replace Dave.

    D. Yes, because Conan, as offeror, is the master of his offer.

40. Assume that a valid contract was created between Conan and Jay, but Conan no longer wants Jay to perform at the Comedy Stop because of Dave's recovery, unless he accepts a much smaller part warming up the audience with a monologue before Dave's act begins. Dave will be paid $25,000.00 per week for his performance and Jay's normal weekly fee is $15,000.00. Conan offers to pay Jay $2,500.00 per week for the monologues. Jay refuses to accept the lesser work and less than $15,000.00 as his fee, and is unable to obtain other work during the five-week run of Dave's act. How much may Jay recover from Conan per week?

    A. $25,000.00

    B. $15,000.00

    C. $12,500.00

    D. $0

41. Arsenio arrives at the Comedy Stop on Sunday, after receiving the letter from Conan on Saturday. He was unaware of the identical letter to Jay and did not notify Conan of his intentions in advance of his arrival at the club. Conan said, "You're too little too late. Dave is funnier than you and he recovered last night, so he'll be performing at the club. I only sent the letter to you because I was in a bind, and I didn't expect you to come without letting me know." Who will prevail if Arsenio sues Conan?

   A. Conan, because a return promise is the only valid method of accepting an offer.

   B. Conan, because a reasonable interpretation of his letter would be that Arsenio was required to accept by way of a timely return promise.

   C. Arsenio, because Conan's letter could be reasonably interpreted to invite acceptance by performance or return promise.

   D. Arsenio, because there was no revocation by Conan before Arsenio had commenced performance.

Questions 42 – 43 are based on the following facts:

Marilyn visited Outpatient Plastic Surgery Clinic ("Clinic") for a rhinoplasty to be performed by Dr. Picasso. After Marilyn was given general anesthesia, and unconscious, Dr. Picasso performed an abdominal liposuction instead. The liposuction was performed because an unidentified employee of Clinic mixed-up Marilyn's chart with the chart of another patient. The mistake was not discovered until after the wrong procedure to Marilyn was completed.

42. If Marilyn sues Dr. Picasso, who will prevail?

   A. Dr. Picasso, unless Marilyn establishes that the doctor was negligent for not verifying her identity.

   B. Dr. Picasso, because he was not responsible for the chart mix-up.

   C. Marilyn, for battery.

   D. Marilyn, for negligence, under the doctrine of res ipsa loquitur.

43. If Marilyn also asserts a personal injury claim against Clinic, who will prevail?

   A. Clinic, unless Marilyn can establish vicarious liability for Dr. Picasso's conduct.

   B. Clinic, because it is without fault.

C. Marilyn, for battery.

D. Marilyn, for negligence, under the doctrine of res ipsa loquitur.

44. Wayne takes his violin to Charles' Violin Shop to have the instrument restrung. After the work was completed, Charles confuses it with another instrument he has for sale and the instrument is sold to Richard for $400.00. Richard believed the violin was owned by Charles at the time of his purchase. When Wayne returns to pick up his instrument, Charles realizes his mistake. If Wayne sues Charles and Richard for conversion, Wayne will be successful against:

A. Richard only, due to his negligence in verifying ownership prior to his purchase.

B. Richard only, because Charles' act is considered mere intermeddling with the violin.

C. Charles only, because Charles was in the best position to authenticate ownership of Wayne's violin.

D. Charles and Richard, because they both have exercised dominion over the violin.

45. George was traveling cross country in his new motor home with the goal of visiting all forty-eight contiguous states before his next birthday. Near the end of the first day of his trip, he came across Marcee, who told George that her car had broken down and that she needed a ride. Not believing Marcee would reimburse him for the expense, George refused to give Marcee a ride back to the nearest town, which he had passed fifty miles earlier. Marcee almost dies from exhaustion and hunger while walking back to town, and requires hospitalization for several weeks, in order to recover. If Marcee sues George to recover for her injuries and damages, who will prevail?

A. George, if he reasonably believed that Marcee would not reimburse him for the expense of returning her to town.

B. George, unless there was a special relationship between George and Marcee.

C. Marcee, if the likelihood of harm to her was greater than the likelihood that she would not reimburse George.

D. Marcee, if she would not have been injured "but for" George's refusal to drive her to town.

46. Larry Liftit is caught stealing a wallet from the pocket of Phil, an off-duty police officer. At time of trial on the charge of larceny, Larry testifies that he had been so intoxicated at the time he took the wallet that he could not have formed the intent to commit the crime. When the jury is instructed on the burden of proof, they should be advised that:

    A. The prosecution must establish beyond a reasonable doubt that Larry had the capacity to form the necessary intent.

    B. The prosecution must establish by clear and convincing evidence that Larry had the capacity to form the necessary intent.

    C. The defendant must establish his diminished capacity by a preponderance of the evidence.

    D. The defendant must establish his diminished capacity by clear and convincing evidence.

Questions 47 – 49 are based on the following facts:

On January 1, Mr. Trumpery entered into a written contract to buy Mr. Ellis' mansion for $2.5 million. Mr. Trumpery requested to delay the closing of the sale until March 15, at which time payment was to be made in exchange for the deed to the property.

47. Assume for this question, that Mr. Ellis conveys the mansion to Mr. Mapple on February 15. Mr. Trumpery now wants to take advantage of Mr. Ellis' conveyance to Mr. Mapple as a reason to get out of his contract with Mr. Ellis so that he may buy a much more modest home and use the remainder of the money to quietly retire in Florida. Is Mr. Trumpery still obligated to perform his contract with Mr. Ellis?

    A. Yes, because Mr. Ellis could still purchase the property back from Mr. Mapple and be able to provide the deed to Mr. Trumpery on March 15.

    B. Yes, because Mr. Ellis is not due to perform until March 15, which means there is no breach until such date, and Mr. Trumpery must remain ready to perform on the contract until then.

    C. No, if Mr. Ellis did not protect Mr. Trumpery's rights as part of the sale of the property.

D. No, but Mr. Trumpery must demand assurance from Mr. Ellis that he will perform on March 15.

48. Assume instead, that on February 15, Mr. Ellis merely tells Mr. Trumpery that he no longer intends to sell his mansion and that he will not convey the deed on March 15. May Mr. Trumpery immediately assert an action for breach of contract?

    A. Yes, because Mr. Ellis' statement was a repudiation of the contract, which permits the immediate filing of litigation by Mr. Trumpery.

    B. Yes, but only if Mr. Ellis has contracted with a new buyer of the property.

    C. No, because Mr. Ellis is not obligated to perform until March 15, so there can be no breach until such date.

    D. No, because Mr. Ellis might retract his repudiation before March 15.

49. Assume for this question, that Mr. Ellis did not deliver or tender the deed on March 15. May Mr. Trumpery bring an immediate action against Mr. Ellis to recover his damages for breach of contract?

    A. No, because he must make a formal written demand for Mr. Ellis' compliance with the contract terms.

    B. Yes, but Mr. Trumpery must have paid the $2.5 million on March 15.

    C. Yes, if Mr. Trumpery tendered payment of the $2.5 million on March 15.

    D. Yes, whether or not Mr. Trumpery either tendered payment or actually paid the $2.5 million on March 15.

Questions 50 – 51 are based on the following facts:

Carl, an assassin, obtained a job as a security guard in an office building because he knew Brandon, his target, worked in the building. After determining Brandon's schedule, Carl intended to kill Brandon as he left work one day. Carl set up an ambush and fired his gun at Brandon, missing him and striking Daniel, but only causing a slight injury to him. Daniel turned around when he was struck and observed Brandon walking with only a briefcase in his hand. Believing it was Brandon who shot him, Daniel severely beat Brandon.

50. Is Carl guilty of attempted murder of Daniel?

    A. Yes, because Carl had the requisite malice aforethought and premeditation.

    B. Yes, because Carl attempted to kill Brandon.

    C. No, because Carl did not intend to kill Daniel.

    D. No, because Daniel received only a slight injury.

51. Is Daniel guilty of battery upon Brandon?

    A. Yes, because Brandon had not committed any crime.

    B. Yes, because Daniel intentionally beat up Brandon.

    C. No, if Daniel reasonably believed Brandon attempted to kill him.

    D. No, if Daniel acted with an imperfect self-defense believing that he was shot by Brandon.

Questions 52 – 53 are based on the following facts:

As a result of negligence, Boyd was involved in a motor vehicle accident with a truck owned by Acme Retail Stores ("Acme"). The property damage to Acme's truck cost $10,000.00 to repair. Risk Managers ("Risk") was a company that operated as third party risk adjusters for business clients, including Acme, which was without its own risk management department. Zeke was the President of Risk. At the time Acme hired Risk to collect money for the property damage from Boyd, Zeke intended to use the money to extinguish a joint debt of Zeke and Risk that was incurred to purchase computers for Risk. An employee of Risk collected the $10,000.00, which was used by Zeke to extinguish the joint debt, less Risk's fees for collecting the money from Boyd. Zeke intended to pay Acme for Boyd's debt when he returned from his Las Vegas vacation in three weeks.

52. What, if any, theft crime was committed by Zeke?

    A. No crime, because the employee of Risk who collected the money was an innocent agent of Risk who did not have the necessary mens rea to commit a crime.

    B. False pretenses from Boyd, because Zeke intended to use the money for his own benefit at the time it was collected from Boyd.

    C. Embezzlement from Acme, because Acme entrusted its money to Risk.

    D. Larceny from Acme, because Zeke intended to keep the money for his own use at the time it was collected from Boyd.

53. If Zeke has committed a crime under the facts above, can Risk also be convicted of the same crime?

    A. No, because Risk, as a corporation, is a fictitious business entity that cannot be sent to prison.

    B. No, because a corporation cannot form the specific intent necessary for conviction.

    C. No, unless there is a contemporaneous conviction of Zeke for the same offense.

    D. Yes, because Zeke was the President of Risk.

54. After years of doing his own taxes, Norm retained Vera, a tax accountant, to prepare his federal tax return because of the increasingly complex federal tax rules. Vera told Norm that he could deduct certain business expenses from the operation of his bar, The Beer Tavern, although she knew her advice was incorrect. Norm signed and filed the erroneous tax return with the Internal Revenue Service. If the U.S. Attorney prosecutes Norm for willful income tax evasion, does he have a valid defense for following his tax accountant's advice?

A. No, if Vera knew her advice was erroneous.

B. Yes, because Norm only signed and filed the tax return.

C. Yes, because the income tax return was prepared by Norm's tax accountant.

D. Yes, if Norm had a reasonable and good faith reliance upon Vera's advice.

55. Hal was hiking in the wilderness in the mountains near his home when he found another hiker, Vic, apparently injured from exposure to the elements. Hal picked Vic up and carried him several miles before coming upon Patrick, who was using a cellular telephone to talk to his stockbroker about some of his investments. When Patrick refused to call for assistance for Vic, Hal drew his knife and threatened to harm Patrick, unless he agreed to let Hal use the telephone. Patrick immediately hung up and permitted Hal to call for assistance. Hal is now being prosecuted for assault with a deadly weapon. Did Hal have any privilege to threaten Patrick with harm?

A. No, if Hal did not know Vic.

B. No, unless there was a special statute in the jurisdiction establishing such privilege.

C. Yes, because Hal was privileged to use deadly force to rescue Vic if necessary to save Vic's life.

D. Yes, because Hal was privileged to threaten the use of deadly force if reasonably necessary to save Vic's life.

Questions 56 – 58 are based on the following facts:

Bill Brown and his wife, Alicia, had decided to purchase a larger home because their family has grown to include three children in the ten years they have been married, and because their income had steadily improved during the same period of time. After deciding on a spacious custom home in a new development across town, they both signed a written contract to buy the home for $300,000.00 with Cathy, who was the developer. The contract stated that the Browns would purchase the home "as long as they sell their present home for $175,000.00 cash, and obtain a new loan within the next 90 days."

56. Because the home the Browns intended to purchase was a bargain price and because Cathy decided against possibly waiting for 90 days to receive the sale proceeds, she told the Browns the sale was off the following day – before the Browns had even put their present home up for sale. Mr. and Mrs. Brown filed a lawsuit against Cathy for breach of contract, but Cathy raised the defense that there was no consideration for the contract. Will she be successful with this defense?

    A. No, because Cathy's promise to sell the new home was consideration for the Browns' promise to sell their present home.

    B. No, because within the Browns' promise to buy the home from Cathy is a condition the Browns make a good faith effort to find a buyer for their present home.

    C. Yes, because the Browns' promise to sell their home within 90 days was not within Cathy's nor the Browns' control.

    D. Yes, because the Browns had not changed their position in reliance on Cathy's promise to sell.

57. For this question, assume that the Browns have not put their home on the market and have refused to purchase the new home from Cathy. Cathy files a lawsuit and presents evidence that the Browns could have found a buyer for their home who would have paid $175,000.00 at the close of escrow. Who will prevail?

    A. Cathy, because the condition of the Browns' promise to sell their present home at the stated terms was excused by their refusal to make it occur.

    B. Cathy, because the terms of the sale of the Browns' home was not a condition but a promise.

    C. The Browns, because the condition of the Browns' promise to sell their home at the stated terms did not occur.

D. The Browns, because they did not make any promise to actually locate a buyer for their home.

58. For this question, assume that the Browns will not follow through on the purchase of the new home from Cathy. When Cathy sues, the Browns defend by asserting the parties had orally agreed that the Browns' obligation to buy the new home was conditioned upon the Browns being able to purchase a small strip of land adjacent to their property so that there was enough space to construct a two-car garage for the home. The written contract was silent on the issue of purchasing the adjacent land. The Browns were unsuccessful in purchasing the adjacent property. When the Browns offered evidence of the condition at trial, Cathy objected on grounds that it violated the Parol Evidence Rule. What is the best argument to avoid prohibiting the evidence on the basis of the Parol Evidence Rule?

   A. The evidence was provided to show a modification of the written contract.

   B. The evidence would be offered to clear up an ambiguity in the written contract.

   C. Evidence of an oral agreement may be offered to establish an oral condition to an integrated written contract.

   D. The written contract was not integrated.

Questions 59 – 60 are based on the following facts:

Dr. Lindy was a veterinarian who believed a pet's fitness was just as important as his owner's fitness. In furtherance of his beliefs, Dr. Lindy regularly jogged several miles in the morning before going into the office, and always with his dog, Flash. The runs took place on Dr. Lindy's thirty-acre estate that was surrounded by chain-link fencing.

One morning as Dr. Lindy and Flash were on their run, Marlon drove by in his car, which was running poorly, when it suddenly backfired loudly. This caused Flash to knock down a section of the 7-foot high perimeter fence. Maggie, who was walking past Dr. Lindy's estate, was bitten by Flash when the dog escaped. There is a statute in the jurisdiction that states all non-commercial passenger vehicles must be in a state of proper tune.

59. If Maggie sues Dr. Lindy for his injuries, who will prevail?

    A. Dr. Lindy, unless Flash had previously displayed a propensity to bite.

    B. Dr. Lindy, unless he was negligent in not preventing Flash's escape.

    C. Maggie, because she was bitten by Dr. Lindy's dog.

    D. Maggie, because Flash escaped from Dr. Lindy's control.

60. If Maggie sues Marlon for her injuries resulting from the dog bite, who will prevail?

    A. Marlon, because the easily-knocked-down fence was an independent, intervening act.

    B. Marlon, because preventing Maggie's dog bite injury was not within the statutory purpose.

    C. Maggie, because of Marlon's violation of statute.

    D. Maggie, because the backfiring caused Flash to escape.

Questions 61 – 62 are based on the following facts:

Sergeant Monday was a detective working bunko division for a major metropolitan police department. Jimmy the Rat, an informant, who has always provided reliable information to Monday, tells Monday that a major crime ring is operating in the west side of the city. The "M.O." of the ring, headed by Cal Worthless, is to set up a valet parking service at established businesses, operating legitimately for a short period of time. Then, at an appropriate date, the car's owners are all swindled out of their vehicles because they are unaware that they have "voluntarily" handed their cars over to the "criminal element." Because of his success in the past, Cal has become so brazen as to take advance orders for vehicles.

Jimmy identifies Cal's current location for Monday so that contact can be made. Monday meets with Cal and "orders" a late model black-and-white Ford sedan, with low mileage and a V-8 engine. One week later, Cal contacts Monday, telling him he has obtained the car. Cal is arrested when he hands the keys over to Monday.

61. If Cal claims the defense of entrapment, will he succeed?

    A. No, because Cal's business was an ongoing criminal enterprise.

    B. No, because Cal was predisposed to take the Ford.

    C. Yes, because Monday unilaterally contacted Cal for a vehicle.

    D. Yes, because Jimmy obtained his information without disclosing that he was an agent of law enforcement.

62. Assume instead, that upon meeting Cal, Monday thought he was a "real sleazeball" who could be convinced to sell some heroin for Monday, which would result in a longer jail sentence than the crimes discussed above. Cal states that he has some contacts and will be able to unload whatever amount of heroin Monday provides. When Cal "buys" his share for distribution, he is arrested. If Cal claims the defense of entrapment under these facts, will he succeed?

    A No, because Cal agreed to sell the heroin.

    B. Yes, if it is reasonably likely that a reasonable person would have purchased the heroin from Monday under the same circumstances.

    C. Yes, because confidence in the police force would otherwise be undermined.

    D. Yes, because the violation of Cal's due process rights, however slight, underlies the defense.

63. Columbo was driving home from the opera early one winter evening when it started to snow. Because the visibility was reduced to an unsafe distance, he decided to stop at The Lieutenant, a restaurant near the opera house, so that he could get some dinner and wait out the storm. At the door, he was requested to check his coat by the maitre d', obtaining a ticket in return. Columbo's coat, while not very valuable, had a lot of sentimental value to him. The ticket, which was read by Columbo, disclaimed liability for any loss or damage to the coat. By the time he had finished his dinner, the storm had let up, and Columbo decided to leave for home. When Columbo presented the ticket and requested his coat, the coat could not be located by the coat clerk. If Columbo brings a conversion action, who will prevail?

   A. The Lieutenant, because the express disclaimer of liability resulted in a waiver of Columbo's rights.

   B. The Lieutenant, if its method of coat check operations maintained reasonable procedures to prevent losses or theft of the checked coats.

   C. Columbo, since the restaurant was unable to return Columbo's coat.

   D. Columbo, unless there was no intrinsic value in the coat.

Questions 64 – 67 are based on the following facts:

Chaulky Cullen, a 5-year-old child movie star, was attending the taping of the David Leatherman show as one of David's guests. Chaulky was brought to David's studio by his mother, Misty Cullen. Because David is very good with children, he frequently has children as guests on his show. Always trying quirky (but usually funny) bits to keep David's show interesting, his director has set up an unusual method of entry for his guests. The method consists of lowering a large cage from the ceiling, out of which the guest steps onto the set. The cage and its mechanism was designed, built and maintained by SBC Enterprises ("SBC"). The studio in which the "cage" and the David Leatherman Show's set is situated is owned by Late Night Productions ("Late Night"). As Chaulky was making his entrance, the cage rapidly dropped to the ground, injuring him. David quickly removed Chaulky from the cage and telephoned for emergency medical care. Chaulky brings an action for personal injury, through his guardian ad litem, against David and SBC.

64. Will Chaulky prevail against David?

   A. No, because the primary duty to supervise Chaulky was by his mother, Misty.

   B. No, unless David failed to exercise reasonable care removing Chaulky from the cage.

C. Yes, because David had a non-delegable duty to make the cage safe.

D. Yes, because Chaulky was a business invitee of the premises.

65. Assume for this question, that the pulley mechanism for the cage was improperly manufactured by SBC, which resulted in the inability to slow the descending cage. On which theories will Chaulky prevail against SBC?

A. Negligence only.

B. Strict products liability only.

C. Strict products liability and strict liability for abnormally dangerous condition.

D. Negligence and strict products liability.

66. Assume that Chaulky suffered from a congenital bone defect that rendered his skeleton susceptible to fracture. As a result of his congenital defect, Chaulky's leg was shattered, requiring a long period of recovery. During the extended recovery period, Chaulky is unable to complete his latest film, "At Home in New York," for which he was to be paid $2 million had he not incurred the injuries. Chaulky is replaced by an unknown young actor, and the film is completed without him, and without paying him the $2 million. Will Chaulky be entitled to recover the $2 million as damages, if David or SBC are found liable?

A. Yes, unless Chaulky's inability to complete the film was the result of an unforeseeable injury.

B. Yes, if the $2 million loss of income was the result of his injuries.

C. No, because as a "thin skull" plaintiff, Chaulky's loss of earnings must be reduced to reflect the probability of a shortened career.

D. No, because Chaulky's congenital defect was a pre-existing condition.

67. If Chaulky obtains a judgment against Late Night and SBC, and Late Night pays the entire judgment, is Late Night entitled to recover any portion of the amount paid from SBC?

A. Yes, because the manufacturer of a product is liable for all proximately caused losses resulting from a defect in its product.

B. Yes, unless Late Night was actively negligent.

C. Yes, because property owners are always entitled to indemnification for the torts of an independent contractor where its duty is non-delegable.

D. No, because plaintiff may choose which, if any, of the "deep pocket" defendants who he wants to proceed against.

68. Late one night in Old Goats Tavern, three unemployed security guards, Bonnie, Clyde, and Ben, were discussing a plan to obtain funds for relocating to the midwest from the east coast. None of them had worked for over six months, resulting in all of them being down to their last few dollars. Wanting to avoid being "street people," they decided to rob the Metropolitan Museum of several famous art works. Ben told Bonnie and Clyde that he would have nothing to do with the actual heist, but would secret them away on his boat once the job was completed. He told Bonnie and Clyde that he could earn his money legitimately this way, and would charge $10,000.00 for the service, payable at time of departure. Bonnie and Clyde steal the art works, immediately fence one Renaissance master painting for $10,000.00 and use the money to pay for their passage on Ben's boat. Has Ben committed any crime?

A. Yes, as a principal in the first degree.

B. Yes, as a principal in the second degree.

C. Yes, as an accessory after the fact.

D. No, because he did not participate in any stage of committing the theft.

Questions 69 – 70 are based on the following facts:

Alfred was taking a late walk one night when he was approached by Batman and Robin. Batman told Alfred that his sons, Bruce and Dick, were being held hostage and would not be released unless Alfred did as he was told. Alfred had no reason to believe Batman's statement was not true. Robin handed Alfred a canister of "Batgas" which, if discharged, can cause nausea, vomiting, and even death. Robin told Alfred to take the Batgas to the meeting of the Philanthropic Society, which was flush with cash from a recent fundraiser, and steal the cash. He also told Alfred, "If you don't do as we say, Robin and I will 'WHAM!' your sons." Alfred went into the society's offices and threatened the staff with the Batgas. A security guard at the society drew his gun and pointed it at Alfred. Alfred dropped the can and was placed in custody until the Gotham City Police Department arrived to arrest him. Alfred is charged with robbery.

69. Alfred will be found:

    A. Guilty, because Alfred intended to obtain the money.

    B. Guilty, because the threat of harm was to third parties.

    C. Not guilty, because he did not complete the robbery.

    D. Not guilty, because Alfred was threatened with harm to a member of his family.

70. Assume for this question that Batman and Robin are charged with attempted robbery. They will be found:

    A. Guilty, there was the requisite meeting of the minds.

    B. Guilty, because Wharton's Rule is irrelevant.

    C. Not guilty, because neither actually committed the act.

    D. Not guilty, because Alfred never completed the robbery.

71. Martha was a confirmed junk food addict and often ate her meals at fast food restaurants, including her favorite, Wiener Hut. One morning, while on her way to work, she stopped at the drive-thru window to order her favorite menu item, scrambled eggs and wienies. After paying for her order, she was given a bag containing her food by the cashier. As Martha drove away, she opened the bag and found not only her meal, but the prior day's receipts. Martha drove off without returning the money. What crime, if any, did Martha commit?

    A. Larceny.

    B. Larceny by trick.

    C. Embezzlement.

    D. None of the above.

72. Dan and Roseanne purchased a home in the new neighborhood, in a developing community, called Bluecollar, which was named for the town's largest employer, a denim manufacturer. Adjacent to their home was the one of the few restaurants in town, a sushi bar, which was not very popular. In order to increase business, Ito, the restaurant's owner, set up a Karaoke machine (which amplified both recorded music and the singer's voice) and marketed the Karaoke as "fabulous family entertainment."

The Karaoke resulted in bringing in a lot of business for Ito. Although there were now long waits and large crowds at the sushi bar, it was the loud, off-key howling of the Karaoke singers that disrupted the solitude of Dan and Roseanne into the late hours each night. Prior to Ito's offering of the Karaoke, a local ordinance was passed prohibiting amplified music in restaurants and bars within town limits. Dan and Roseanne ask Ito to cease the "entertainment." If Dan and Roseanne file a nuisance action against Ito, will they prevail?

A. Yes, because Ito is violating the ordinance.

B. Yes, because Dan and Roseanne will suffer a substantial and unreasonable harm in the use and enjoyment of their land.

C. No, because Dan and Roseanne assumed the risk of being annoyed by the operation of Ito's restaurant by coming to the nuisance.

D. No, unless the annoying sounds are accompanied by trespass by Ito's patrons.

Questions 73 – 75 are based on the following facts:

After failing to obtain a promotion to the level of production manager for The Daily Planner, the manufacturer of time management materials, Jimmy decided to work even harder in the hopes of earning a future promotion. However, on the day that he learned that he was not selected for promotion, he watched as the new production manager, Clark, left for a workout at the gym with the plant foreman, Lois, which upset him very much.

Following Clark and Lois from a distance to avoid detection, Jimmy watched as Clark and Lois entered the gym holding hands. Infuriated, he wanted to scare Clark by driving his car at him at full speed, then turn away suddenly once he was close to Clark.

73. When Jimmy drove his car at Clark, Clark was able to jump out of the path of the vehicle, except for Clark's gym bag that was knocked out of his hand when it was struck by the front fender of Jimmy's car. Which crimes did Jimmy commit?

    A. Attempted murder, assault with a deadly weapon, and battery.

    B. Attempted murder and assault with a deadly weapon.

    C. Assault with a deadly weapon, and battery.

    D. Battery.

74. If Clark was struck and killed by Jimmy's car, what is the most serious crime of which Jimmy will be convicted?

    A. Involuntary manslaughter.

    B. Voluntary manslaughter.

    C. Second degree murder.

    D. First degree murder.

75. Assume for this question, that Jimmy intentionally ran over Lois believing that if he did not get the promotion, neither should Lois. Unknown to him, Lois was pregnant with Clark's baby. Although Lois survived, the baby did not. Will Jimmy be found guilty if charged with homicide of the baby?

    A. Yes, of first degree murder since he intended to kill Lois.

    B. Yes, of involuntary manslaughter based upon the transferred intent doctrine.

    C. Yes, of first degree murder since confirmation of Lois' pregnancy is medically feasible.

    D. No, because a fetus is not a living "human being."

Questions 76 – 79 are based on the following facts:

As Ruth approached her eighteenth birthday, she decided to sell the car she has owned since her sixteenth birthday. Although Sandra is 10 years older than Ruth, she is buying her first car. Sandra takes Ruth's car for a test drive. Sandra notices that the car bounces and vibrates severely at freeway speeds, but is told by Ruth that the vibration merely means the tires need to be balanced. What Ruth failed to tell Sandra (and which was known to Ruth) is that the vibration was from worn shocks and a bent frame, which are costly to repair. Sandra agrees to buy the car for $2,500, and signs an agreement that, in part, states she will pay Ruth and pick up the car the following Friday. Sandra contacts a car repair shop to set an appointment for tire balancing, only to learn the true nature and cost of the problem.

76. If Ruth sues Sandra for breach of contract, because Sandra refuses to follow through with the purchase, will Ruth prevail?

    A. Yes, because only Ruth can void the contract based upon Ruth's infancy.

    B. Yes, because Sandra's reliance on Ruth's representations were unreasonable.

    C. No, because the contract is voidable due to Ruth's incapacity to contract.

    D. No, because she materially misrepresented the car's condition.

77. Assume for this question only, that Sandra told Ruth that she knew the shocks were worn and that visible body damage indicated the frame was bent, but she agreed to purchase the car anyway. After agreeing to the sale, Ruth decides to keep the car. Sandra sues Ruth to enforce the terms of the contract. Will Sandra prevail?

    A. Yes, because any claim that Ruth misrepresented the condition of the car would be unreasonable.

    B. Yes, because Sandra is estopped to avoid the contract.

    C. No, because Ruth may avoid the contract because she is a minor.

    D. No, because a contract based on a material misrepresentation is void ab initio.

78. Assume for this question that Ruth had two cars, each with personalized license plates. The car for sale had plates stating, "Ruth I", and the other car had, "Ruth II". Assume the written agreement between Ruth and Sandra purports to identify the car by license number, and Ruth enters "Ruth II" where the license number information is requested. The error is not noticed until Sandra is to take delivery of the car. Ruth delivers the "Ruth I" vehicle to Sandra, who refuses to accept it. Because she only needs one car, Ruth returns with "Ruth II" and tenders it to Sandra, who refuses to accept delivery of it as well. The "Ruth II" vehicle is the same year, make, and model of the "Ruth I" car, but without the defects. If Ruth sues Sandra for her refusal to accept "Ruth II," who will prevail?

   A. Sandra, because the Parol Evidence Rule does not bar evidence that Sandra never agreed to purchase "Ruth II."

   B. Sandra, because a written agreement entered on the basis of fraudulent representations fails to satisfy the Statute of Frauds, and is thereby voidable.

   C. Ruth, because the Parol Evidence Rule prohibits evidence that "Ruth II" was not the actual subject matter of the parties' agreement.

   D. Ruth, if the reasonable value of "Ruth II" was $2,500.

79. Assume the same facts as in the preceding question, except that Sandra knew of the transcription error by Ruth at the time their agreement was reduced to writing. Although Sandra requests delivery of "Ruth II," Ruth refuses. Sandra files a breach of contract action against Ruth seeking to enforce the agreement as written. Who will prevail?

   A. Sandra, because the Parol Evidence Rule bars evidence of the misidentification of the car Ruth had put up for sale.

   B. Sandra, because the unilateral mistake was not known to exist by Ruth.

   C. Ruth, because there was no agreement to sell "Ruth II" to Sandra.

   D. Ruth, because there was a mutual mistake.

80. Seller transferred title to his vacant lot in Sunny Ville to Buyer for $78,000. Buyer purchased land on the representation made by Seller that the property was unencumbered, except for a mortgage for $15,000. However, Seller did not disclose that the property was encumbered by an easement which restricted the use of the land. The easement will not interfere with the use Buyer intends for the land. The lot subject to the encumbrance is worth $93,000, but without the encumbrance the worth is $98,000. If Buyer asserts a claim against Seller for damages, will Buyer prevail?

A. Yes, because the land is worth $98,000 without the encumbrance.

B. Yes, unless Buyer reasonably could have discovered the easement against the property.

C. No, because Buyer can make full use of the land as intended.

D. No, if the reasonable value of the property is $93,000.

Questions 81 – 84 are based on the following facts:

Skip arrived at the airport intending to depart on a well-deserved vacation. After confirming his flight, he observed Shirley, who was overloaded with baggage, negligently fall down some stairs leading to the baggage pick-up area. Observing that Shirley was hurt, Skip ran into the airport's restaurant, Fly-N-Again, to telephone for medical assistance, only to slip and fall in some crushed ice on the floor, sustaining a broken wrist. Restaurant personnel and management did not have any knowledge of the presence of the ice on the floor prior to Skip's fall.

81. If Skip sues Shirley on a negligence theory, and Shirley does not raise the affirmative defense of contributory negligence, will he prevail?

A. Yes, because of the good samaritan rule.

B. Yes, because Skip's conduct in attempting to summon help for Shirley was foreseeable.

C. No, because the injury to Skip was not a foreseeable risk posed by Shirley's negligence.

D. No, because of Fly-N-Again's intervening negligence.

82. If Skip sues Shirley on a negligence theory, and Shirley raises the affirmative defense of contributory negligence, which of the following facts are relevant in determining whether Shirley will prevail on her affirmative defense?

I. Skip did not observe the crushed ice.

II. Skip had observed that Shirley was in serious condition.

III. Skip was only 12-years-old.

A. I and III only.

B. I and II only.

C. II and III only.

D. I, II and III.

83. If Skip sues Fly-N-Again on a negligence theory and Fly-N-Again does not assert assumption of risk as a defense, will Skip prevail in his action?

A. No, because Skip was not an invitee of Fly-N-Again when he fell.

B. No, if a customer of Fly-N-Again spilled the ice moments before Skip's fall.

C. Yes, because the owner or operator of premises has the duty to inspect and correct defects thereon.

D. Yes, because the risk of having crushed ice on the floor is outweighed by the utility of having frequent inspections of the premises.

84. If Skip sues Fly-N-Again on a negligence theory for failure to clean up the crushed ice and Fly-N-Again asserts that Skip assumed the risk of injury, will Skip prevail in his action?

A. No, if Skip did see the crushed ice.

B. No, if Skip was a minor.

C. Yes, if Skip should have seen the crushed ice.

D. Yes, if Skip was in a hurry.

Questions 85 – 88 are based on the following facts:

Sam is a private detective who often crosses the line of the law when conducting investigations for his clients, but he is well-paid and frequently sought out for this reason. Because Sam was going out of town on a case, and a client needed quick results, Sam attempted to contact Nick, another private detective who was unafraid of performing the same types of investigations as Sam, to perform the necessary work.

Sam left a note intended for Nick, of Nick and Nat Detective Agency, stating that he would have to break and enter the local prosecutor's office and recover a handgun tying Sam's client to a string of murders, but that care should be taken during the job to avoid detection by, and injury to, anybody who might discover the break-in activity. Despite the brutality of the crimes and large amount of press coverage, the prosecutor kept the gun in a shoebox on a shelf in his office. Instead of being found by Nick, the note was found by Nat, who also knew Sam and who thought the note was intended for him. That evening, Nat broke into the prosecutor's office to retrieve the gun. As Nat was obtaining the handgun, he was discovered by the janitor. Nat used a non-lethal pepper spray to disable the janitor, but the janitor was asthmatic and died of asthmatic seizure an hour after he was sprayed.

85. Is Sam guilty of soliciting Nat to perform an unlawful act?

    A. No, because he did not intend that Nat perform the act.

    B. No, unless Nat was reasonable in believing the note was intended for him.

    C. Yes, because Sam asked that the incriminating evidence be recovered.

    D. Yes, because Nat performed the act as requested in the note.

86. Assume that Sam telephoned Nick at his portable telephone number to confirm that he had received the note. Nick told Sam that he had not been to his office, but based on their discussion, he would be able to recover the handgun the following day. Is Sam guilty of soliciting Nick to perform an unlawful act?

    A. No, because Nick did not receive the request before Nat had acted on the note.

    B. No, because Nat believed the note was intended for him.

    C. Yes, when Sam told Nick over the telephone that he wanted the incriminating evidence recovered.

    D. Yes, because Sam's note was intended for Nick.

87. Was there a conspiracy to unlawfully recover the incriminating handgun?

    A. Yes, between Sam and Nat.

    B. Yes, between Sam and Nick.

    C. Yes, between Sam, Nat and Nick.

    D. No.

88. May Sam be held criminally liable for the death of the janitor?

    A. No, because Sam had requested that care be taken to avoid harm to others.

    B. No, because Sam did not intend that anybody be killed during the recovery of the handgun.

    C. Yes, because of Blackstone's Rule.

    D. Yes, because Sam's actions were the cause in fact of Nat's presence at the prosecutor's office.

89. Jake Quick is the director of a series of successful motion pictures for Supremacy Studios. His latest film, "It Never Happened!", purports that the Holocaust never occurred. The film was reviewed by Jean Siskbert as part of her weekly television show dedicated to the review of films. Jean stated that the movie's premise was an intentional distortion of the truth, Jake's motives for making such propaganda were his bigotry and racism, and he was using the film as a springboard for Jake's recently-announced candidacy for state congressman. Despite Jean's review, the film has done very well at the box office. If Jake sues Jean for defamation, will he prevail?

    A. No, because Jake's film was doing very well.

    B. No, because Jean's critique was merely an expression of her opinion.

    C. No, because Jake is a public figure.

    D. No, unless Jean acted with reckless disregard of the truth.

90. Tawnya Tattles is an investigative reporter for the investigative newspaper, National Star. In a recent article, Tawnya reported that Lee Coco, the president of a national military defense company, was being fired for his role in the manipulation of the company's stock for personal profit and for attempting to hide cost overruns on the Quasar, a fighter jet using environmentally-safe weapons. Lee, in fact, had left his position as president of the company to work for Replenish, an organization dedicated to reversing environmental destruction that has occurred during the industrialization of the world during the 20th Century. If Lee files a defamation action against Tawnya, will Lee prevail?

A. No, if Tawnya used reasonable care in her investigation for the article on Lee.

B. No, if Tawnya believed the article was true.

C. No, if Tawnya promptly issued a retraction in the paper that reasonably would be seen by readers of the paper.

D. No, if Tawnya did not intend ill will towards Lee.

Questions 91 – 94 are based on the following facts:

When Mitch's parents decided to move to a sunnier climate upon their retirement, they sold their home. The large amount of furniture that once occupied the home was given to Mitch. Because he was in need of money to defray his college education costs, Mitch decided to place the following advertisement on the local cable channel: "Special prices this weekend only. Furnish your home with our couches – $299.00." Mitch had no experience selling furniture, but was able to rent a temporary space in a vacant store located in the center of town, to display and sell the furniture.

91. Assume that Rhoda responded to the advertisement. When she arrived at the store, she saw three couches, one of which was of much higher quality than the other two. She handed Mitch $299.00 cash, telling him that she wanted the higher quality couch. Mitch refused to accept Rhoda's money, and told her she had chosen the couch with a price of $1,499.00. If Rhoda sues Mitch for breach of contract, who prevails?

A. Mitch, because $299.00 was not sufficient consideration for the couch.

B. Mitch, because the advertisement did not constitute an offer.

C. Rhoda, because she objectively manifested her intent to purchase the higher quality couch.

D. Rhoda, because Mitch's advertisement was an offer that was accepted upon Rhoda's tender of the $299.00.

92. Assume that Priscilla comes into Mitch's shop and agrees to purchase the higher quality couch for $1,499.00, payment within seven days. Priscilla is a private investor in furniture, and recognizes the couch as one that formerly graced the home of Elvis Presley and was worth at least $15,000.00. The original cost of the couch was only $125.00. Mitch confirmed the terms of sale by sending a remittance invoice to Priscilla, which was signed and dated the date Priscilla visited the store. He also places a "sold" sign on the couch. Although Priscilla received the invoice, she had changed her mind about the couch, and discarded the document. Mitch sues Priscilla for breach of contract, but she raises the Statute of Frauds as a defense. Will she prevail?

A. No, because the remittance invoice signed by Mitch satisfies the Statute of Frauds writing requirement.

B. No, because she failed to object to the terms of the sale as set forth in the invoice.

C. Yes, because Priscilla is not a merchant and there is no writing signed by her.

D. Yes, because Mitch's writing was not contemporaneous with the agreement, thereby permitting fraud or mistake to enter into the writing.

93. Assume the same facts as Question 92, except that Priscilla asserts the defense that there was not adequate consideration for her promise to pay $1,499.00. Will this defense be successful?

A. No, because Mitch detrimentally relied when he marked the couch "sold," thereby restricting it from further sale.

B. No, because Mitch's promise to tender the couch upon receipt of the $1,499.00 was sufficient consideration.

C. Yes, because the agreement is unenforceable when the comparing the valuation of the couch to the original price of $125.00.

D. Yes, because Mitch did not change his position in reliance on Priscilla's promise to pay $1,499.00.

94. Assume that a valid contract was created between Mitch and Priscilla for the sale of the couch, but before Priscilla pays for it, the federal government declares that all commercial sales and private use of the former possessions of Elvis Presley are illegal, and that such former possessions are declared national treasures. What is the most correct statement regarding the rights of Mitch and Priscilla?

   A. Mitch is in breach for his inability to tender the couch because Priscilla's payment of cash is not prohibited.

   B. Priscilla will be entitled to the benefit of the bargain damages from Mitch in the amount of $15,000.00.

   C. Mitch is entitled to the purchase price, but Priscilla is not entitled to the couch because of the fortuitous nature of the federal action.

   D. Mitch is excused from tendering the couch, and Priscilla is not obligated to pay the purchase price.

Questions 95 – 99 are based on the following facts:

Bob is a crane operator for his employer, Skyhigh Commercial Construction ("Skyhigh"). Skyhigh has provided the crane used by Bob, which was purchased from Casey Equipment, a heavy equipment manufacturer owned by Casey. As Bob was operating the crane one day, the crane tipped over, resulting in injuries to him. Bob does not have any knowledge of his conduct immediately before the accident, but a witness steps forward who states that the crane suddenly fell over when Bob slowly extended the boom of the crane without any load attached. Bob sues Casey for $50,000, on the basis of defective manufacture and design of the crane. Another witness states that Bob had ignored warnings that his load was too heavy and he had released his load only after the crane started to severely tilt to one side. After obtaining the witness statements, but before trial, Casey offers to settle Bob's claim for $20,000, which Bob accepts.

95. Assume that Casey refuses to pay the $20,000 before any other action is taken by Bob. If Bob sues Casey for $20,000, what result?

   A. Casey prevails, because Bob's claim was based on evidence that directly conflicts with the evidence of Casey, and Bob has the burden of proof on the issue of liability.

B. Casey prevails, because an executory contract is not enforceable as an accord and satisfaction.

C. Bob prevails, because the settlement agreement was enforceable as a compromise of a disputed claim.

D. Bob prevails, because tort liability is enforceable without consideration.

96. Assume the same facts as above, except that Bob sues Casey for the $50,000 he initially demanded. Casey defends on the grounds that his obligation to pay $20,000 in settlement replaced any liability that may be proven-up at trial. Will Casey's defense succeed?

A. No, because Casey's promise to pay $20,000 in settlement was void ab initio.

B. No, because Bob has the option of suing on the settlement agreement or the tort theory alleged in his complaint.

C. No, because its promise was made in compromise of a disputed claim.

D. No, because its promise to pay is enforceable without consideration.

97. Assume that after the settlement agreement is entered into, the witness, who is favorable to Bob, admits to Casey that he made up his story, but that Bob did not know he had done so. Bob has already dismissed his complaint. Casey now refuses to pay Bob the settlement amount. If Bob sues Casey for Casey's refusal to pay the settlement amount, what result?

A. Bob prevails, because the settlement was an accord and satisfaction.

B. Bob prevails, because he did not have knowledge of his witness' false statement when he entered the settlement with Casey.

C. Casey prevails, because an executory contract is not enforceable as an accord and satisfaction.

D. Casey prevails, because the recanted evidence of Bob's expert indicates there is no longer consideration for the settlement agreement.

98. Assume that after Casey entered into the settlement agreement with Bob, he became unable to pay the $20,000. Bob threatened to file another lawsuit against Casey, since he had dismissed his prior action. Frank hears of Casey's predicament and tells Bob that he will pay Bob the $20,000, if Bob agrees not to file the new lawsuit. Frank is a contractor that has been purchasing Casey's equipment for years, and has agreed to the payment out of loyalty to Casey. Bob agrees, and refrains from filing the new action. The following day, Frank informs Bob that he has had a change of heart and would not be paying the money. If Bob sues Frank for $20,000, who prevails?

   A. Bob prevails, because his agreement to forbear to sue Casey is adequate consideration for his promise.

   B. Bob prevails, because Frank's loyalty to Casey is sufficient consideration for Frank's promise.

   C. Frank prevails, because his promise is not supported by consideration.

   D. Frank prevails, because the rule on contribution requires that Bob must first sue Casey and receive judgment before he can sue on Frank's promise to pay.

99. Assume the same facts as in Question 98, but that Frank defends on the grounds that the statute of frauds will prevent enforcement of the Bob-Frank agreement. Will Frank prevail on this ground?

   A. Yes, because a promise to forbear to sue for an amount in excess of $500 must be evidenced by a writing.

   B. Yes, because the promise to pay the debt of another must be evidenced by a writing.

   C. Both A and B are correct.

   D. No, because Frank's promise does not require a writing under the Statute of Frauds to be enforceable.

100. Derrick contacted his friend, Brock, and asked Brock to loan him $2,000, to purchase some equipment in order to manufacture illegal drugs for sale, and to become a 50-50 partner in the enterprise. After Brock gave Derrick the money, Derrick decided to use the $2,000 for a vacation in Hawaii instead. What crime did Derrick commit when he failed to repay the money to Brock ?

   A. Larceny.

   B. Obtaining money by false pretenses.

C. Embezzlement.

D. Conspiracy to manufacture illegal drugs.

END OF QUESTIONS

SIMULATED BAR ANSWERS

1. C is the correct answer. Art was under a pre-existing duty to construct the home as agreed. Although the tiles would be difficult to obtain, Art's performance will not be excused under the doctrine of unanticipated circumstances. A, B and D are incorrect for the reasons stated in answer C.

2. A is the correct answer. Though Bob's act of meeting with the IRS and reaching a favorable resolution for Art may have resulted in Art's promise, the promise was not supported by any consideration. Thus, Bob's promise to install a Genie door raiser for Art is purely gratuitous and is unenforceable. B is incorrect because the parole evidence rule only applies when a full, complete integrated written contract is entered into between the parties. C is incorrect for the reasons stated in answer A. D is incorrect because promissory estoppel is triggered when a gratuitous promise is likely to, and does, induce the promisee to rely. Here, the facts state that Art's promise followed Bob's act; therefore, Bob was not induced by the promise.

3. D is the correct answer. Where a contract contains gaps in the terms to be performed, the court will ordinarily fill in such gaps by implication, e.g., requiring a garage door opener of the power rating that is reasonably required. Although Art refused to install the more powerful motor, he is entitled to payment of the contract price for his substantial performance, less Bob's damages for Art's failure to install the appropriate motor.

4. C is the correct answer. When a partially constructed home is destroyed accidentally, through no fault of the parties to the contract, the party constructing the home cannot recover for the work, including material and labor that was destroyed, because no benefit has been conferred upon the owner. Therefore, Art may not recover for previously completed work. A and B are incorrect for the reasons stated for answer C. D is incorrect because the duty of a contractor to perform on time may be excused by destruction of the home.

5. A is the correct answer. An express condition that performance must be to the satisfaction of a third person requires that the third person's decision be honest and in good faith. However, where the third person's dissatisfaction is a gross mistake, the condition of personal satisfaction will be excused. B, C and D are incorrect for the reasons stated in answer A.

6. C is the correct answer. Where a plaintiff in default (here, University is standing in Art's shoes as plaintiff) sues to recover damages, the plaintiff's recovery is measured by the amount of defendant's enrichment, but not more than the contract price. A, B and D are incorrect for the reasons stated in answer C.

7. D is the correct answer. False imprisonment requires a showing of physical or psychological confinement of another who is conscious of or injured by the confinement. Because Milton was not aware of his confinement since he was asleep, and there are no facts suggesting injury due to the confinement, Florence is not liable for false imprisonment. A and B are incorrect for the reasons stated in answer D. C is incorrect because Florence may be found liable absent force or threats by creating a physical barrier of confinement, e.g., locking the door.

8. A is the correct answer. Robin must show that Bank's failure to provide a security guard or post a sign was the actual and proximate cause of Mark's death, in order to impose liability. B is incorrect because a lack of prior occurrences is no defense. C is incorrect because comparative negligence does not necessarily provide a complete defense. D is incorrect because the law as described did not violate the U.S. Constitutional prohibition against ex post facto laws.

9. C is the correct answer. Plaintiff may recover damages for severe emotional distress caused by observing the negligently inflicted injury of a third person if, but only if, plaintiff is closely related to the injured victim, present at the scene of the injury-producing event at the time it occurs, aware that the victim is being injured, which results in plaintiff suffering serious emotional distress. A and B are incorrect for the reasons stated in answer C. D is incorrect because for negligent infliction, foreseeability is not an element of the tort.

10. C is the correct answer. A conspiracy is an agreement between two or more persons to do an unlawful act. Because Max did not willingly agree to perform the robbery, but was under the compulsion of duress, there was not an agreement between Siegfried and Max such that it amounted to a conspiracy. A, B, and D are incorrect because C is correct.

11. B is the correct answer. The defense of duress applies where the conduct of another caused the defendant to reasonably believe that, unless he committed the crime, he or a third person would suffer death or serious bodily harm. The defense of duress applies here because Siegfried threatened to blow up the briefcase attached to Max's arm, which if filled with explosives would most likely result in his death. Max's reasonable belief that the briefcase contains explosives means that the defense applies, even though the briefcase contained a harmless material. A, C and D are incorrect because B is correct.

12. D is the correct answer. A person can commit a crime through an innocent agent and be subject to conviction as though he committed the crime himself. A, B and C are incorrect for the reasons stated in answer D.

13. A is the correct answer. Pursuant to U.C.C. 2-206, an offer to buy goods shall be construed as inviting acceptance either by a prompt promise to ship or act of shipment. However, the act of shipping non-conforming goods is not only acceptance of the offer, but also a breach of the accepted contract. B is incorrect because upon accepting the goods, a contract was formed and would place CompuPlay in breach of contract. C is incorrect because the seller must seasonably notify the buyer that the shipment is offered as an accommodation only. D is incorrect because a buyer is entitled to a reasonable opportunity to inspect goods.

14. D is the correct answer. Negligence is defined as conduct which falls below a standard of care established by law for the protection of others from an unreasonable risk of harm. Phil must show that Continental failed to exercise due care in maintaining the pipeline before liability will be imposed. A is incorrect because the facts state there was no danger to Phil presented by the leaking pipeline. B is incorrect because Torts Restatement 402(A) provides that liability is limited to persons who sell, produce, or distribute the product. Continental merely owned and operated the pipeline. C is incorrect because Phil must show he suffers an injury peculiar in kind.

15. D is the correct answer. A property owner may use reasonable (non-deadly) force to protect his property from intruders. Here, the facts state Buck's fence only gave a mild shock. A and B are incorrect for the reasons stated in answer D. C is an incorrect statement of law.

16. D is the correct answer. At common law, a burglary is the nighttime breaking and entering into the dwelling house of another with the intent to commit a felony therein. Because Sue entered Jeff's home to retrieve her own property, she entered without the requisite intent necessary to have committed a burglary. A, B and C are incorrect for the reason stated in D.

17. D is the correct answer. A private citizen is privileged to use deadly force to avert the perpetration of an inherently dangerous felony which involves a substantial risk of death or serious bodily harm to others and that the person against whom the force was used is guilty of that crime. A, B and C are incorrect since crime prevention, under these facts, is a valid defense.

18. B is the correct answer. Larceny is defined as the trespassory taking and carrying away of the personal property of another with the intent to permanently deprive. When Amy had decided to keep Mr. Ed, before obtaining possession of him, she was in unlawful possession of him in violation of the ownership rights of Wilbur at the time she was given such possession. A is incorrect because a larceny was committed at the time Amy received Mr. Ed. C and D are incorrect for the reasons stated in answer B.

19. D is the correct answer. Under U.C.C. section 2-306, a requirements contract measures the quantity of goods by the "requirements" of the buyer. The party who will determine the quantity amount is required to exercise good faith and the contract does not lack mutuality since the requirement of good faith is imposed upon the party determining quantity. A contract whereby the parties make an agreement to buy all that is required and an agreement to supply all that is required, is sufficient consideration in a requirements contract. A, B and C are incorrect for the reasons stated in answer D.

20. A is the correct answer. Pursuant to U.C.C. section 2-306(1), no quantity unreasonably disproportionate to any stated estimate, or in the absence of a stated estimate to any normal or otherwise comparable prior output or requirement contract, may be tendered or demanded. Roach Coach's demand for 20 dozen sandwiches was unreasonably disproportionate to its prior year's requirements of seven dozen sandwiches per week. B is legally incorrect as contemplation by the contracting parties is not the proper test under U.C.C. section 2-306(1). C and D are incorrect for the reasons stated in answer A.

21. A is the best answer. Under U.C.C. section 2-306, a party who will determine the quantity amount is required to exercise good faith. A contract where a party makes an agreement to buy all he requires and that party fails to buy all his requirements is not acting in good faith (absent additional facts) and, therefore, is in breach of contract. B, C and D are incorrect for the reasons stated in answer A.

22. C is the correct answer. Requirements contracts generally are not assignable because the assignee (Ken) may have significantly different requirements than the assignor (Bugs), thereby materially changing the duty of the obligor (Fresh Foods) under the contract. A is an incorrect statement of law. B and D are incorrect for the reasons stated in answer C.

23. D is the correct answer. A novation is a three-party agreement by which the obligee (Fresh Foods) agrees to accept a new obligor (Ken) in place of the original obligor (Bugs). The novation results in a discharge of the original obligor from his duties under the original contract. A and B are incorrect for the reasons stated in answer D. C is incorrect because in the absence of a novation, Bugs is not discharged from his duties under the original contract.

24. B is the correct answer. A manufacturer, retailer, or supplier of a product who places an unreasonably dangerous product into the stream of commerce will be held strictly liable for injuries to a consumer or user of the product. A is incorrect because liability for a defective product will not be imposed if the product was not unreasonably dangerous. C is incorrect because the plaintiff need not be the purchaser of the product to recover. D is incorrect because contributory negligence is generally not a defense to a strict products liability cause of action, unless there are facts to support a finding of unreasonable misuse of the product. Such facts are not present in the situation above.

25. C is the correct answer. A manufacturer, retailer, or supplier of a product who places an unreasonably dangerous (defective) product into the stream of commerce will be strictly liable for injuries to a consumer or user of the product. This doctrine applies to retailers and distributors as well as manufacturers because each party is an integral part of the marketing enterprise enabling them to share the risk of liability with the manufacturer. A is incorrect for the reasons stated in answer C. B is incorrect because no privity is required to impose liability under the theory of strict products liability. D is an incorrect statement of law.

26. B is the correct answer. Under a negligence products liability theory, a commercial supplier generally has no duty to inspect, test, or provide warnings in regard to products manufactured by another prior to selling the product, unless the seller has reason to know that the product is dangerously defective. A is incorrect for the reasons stated for answer B. C and D are incorrect because they are not supported by the facts.

27. D is the correct answer.□To place liability upon a manufacturer under the theory of strict liability in tort, a showing that the product was defective and a causal relationship to the injuries suffered is required. Here, Tina only suffered emotional injuries from her observance of the injuries to Christopher, which are not recoverable unless the injured third person has a close relationship to the plaintiff. A, B and C are incorrect for the reasons stated in answer D.

28. A is the best answer. An individual is criminally liable as an accomplice of a crime performed by another if, with the intent to facilitate the crime, encouragement or assistance was given, or he failed to perform a legal duty to prevent the crime of another. Al assisted Marcey and Jefferson to kill Peggy by leaving the window open. Therefore, Al is guilty as an accomplice to the murder. B is incorrect because it does not address Al's participation in the crime. C and D are incorrect for the reasons stated in answer A.

29. D is the correct answer. At common law, a burglary is defined as the nighttime breaking and entering into the dwelling house of another with the specific intent to commit a felony therein. A breaking is established with the use of actual or constructive force. Since Al left the bedroom window open and Jefferson threw the broom through an open window, no actual or constructive force was used to create an opening to obtain entry. Thus, there was no breaking and Jefferson is not guilty of burglary. A and B are incorrect for the reasons stated in answer D. C is incorrect because an entry can be accomplished by the defendant's insertion of a tool or other instrumentality for the purpose of committing the intended felony.

30. C is the correct answer. At common law, arson is defined as the malicious burning of the dwelling of another. The key to this question is to realize that the dwelling did not "burn," the dwelling only had smoke damage. Thus, at common law, no arson occurred. A is an insufficient response since there was no actual burning of the structure. B and D are incorrect because specific intent is not a necessary element and are not responsive to the question.

31. D is the correct answer. Where a defendant agrees to provide goods or services for consideration which he knows are to be used to further an unlawful objective, he is liable for conspiracy for providing such goods or services. Lovejoy refurbished the table and would be paid out of the proceeds of the table's sale, and is, therefore, liable for conspiracy. A and B are incorrect for the reasons D is correct. C is incorrect because it does not recognize the element of "consideration" to be received by Lovejoy.

32. C is the correct answer. A defendant is entitled to use reasonable force in self defense to the extent such force is not likely to cause serious bodily injury or death unless defendant is being threatened with serious bodily injury or death. Thus, Hugo will be liable to George if the force used by Hugo is unreasonable. A is incorrect because Hugo was entitled to defend himself from George's physical confrontation. B is incorrect because there is generally no duty to retreat. D is incorrect because the answer fails to address whether Hugo had knowledge of George's susceptibility.

33. B is the correct answer. The most likely theory that George would allege against Drama School would be negligence, which has elements of duty, breach, actual and proximate causation, and damages. A breach of duty would occur if Drama School failed to use reasonable care to supervise its premises. The other answers do not properly address the elements of a negligence cause of action.

34. A is the correct answer. An individual may recover damages for the unauthorized use by defendant of the individual's name or likeness for a commercial purpose. This is particularly true where plaintiff is a celebrity such that plaintiff's name or likeness would have commercial value. Because Gear did not agree to permit his picture to be used in Nogo's advertisements, he may recover his damages for Nogo's unauthorized use of his likeness. B is incorrect for the reason stated for answer A. C is incorrect because Gear was photographed in a public place. D is incorrect because Nogo's commercial use was improper, while Pleasure's noncommercial use is not actionable.

35. C is the correct answer. Gear may recover for a defendant's highly offensive intrusion into his private life, whether the intrusion was intentional or negligent in nature. However, Gear was driving his convertible on a public roadway and had no reasonable expectation that he would not be intruded upon by Phil. A, B and D are, therefore, incorrect.

36. C is the best answer. Where property is lost or mislaid, the property is considered to be in the constructive possession of the true owner. When property is found by a third party, that party has a clue to the identity of the property's owner, and decides to keep the property, she has committed a larceny. When Julia found the diary, she intended to keep it even though she had a clue to ownership when she discovered the bookmark with the owner's name on it. Based on these facts, Julia has committed a larceny. A is incorrect because Julia formed the intent to keep the book upon finding it. B is clearly wrong. D is incorrect because Julia was never entrusted with the property, nor did she ever intend to return it.

37. B is the correct answer. The crime of larceny requires a taking of the personal property of another with the intent to permanently deprive. Although Wayne was voluntarily given possession of the bicycle by Chuck, a taking with the victim's permission is larceny where the permission was obtained by fraud or deception, such as the deception used by Wayne. A and C are incorrect because Wayne did not obtain lawful possession. D is an incorrect statement of the law.

38. B is the correct answer. Under the "mailbox rule," where the use of U.S. mail, telegram, or overnight mail services is a reasonable method of communicating an acceptance, such acceptance is generally effective upon dispatch and a revocation is generally effective upon receipt. Thus, even though Jay received Conan's attempted revocation before Conan received Jay's acceptance, a contract was formed. Note that although an offer may invite acceptance by either a promise or an act, and on its face Conan's offer arguably contains language that invites acceptance by performance, a reasonable interpretation of Conan's offer was that he required to be contacted prior to Sunday for acceptance. A is incorrect because the method of revocation is generally not limited to the same method as the communication method of the offer. C is incorrect because Jay's normal fee can be objectively determined. D is incorrect because a request using such language as "I wish" or "I hope" is considered to be mere inquiry.

39. A is the correct answer. An offer is an outward manifestation of present willingness to enter into a bargain, made in such a way that the person to whom it is addressed reasonably believes that he could accept the offer by assenting to the stated terms. Because Jay had no knowledge that Arsenio received an identical offer, he reasonably believed that he could accept the offer by sending a telegram to Conan. B, C and D are incorrect.

40. B is the correct answer. Where an employer wrongfully terminates an employment contract, the employee must undertake reasonable efforts to seek employment of the same caliber and type. Although Jay was offered alternative employment, he was not required to accept such employment, which was of significantly lesser caliber and arguably of a different type than that originally contracted. Upon an employer's breach, the employee is entitled to recover expectation damages (i.e., the benefit of the bargain under the contract), so Jay may recover $15,000.00. A, C and D are, therefore, incorrect.

41. B is the best answer. Although an offer may invite acceptance by either a promise or an act, and on its face Conan's offer arguably contains language that invites acceptance by performance, a reasonable interpretation of Conan's offer was that he required to be contacted prior to Sunday for acceptance. Arsenio should know that if Conan was not contacted by Arsenio that Conan would continue his efforts to secure a replacement act for Dave, or else he could not open the following week. A, C and D are incorrect.

42. C is the correct answer. A battery is the harmful or offensive touching of plaintiff without privilege or consent. Because Marilyn only consented to the rhinoplasty, Dr. Picasso exceeded the consent he was granted and is liable for battery. A, B and D are incorrect.

43. D is the correct answer. The doctrine of res ipsa loquitur has been held to apply to establish "exclusive control" in a group of medical personnel when an unconscious plaintiff suffers harm of a type that might be attributable to someone's negligence. Thus, Clinic may be held liable for Marilyn's injuries even though she cannot establish who was responsible for her injuries. A, B and C are incorrect.

44. D is the correct answer. Although Charles was mistaken as to his ownership of the violin at the time of sale, and Richard in good faith believed the violin was owned by Charles, the intent required for conversion is the tortfeasor's intent to deal with the chattel in a manner that exercises dominion and control over the chattel of another. Thus, it is no defense that defendants are not conscious wrongdoers. A, B and C are incorrect for the reason stated for answer D.

45. B is the correct answer. The general rule is that a defendant who did not place another individual in a position of peril owes no duty to provide assistance to that person in an emergency. However, defendant must provide assistance to another individual in an emergency where a special relationship exists, e.g., family members, employer-employee, etc. A, C and D are incorrect for the reason stated for answer B.

46. A is the correct answer. The burden is on the prosecution to establish beyond a reasonable doubt the elements of a criminal cause of action, including the specific intent to commit a crime where such intent is a necessary element of the crime.

47. C is the correct answer. Where a party to a contract will be unable to perform at the time set for his (Mr. Ellis') performance, i.e., there is a prospective inability to perform, the other party (Mr. Trumpery) is excused from holding himself ready to perform, rendering performance, or tendering performance, as an implied condition to the duty of the party who is unable to perform. A, B and D are incorrect for the reasons stated for answer C.

48. A is the correct answer. Where a party repudiates a contract in advance of the date set for his performance, the innocent party is excused from holding himself ready to perform, rendering performance, or tendering performance. In addition, the innocent party may generally treat the anticipatory repudiation as a present material breach of the contract and bring an immediate action to recover his damages. B, C and D are incorrect for the reasons stated for answer A.

49. C is the correct answer. When a contract fixes the same time for performance by the parties to the contract, tender of such performance by each party is an implied condition of the other party's duty to perform (concurrent conditions). Thus, Mr. Trumpery must tender the $2.5 million to Mr. Ellis in order for Mr. Ellis' duty to perform to arise. A, B and D are incorrect for the reasons stated for answer C.

50. C is the correct answer. Attempted murder requires the specific intent to cause the death of another, and since Carl did not intend to kill Daniel, he is not guilty of attempted murder of Daniel. A, B and D are incorrect for the reasons supporting answer C.

51. C is the best answer. Self-defense does not require a correct belief that such is necessary to protect oneself, but only a reasonable belief. Therefore, A is an incorrect statement. B is incorrect because one who is defending him or herself may attack the assailant intentionally. D is an incorrect statement of law; imperfect right to self-defense is relevant only to murder.

52. C is the best answer. Embezzlement is the fraudulent conversion of rightfully entrusted personal property. Because Zeke intended to extinguish the joint debt, and subsequently did so, with the money collected from Boyd, an embezzlement occurred. A is incorrect because of the explanation above. B is incorrect because Zeke did not obtain title of the money received. D is incorrect because the money was in the "possession," not "custody," of Risk employee. Thus, there was no "trespass" and no larceny.

53. D is the best answer. A corporation may be liable for a criminal act, under all jurisdictions, where the act involves a specific intent crime and is authorized, performed or at least tolerated by the board of directors or a high managerial agent acting on behalf of the corporation within the scope of his employment. Since Zeke used the money to extinguish the joint debt of Risk in his capacity as corporate president, Risk is liable for the crime. A is incorrect because it presumes a corporation cannot be convicted of crime. B is incorrect because a corporation can be convicted of a specific intent crime. C is incorrect because the conviction of Risk and Zeke would not have to be contemporaneous.

A

SIMULATED BAR

54. D is the correct answer. Generally, ignorance or a mistaken belief as to the law is no defense to criminal liability. Although such ignorance/mistaken belief is based on the good faith reliance on an attorney's advice, or as in this case of defendant's tax accountant, it is no defense. However, where defendant's good faith reliance is such that he did not have the necessary mens rea to commit the crime, such reliance will act as a defense. If Norm believed in good faith that Vera's advice was correct, Norm did not have the necessary "willfulness" to evade payment of taxes required under the statute. A and C are incorrect statements of the law. B is incorrect because it is factually correct. Where there is a legal vs. factual answer, the legal answer is the best response.

55. D is the best answer. In general, where defendant criminally acts under the reasonable belief that his actions will prevent the occurrence of a greater harm, the defense of necessity will keep the defendant from criminal liability. Thus, when Hal threatened Patrick in order to call for emergency assistance to save Vic's life, no criminal liability will result to Hal for such actions. A is incorrect because there is no requirement that the act be performed for the necessity of an acquaintance. B is incorrect because no special statute is required to permit raising the defense of necessity. C is an incorrect statement of the law, because Hal only used the threat of deadly force against Patrick. Had Hal used deadly force under the circumstances, the defense would not have been available.

56. B is the best answer. A conditional promise means that the promisor only needs to perform if a specified condition occurs, and is recognized as sufficient consideration for a contract where not illusory. Further, every contract imposes upon each party a duty of good faith and fair dealing in its performance and its enforcement. Thus, the Browns must use good faith efforts to sell their present home, and although they are not obligated to buy the home from Cathy unless their present home is sold, their promises are sufficient consideration to form a contract.

57. A is the correct answer. A condition will be excused where a party who is favored by the condition wrongfully prevents or hinders the completion of the condition. Thus, Cathy does not need to provide evidence that a ready and willing buyer for the Browns' home for $175,000.00 existed. B is an incorrect statement of law. C and D are incorrect for the reasons stated for answer A.

58. D is the best answer. Although the Statute of Frauds will most likely require all contract terms to be in writing to be enforceable, the Parol Evidence Rule provides that where there is a fully integrated contract, parol evidence will not be allowed into evidence to vary, add to, or contradict the terms of a written contract. Since this answer presupposes that full integration is not present, parol evidence cannot be excluded based on the Parol Evidence Rule. A is incorrect because the condition was not a modification, but was part of the original contractual agreement. B is incorrect because there is no ambiguity. C is incorrect statement of the law.

59. B is the best answer. Under general tort principles, a possessor of a domestic animal that has not previously exhibited dangerous propensities is not held strictly liable for the acts of the animal, so long as the possessor was exercising due care at the time. Since Dr. Lindy was not negligent in allowing Flash to escape, he is not liable for Maggie's injuries. A is incorrect for the rule stated above. C and D do not require any culpable conduct, such as negligence by Dr. Lindy, and are, therefore, incorrect.

60. B is the best answer. Liability under the principles of negligence per se for violation of statute requires violation of a statute passed for the purpose of preventing the injury suffered by plaintiff and that plaintiff was within the class of persons sought to be protected by the statute. Although plaintiff is probably within the class of persons sought to be protected by the statute violated by Marlon, the most likely injury sought to be prevented is damage to plaintiff's lungs. Therefore, this response addresses that issue. A, C and D are incorrect statements.

61. B is the best answer. Under the traditional (subjective) rule, the defense of entrapment will be available where a law enforcement officer has instigated the defendant's illegal conduct, and the defendant was not predisposed to commit the crime. Under the facts, Cal was predisposed to commit the crime. Monday's request for a specific type of vehicle did not subjectively create the intent for Cal to commit the crime. A is incorrect because B is the better answer. C is incorrect for the reason stated for answer A. D is an incorrect rule of law.

62. B is the best answer. The minority (objective) standard for the defense of entrapment looks to whether the crime was performed in response to law enforcement activity that was reasonably likely to cause a reasonable, but unpredisposed, person to commit a crime, which is the rule set forth in this answer. Also, none of the choices address the traditional (subjective) rule. A, C and D are incorrect statements.

63. The best answer is C. Conversion is the intentional exercise of dominion and control over the chattel of another. When a bailee receives possession of the chattel of another and uses the chattel in such a way as to materially breach the scope of his authority over the chattel, a conversion has occurred. When the coat clerk could not produce Columbo's coat when presented with the ticket, a material breach of his authority, and, therefore, a conversion, had occurred. A is incorrect because waiver does not apply as a defense under the facts given. B is incorrect because where the defendant intends to deal with the chattel in the manner in which resulted in the loss of the coat, even if he did not consciously commit a wrongdoing (permit theft or gave the chattel to the wrong person), he is liable for conversion. The Lieutenant is vicariously liable for the coat clerk's conduct. D is incorrect because it merely addresses the amount of recoverable damages.

64. B is the correct answer. An owner or occupier of land has the duty to inspect and discover any dangerous conditions or activities on the land, and to correct or warn of such conditions or activities. However, the question asks about the liability of David, who is not the land owner or occupier. Since this answer is the only one given that addresses a possible situation in which David could be held liable, it is the only possible correct answer. A is incorrect because Chaulky's mother does not have the same duty as the owner or occupier of land because of her status as parent of a minor child. C and D are incorrect for the reasons stated for answer B.

65. D is the correct answer. A manufacturer of a product may be held liable for its negligence which results in its product being unreasonably dangerous. A manufacturer of a defective product is also strictly liable to consumers and users for injuries caused by the defect. However, a manufacturer is not liable under a premises liability theory ("abnormally dangerous condition") for defects in a product. A, B and C are incorrect for the reasons stated.

66. B is the correct answer. In cases involving a "thin skull" plaintiff, all courts will hold defendant liable for the full extent of plaintiff's damages, under the rationale that a defendant takes the plaintiff as he finds him. Therefore, defendant(s) will be liable for the actual amount of lost income resulting from his inability to complete the film. A is an incorrect statement of the law. C is incorrect because the loss of earnings to Chaulky has no relationship to a shortened lifespan. D is an incorrect statement of the law.

67. B is the correct answer. Generally, a defendant who is only secondarily liable for plaintiff's damages is entitled to indemnification, for the amount of any judgment paid, against the party primarily responsible for plaintiff's damages. However, indemnity is also available where defendants are directly liable to plaintiff, but there is a great degree of difference between the culpability of the liable parties. Since this answer attributes active negligence against the premises owner, Late Night, it is not entitled to recover any amount of the judgment paid. A and C are incorrect statements of the law, because they do not permit the existence of any exceptions to the purported rules given. D is incorrect because it fails to recognize the principles of contribution and indemnity.

68. C is the correct answer. An accessory after the fact is a person who receives, comforts, or assists another to avoid arrest, prosecution, or conviction, knowing that the other has committed a felony. Since Ben knew of the theft (and in fact was paid for his services out of the spoils of the theft), and was acting to avoid Bonnie and Clyde's arrest, he is guilty of being an accessory after the fact. A is incorrect because a principal in the first degree is someone who actually commits the crime by his acts, or through the acts of an innocent person or inanimate agent. B is incorrect because a principal in the second degree is someone who incites or abets the commission of the crime, and is actually or constructively present at the scene of the crime. D is incorrect because of the reasons stated for the correct answer.

69. C is the correct answer. Robbery is the trespassory taking and carrying away of the personal property of another, from the person or their presence, by force or threat of force, with the intent to permanently deprive. All elements must be present. Here, there was no taking (control) of the property-so there was no robbery. A is incorrect because it addresses only one element of the crime. B is an incorrect statement of law-the threat can be to third parties. D is not the best answer because it is better to choose an answer which eliminates an element of the actus reas than an answer which raises a possible defense of duress.

70. A is the best answer because there is an agreement between Batman and Robin to commit the unlawful act of robbery. This is a question which does not offer a correct answer. Conspiracy does not require action on the part of all co-conspirators, nor does it require completion of the crime. Thus, we are left with choices A and B. A is the better answer because it is more relevant to this fact pattern. Wharton's Rule only concerns those crimes which, by definition, require multiple perpetrators. Robbery is not such a crime. C and D are incorrect statements of law.

71. A is the correct answer. Larceny is the trespassory taking and carrying away of the personal property of another. In circumstances where the owner has lost or mislaid the property, a larceny has occurred if there is a clue to ownership of the property and the intent to permanently deprive exists at the time defendant takes possession of the property. Since Martha received the money in a Wiener Hut bag from a Wiener Hut cashier, and immediately discovered the money before driving away with it, she is guilty of larceny. B is incorrect because the property was not taken by fraud or deception. C is incorrect because embezzlement requires the defendant to obtain lawful possession; however, lost or mislaid goods remain in the constructive possession of the owner. D is incorrect because A is the correct answer.

72. B is the best answer. Private nuisance is the nontrespassory invasion of the use and enjoyment of plaintiff's land. In order for an interference to permit recovery for damages, the interference must result in substantial and unreasonable harm in the use and enjoyment of realty, which is the rule set forth in the correct answer. A is incorrect because a violation of the ordinance does not necessarily constitute a nuisance. C is incorrect because Dan and Roseanne did not come to the nuisance. The noise and crowds did not occur until after they moved in. D is an incorrect statement of the law in that actual trespass is not required for recovery under a private nuisance theory.

73. The correct answer is C. Generally, an assault with a deadly weapon is intentionally placing another person in fear of a battery or an attempted battery, through the use of an instrumentality calculated to cause severe harm or death. A battery is the intentional and unlawful application of force to another person. Since Jimmy intentionally drove at Clark with his car (the deadly weapon), only to have Clark jump out of the way, Jimmy is guilty of the assault with a deadly weapon. Although Jimmy did not strike the actual person of Clark, striking and knocking an object out of Clark's hand is sufficient to constitute a battery. Attempted murder is the specific intent to kill coupled with an act in perpetration to complete the killing. The facts are absent any indication that Jimmy intended to kill Clark. Based on the explanation, A, B, and D are incorrect.

74. C is the correct answer. D is incorrect because first degree murder is the premeditated intentional killing of a human being, or via felony-murder. Here, since Jimmy only intended to scare Clark, there was no specific intent to kill with premeditation or deliberation. Further, felony-murder cannot be used when the underlying felony involves an attack on the person, such as the facts indicate here. (This is called the merger rule). Second degree murder requires, essentially, either an intent to kill, or a reckless killing— such as these facts indicate. Voluntary manslaughter, choice B, is a killing that would be murder except for the fact it was committed with adequate provocation thereby mitigating the defendant's culpability. There was no reasonable provocation here. Involuntary manslaughter, choice A, is an unintended killing that occurs during a criminal act or as the results of criminal negligence. Although this crime is present, always the more serious crime should be chosen, thus, C is a better answer.

75. D is the correct answer. For purposes of criminal homicide, unless the victim is a living human being, there can be no homicide. However, most courts do not recognize that a viable living fetus is a "living human being" such that the killing of the fetus would be homicide. A, B and C are incorrect for this reason.

76 . D is the correct answer. Where one party to a contract has made a material misrepresentation regarding the subject of the contract, the contract is voidable by the innocent party. Since Ruth's statement regarding the defects in her car were likely to induce Sandra (or a reasonable person) to purchase the car, the misrepresentation is material. A is incorrect because it reaches the wrong conclusion and the contract can be avoided on grounds other than infancy. B is incorrect because Sandra's reliance was reasonable since no facts suggest that Sandra should have known of the misrepresentation, and because it was to be her first car purchase – which indicates lack of sophistication. C is incorrect because minors may enter into a contract. The contract is merely voidable, but may be enforceable if the minor chooses not to avoid it.

77. C is the correct answer. A contract entered into by a minor is voidable at the minor's choice, even though the minor may enforce the contract against an adult. Since Ruth is a minor and has stated that she wants to avoid the contract, the contract is not enforceable in favor of Sandra. A and B are incorrect because these answers are couched in language as if Sandra seeks to avoid the contract, and because of the incorrect conclusion of enforceability. D is incorrect because a contract based on material fraudulent representations is merely voidable.

78. A is the correct answer. Parol evidence is admissible to show the existence a mistake in the transcription of the terms of an oral agreement that was subsequently reduced to writing, where the terms of the agreement were not correctly transcribed to reflect the agreement of the parties. Since Ruth and Sandra agreed that Sandra would purchase "Ruth I," parol evidence that Sandra did not agree to purchase "Ruth II" is admissible. B is incorrect because the error in transcription was not because of any fraud and because it is any incorrect rule of law. C is an incorrect rule of law. D is incorrect because Sandra is not required to purchase "Ruth II" as set forth in the explanation for answer A.

79. C is the correct answer. As stated in the answer to question 78, parol evidence is admissible under the circumstances to prove that the parties oral agreement was transcribed incorrectly when it was reduced to a writing. A is incorrect because of the reason answer C is correct. B is incorrect because where only one party knows that a mistake has been made, that party cannot snap up an offer that was made in mistake. D is incorrect because it misstates the facts; there was no mutual mistake.

80. A is the correct answer. Since a party to a contract is entitled to receive the benefit of his bargain, where the other party to the contract induces the injured party to enter the contract by making fraudulent representations, the injured party is entitled to recover his damages to the extent there is a difference between what he was offered and what he received. B is not held to a reasonable discovery standard where his reliance was obtained by fraud. C and D are incorrect because Buyer has not received the full benefit of his bargain.

81. B is the correct answer. Where a defendant owes a duty to an individual, defendant also owes a duty to someone who reasonably goes to the rescue to the person defendant has placed in peril by her negligence. This rule applies even if defendant is the victim of her own negligence. Therefore, Shirley is liable for injuries sustained by Skip when he reasonably attempted to obtain assistance for Shirley. A is incorrect because it does not correctly identify the rule. C is incorrect because B is the correct answer. D is incorrect because intervening negligence does not necessarily exculpate Shirley from liability.

82. D is the correct answer. Choice I concerns whether Skip acted reasonably in light of the presence of the ice. Choice II concerns the swiftness with which medical care is required and the reasonableness of acting hastily when summoning such medical care. Choice III addresses the level of care to which tort law requires of Skip to have been acting in a reasonable manner. Therefore, all choices are relevant in determining whether Skip acted reasonably to prevent injury to himself, or, alternatively, whether Skip was contributorily negligent. A, B and C are incorrect since D is correct.

83. B is the correct answer. An owner or operator of premises owes an invitee the duty of care to inspect the premises for dangerous conditions and to correct or warn of such conditions. Thus, a premises owner or occupier must correct or warn of conditions which he knew or should have known about. Because a customer spilled ice moments before it was slipped in by Skip, Fly-N-Again did not have a reasonable period of time to discover the dangerous condition and will, therefore, not be held liable under the theory of negligence. A misstates Skip's status, and is, therefore, incorrect. C is an incomplete statement of the duty for a premises owner or operator. D is an incorrect application of the law in the premises liability area.

84. A is the correct answer. Implied assumption of risk will be a defense where plaintiff was actually aware of the particular risk involved and voluntarily encountered the known risk. Since Skip must have had actual knowledge of the particular risk, the defense will not apply because he had no such knowledge. B is incorrect because a minor may assume the risk where he fully appreciates the risks involved. C is incorrect because the test is not an objective, but a subjective, standard. D is incorrect because it addresses the reasonableness of Skip's conduct, not whether he voluntarily encountered a known risk.

85. A is the correct answer. Where defendant counsels, incites or induces another to commit or join in the commission of a crime, he is guilty of solicitation. However, where the solicitation is directed to a specific person, but defendant did not intend to solicit the person who actually received the communication, there is no crime of solicitation as to the person (Nat) who received such communication.

86. D is the best answer. Solicitation is the intentional enticement, advisement, incitement or other encouragement of another to commit a crime. When Sam left the note for Nick, requesting that he steal evidence of a crime that would implicate Sam's client, a solicitation occurred. It does not matter that Nick did not receive the note, the solicitation occurred when it was left at his office. A and B are incorrect because the fact that Nat believed the note was for him and acted on that belief does not affect Sam's guilt for soliciting Nick. C is incorrect because Nick had already been solicited by Sam before the telephone conversation.

87. B is the correct answer. Conspiracy is an agreement between two or more persons to accomplish a lawful act by unlawful means or accomplish an unlawful purpose. When Nick agreed to obtain the gun at Sam's request, a conspiracy was formed. A and C are incorrect because there was no intent to agree with Nat by either Sam or Nick. D is incorrect because B is correct.

88. D is the correct answer. A defendant will be liable under the theory of vicarious liability for the crimes committed by another person when such is within the scope of a solicitation or conspiracy. In such instance, causation is established. Although this is a close call, since it was stipulated the spray was non-lethal and since a different party carried out the plan, D is, nevertheless, the best choice. A and B are incorrect for the same reasons that D is correct. C is incorrect because there is no "Blackstone's Rule."

89. D is the best answer. Defamation of a public person is constitutionally privileged, unless published with knowledge of falsity or reckless disregard of the truth. Since this answer assumes Jean acted with reckless disregard of the truth, she violated constitutional standards and is, therefore, liable for defamation. A is incorrect because the fact that Jake's film was doing well does not mean that Jake did not suffer any damages as a result of Jean's statements. B is incorrect because, although opinions generally have constitutional protection, opinions are actionable when they contain known false statements or the statement was made with reckless disregard for the truth. C is incorrect because D is correct.

SIMULATED BAR

A

90. A is the correct answer. Defamation of a public person is constitutionally privileged, unless published with knowledge of falsity or reckless disregard of the truth. Since this answer presumes that Tawnya used reasonable care in investigating Lee, her conduct is not such that it violated the constitutional standard of knowing falsity or reckless disregard for the truth. B is incorrect because Tawnya will be liable, despite her belief in the truth, if she exhibited a reckless disregard for the truth. C is incorrect because the defamation has already occurred, and a retraction is usually only effective in limiting general, but not special, damages. D is incorrect because it sets forth the incorrect standard for liability.

91. B is the correct answer. The general rule is that an advertisement is not an offer because it is usually too indefinite and is construed as an invitation to deal. Since Mitch's ad did not specify which couches were offered at the $299.00 price, the ad could not be construed to invite acceptance to purchase the higher quality couch at the sale price. A is incorrect because consideration is not normally reviewed by the courts for adequacy as long as the contract is not unconscionable. It is unlikely the court would find it unconscionable to pay $299.00 for a couch listed at $1,499.00, particularly since no value of the higher quality couch is given in the facts. C and D are incorrect because the advertisement is not an offer such that Rhoda may accept the terms of it.

92. C is the correct answer. The Statute of Frauds requires that a contract for the sale of goods for $500.00 or more must be in writing, signed by the party to be charged, to be enforceable. One exception to this rule is when both parties are merchants, and one party sends the other party a written confirmation which satisfies the Statute of Frauds as to the sender, and the party receiving the confirmation does not send a written objection within 10 days (U.C.C. 2-201). Since Priscilla is not a merchant, and she did not sign any writing evidencing the terms of the contract, the contract is unenforceable. A and B are incorrect for the reasons C is correct. D is an incorrect statement of the applicable law.

93. B is the correct answer. Again, the court ordinarily will not evaluate the adequacy of consideration between parties, as long as the contract is not unconscionable. Arguably, payment of $1,499.00 for a couch valued at $15,000.00 is not unconscionable such that the contract is lacking sufficient consideration. A is incorrect because there are no facts evidencing detrimental reliance (such as the loss of a sale of the subject couch) whereby promissory estoppel would apply. C is incorrect for the same reason that B is correct. D is factually correct, but reaches the wrong conclusion on the issue of adequacy of consideration.

94. D is the best answer. Where performance of a contract becomes illegal as a result of a supervening change in the law after the contract was entered into, the promisor's performance is excused. Thus, Mitch is not obligated to deliver the couch and Priscilla is not obligated to pay for it. A, B and C are incorrect for the same reasons D is correct.

95. C is the correct answer. Public policy favors compromise settlement of disputed claims, and a settlement agreement is enforceable under contract law. Therefore, Bob may bring an action to enforce the Bob-Casey settlement agreement. Answer A merely sets forth that a disputed claim exists, but reaches the wrong conclusion because Bob will prevail. B is incorrect because an executory settlement agreement is enforceable. D is an incorrect statement of the law.

96. B is the correct answer. After Casey repudiated the settlement agreement, Bob has the option of suing on either his original claim or on the terms of the settlement. A and D are incorrect statements of the applicable law. C is incorrect because settlement agreements on disputed claims are enforceable, and for the reasons supporting answer A.

97. B is the best answer. The court will uphold the Bob-Casey agreement because the agreement was not based on any known misrepresentations of Bob. A is incorrect because under the facts there has been no satisfaction. C is incorrect because courts will usually enforce executory settlement agreements. D is incorrect because the parties were not aware of the false statements at the time they entered into their agreement.

98. A is the correct answer. A bargained-for promise to forbear from bringing a reasonable and good faith claim constitutes consideration. Therefore, Frank's promise to pay the settlement amount in exchange for Bob's promise to forbear to sue Casey forms an enforceable contract. B is incorrect because loyalty does not constitute consideration. C is incorrect because A is correct. D is incorrect because the Bob-Frank agreement is a contract that is enforceable in and of itself, and therefore, Bob does not have to first seek his remedy from Casey.

99. D is the correct answer. A promise to pay an amount in exchange for a promise to forbear from asserting a legal claim does not fall within the Statute of Frauds, and, therefore, is not required to be in writing to be enforceable. This should not be confused with the promise to pay the debt of another under a surety arrangement. A, B and C are incorrect because D is correct.

100. C is the correct answer. Embezzlement is the fraudulent conversion of rightfully entrusted property. Since Brock voluntarily gave Derrick the $2,000 for Derrick's intended illegal drug purchase, Derrick was in rightful possession of the money. Derrick's subsequent taking of the money, therefore is embezzlement. A is incorrect because a larceny requires that the property is not in the rightful possession of defendant. B is incorrect because it requires a false statement intended to obtain title and possession. There was no false statement at the time possession was obtained, and legal title was never obtained. D is incorrect because it does not address the issue of failure to repay the money, although it is a legally correct answer.

END OF ANSWERS

PROFESSIONAL RESPONSIBILITY

PROFESSIONAL RESPONSIBILITY – QUESTION BREAKDOWN

1. Judicial Conduct – Character Witness
2. Judicial Conduct – Government Commission
3. Judicial Conduct – Juror Commission
4. Judicial Conduct – Election
5. Avoiding Impropriety – Advertisements
6. Bar Admission
7. Failure to Disclosure
8. Attorney Misconduct
9. Judicial Conduct – Character Witness
10. Judicial Conduct – Juror Commission
11. Judicial Conduct
12. Judicial Conduct – Investments
13. Judicial Conduct – Gifts
14. Judicial Conduct – Campaigning for Office
15. Competence
16. Failing to Act Competently
17. Competence – Case Strategy
18. Avoiding Impropriety – Perjured Testimony
19. Availability of Legal Services – Fees
20. Availability of Legal Services – Solicitation
21. Availability of Legal Services – Fees
22. Availability of Legal Services – Fees
23. Accepting Employment – Retainer Contract
24. Accepting Employment
25. Accepting Employment – Contingency Fee
26. Accepting Employment – Fees
27. Accepting Employment – Fee Splitting
28. Accepting Employment
29. Accepting Employment – Fees
30. Conflict – Fee Dispute
31. Disclosure – Future Criminal Conduct

32. Disclosure – Confidences
33. Accepting Employment – Multiple Clients
34. Conflict of Interest
35. Business Transaction
36. Malpractice Liability
37. Availability of Legal Services – Fees
38. Accepting Employment – Imputed Disqualification
39. Accepting Employment – Imputed Disqualification
40. Accepting Employment – Imputed Disqualification
41. Accepting Employment – Imputed Disqualification
42. Accepting Employment – Imputed Disqualification
43. Accepting Employment – Fraudulent Conduct
44. Accepting Employment – Fraudulent Conduct
45. Who is the Client
46. Trust Account
47. Availability of Legal Services – Fees
48. Distribution of Settlement
49. Availability of Legal Services – Disputed Funds
50. Availability of Legal Services – Commingled Funds
51. Commingled Funds
52. Attorney-Client Relationship
53. Frivolous Claims
54. Standard of Prosecutors
55. Disclosure
56. Perjury
57. Material Evidence
58. Avoiding Impropriety
59. Testimony of Lawyer
60. Communication
61. Avoiding Impropriety – Fraud
62. Professional Conduct
63. Practice of Law
64. Practice of Law

PROFESSIONAL RESPONSIBILITY QUESTIONS

1. Appellate Judge Bilbo learns that his old grammar school friend, Trol, is being charged with receiving stolen property. Trol asks Bilbo to testify, as a character witness, at his criminal trial. Bilbo asks the chief appellate judge's permission. Judge Elfkin, the chief judge, after careful deliberation approves. Is Bilbo subject to judicial discipline?

   A. No, because all judicial rules are discretionary.

   B. No, because he obtained proper consent.

   C. No, because judges cannot be disciplined.

   D. None of the above.

2. Supreme Court Justice Vader is asked to serve on a governmental commission regarding the reinvestigation of the assassination of President Kennedy. Is it proper for Vader to serve?

   A. Yes, because such a task requires judicial temperament.

   B. Yes, provided he is not paid.

   C. No, because it appears improper.

   D. No, because it is undignified.

3. After a 10-month trial, Judge Karnit criticizes the jurors for their inability to reach a verdict and then individually speaks to each juror, with no one else present. Karnit is subject to judicial discipline for:

   A. The criticism and the ex parte conferences.

   B. The criticism, only.

   C. The ex parte conferences, only.

   D. Neither the criticism nor the ex parte conferences.

4. Judge Doe, running for reelection, promises to order capital punishment "in every case." Is this a proper campaign pledge?

   A. Yes.

   B. Yes, because it is First Amendment protected.

   C. No.

   D. None of the above.

5. Lawyer Quinn places an advertisement in a raunchy magazine. In the ad, he states that he has never lost a drunken driving case. Quinn is subject to discipline because:

A. Advertising is per se unlawful.

B. Advertising is per se in violation of the rules.

C. The ad must be in a dignified forum.

D. The ad is misleading.

6. Many years ago, in college, Linda was suspended for being caught with a small amount of marijuana on her person. She was suspended for one semester, then later returned, to graduate with honors. On Linda's bar application, she is asked if she was ever suspended from any school. Linda writes "no." Five years after being admitted, a former boyfriend of Linda makes a tip to the bar. The bar investigates and finds that Linda knowingly lied. Linda is suspended from practice for 6 months. Is the suspension lawful?

   A. No, because of the statute of limitations.

   B. No, because it is unrelated to present moral turpitude.

   C. Yes, because such is a very clear violation of the rules.

   D. None of the above.

7. Lawyer Joe learns that his boss is embezzling funds. Because Joe fears for his job, he does nothing. Joe's silence is:

   A. Proper.

   B. Improper.

   C. In violation of the norms of professional responsibility.

   D. In good faith, thus excusable.

8. Lawyer Manson goes on a hunting trip to Canada. One evening, he gets in a bar room brawl and kills two men. He is convicted of two counts of involuntary manslaughter. Manson's home state of M decides to discipline him. Is this permissible?

   A. No, because it was outside the state.

   B. No, because it was outside the country.

   C. No, because the actions were unrelated to the practice of law.

   D. Yes.

9. Slip is in a major difficulty. He is on trial for willful tax fraud. His old friend, Thomas, who is a municipal judge, knows that Slip is of the highest moral character. Slip could really use Thomas's testimony – but only as it relates to Slip's good character. Should Thomas so testify?

   A. No, because such appears improper.

B. No, because judges can never be witnesses.

C. No, because Slip may be of bad character.

D. Yes.

10. Juror Josie has a problem at the trial of which Joe Judge is the judge. One morning, before the trial is to begin, Josie comes in to Joe's chambers and tells him that he remembers the defendant from youth. Joe says, "Why didn't you tell us that before trial?" Josie says, "I forgot." Because it is such an important trial, Joe says, "Just forget we ever had this conversation." Joe's conduct was:

A. Proper.

B. Not proper.

C. Proper, if the error was harmless.

D. Proper, if Josie was not biased.

11. Maria is a state appellate judge. She teaches law for a local law school, and is paid for her teaching. Which of the following are true?

I. She should report her income.

II. She should not be paid.

III. She should not be teaching law.

A. I and II only.

B. II only.

C. I only.

D. III only.

12. Judge Gerard invests in the stock market for herself and her immediate family. She does quite well. Is such permissible?

A. Yes, because she does well.

B. Yes, because judges can do anything they want.

C. Yes, because a judge can manage her own finances.

D. Yes, because this business is unrelated to the practice of law.

13. Judge Lou is having his 50th birthday party. Lou is very popular and receives about 200 gifts, worth over $5000. Has Lou behaved improperly in accepting these gifts?

A. No, unless a particular gift is very valuable.

B. No, unless more than one gift is particularly valuable.

C. No, unless the gifts appear to create partiality on Lou's part to a lawyer likely to appear in Lou's court.

D. Yes.

14. Willie is campaigning for judicial office. It is a tough race. Willie thus pledges that, "If there is any doubt, I will order the maximum sentence." Is this proper?

    A. Yes.

    B. No.

    C. More facts are needed.

    D. It depends on the jurisdiction.

Questions 15 – 16 are based on the following facts:

Lawyer Breebar has just passed and been admitted to the bar, after having failed it three times prior. Breebar decides to set up his own personal injury practice, even though he has virtually no experience in this area.

Breebar rents office space, hires a secretary and places advertisements. Soon thereafter Client Herb calls Breebar regarding an auto accident case. The case seems relatively straightforward, so Breebar accepts the representation. However, the more Breebar looks into the facts, the more confused he becomes.

Months pass. Herb calls Breebar repeatedly, but Breebar does not return his phone calls. Instead Breebar consoles himself by hanging out at the beach. Breebar ultimately decides to get out of law and become a professional surfer.

15. When Breebar opened up a law office immediately after being admitted to the bar, he is:

    A. Subject to discipline because he is per se incompetent in this legal matter.

    B. Subject to discipline because he is actually incompetent in this matter.

    C. Not subject to discipline because he is presumed competent.

D. Not subject to discipline because he is actually competent.

16. When Breebar did not return Herb's phone calls, he is:

    A. Subject to discipline based on a theory of neglect.

    B. Subject to discipline because he has decided not to practice law.

    C. Not subject to discipline because there is no actual prejudice.

    D. Not subject to discipline because Breebar is no longer functioning as a lawyer.

Questions 17 – 18 are based on the following facts:

Lawyer Rob represents Client Loon. Loon is charged with the statutory offense of "Driving an Automobile while under the Influence of Alcohol." Rob has performed an excellent job. He has investigated the arresting officer, has had an expert examine the breathalyzer test utilized by the police, and has assembled a host of witnesses indicating that Loon is personally against the use of all drugs, including alcohol. However, there is one problem. Loon talks with a slight lisp and tends to be snide when he is questioned. Rob, therefore, decides that Loon must not take the stand in his own defense. Loon insists that he be so allowed. The trial ends with Loon fully acquitted - even though he does not take the stand.

17. Should Rob have let Loon take the stand?

    A. Yes, because this is an area of client decision.

    B. Yes, because a client's fundamental desires should always be followed.

    C. Yes, because the jury may have drawn an adverse conclusion from Loon's silence.

    D. No, because this was an area of attorney strategy.

18. Assume for this question only, that Loon admits to Rob that he was drinking heavily. If Ron coaches Loon as to how to best lie on the stand, Ron is:

    A. Behaving within the norms of the profession.

    B. In technical violation of the norms, but is not subject to discipline.

    C. Subject to discipline.

    D. Not subject to discipline.

Questions 19 – 20 are based on the following facts:

Lawyer Epsilon is in solo practice. One of the matters Epsilon routinely handles is the drafting of simple wills. In order to increase his business, Epsilon does these simple wills for only $25; thus intentionally undercutting the price of his peer lawyers. Two weeks after preparing the last of such wills for Client Andropov, Andropov's sole beneficiary dies. Epsilon has not made subsequent contact with Andropov.

19. Epsilon's undercutting the price of his peer lawyers is:

    A. In technical violation of the disciplinary norms.

    B. In substantial violation of the norms.

    C. Proper.

    D. Improper.

20. Which of the following are true?

    I. It is proper for Epsilon to contact Andropov regarding changing the will.

    II. Epsilon should contact Andropov regarding changing the will.

III. Epsilon will be disciplined for his failure to contact Andropov.

A. I only.

B. I and II only.

C. III only.

D. None of the above.

Questions 21 – 30 are based on the following facts:

Lawyer Linda is in practice in a large city. She charges $10,000 to go to trial on a charge of drunk driving. She requires this money be paid up front. Linda has been in practice for 15 years and enjoys a fine reputation in the community. Fifty miles outside of the city Lawyer Chip does the same work for $2,000. Linda seals her client contracts with a handshake, only. Chip always commits his contracts to writing.

On one occasion, Client Bingo sought the services of Linda. Linda refused because Bingo could not afford the $10,000. Bingo then sought the services of Chip. Bingo told Chip that he could not afford even $2,000. Chip felt sorry for Bingo and agreed to defend him against the charge of drunk driving "for $500 now and if you are acquitted you can pay me $1500 when you are able." Bingo is convicted and Chip does not bill him for the $1500.

A short time later, Client Moxy seeks the services of Linda. Linda decides to represent Moxy against a drunk driving charge for only $1000. Linda does this because Moxy is hard-pressed to find the money.

After the Bingo case, Client Rex comes in to see Chip, with a similar problem. Because Rex is wealthy and because Chip is having a cash-flow problem, Chip decides to bill Rex $5000 for the defense. This fee is not unusual for Chip's community, but it is the first time Chip has set his billing so high.

Unfortunately, the Rex case turns out to be highly complex. Chip calls Linda to see if she is willing to help out. Linda agrees, as does Rex. The fee is not raised and the client agrees to this arrangement in writing. Chip and Linda spend equal time on Rex's case and split the fee equally.

21. Linda's charging of $10,000 for a routine defense of drunken driving:

    A. May be excessive and thus subjects her to possible discipline.

    B. Is probably not excessive and thus is proper.

    C. Is totally within his own discretion.

    D. Is improper.

22. In order to discipline Linda for charging an excessive fee, which of the following are relevant:

    I. Her expertise.

    II. Her reputation.

    III. The difficulty of the case.

    IV. The fees of similarly situated attorneys.

    V. Chip's fees.

    A. I, II and III only.

    B. III and IV only.

    C. I, II, III and IV only.

    D. I, II, III, IV and V.

23. Linda's method of sealing her contracts with a handshake only is:

    A. In violation of the rules.

    B. Proper, but not preferred.

    C. Proper, and preferred.

    D. Improper.

24. Linda's refusal to represent Bingo:

    A. Is proper because rarely are attorneys required to accept clients.

    B. Is in technical violation of the rules.

    C. Depends on whether this jurisdiction follows the ABA Model Rules.

    D. Is in violation of the disciplinary rules, because she represented Moxy for only $1000.

25. Chip's fee agreement with Bingo:

    A. Was in good faith, thus Chip is not subject to discipline.

    B. Is a violation of the ethical norms, only if Chip was in good faith.

C. Is a violation of the rules, under the Leon case.

D. Subjects Chip to discipline.

26. Chip and Linda's billing some clients more money than others:

I. Is proper because attorneys need not bill the same amounts.

II. Subjects each of them to discipline, because although different attorneys can bill different amounts to different clients, each individual attorney must bill the same amount to every client who has similar legal work.

III. Is a violation of the Equal Protection Clause.

A. I only.

B. II and III only.

C. II only.

D. III only.

27. Based on the above facts, is Chip subject to discipline for utilizing Linda's services on the Rex case?

A. Yes, because fee splits, with attorneys outside the firm, are per se violative of the norms of the profession.

B. Yes, because the fee split was not in proportion to the actual work performed.

C. Yes, because Rex did not consent to the fee split.

D. No.

28. With regard to Chip's fee split with Linda, it would have been preferable for Chip:

I. To have asked Rex if he could call another attorney before so doing..

II. To have withdrawn entirely.

III. To have given Linda the greater portion of the fee.

A. I only.

B. I and II only.

C. I and III only.

D. I, II and III.

29. Assume for this question only, that instead of $1000, Linda received as full payment from Moxy her engagement ring, which was worth approximately $1100. Such a fee arrangement is:

    A. Improper.

    B. Proper.

    C. A disciplinary rule violation.

    D. None of the above.

30. Assume for this question only, that Rex is convicted and then demands the return of his $5000. What should Linda and Chip do?

    A. Nothing.

    B. Return the fee.

    C. Tell the prosecutor.

    D. Recommend arbitration of the dispute.

Question 31 – 32 are based on the following facts:

Kibbles approaches Lawyer Alfalfa in order to secure her services. Alfalfa agrees to represent Kibbles. The case involves a complex civil suit based on an alleged contractual misrepresentation Kibbles made to Sprout. At one point, Kibbles says, "If this [expletive] continues, I'm going to have to get someone to kill Sprout."

Alfalfa tells Kibbles, "Do not do that. It will only make your problems worse."

Kibbles responds, "Perhaps so, but I'm getting very close to having him taken out, and I mean it."

Alfalfa does nothing, and unfortunately Sprout is murdered, apparently by Kibbles.

31. Which of the following is most correct?

    A. Alfalfa is subject to discipline, because she was required to reveal the danger to Sprout.

    B. Alfalfa is subject to discipline, because she was required to withdraw from the case.

    C. Alfalfa behaved properly, because the crime was not reasonably apparent.

    D. Alfalfa behaved properly, because Kibbles was her client.

32. Assume for this question, that Alfalfa is called before the state disciplinary board regarding the Sprout killing. Which of the following are correct statements?

    I. Alfalfa is not subject to discipline.

    II. Alfalfa is subject to discipline.

    III. Alfalfa is permitted to reveal the conversation between herself and Kibbles, if such is relevant to her defense – because such was only a "secret."

    IV. Alfalfa is permitted to reveal the conversation between herself and Kibbles, if such is relevant to her defense.

    A. I and III only.

    B. I and IV only.

    C. II only.

    D. III only.

33. Lawyer Tron agrees to represent A, B and C on a personal injury lawsuit based on the automobile accident they had with D. As the case progresses, it is clear that D's policy will not cover the extent of the injuries suffered by B – although the policy is ample to cover the damages of A and C. D's insurer makes an offer of settlement which A and C accept. B, however, rejects the offer. At this juncture, Tron, in all probability, must:

    A. Try to compromise his clients' competing interests.

    B. Withdraw from representing B.

    C. Withdraw entirely.

    D. None of the above.

34. Lawyer Omega is a property law expert. Ten years ago, he argued a case for Zed, taking the position that the Rule Against Perpetuities was applicable. Omega was successful. Presently, on a remarkably similar fact-pattern, involving entirely different parties, Omega is asked to argue the opposite legal position. Assume that the Zed case has no precedential weight because it was not selected for official publication by the state supreme court. Is Omega permitted to argue the instant case?

    A. No, because such appears improper.

B. No, because such is an act involving moral turpitude.

C. Yes, because the parties are different.

D. Yes, because it was stipulated that the prior case was de-published.

35. Lawyer Pimbar practices corporate law. One of his clients, Nebber, invests in new business ventures. Pimbar has worked for Nebber, intermittently, for about 10 years. Pimbar has noted Nebber's great success and one day approaches Nebber regarding the possibility of Pimbar working with Nebber on "some kind of business deal." Because Pimbar has been a good lawyer, Nebber agrees and includes Pimbar in a deal which is highly profitable. Which of the following are correct propositions?

I. Pimbar is subject to discipline.

II. Pimbar's behavior was proper.

III. Pimbar should have committed the agreement to writing.

IV. Pimbar should have told Nebber that doing this business together was not necessary in order to secure Pimbar's continued services.

V. Pimbar should have made sure that Nebber truly wanted to do this business together.

VI. Pimbar should have kept a copy of the business deal for two years.

A. I only.

B. III, IV, V and VI only.

C. II, III, IV, V and VI only.

D. II, III, IV and V only.

36. Lawyer Delta operates a low cost legal services office. Delta has been in business for four years. Delta prepares simple wills, files non-contested divorces, and handles the defense of simple misdemeanors. Delta's fees are the lowest in town. Somewhat surprisingly, there have been no complaints whatsoever against Delta. In fact, he has been independently rated by one of the city's magazines as one of the top three lawyers in town.

One of the ways that Delta keeps his costs down is to not purchase any malpractice insurance. In order to safeguard himself against a calamity, he takes the following precautions: he has a triple fail-safe system so that no statutes of limitations are missed, he oversees all work, and he requires all clients to waive the right to sue him for malpractice "as a condition for receiving a 30% discount." Delta is subject to discipline because:

A. He undercut the prices of his peers.

B. He allowed the magazine to be his "runner."

C. He allowed the magazine to be his "capper."

D. He improperly limited malpractice liability.

37. Lawyer Guillaumet agrees to represent Client Kyle on a murder case. Kyle is indigent, so Guillaumet agrees to do the case for 50% royalties on a book that "Guillaumet may write after the trial is complete." Before the trial, Kyle pleads guilty to negligent homicide. Guillaumet never writes the book and, thus, receives no fee. Guillaumet's fee agreement is:

A. Proper, because Kyle consented.

B. Proper, because there was no actual prejudice.

C. Proper, but only because the book was never written and the case did not go to trial.

D. None of the above.

Questions 38 – 41 are based on the following facts:

Lawyer Gloria used to work for the law firm of Snow and White. Because of an excellent offer, she decides to work for the firm of Smith and Jones. While at Snow and White, Gloria had a minor role in a suit against Franklin by Kingsley. In the course of that suit, Gloria learned some confidential information about Kingsley, her then client. Presently, Baxter approaches Gloria regarding representing her in a suit against Kingsley. The suit is somewhat related to the earlier case.

38. If Gloria accepts the case, she is:

    A. Subject to discipline.

    B. Subject to discipline, only if she compromises anything she learned about Kingsley.

    C. Subject to discipline, unless she voluntarily screens herself off the case.

    D. Not subject to discipline.

39. Assume for this question, that Gloria tells the two partners of the firm, Smith and Jones, about her potential conflict of interest. By doing which of the following, will Smith and Jones not be subject to discipline?

    I. Immediately terminating Gloria, then taking the case.

    II. Screening Gloria off of the case.

    III. Obtaining written conscent from all involved.

    A. I only.

    B. II only.

    C. I, II and III.

    D. I or II.

40. Assume for this question only, that Smith and Jones do not take the case, and that a short time later Lawyer Smith leaves the firm, to form a new firm called Smith and Klinghoofer. May Smith and Klinghoofer take the Baxter case against Kingsley?

    A. Yes, because there is no longer imputed disqualification.

    B. Yes, because the rules now so permit.

    C. Yes.

    D. No.

41. Assume for this question only, that Kingsley's lawyers contacted the firm of Smith and Jones and said, "We are aware of the conflict because of your hiring Gloria. If you screen Gloria off the case, we have no problem with your representing Kingsley." In such instance:

    A. Kingsley's lawyers are subject to discipline.

    B. Smith and Jones are permitted to take the case.

    C. Gloria is subject to discipline if Smith and Jones take the case.

    D. Gloria is subject to discipline since she will likely help Smith and Jones on the case.

42. Attorney Arlen is District Attorney for Medium City. He has direct responsibility for the handling of all criminal cases in the city. Arlen decides to go into private practice and joins the firm of Doe and Foe. Several of Doe and Foe's cases were filed through Arlen's office prior to Arlen's resignation. Are Doe and Foe permitted to retain these cases even though there is a potential/actual conflict of interest?

    A. Yes, because no actual conflict has been shown.

    B. Yes, because there is only a potential conflict of interest.

    C. Yes, if Arlen is screened off any case, is given no compensation for these cases, and the other side is informed.

    D. Yes, because attorneys must be allowed mobility to change jobs.

Questions 43 – 45 are based on the following facts:

Lawyer Angel is in the employ of Rockford Corp. Rockford president Jim is contemplating a complex business transaction which Angel believes to be fraudulent. Angel tells this to Jim and Jim says, "I think we'll go ahead anyway."

43. What should Angel do?

    A. Withdraw from further representation of Jim.

    B. Withdraw from further representation of Rockford Corp.

    C. Suggest Jim reconsider and obtain another lawyer's advice.

    D. Blow the whistle on Rockford Corp.

44. Assume for this question, that Jim is adamant about going ahead with the arguably fraudulent conduct and that Angel has asked him to seek another's attorney's advice. If Angel goes directly to the Board of Directors, requesting that they override Jim's decision, Angel is:

    A. Behaving properly.

    B. Subject to discipline.

    C. Behaving improperly.

    D. None of the above.

45. Assume for this question only, that Rockford employee Dodd approaches Angel about fraudulent acts that Jim has requested Dodd to perform, some of which Dodd has performed. The most important thing that Angel should do is:

    A. Withdraw from future employment.

    B. Counsel against the fraud.

    C. Tell Dodd that Angel is not his attorney.

    D. Give Jim an ultimatum that this conduct must cease.

46. Attorney practices law in State X. Occasionally, he receives an "advance of fees" which he puts in a client trust account in State Y. Attorney does this because the interest rates are substantially higher in State Y. Attorney's handling of client funds is best labeled:

    A. Fraudulent.

    B. Proper, but not preferable.

    C. In violation of the codes.

    D. Intelligent.

47. Attorney Midas agrees to represent Drugger. Since Drugger is hard-pressed for cash, Midas agrees to accept a Rolex watch as an advance of the first $10,000 owed. Since Midas has not earned the $10,000 yet, he is in a quandary as to what to do with the watch. What is Midas's best course of conduct?

    A. Wear the watch.

    B. Sell the watch and put the $10,000 in his client trust account.

    C. Place the watch in a client-only safety deposit box.

    D. Call the state bar for help.

Questions 48 – 51 are based on the following facts:

Lawyer Sable has just settled a case for Client for $220,000. Client has accepted this settlement. Outstanding liens and costs total $20,000. Sable agreed to a contingency fee of 25%.

48. Client says to Sable, "Don't pay off the $20,000 to the doctors - they didn't earn it." What should Sable do?

    A. Pay the $20,000 since it truly was owed.

    B. Give notice to the debtors and keep the money in his trust account.

    C. Pay the $20,000 to Client since it is ultimately his choice.

    D. Seek arbitration.

49. If Client tells Sable, "You are overpaid. You didn't earn $50,000. You earned $10,000, at most." Sable then recommends Client arbitrate or sue. Sable keeps the entire $220,000 in his trust account. Is Sable subject to discipline?

    A. No, because there was an ongoing dispute.

    B. No, because a 25% contingency fee is generous.

    C. No, because there has been no misappropriation of property.

D. None of the above.

50. Assume for this question only, that Sable, unknown to Client, invests the entire $220,000 in a business gamble and wins big. He then confesses this to Client and offers Client half of his profits ($100,000) in addition to the $150,000 owed. Is Sable subject to discipline?

    A. Yes, because he has commingled funds.

    B. Yes, because lawyers must not gamble.

    C. No, because there was no harm.

    D. No, because Client profited substantially.

51. Assume for this question only, that Client agrees to the fee division and is promptly paid the $150,000. Sable, however, leaves his fee, $50,000, in the trust account for two months so as to avoid paying taxes on that amount for the calendar year just ending. If Sable is called up for discipline, his worst defense is:

    A. There was no harm to the client.

    B. There was no commingling.

    C. It was a first-time good faith mistake.

    D. He was very sick and thus could not remove the funds.

52. Lawyer Snobble is representing Client Meek on a "slip and fall" case. Snobble is performing excellent work and is nearing settlement of the case. For no good reason, Meek terminates the employment of Snobble. Under these circumstances, Snobble:

    A. Should withdraw.

    B. Shall withdraw.

    C. May withdraw.

    D. Should seek arbitration.

53. Lawyer Vardon is an excellent and tough attorney. She is representing Client Don in a civil rights action. In order to motivate the opposing party Lon to settle, she attempts to "wear down" his desire to sue. She does this by opposing every discovery request and by making several discovery requests which are not necessary. Is Vardon subject to discipline?

    A. No, because this is an acceptable tactic.

    B. No, because ours is an adversary system.

    C. No, because discovery is, per se, acceptable.

D. Yes.

54. Prosecuting attorney Notch decides to prosecute Gung to "send out a message to all gang members." There is a terrible gang problem. In the particular case against Gung, the evidence is amorphous. Notch believes he will likely not obtain a conviction, but is nevertheless hopeful. Notch's prosecution of Gung:

    A. Subjects Notch to discipline.

    B. May subject Notch to discipline – depending on whether or not a conviction is obtained.

    C. Is proper.

    D. More facts are required.

55. Lawyer Penelope is representing Phyllis in a complex securities case. The opposing counsel has missed two cases on two different points. Both are directly on point. One case is in State P (where this case is being litigated.) The other case is in sister State Q (State P usually follows the lead of State Q.) Penelope reveals neither case to the court. Moreover, in closing argument, Penelope alludes to facts which she did not offer in the case-in-chief (she believes she can "get this by" the inattentive and ill-informed jury.) The opposing party prevails in the verdict. Which of the following will not subject Penelope to discipline?

    I. Losing the case.

    II. Not revealing the State Q case.

    III. Not revealing the State P case.

    IV. Her closing argument.

    A. III and IV only.

    B. I and II only.

    C. I only.

    D. IV only.

56. Client Winston tells his Lawyer Shannon that he must perjure himself regarding the use of self-defense. Shannon tries to convince Winston not so proceed, but Winston is adamant. Shannon makes a decision that it is better that she help. She, thus coaches Winston on the best method to utilize this defense. Utilizing the perjury, Winston is acquitted.

    A. Shannon is subject to discipline, but is not subject to malpractice liability.

    B. Shannon is not subject to discipline, but is subject to malpractice liability.

    C. Shannon is subject to discipline and is also subject to malpractice liability.

D. Shannon is neither subject to discipline nor to malpractice liability.

57. Lawyer O'Mallory has a document given to him by his client Cohn. The document indicates that Cohn is civilly liable. The document is a memorandum of agreement between Cohn and the plaintiff in this case, Bush. Evidently, Bush has no copy of the agreement. Cohn asks O'Mallory what he should do with the document. Which of the following are acceptable responses?

I. Do not admit that you have such a document.

II. Only admit you have it if asked.

III. Make it available to the opposing party.

IV. Do not destroy it.

V. It is better to make it available to Bush. If you give it to me, I will, but I cannot make you furnish it.

A. I and V only.

B. II and V only.

C. III and IV only.

D. III, IV and V only.

58. Lawyer Flash holds a pretrial news conference regarding his client's case. Client Jed was allegedly beaten up by the police without provocation. Flash's motivation for holding the news conference is to motivate the other side to settle. On these facts alone, Flash's conduct is:

A. Proper.

B. Not proper.

C. In violation of the disciplinary rules.

D. None of the above.

59. At the close of Lawyer's case, after a verdict has been obtained in favor of Lawyer's client, Lawyer takes the stand to state her fees (which the losing party must pay). Such is:

A. Proper.

B. Not proper.

C. In violation of the disciplinary rules.

D. None of the above.

60. Lawyer Tetra is representing Client Tantra, in a case against Yantra. Yantra is being represented by Sinnic. Tetra calls Sinnic repeatedly, to make an objectively very fair offer of settlement. Sinnic does not return her calls. Tetra then makes a written settlement offer, with the request that even if the offer is rejected, that Sinnic make phone or written contact. Still, Sinnic makes no contact. Finally, Tetra contacts Yantra directly. Yantra is shocked that such generous offers were made and that Yantra had never heard about them. Sinnic files a complaint with the state bar against Tetra for "interfering in the sacrosanct attorney-client relationship." This complaint will:

A. Fail, because of Sinnic's bad faith.

B. Fail, because Tetra had no reasonable alternative.

C. Fail, because no settlement was actually made.

D. None of the above.

Questions 61 – 62 are based on the following facts:

Lawyer Young works for Partner Old. Old tells Young to mislead the opposing party. Young believes that such is against the rules of the state bar. However, Old insists.

61. If Young acquiesces, he is:

A. Subject to discipline.

B. Not subject to discipline.

C. Civilly liable.

D. Not civilly liable.

62. Old is subject to discipline for which of the following:

I. Vicarious violation of the norms.

II. Failure to adequately supervise underlings.

A. I only.

B . II only.

C. I and II.

D. Neither I nor II.

63. Lawyer Bob is licensed in 16 states. He has decided to relocate to State Q. State Q will waive Bob in, for a nominal fee, without the need for Bob to sit for the bar examination. Bob relocates to state Q. While waiting to be sworn in, Bob does a few simple wills, without being paid, primarily as favors. Is Bob subject to discipline?

    A. Yes, because he was practicing law without a license.

    B. No, because in effect he had a license.

    C. No, because he had no pecuniary motive.

    D. No, because he did not appear before a court.

64. Lawyer Fred signs up to work in the "Law Offices of Ben Bigger," a very influential attorney. Fred knows very little. Bigger has much knowledge, and many innovative techniques. Bigger requires not only Fred, but all of his new associates, to agree not to compete for five years, in order to work for him. Is Bigger subject to discipline?

    A. No, because under the circumstances, such is reasonable.

    B. It depends on other facts.

    C. There is a code split.

    D. None of the above.

END OF QUESTIONS

PROFESSIONAL RESPONSIBILITY ANSWERS

1. D is the correct answer. A judge, even with another judge's approval, is not permitted to be a character witness. See, ABA Model Code of Judicial Conduct [CJC] 2B. As such, a judge has unnecessarily put him or herself in a position of appearing biased or prejudiced and has placed him or herself in a role more of a lay citizen. A is incorrect under the ABA Code because not all judicial rules are discretionary. B is incorrect because consent of a superior does not relieve a lawyer or a judge from personal responsibilities. C is incorrect because judges certainly can be disciplined.

2. C is the correct answer. CJC 4C(2) indicates that it is improper for a sitting judge to serve on a government commission. Although the prestige of the judge's position will add weight to the credibility of the commission, again this is thought to be a compromise of judicial impartiality. A, though arguably giving a correct statement of interpretation, is incorrect because the rules are to the contrary. B is incorrect because the mere fact that the judge is not paid does not relieve the judge of his or her ethical responsibility. D is incorrect because serving on such a commission is not, per se, undignified.

3. A is the correct answer. Judges must refrain from criticisms of jurors and must also refrain from ex parte conferences absent exigencies (and there was no exigency here). CJC 3B(7)(a); 3B(10). Judges must maintain demeanor and professionalism. Criticism of any party absent their misconduct destroys that professionalism. Further, under our adversary system, ex parte conferences are believed to create not only an appearance of impropriety but actual impropriety in that the other advocate does not have a chance to defend his or her position. B, C and D are incorrect for the same reasons that A is correct.

4. C is the correct answer. A judge who must seek reelection is permitted to promise impartiality. He or she is not permitted to promise a result in a specific case. CJC 5A(3)(d)(i). A and D are incorrect for the same reasons that C is correct. B is incorrect because although a judge is granted certain first amendment freedom of speech protection, this radical promise is beyond the first amendment freedom allowed.

A PROFESSIONAL RESPONSIBILITY

5. D is the correct answer. Advertisements must not be misleading. ABA Model Rules of Professional Conduct Model Rule [MR] 7.1; ABA Model Code of Professional Responsibility, Disciplinary Rule [DR] 2-101. Since a statement that a lawyer has never lost a case, even if true, is misleading – since it sets up an unreasonable expectation regarding cases which no lawyer could win; Quinn's ad is in violation of the rules. A and B are incorrect because lawyer advertising is given limited First Amendment protection. C is incorrect because there is no requirement, as yet, that lawyer ads appear in a dignified forum. Such is, of course, preferable, but it is not mandatory.

6. C is the correct answer. Lawyers must not lie on their bar applications. Such shows a lack of good character, which subjects an attorney to discipline. MR 8.1; DR 1-101(A). Discipline is not for the purpose of punishment. Rather, it is to protect the public from dangerously inept or corrupt attorneys. Moreover, there are no statutes of limitations regarding disciplining attorneys. Thus, C is correct and A and D are incorrect. B is incorrect because it is permissible to discipline an attorney for past acts unrelated to her present psychological state.

7. C is the correct answer. A lawyer must turn in his delinquent peers provided what they know is unprivileged. MR 8.3(a); DR 1-103(A). Thus, C is correct and A and B are incorrect. D is incorrect for two reasons: first Joe is not in good faith and second, good faith is not an excuse for this kind of violation. (Note: California has no like requirement.)

8. D is the correct answer. A state can discipline a lawyer for actions performed anywhere, if such actions involve moral turpitude. Since manslaughter is morally wrong, discipline is acceptable. MR 8.4; MR 8.5; DR 1-102(A)(3). Therefore, D is correct and A and B are incorrect. C is incorrect because the actions of moral turpitude need not be directly related to the practice of law.

9. A is the correct answer. Judges should not be character witnesses. Such appears improper. CJC 2B. Therefore A is correct and D is incorrect. B is incorrect because judges may on occasion be required to testify, e.g., if they are a party to their own litigation. C is incorrect because Slip's good or bad character is not the issue. The issue is whether the judge is permitted to testify.

10. B is the correct answer. Ex parte communications between a judge and juror are not preferable. If such occur, all parties to the litigation should be given notice. CJC 3B. Thus, B is correct and A, C and D are incorrect.

11. C is the correct answer because only choice I is correct. A judge is permitted to teach law and be paid. Thus, II and III are incorrect and I is correct. However, judges should make a public report of their extra judicial income. CJC 4B, H.

12. C is the correct answer. Judges are permitted to manage and participate in a business primarily engaged in investment of the judge's financial resources. Thus, C is correct and A and B are incorrect. D is incorrect because the business can be related to law, e.g., law teaching. CJC 4D.

13. C is the correct answer. Judges are permitted to receive gifts related to ordinary hospitality such as birthday presents. Only when the gift creates an appearance of impropriety should it be refused. CJC 4D. A, B and D are, therefore, incorrect and C is correct. (Note: the call of this question is phrased in the negative.)

14. A is the correct answer. Judges, when campaigning for office, generally should not make pledges regarding the way they would sentence CJC 5A. However, the first amendment is applicable to judges – so judges can take a "law and order" stance. Thus, B is incorrect. C is incorrect because ample facts were given. D is incorrect because the first amendment controls.

15. C is the correct answer. Passing the bar exam, on its face, is proof of reasonable competence. Perhaps where the law is complex, a new lawyer could not begin practice in that area. But in any general area of law, new lawyers are permitted to start right out. MR 1.1; DR 6-101. A is incorrect for the same reason that C is correct. B is incorrect because no facts indicate that Breebar is actually incompetent. D is incorrect because no facts indicate that Breebar is actually competent.

16. A is the correct answer. Lawyers must neither neglect cases nor neglect their clients. MR 1.3; DR 6-101(A)(3); American Bar Association Model Code of Professional Responsibility Ethical Consideration [EC] 6-4. Not returning client calls for months, as stipulated here, is just cause for discipline. B is obviously incorrect because lawyers are free to discontinue their practice of law. C is incorrect because the issue of injury to the client is more an issue of tort (malpractice) liability. There need be no client prejudice for discipline to follow. D is incorrect because, although it is permissible for a lawyer to discontinue the practice of law, he must take reasonable steps to insure that his clients are well taken care of. Breebar just "goofed off."

17. A is the correct answer. As a general rule, strategy is entirely within a lawyer's discretion. There are, however, certain fundamental choices which are entirely to be made by the client. Whether or not to take the stand is one of those areas. MR 1.2(a); EC 7-7. Thus, Rob should have let Loon testify. Here the Model Rules require that the attorney abide by the client's wishes regarding whether or not to testify. (Under the old Model Code, it is discretionary.) B is incorrect because if a client disagrees as to strategy, the lawyer may follow his own decisions and desires. C offers a correct analysis of what the jury might think regarding a defendant's silence. But C is incorrect because the real issue is not what the jury will think – it is who gets to make the decision. D is incorrect for the same reasons that A is correct.

18. C is the correct answer. A lawyer must not make use of perjured testimony. MR 3.3(a)(4); DR 7-102(A)(4.) Rob not only makes use of the testimony – he also aids in the fraud on the court. A and D are incorrect for the same reason that C is correct. B is incorrect because a technical violation of the mandatory rules subjects an attorney to discipline. Of course, if it is merely a technical violation, the discipline will probably be light, e.g., private reprimand only.

19. C is the correct answer. There is nothing in the code which prohibits a lawyer from charging low fees. To the contrary, lawyers are encouraged to compete and to do work for free. MR 6.1; EC 2-25. Thus, Epsilon's behavior is within his own discretion and is, thus, "proper." Choices A, B and D are incorrect for the same reasons that C is correct.

20. B is the correct answer, because choices I and II are correct. Choice I is correct because there is an exception to the rule barring solicitation of clients when the solicitation concerns a related matter to which the lawyer had previously performed work. MR 7.3; DR 2-104(A)(1). Choice II is correct because when a client is to be prejudiced, the best course of conduct is for the attorney to initiate contact with that former client (on the related matter). MR 1.3. Choice III is incorrect because, although lawyers "should" contact clients in like situations; such is within their discretion – unless, of course, they tell the client that they will periodically inspect the legal document.

21. B is the correct answer. For the most part, attorneys can set their own fees which are permitted to be substantial, within the broad parameters of reasonableness. MR 1.5; DR 2-106. A and D are incorrect because although excessive fees will subject an attorney to discipline, this fee was likely not excessive. C is incorrect because attorney fees must be reasonable.

22. C is the correct answer, because choices I, II, III and IV are correct. I is correct because expertise is a factor in whether the attorney fee is excessive v. reasonable. II is correct because the attorney's fame (reputation) is another legitimate factor. III is obviously correct, because the more difficult is the case, the higher the fee can be. IV is correct because, although not completely controlling, the fees of similarly situated attorneys is relevant in adjudging whether a particular attorney's fee is excessive. Choice V is incorrect because Chip, a small town attorney, is not similarly situated to Linda. Thus, his fees are not relevant. See generally MR 1.5; DR 2-106(A).

23. B is the correct answer. Although it is preferable to reduce contracts with new clients to writing, such is not mandatory. MR 1.5(b); EC 2-19. A, C and D are incorrect for the same reasons that B is correct. (Note: California law requires fees of $1000 or over generally be put in writing; the MPRE does not test California law.)

24. A is the correct answer. Nothing in the ABA code requires an attorney to accept all walk-in clients. Thus, B and C are incorrect. D is incorrect because nothing in the code requires an attorney to bill all clients the same amount for similar work. The fees need only be reasonable – but not equal. MR 1.5; DR 2-106; EC 2-17. Such is obviously the case because attorneys are encouraged to perform some legal work for the poor for no charge. MR 6.1; EC 2-25.

25. D is the correct answer. Allowing Bingo to pay an additional $1500 only if he is acquitted is essentially a contingency fee contract. Contingency fee contracts in criminal cases are per se prohibited. MR 1.5(d)(2); DR 2-106(C). Chip's good faith is no defense – thus, A and B are incorrect. C is incorrect because there is no Leon case relevant here. (Note: California law does not, per se, prohibit such an arrangement.)

26. A is the correct answer, because only choice I is correct . Attorney fees need only be reasonable, not equal – thus, I is correct. MR 1.5; DR 2-106; EC 2-17. II is incorrect for the same reason that I is correct. III is incorrect because there is no state action; thus, the Equal Protection Clause is not relevant.

27. D is the correct answer. Fee splits are acceptable with attorneys outside the firm if the client consents and the fee is not raised. MR 1.5(e); DR 2-107(A). A is incorrect for the same reasons that D is correct. B is incorrect because it misreads the facts. This fee split was in proportion to actual attorney work performed. (Please note: the Model Code requires an equal fee split; but the Model Rules do not. Regardless of this code difference, this answer is incorrect because it misreads the facts.) C is incorrect because Rex did consent.

28. A is the correct answer because only choice I is correct. I is correct because Chip really should have asked his client prior to investigating the possibility of bringing another attorney aboard. MR 1.5(e); DR 2-107(A). II is incorrect, because withdrawal is not necessary. III is incorrect because the code does not suggest that disproportionate attorney fee splits are always preferable.

29. B is the correct answer. Although the receipt of client chattels as fee is not preferable, such is not prohibited. See MR 1.5, Comment [2]. A, C and D are incorrect for the same reason that B is correct.

30. D is the correct answer. When there is a fee dispute between the lawyer and client, the lawyer should recommend arbitration. Such, however, is not required. See MR 1.5, Comment [5]. [Note: it would be a different fact-pattern entirely, where the fee is in the trust account of the attorney. Such is not the case when the fee is paid up front, as here.] A is incorrect for the same reason that D is correct. B is incorrect because attorneys need not return fees which they reasonably believe they have earned. C is incorrect because attorneys must not threaten or harm clients so as to keep their fees which are in dispute.

31. D is the correct answer. Somewhat surprisingly, there is no requirement that an attorney reveal an intended future crime of her client. The option is given if the crime involves physical danger or corporate fraud under MR 1.6. Therefore, D is correct. A is incorrect for the same reason that D is correct. B is incorrect because an attorney need only withdraw when the crime (or fraud) is on the court itself. C is incorrect because it misreads the facts – the crime was reasonably apparent.

32. B is the correct answer because only choices I and IV are correct. I is correct because an attorney is permitted to keep to herself her client's spoken intent to commit a future dangerous crime. MR 1.6(b)(1); DR 4-101(C)(3.) IV is correct because an attorney is permitted to reveal a confidence if such is reasonably related to and reasonably necessary to defense of herself. MR 1.6(b)(2); DR 4-101(C)(4.) II is incorrect for the same reasons that I and IV are correct. III is incorrect because it gives the wrong reason for the permission to reveal data necessary to defend oneself. It does not matter whether the revelation involves a confidence (testimonial-type information received from the client) or a secret (non-testimonial observations made by the attorney of the client). In either case, the attorney may reveal such to defend herself or protect another party from violence. But, outside of these exceptions, neither confidences nor secrets are permitted to be revealed.

33. C is the correct answer. Although an attorney is permitted to represent multiple clients in one cause of action, if a conflict develops between any of the clients, the attorney must withdraw from all. MR 1.7(b); DR 5-105(C.) A, B and D are incorrect for the same reason that C is correct.

34. C is the correct answer. Since the parties, the court, and the time-frame are all different there is no real conflict of interest in taking an opposite legal position some time in the future. See MR 1.7, Comment [9]. A and B are incorrect for the same reasons that C is correct. D is incorrect because it is irrelevant whether or not the case was de-published. The issue is whether the attorney misbehaved – not whether the case has precedential weight.

35. D is correct because only choices II, III, IV and V are correct. II is correct because business transactions between lawyers and their clients are not prohibited completely. MR 1.8(a); DR 5-104(A.) III is correct because, under MR 1.8(a)(3) written client consent is required, but there is no such requirement in the Model Code of Professional Responsibility. Therefore, the correct answer for the MPRE uses discretionary language, such as the word "should." IV is correct because telling the client that he need not do business with the lawyer insures that the client's participation is voluntary and that there is no attorney over-reaching. MR 1.8(a)(1); DR 5-104(A); EC 5-3. V is correct for the same reasons that IV is correct.

36. D is the correct answer. Under MR 1.8(h), a lawyer is permitted to prospectively limit his malpractice liability only if the client receives independent legal advice recommending such. There was none here. (Under DR 6-102(A), such a waiver is, per se, banned.) Thus, D is correct. A is incorrect because attorneys are permitted to lower prices so as to compete with their peers. B and C are incorrect because no facts indicate that Delta paid the magazine reporter to stir up business for him.

37. D is the correct answer. An attorney is not permitted to receive as his fee rights to a book about the subject matter of the litigation. MR 1.8(d); DR 5-104(B). Thus, A, B and C are incorrect; and D is the best answer. (Note: California law may permit such an arrangement.)

38. A is the correct answer. When a lawyer has learned something confidential and relevant about a client, she is not permitted to oppose that client in a later case. MR 1.9(a); EC 4-6. B is incorrect because it misreads the facts. The facts indicate that the prior confidence is "somewhat related," thus, the best answer is that Gloria cannot take the case. C is incorrect because screening Gloria off the case is not an available option under the facts. D is incorrect for the same reason that A is correct.

39. C is correct because choices I, II and II are correct. When a lawyer in a firm is disqualified, generally all lawyers in the firm are disqualified. MR 1.10; DR 5-105(D). Although terminating Gloria is harsh and may open Smith and Jones to civil liability for wrongful termination; the termination will remove the conflict of interest. Screening Gloria off the case is acceptable, provided there is written consent.

40. A is the correct answer. A vicariously disqualified attorney (here Smith) is no longer disqualified if he discontinues association with the actually disqualified attorney. See generally MR 1.10; DR 5-105(D). B and C are correct answers, but they are less specific and, thus, less preferable to choice A. D is incorrect for the same reason that A is correct.

41. B is the correct answer. Actual or imputed disqualification can be waived by the opposing party. Thus, since such occurred here, B is the correct answer. MR 1.10(d). A is incorrect because in no way does it appear that Kingsley's lawyers compromised his case – Gloria had to be screened off the case. C is incorrect because whether or not Smith and Jones take the case, Gloria has performed up to the standards by making the conflict known and apparently taking no part in the case. D is incorrect since no facts whatsoever suggest that Gloria will compromise Kingsley's position.

42. C is the correct answer. MR 1.11(a) permits the new firm not to be disqualified if the former government attorney is screened off the case and the opposing party is given notice. This rule allows government attorneys mobility and is probably a necessity due to the large volume of cases that government attorneys deal with. A and B are incorrect because they avoid discussing the particulars of the rule which governs this situation. D is an incorrect answer because, although it correctly states the policy behind the rule, it does not state the rule itself. As always, a more specific answer is to be chosen over a correct but more general answer.

43. C is the correct answer. When a lawyer works for a business entity and a director of that entity indicates the desire to perform an act involving fraud, the first thing the attorney should do is ask this individual to reconsider and seek a second opinion from another attorney. See MR 1.13(b); EC 5-18; EC 5-24; DR 5-107(B). Thus, C is correct. Since withdrawal at this point is not required, both A and B are incorrect. D is incorrect because a breach of the confidence is not acceptable.

44. A is the correct answer. Going over the head of the individual in the business entity who intends to do the fraud is the correct course of conduct. Thus, A is correct. MR 1.13(b). B, C and D are incorrect for the same reason that A is correct.

45. C is the correct answer. Angel is in a difficult position. Not only should he counsel Jim and Rockford Corp., but he also may have some duties to Dodd – who apparently is seeking Angel's legal advice. Since what Dodd says may hurt Dodd if revealed – but may possibly aid Rockford Corp., Angel should as soon as possible tell Dodd that he represents Rockford not Dodd. Otherwise, there might arise an impermissible conflict of interest between the duties owed to Rockford and those owed to Dodd. Without this kind of warning, Dodd's interests might severely be compromised. See MR 1.13, Comment [8]. Although withdrawing would be permissible, Dodd's interests are more imminent and, thus, important, thus, C is a better answer than A. Similarly, although counseling against future fraud is important, Dodd should be told by Angel that Angel is not his attorney – and, thus, their conversation is not privileged. Therefore, again, C is a better answer than B. For similar reasons of imminence and the immediacy of Dodd's problems, C is a better answer than D.

46. C is the correct answer. Although this attorney is in good faith and has made a legitimate economic decision; nevertheless the code is quite unforgiving. It is required that the trust account be in the state in which the attorney practices law. MR 1.15; DR 9-102(A). A is incorrect because the conduct is not fraudulent. B is incorrect for the same reason that C is correct. Although the attorney's choice may be economically intelligent, it is legally stupid to overtly violate the code. [Please note: the student may have noted an inordinate number of C choices as the correct answer. This was purposeful, on the part of the drafter. Students should not be attempting to "fudge" answers such that there are 25% of each choice.]

47. C is the correct answer. Although receiving property as advance payment of fees from a client is not preferred, it is acceptable if such is kept separate from the property of the attorney. Putting the property in a client-only safety deposit box is the ideal method. See MR 1.15, Comment [1]; DR 9-102(B)(2). A is incorrect for the same reason that C is correct. B is incorrect because a problem will arise if less money is earned than the value of the watch. D is correct, but C is a more specific, thus, better answer.

48. B is the correct answer. The Model Rules recommend the procedure offered in choice B. See MR 1.15(c) and Comment [3]. A is incorrect because it entirely disregards the client's wishes which may have a reasonable basis. B is incorrect, since by paying the client, the attorney may be furthering a fraud. D is incorrect only because the attorney has no claim to the funds and, thus, is not a necessary party to the arbitration.

49. D is the correct answer. A is incorrect because it is in dispute that $150,000 is owed to client. Such must be paid. Only $40,000 is in dispute. B and C are incorrect because it is not a defense to taking disputed funds out of the trust account that the client is acting irrationally.

50. A is the correct answer. That the client is not injured is irrelevant to the rule prohibiting commingling. Since taking Client's funds was without consent, it is commingling. B is incorrect because lawyers are permitted to gamble with their own money, outside of their practice of law. C and D are incorrect for the same reasons that A is correct.

51. B is the correct answer. There was certainly commingling and this is certainly prohibited. Since harm to the client is irrelevant when there is commingling, A is a poor choice. C is incorrect because there is no good faith exception to the rule prohibiting commingling. However, in passing, it is noted that the state disciplinary board may consider the good faith when doling out the punishment. D is incorrect because illness on the part of the attorney may be a mitigating factor. See generally MR 1.15, DR 9-102. [Please note: the call of this question was phrased in the negative.]

52. B is the correct answer. Because the attorney-client relationship is fiduciary in nature and because it is the client who is in the position of trust, clients are generally permitted to terminate the services of their attorneys "at will" with little or no penalty. MR 1.16(a)(3); DR 2-110(B)(4). Attorneys, when terminated, as a general rule, must withdraw; thus, B is the correct answer. A and C are incorrect for the same reasons that B is correct. D is incorrect because there is no need for arbitration as to whether the attorney must withdraw after being fired by the client – the lawyer shall withdraw.

53. D is the correct answer. Attorneys must not either harass an opposing party or pursue a frivolous argument. MR 3.1; DR 7-102(A)(1). Since it is stipulated that Vardon merely desired to "wear down" the opposing party, such action is definitely prohibited, and, thus, only D is the correct answer. A, B and C are incorrect for the very same reason that D is correct.

54. A is the correct answer. Prosecutors have a higher duty of "justice" than other attorneys – not only must they obey the applicable code of legal ethics and do a good job but they also must personally and reasonably believe that she who the prosecutor is prosecuting is more likely than not guilty. Prosecutors do not have the luxury of simply trying "pretty good" cases. MR 3.1; See generally 7-102. Thus, A is correct, and B, C and D are incorrect.

55. B is the correct answer because only choices I and II are correct. I is correct because attorneys are generally not disciplined for simply losing cases. There must be another factor, such as neglect. II is correct because attorneys need not reveal cases on point which are outside the jurisdiction. However, attorneys must reveal cases within the jurisdiction which are directly on point; thus, III is incorrect. MR 3.3(a)(3); DR 7-106(B)(1). (Note: there is no such requirement to reveal contra cases in California.) IV is incorrect because attorneys must not purposely mislead the jury in closing argument. MR 3.3(a)(1); DR 7- 102(A)(5). (Note: the call of this question is phrased in the negative.)

56. A is the correct answer. An attorney must not help a client commit perjury. MR 3.3(a)(4); DR 7-102(A)(4). Since Shannon did this, she is subject to discipline. In order for an attorney to be civilly liable for malpractice, there must occur two elements: 1) an attorney error (usually shown by referring to the state's code of ethics) and 2) harm/damages to the client. Since Winston was acquitted, prong 2 is lacking and there is no malpractice liability. Only choice A includes the above two propositions (discipline but no malpractice.) Thus, B, C and D are incorrect.

57. D is the correct answer because only choices III, IV and V are correct. An attorney must counsel his client to furnish to the opposing party all material evidence. MR 3.4(a); DR 7-109(A.) Since the document is certainly material evidence, O'Mallory must advise his client to make such available. I and II are, thus, incorrect and III and IV are, thus, correct. V is correct because in the event that the client refuses to turn over material evidence the attorney cannot blow the whistle. Moreover, attorneys are permitted to tell clients the attorney's ethical duties.

58. A is the correct answer. Attorneys enjoy a real degree of First Amendment free speech protection; thus, they are permitted to speak to the press pre-trial. Attorneys can be disciplined only if they intend or should have known that their comments will prejudice the trial. Since Flash's conduct fell short of that, it was proper. B, C and D are incorrect for the same reasons that A is correct. See generally MR 3.6(a); DR 7-107.

59. A is the correct answer. A lawyer is permitted to testify as to the value of her legal services, thus, A is the correct answer. MR 3.7(a)(2); DR 5-101(B)(3). B, C and D are incorrect for the same reason that A is correct.

60. D is the correct answer. A lawyer must not communicate with a represented party absent the opposing lawyer's consent or judicial order. MR 4.2. There was no order here. Thus A, B and C are incorrect.

61. A is the correct answer. It is no defense to a charge of discipline that the charged lawyer was simply obeying the orders of his superior. MR 5.2(a). It is a disciplinary violation to intentionally mislead the opposing party. MR 4.1; DR 7-102. Thus, A is correct and B is incorrect. C and D are incorrect because more facts are needed as to whether there is tort liability, e.g., were there damages?

62. C is the correct answer because both choices I and II are correct. A lawyer is responsible when he directs another lawyer to violate the rules of ethics. Thus, I is correct. Similarly, a lawyer must supervise underling employees. Thus, II is correct. See generally MR 5.1.

63. A is the correct answer. Until a lawyer has been sworn in, he is not licensed to practice law. Since Bob was not sworn in, did not receive a waiver from he court, was not practicing with a licensed attorney of record and was within no other exception – he was practicing law without a license. B is incorrect because he did not have a law license – he was waiting. C is incorrect because profit-motive is not the test for the unauthorized practice of law. D is incorrect because a lawyer need not be in court to be practicing without a license. MR 5.5; DR 3-101(B).

64. D is the correct answer. A lawyer must not restrict the rights of other lawyers to practice law, when they are no longer in the same firm. MR 5.6(a); DR 2-108. A is incorrect because such arrangements are per se unreasonable. B is incorrect because the facts are explicit – there was such a requirement. C is incorrect because both codes are in complete agreement.

END OF ANSWERS

FLEMING'S FUNDAMENTALS OF LAW

Prices Effective – August 1, 2005

FFOL BAR REVIEW COURSES:

Long Term Live Bar Review Course	$2650
Long Term Home Study Bar Review	$2925
Ultimate Bar Tutorial	$5500
Short Term Live Bar Review Course	$2450
Short Term Home Study Bar Review	$2725

FFOL EXAM SOLUTION® REVIEW COURSES:

With 4 Hour CDs, Outline, Hypotheticals & A Sample Written Model Answer Included For Attached Hypothetical. Audio Cassettes also available upon request.

	FFOL Bar Student @ 20% Discount	Non Bar Student
Civil Procedure I	**$56**	$70
Civil Procedure II	**$56**	$70
Community Property	**$56**	$70
Constitutional Law I	**$56**	$70
Constitutional Law II	**$56**	$70
Contracts I – U.C.C.	**$56**	$70
Contracts II – U.C.C.	**$56**	$70
Corporations	**$56**	$70
Criminal Law	**$56**	$70
Criminal Procedure	**$56**	$70
Evidence	**$68**	$85
Professional Responsibility for the MPRE Exam	**$68**	$85
Property I	**$56**	$70
Property II	**$56**	$70
Remedies	**$68**	$85
Torts I	**$56**	$70
Torts II	**$56**	$70
Trusts	**$56**	$70
U.C.C. Outline Only	**$20**	$25
Wills	**$56**	$70
Outlines only for individual subjects listed (excluding PR for MPRE Exam)	**$20**	$25

FFOL COURSES AND SEMINARS:

	FFOL Bar Student	Non Bar Student
Legal Examination Writing Workshop		
• Live Program	**$156**	$195
• Home Study Program	**$164**	$205
Performance Review – 4 Days		
• Live Program	**$316**	$395
• Home Study Program	**$360**	$450
Baby Bar Review		
• Live Program	**$340**	$425
• Home Study Program	**$360**	$450
Final Review Videos (viewed in Main office)	**$28**	$35

FFOL PUBLICATIONS & STUDY AIDS:

	FFOL Bar Student	Non Bar Student
Essay Examination Writing Workbook Volume 1 (Torts, Contracts/UCC, Criminal Law)	**$24**	$30
Essay Examination Writing Workbook Volume 2 (Evidence, Property, Civil Procedure)	**$24**	$30
Essay Examination Writing Workbook Volume 3 (Con Law. Crim. Pro., Corps.)	**$24**	$30
Essay Examination Writing Workbook Volume 4 (Com. Prop., Wills, Trusts, Remedies)	**$24**	$30
FFOL Multistate Examination Workbook Volume I (Contracts/UCC, Crim. Law, Torts, Prof. Resp., Simulated Exam)	**$24**	$30
FFOL Multistate Examination Workbook Volume II (Civ. Pro., Con. Law, Crim. Pro., Evidence, Property)	**$24**	$30
Performance Exam Solution (CD's And Workbook)	**$84**	$105
Professional Responsibility Essay Writing Workbook	**$24**	$30

JOIN TODAY

With a $200 non-refundable deposit towards any future FFOL Bar Review, you will receive the following benefits:

- ✓ **Free Exam Solution Outlines®** for the semester in which you join FFOL.
- ✓ A **20% discount** given on all future FFOL courses and materials during law school.
- ✓ Attend all **Final Review Courses free** in your last semester of law school.
- ✓ **Free set of Exam Solution Outlines®** in your last semester of law school.
- ✓ **Your space is reserved** in the bar review and the **course price is frozen.**

Prices DO NOT INCLUDE sales tax, shipping & handling. PRICES ARE SUBJECT TO CHANGE WITHOUT NOTICE.
Visa, Mastercard, American Express, and Discover accepted. No COD's.

23166 Los Alisos Boulevard, Suite 238 Mission Viejo, CA 92691
1-800-**LAW-EXAM** (CA ONLY) • 949-770-7030 • FAX 949-454-8556
EMAIL: flemings1@aol.com • WEB: www.lawprepare.com

Price List 8/1/05